TREES OF CENTRAL TEXAS

DATE DUE

BRODART, CO.   Cat. No. 23-221

Trees of Central Texas

BY ROBERT A. VINES

 UNIVERSITY OF TEXAS PRESS, AUSTIN

Eighth printing, 2004

Requests for permission to reproduce material from this
work should be sent to Permissions, University of Texas Press,
Box 7819, Austin, Texas 78713-7819.

⊗ The paper used in this publication meets the minimum require-
ments of American National Standard for Information Sciences—
Permanence of Paper for Printed Library Materials, ANSI Z39.48-1984.

Library of Congress Cataloging-in-Publication Data

Vines, Robert A., 1907–1978
    Trees of central Texas.

    "Third volume in a series of field manuals extracted from Trees,
shrubs, and woody vines of the Southwest"—
    Includes index.
    1. Trees—Texas—Edwards Plateau Region—Identification.
1. Vines, Robert A., 1907–1978. Trees, shrubs, and woody vines of the
Southwest. II. Title.
QK484.T4V517 1984   582.1609764   84-2316
ISBN 0-292-78058-3 (pbk.)

CONTENTS

Publisher's Note   ix

Acknowledgments   x

Introduction   xi

Podocarpus Family (Podocarpaceae)   1

Pine Family (Pinaceae)   2

Taxodium Family (Taxodiaceae)   6

Cypress Family (Cupressaceae)   8

Lily Family (Liliaceae)   17

Willow Family (Salicaceae)   23

Garrya Family (Garryaceae)   43

Walnut Family (Juglandaceae)   45

Beech Family (Fagaceae)   54

Elm Family (Ulmaceae)   88

Mulberry Family (Moraceae)   108

Barberry Family (Berberidaceae)   118

Laurel Family (Lauraceae)   119

Junco Family (Koeberliniaceae)   124

Witch Hazel Family (Hamamelidaceae)   125

Sycamore Family (Platanaceae)   127

Rose Family (Rosaceae)   130

Legume Family (Leguminosae)   174

   Subfamily Mimosoideae   174

   Subfamily Caesalpinioideae   198

Subfamily Papilionoideae   207

Caltrop Family (Zygophyllaceae)   222

Rue Family (Rutaceae)   224

Quassia Family (Simarubaceae)   232

Mahogany Family (Meliaceae)   235

Euphorbia Family (Euphorbiaceae)   236

Sumac Family (Anacardiaceae)   240

Holly Family (Aquifoliaceae)   256

Maple Family (Aceraceae)   261

Buckeye Family (Hippocastanaceae)   263

Soapberry Family (Sapindaceae)   268

Buckthorn Family (Rhamnaceae)   273

Linden Family (Tiliaceae)   289

Mallow Family (Malvaceae)   290

Chocolate Family (Sterculiaceae)   292

Tamarisk Family (Tamaricaceae)   294

Cactus Family (Cactaceae)   299

Loosestrife Family (Lythraceae)   302

Pomegranate Family (Punicaceae)   304

Dogwood Family (Cornaceae)   306

Heath Family (Ericaceae)   308

Sapodilla Family (Sapotaceae)   310

Persimmon Family (Ebenaceae)   314

Storax Family (Styracaceae)   318

Ash Family (Oleaceae)   322

Dogbane Family (Apocynaceae)   347

Borage Family (Boraginaceae) 349

Verbena Family (Verbenaceae) 351

Trumpet-creeper Family (Bignoniaceae) 353

Madder Family (Rubiaceae) 357

Honeysuckle Family (Caprifoliaceae) 359

Diagrams of Inflorescence; Leaf Apices, Margins, and Forms; and Flower Parts 363

Glossary 367

Index 391

PUBLISHER'S NOTE

Trees of Central Texas is the third volume in a series of field manuals extracted from *Trees, Shrubs, and Woody Vines of the Southwest,* written by Robert A. Vines and published by the University of Texas Press in 1960. *Trees of East Texas* and *Trees of North Texas* were published in 1977 and 1982, respectively. Prior to his death in 1978, Mr. Vines had prepared the outline for the content of these volumes and others on the western and southern portions of the state. The Press' managing editor, Barbara N. Spielman, worked closely with Mr. Vines on both the books and the outlines and will continue to oversee future volumes in the field-guide series.

ACKNOWLEDGMENTS

Special thanks are acknowledged herewith to the staffs of various herbaria for the loan of plant materials for study. Without such assistance this work would have been impossible. These include the United States National Herbarium, United States National Arboretum, New York Botanical Garden, Missouri Botanical Garden Herbarium, Harvard University Gray Herbarium, Southern Methodist University Herbarium, Chicago Museum of Natural History Herbarium, and University of Texas Herbarium.

Marshall Conring Johnston of the University of Texas Department of Botany has been very helpful in providing plant material, but most helpful of all has been the book he coauthored with Donovan Stewart Correll, *Manual of the Vascular Plants of Texas*. This excellent work substantiated and clarified many things for me.

Also, I wish to give special thanks to Cornelius H. Muller for his advice on the revision of the oaks of Texas. George Avery of Miami, Florida, has been very helpful in providing information on the subtropical plants.

My thanks should also go to the various artists who prepared the illustrations, namely Sara Kahlden Arendale, Margaret Beggins, Pat Beggins, Jan Milstead, Felicia Bond, and Michele Cox.

INTRODUCTION

The purpose of this field guide is to identify by full descriptions and illustrations all the native and naturalized trees of central Texas. The very nature of a field guide, however, limits the amount of material it can contain and still be easily carried and used in the field. Because of this limitation, detailed data on the varieties, horticultural forms, propagation, and medicinal uses of the trees have been omitted. The reader who seeks a more in-depth discussion is referred to the author's *Trees, Shrubs, and Woody Vines of the Southwest*, upon which this guide is based.

Central Texas, roughly the area of the Edwards Plateau, is bordered by the Balcones Escarpment on the south and east, the Pecos River on the west, and the Texas Plains and the Llano Uplift to the north.

What Is a Tree?

A native tree is one that grows without cultivation. A naturalized tree is one that is introduced from other regions, but one that escapes cultivation and grows freely. A somewhat general definition of a tree has been suggested by some authorities but is not accepted by all. The definition often given is that a tree is a plant with a single woody trunk at least four inches in diameter four feet above the ground, with a definite branched crown, and with a height not less than twelve feet.

This rule may have some exceptions because some trees may have several trunks growing from the base, and some are tall enough but fail to attain the stipulated trunk diameter. Also, some shrubs are treelike but have a number of stems rising from the base. Under unfavorable conditions of soil or climate a true tree may become shrublike, or in favorable circumstances a shrub may become treelike. Also, some species are fast growing and reach maximum tree size much quicker than other species. Individual trees vary in size within the same species.

Conservation Importance

Many organizations have contributed to the overall land-use program of soil conservation: federal bureaus, state agencies, district and county governments, timber producers, processors, and wood products manufacturers. The Texas Parks and Wildlife Department has coordinated the wildlife and park management. It should certainly be fully recognized that trees are of great value for purposes other than providing wood products. Humans, animals, and birds eat the seeds, fruit, and sap. Trees furnish drugs, dyes, and resins, prevent erosion, are good sound barriers, reinstitute the oxygen in the air, and are much used for street, park, and home beautification, for shade, and for shelter-belt planting. All these uses are justifiable reasons for forest conservation and for the protection of all woody species.

Central Texas Tree Zone Defined

For the purposes of this publication the central Texas tree zone is that section called the Edwards Plateau (see section H on map 1).

Central Texas is often called the Edwards Plateau because of Edwards limestone outcrops above ground or somewhat below the surface. Many millions of years ago marine organisms formed a thick limey ooze on the sea bottom, which was uplifted to form the present-day limestone. It forms a somewhat flattened plateau, cut with canyons and crenulations. It covers approximately 24 million acres. The plateau rises gradually from about 1,000 feet high on its southern edge to about 2,410 feet in the north-central area. Uvalde, Real, and Bandera counties are especially rugged, and the land continues to be rugged toward the Rio Grande and the Pecos and Devil's rivers. On the eastern and southern edge of the area lies a prominent geological discontinuity known as the Balcones Fault. Here the

strata are broken by the uplift of the plateau. Springs flow
from the broken strata. Some of these are the Comal Springs
at New Braunfels, Goodenough Springs at Comstock, San
Marcos Springs at San Marcos, San Felipe Springs at Del
Rio, and Barton Springs at Austin. Large springs near San
Antonio are the source of the San Antonio River.

A great mass of igneous rocks was thrust up in the north-
east corner of the Edwards Plateau, known as the Llano
Uplift. It is bordered on the west by Menard County, on the
north by San Saba and Mills counties, on the east by Burnet
County, and on the south by Gillespie and Blanco counties.
This area is famous for its numerous varieties of minerals.
Upland soils are of dark calcareous clays and clay loams.
Often the soils have an overlay of gravel or stones. Bottomland soils are dark, clayey, and alluvial or sandy. Some
deeply cut canyons and stream bottoms contain large boul-
ders and stones rounded from water wear.

Rainfall on the Edwards Plateau decreases from east to
west. Boerne averages 32.70 inches annually, Junction
26.29, Ozona 19.50, and from Pecos westward 19.50 or less
(see map 2). Rains often come as sudden thunderstorms
with force that the sparse vegetation cannot slow and the
canyons and arroyos cannot hold. However, in some areas
the calcium in the limestone is soluble, and many underground caverns are formed. The colder parts of the area
are in the northwest, and the moderate parts toward the
southeast.

There are approximately 186 species of trees on the Edwards Plateau, several of which are not found elsewhere.
Mesquite, cedar, and a number of oaks are present. Various
species of acacia, sumac, buckthorn, and buckeye are
found, with willows, cottonwoods, walnuts, and pecans
along the streams. Many grass species occur between the
patches of shrubs and trees. These open areas sustain cattle, sheep, goats, and numerous deer. The last two also
browse the shrubs. In the drier western areas, sotol, yucca,
bear grass, and cactus are mixed with the grasses.

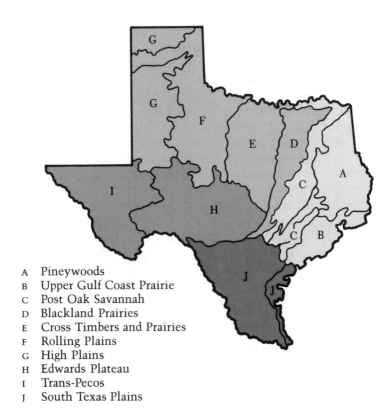

A   Pineywoods
B   Upper Gulf Coast Prairie
C   Post Oak Savannah
D   Blackland Prairies
E   Cross Timbers and Prairies
F   Rolling Plains
G   High Plains
H   Edwards Plateau
I   Trans-Pecos
J   South Texas Plains

MAP 1. Texas tree zones

MAP 2 (*opposite*). Mean annual temperatures by climatic divisions (1941–1970) and mean annual precipitation by climatic divisions (1941–1970)

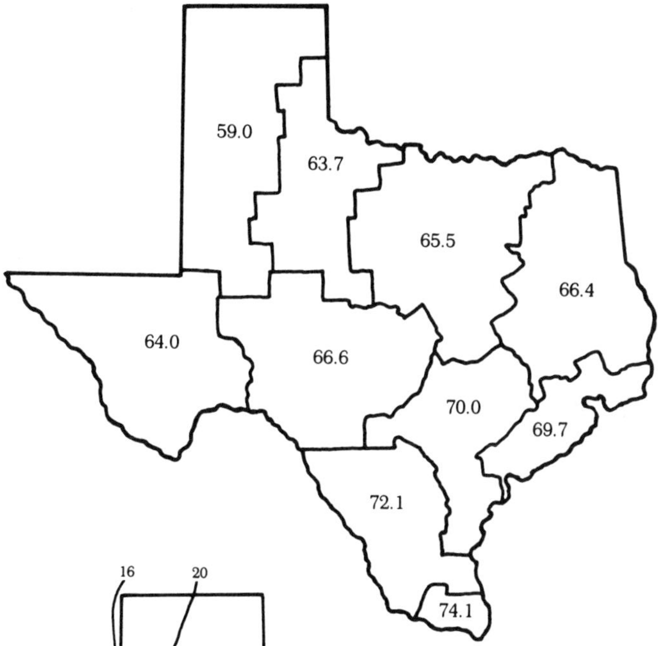
59.0
63.7
65.5
66.4
64.0
66.6
70.0
69.7
72.1
74.1

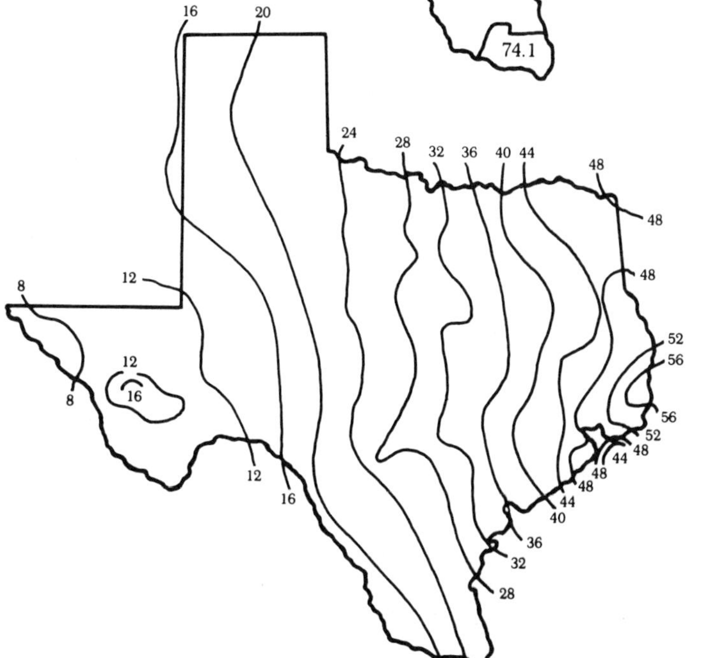
16
20
24
28
32
36
40
44
48
48
48
12
8
12
16
8
52
56
56
52
48
44
48
48
44
40
36
32
28
12
16
20
24

TREES OF CENTRAL TEXAS

PODOCARPUS FAMILY (Podocarpaceae)

Japanese Yew

Podocarpus macrophylla D. Don [H]

Field Identification. A cultivated, evergreen resinous tree to 50 ft tall or more. The branches are spreading, and the bark is brownish or gray and shreddy. The dense narrow leaves are glossy, and the staminate and pistillate flowers are usually on separate trees. The fruit is an oblong, fleshy, purplish drupe.

Flowers. Dioecious or, rarely, monoecious. Staminate catkins sessile, fascicled or solitary, 1–1½ in. long, composed of spirally disposed 2-celled anthers; pistillate on leafy shoots, axillary, solitary, scale-like, enclosing the ovule with several bracts at its base, with 1 or more carpels and 1 ovule.

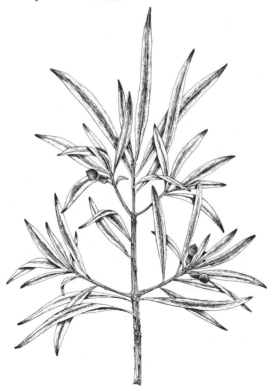

Fruit. Drupe-like, ovoid or oblong, ⅓–½ in. long, the fleshy aril greenish or purplish; seed nutlike.

Leaves. Dense, alternate or opposite, somewhat whorled; shape linear-lanceolate, 3–4 in. long, ⅓–½ in. wide; apices acute or obtuse; upper surface dark glossy green; lower surface paler, greenish yellow, or somewhat glaucescent; midrib distinct, other veins obscure; petioles very short or leaf base narrowly winged and sessile.

Twigs. Stout, when young green, glabrous, and somewhat sulcate; when older light to dark brown, tending to break into shreddy thin scales.

Range. A native of Japan. Often cultivated for ornament in the southern United States.

Remarks. The genus name, *Podocarpus*, is from the Greek meaning "foot" and "fruit," referring to the fleshy fruit stalk. The species name, *macrophylla*, is for the large leaves. It is also listed under the names of *P. longifolia* Hort. and *Taxus macrophylla* Thunb. It was introduced into cultivation in 1804.

PINE FAMILY (Pinaceae)

Pinyon Pine

Pinus edulis Engelm. [H]

Field Identification. Conifer to 50 ft, with a rounded or pyramidal shape. The trunk is short and the lower branches often wide spreading.

Flowers. In unisexual cones, perianth absent; staminate clusters short, dense, stamens spirally disposed; pistillate clusters red, scales spirally disposed with 1–2 ovules at base.

Leaves. Thickly covering the twigs, persistent, bluish green, glaucous, somewhat curved, ¾–1¾ in. long, slender, in clusters of 2–3, mostly threes.

Fruit. Cones mature August–September, soon falling, ovoid to globose, 1–1¾ in. long; scales large, thick and fleshy when green, reddish brown later, irregularly pyramidal, strongly keeled, and resinous; seed borne in cavities usually at the base of the middle

scales that spread widely at maturity, diversely shaped, triangular to rounded, somewhat flattened or rounded at the base, ½–¾ in. long, oily, brown to black, wing rudimentary, edible.

Twigs. Branches rough and scaly, young twigs very smooth, gray, leaf scars and lenticels numerous.

Bark. Reddish brown to almost black on old trunks, broken into thick broad plates with smaller thin scales and deep fissures.

Wood. Yellow, soft, light, close-grained, somewhat fragrant when burned, specific gravity 0.65.

Range. Pinyon Pine is found usually at higher elevations of 4,000–7,000 ft in west Texas, New Mexico, and Arizona to California. South into Mexico in Chihuahua to Baja California and Hidalgo.

Remarks. The genus name, *Pinus*, is the classical name, and the species name, *edulis*, describes the edible large seeds. Some authors refer to it under the names of *Pinus cembroides* Zucc. and

Pinus cembroides var. *edulis* Voss. Other vernacular names are Piñon, Pino, Nut Pine, Indian Nuts, Piñones, and Ocote. The tree is valued for its edible seeds that are gathered and sold in great quantities by the Mexican and Indian people. The seeds are eaten raw or roasted and have an excellent flavor. The seeds are consumed by many species of ground squirrels, chipmunks, porcupine, black bear, Mearn's quail, Merriam's turkey, and the thick-billed parrot. Goats and mule deer browse the foliage. A resin obtained from the tree is used as a waterproofing material and cement for pots and baskets, and for mending articles of jewelry. The wood is used for fuel and posts but rarely for lumber. The tree is usually of slow growth.

Deodar Cedar

Cedrus deodara (Roxb.) Loud. [H]

Field Identification. A cultivated, ornamental, cone-bearing large tree. Attaining a height of 150 ft (or more in its native habitat) but usually considerably smaller in cultivation. Branches wide spreading but drooping at the ends, more or less forming a conical crown. Said to attain an age of 600 years. Bark light to dark gray or brownish, smooth when young, but with age thick, furrowed vertically, and cracked transversely.

Flowers. Borne September–October, monoecious or dioecious. Catkins at the ends of arrested branchlets or spurs. Petals and sepals absent. Staminate catkins erect, cylindric, about 1–2 in. long, consisting of more or less antheriferous scales (stamens), bearing 2 or more anther cells on the back (underside). Pistillate flowers ovoid, purplish, about ½ in. long, consisting of numerous 2-ovuled scales subtended by small bracts.

Fruit. Cones usually ripen in autumn of the second year, about 13 months after flowering; barrel shaped to ovoid or ovoid-oblong. Cones reddish brown, erect, from 3½–5 in. long and 2–3½ in. in diameter; apices rounded or obtuse. Consisting of ovuliferous scales (open carpels), these closely imbricate, broadly cuneate, upper edge thin and rounded, broader than long, deciduous. The columnar axis of the cones erect and persistent when the scales have fallen. Seeds concealed by the cone scales, about ¼ in. long, with a triangular wing and rounded sides, to ⅔ in. long. Cotyledons usually 10.

Leaves. Persistent from 3–5 years with very short sheaths. Alternate and single on elongated shoots and on seedlings, otherwise in dense fascicles on arrested, spurlike branchlets. Color dark green to bluish or glaucous green; acicular with acute apices, not very rigid; triquetrous, about as thick as broad; from ¾–1½ in. long. Resin canals lined with small, thin-walled secreting cells.

Twigs. Leading shoot and branchlets pendulous; young pubescent, greenish to light brown, when older glabrous and dark brown to black or gray, roughened by the bases of the old deciduous leaves.

Range. Native to Afghanistan and India. Krum Valley from altitude of 7,500–10,000 ft. Chitral. Northwest Himalaya, 4,000–10,000 ft, ascending in places to 12,000 ft in the basin of the principal tributaries of the Indus, Tous, Jumna, and Bhagirati rivers. On two feeders of the Alaknanda. Cultivated in Kumson and in Nepal.

Generally cultivated from the northern sections of the Gulf Coast states and southward. Occasionally grown as a yard tree in Houston. Its close relatives Lebanon Cedar (*C. libani*) and Atlas Cedar (*C. atlantica*) can be grown somewhat more northward.

Remarks. The genus name, *Cedrus*, is from *Kadrus*, the ancient Greek name. The species name, *deodara*, is a native Himalayan name.

The Deodar Weevil chews on the bark and twigs, and the larvae girdle the twig and frequently kill the leader. The tree is also subject to damage by the Atlas Cedar aphid, which has been controlled by spraying Malathion on the plant.

The heartwood is yellowish brown, strongly scented, very durable, with the vessels on a transverse section without pores. It consists of medullary rays and of long, thick-walled tracheids, arranged in radial lines, with large bordered pits, usually on their radial walls only. In the earliest formed wood, contiguous to the pith, the tracheids have a spiral or annual thickening of their walls. The annual rings are distinctly marked by belts of very thick-walled tracheids in the outer (autumn) wood and by thinner walled tracheids in the spring wood of the succeeding year. Resin glands are found in the bark and the wood. In the wood they are vertical among the tracheids and horizontal in the medullary rays. The wood is used for building and many purposes in India. Also an aromatic oil is distilled from it.

Young trees require shelter and a great deal of shade. In the United States Deodar Cedar is grown only as an ornamental tree for parks, streets, or larger yards. It is sometimes almost as wide as tall and needs plenty of room. It is very attractive, and the lower branches often sweep the ground.

TAXODIUM FAMILY (Taxodiaceae)

Common Bald Cypress

Taxodium distichum Rich. [H]

Field Identification. Deciduous conifer growing in swampy grounds, attaining a height of 130 ft and a diameter of 8 ft. It is reported that some trees have reached an age of 800–1,200 years. The trunk is swollen at the base and separated into narrow ridges. Curious cone-shaped, erect structures called "knees" grow upward from roots of trees growing in particularly wet situations. Branches horizontal or drooping.

Flowers. March–April, staminate cones brownish, 3–5 in. long; stamens 6–8, with filaments enlarged and anthers opening lengthwise; pistillate cones solitary, or 2–3 together, clustered in the

leaf axils, scaly and subglobose; scales shield shaped, with 2 ovules at the base of each.

Fruit. Ripening October–December, cone globose, closed, rugose, ¾–1 in. in diameter, formed by the enlargement of the spirally arranged pistillate flower scales; scales yellowish brown, angular, rugose, horny, thick; seeds 2-winged, erect, borne under each scale, dispersed by water or wind; large crops occur every 3 to 5 years with lighter crops between.

Leaves. Deciduous, alternate, 2-ranked, ½–¾ in. long, flat, sessile, entire, linear, acute, apiculate, light green, lustrous, flowering branches sometimes bear awl-shaped leaves, deciduous habit unusual for a conifer.

Twigs. Green to brown, glabrous, slender, flexible, often deciduous.

Bark. Gray to cinnamon brown, thin, closely appressed, fairly smooth, finely divided by longitudinal shallow fissures.

Wood. Light or dark brown, sapwood whitish, straight grained, moderately hard, not strong, very durable, weighing 28 lb per cu ft, not given to excessive warping or shrinking, easily worked; heart often attacked by a fungus, the disease being known as "peck."

Range. Texas, Oklahoma, Arkansas, and Louisiana; eastward to Florida, northward to Massachusetts, and west to Missouri.

Remarks. The genus name, *Taxodium*, is from the Greek and means "yewlike," in reference to the leaves, and the species name, *distichum*, means "2-ranked," and also refers to the leaves. Other vernacular names are White Cypress, Gulf Cypress, Southern Cypress, Tidewater Red Cypress, Yellow Cypress, Red Cypress, Black Cypress, Swamp Cypress, and Sabino-tree. Cypress wood is used for making boats, ties, docks, bridges, tanks, silos, casks and tubs, posts, shingles, interior finishes, cars, patterns, flasks, greenhouses, cooling towers, and stadium seats, for example. It is very durable in contact with soil and water. It is easily worked and takes a good polish. The knees are sometimes made into souvenirs, and the cone resin used as an analgesic for wounds. The conical erect knees serve as a mechanical device for anchoring the tree in soft mud, and some authorities believe that the knees also aerate the roots. The seeds are eaten by a number of species of birds, including wild ducks. Common Bald Cypress is often planted for ornament and has been in cultivation in Europe since about 1640. Fossil ancestors of Bald Cypress covered the greater part of North America in company with the ginkgoes, sequoias, and incense-cedars. At present it is concentrated in the swamps of the southern states and middle to lower Mississippi Valley. Florida has about one third of the total amount of acreage of Common Bald Cypress.

CYPRESS FAMILY (Cupressaceae)

Italian Cypress

Cupressus sempervirens L. [H]

Field Identification. A cultivated evergreen, resinous tree up to 70 or 80 ft high with erect or ascending branches. The bark is thin, gray, and nonexfoliating.

Flowers. Terminal or axillary, monoecious-diclinous or dioecious, solitary, small; staminate flowers oblong-cylindric, ⅙–⅕ in. long,

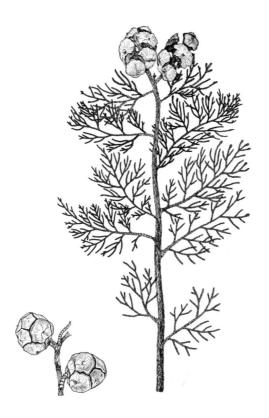

of 6–12 decussate stamens, yellow, with short filaments and 4–6 pollen sacs; pistillate subglobose, the scales with numerous erect ovules.

Fruit. A woody dehiscent cone, subglobose to ellipsoid, ¾–1½ in. in diameter; maturing the second year, with 8–14 peltate scales, a short thin boss on back, and winged seeds numerous under each scale.

Leaves. Scalelike, minute, closely appressed, dark green, rombic, obtuse at apex, glandular on back, minutely denticulate.

Twigs. Stiff, slender, cylindrical or 4-winged, brown or gray.

Range. A native of southern Europe and western Asia, often cultivated in the United States for ornament. Cultivated for many centuries in Europe. It is the classical slender cypress of the Greek and Roman writers.

Remarks. The genus name, *Cupressus*, is the classical name. The species name, *sempervirens*, refers to its evergreen habit. Varieties often planted for ornament are the Columnar Italian Cypress, *C. sempervirens* var. *fastigiata* Hansen (*C. sempervirens* var. *stricta* Ait.), which has erect branches forming a very slender columnar upright head.

Spreading Italian Cypress, *C. sempervirens* var. *horizontalis* Gord (*C. horizontalis* Mill.) has branches spreading horizontally to form a broad pyramidal head.

Oriental Arbor-vitae

Thuja orientalis L. [H]

Field Identification. A cultivated evergreen, resinous shrub, or small pyramidal or bushy tree to 25 ft. The branches are spreading and ascending, with very flat frondlike leafy branchlets. Bark thin, reddish brown, and scaly. Trunk usually branching near the base. Very variable and known under many horticultural form names.

Flowers. Terminal, minute, solitary, monoecious-diclinous. Staminate flowers yellow, of 6–12 decussate stamens. Pistillate flowers subglobose, with 8–12 scales in opposite pairs, with 2 erect ovules at base inside.

Fruit. Cones ovoid-oblong, erect, ½–1 in. long, fleshy and bluish before maturity. Scales usually 6, ovate, obtuse, with thickened ridge or hooked umbo at apex, the upper pair sterile. Seeds 2 to each scale, ovoid, brown, thick, and wingless.

Leaves. Bright green, nearly alike on both sides; scalelike, opposite in pairs, appressed; those of main axes glandular with free spreading apex; those of lateral branches closely appressed and glandular; juvenile leaves needlelike.

Twigs. Very slender, leafy branchlets flattened in one plane.

Range. Native to northern and western China and Korea. Cultivated in many horticultural variations of size, leaf color, and shape, especially grown in the United States and Japan.

Remarks. The genus name, *Thuja*, is the classical name. The species name, *orientalis*, refers to its eastern origin. Many other horticultural forms have been developed and are sold but have not been officially recorded in botanical literature. Some of these may well be duplicates of forms already known under other names.

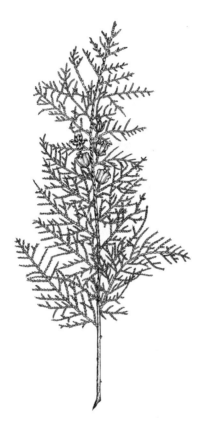

The wood is light, soft, brittle, and rather coarse-grained, durable in contact with the soil. It is used for construction, cabinet-making, and cooperage.

These trees are useful for dense hedges or as specimen plantings in the open. They do well in moist loamy soil and are easily transplanted. For propagation, seeds are sown in spring or cuttings obtained in late summer and wintered in a cool greenhouse. Also grafting on seedling stock in spring or early summer.

Eastern Red-cedar

Juniperus virginiana L. [H]

Field Identification. Evergreen tree of variable shape, attaining a height of 50 ft or, rarely, more. Leaves of two kinds, either scale-like and appressed, or awl-shaped and spreading.

Flowers. March–May, dioecious, catkins small and terminal; staminate catkins oblong or ovoid; stamens 10–12, golden brown, pollen sacs 4; female cones globular; scales spreading, fleshy, purplish, bearing 1–2 basal ovules.

Fruit. Ripening September–December, cone berrylike, on straight peduncles, pale blue, glaucous, subglobose, ¼–⅓ in. in diameter, sweet, resinous; seeds 1–2, ovoid, acute, ⅙–⅛ in. long, smooth, shining.

Leaves. Of two kinds: one kind scalelike, appressed, glandular, dark green, acute or obtuse, about 1/16 in. long, 4-ranked; the other awl-shaped, sharp pointed, glandless, glaucous, 1/2–3/4 in. long; some of the leaves are intermediate between the two forms.

Twigs. Reddish brown, round or angled.

Bark. Light reddish brown, separating into long fibrous strips; trunk more or less fluted and basally buttressed.

Wood. Red, sapwood white, knotty, light, brittle, soft, evenly textured, compact, weighing about 30 lb per cu ft, shrinks little, very resistant to decay.

Range. Growing in all types of soil, on hilltops or in swamps. Almost throughout the eastern United States. West into Texas, Oklahoma, Arkansas, Kansas, Nebraska, and North and South Dakota.

Remarks. *Juniperus* is the classical name, and the species name, *virginiana*, refers to the state of Virginia. Other names are Red Savin, Carolina Cedar, Juniper-bush, Pencil-wood, and Red Juniper. The capital of the state of Louisiana, Baton Rouge (Red Stick), gets its name from the red wood. The wood is used for novelties, posts, poles, woodenware, millwork, paneling, closets, chests, and pencils. The aromatic character of the wood is considered to be a good insect repellent. The extract of cedar oil has various commercial uses. The tree is host to a gall-like rust that in certain stages attacks the leaves of apple trees. Twig-laden bagworm cocoons are also frequent on the branches. A few borers attack the tree, and it suffers greatly from fire damage. It is sometimes used in shelter-belt planting and has been cultivated since 1664. The fruit is eaten by at least 20 species of birds and the opossum.

Rocky Mountain Juniper

Juniperus virginiana var. *scopulorum* (Sarg.) Lemmon [H]

Field Identification. Shrub on high, dry slopes, or a tree to 50 ft and 15–30 in. in diameter. Trunk usually short and dividing into stout branches to form an irregular round-topped crown.

Flowers. In spring, cones small, inconspicuous, yellowish, staminate and pistillate borne separately; staminate with about 6 stamens, connectives entire, anther sacs 4–5; pistillate scales spreading, acute or acuminate, obscure on the mature fruit.

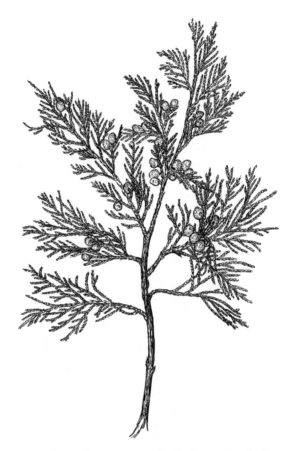

Fruit. Scales of pistillate cones gradually becoming fleshy and uniting into a berrylike, indehiscent conelet, November–December, ripening at the end of the second season, subglobose, ¼–⅓ in. in diameter, bright blue and very glaucous, flesh resinous and sweet; seeds 1–2, about 3/16 in. long, grooved and angled, acute; outer coat thick and bony, inner coat thin and membranous, hilum 2-lobed, endosperm fleshy, embryo straight.

Leaves. Scalelike, 1/25–⅙ in. long, closely appressed, opposite or in threes, rhombic-ovate, acute or acuminate, entire, obscurely glandular dorsally, dark green to yellowish green, often pale or very glaucous, leaves of young shoots often awl-shaped and sharply pointed.

Twigs. Slender, angular and flattened at first, rounded later, brown or gray, scaly with age.

Bark. Reddish brown to gray, fibrous, thin, fissures shallow, ridges flat and interlacing, breaking into shreddy scales.

Wood. Generally the same as that of Eastern Red-cedar, knotty, heartwood in varying shades of brown to red, or streaked lighter, sapwood thin and nearly white, texture rather fine and even (except at knots), specific gravity about 0.49, moderately weak in bending, fairly strong in endwise compression, works rather easily, shock resistance high, shrinks very little in drying, resistant to decay.

Range. Gravelly or rocky soils, dry ridges or bluffs. At altitudes from sea level to 9,000 ft. The most widely distributed juniper of the West. Western Texas, New Mexico, Arizona, Colorado, Nebraska, Nevada, South Dakota, Oregon, Washington, British Columbia, and Alberta.

Remarks. *Juniperus* is the classical Latin name; the species name, *virginiana*, is for the state of Virginia; and the varietal name, *scopulorum*, refers to its habitat of rocky cliffs and crags. Also known under the vernacular names of Western Juniper, River Juniper, Western Red-cedar, Red-cedar, Mountain Red-cedar, Colorado Red-cedar, and Cedro Rojo. The tree is slow growing and long-lived. It is used for reforestation to some extent and for shelter-belt planting on prairies and plains. It also has value in ornamental planting and has been cultivated since 1836. The wood is used for chests, closets, millwork, interior finish, posts, poles, pencils, water buckets, woodenware, novelties, and fuel and is reputed to have insect-repellent properties. The fruit is eaten by a number of species of birds and grazed by bighorn sheep.

Ashe Juniper

Juniperus ashei Buchholz [H]

Field Identification. Shrub or evergreen tree rarely over 30 ft. Usually irregular, leaning, low-branched, with a fluted and twisted trunk.

Flowers. Minute, dioecious, terminal; staminate oblong-ovoid, about ⅙ in. long, stamens 12–18; filaments enlarged into connectives that are ovoid, obtuse, or somewhat cuspidate, pollen sacs near the base; pistillate $\frac{1}{12}$–⅛ in. long with ovate, acute spreading scales that are 1–2-ovuled at the base. The fruit is formed by the cohesion of the enlarged fleshy scales.

Fruit. August–September, sessile or short-peduncled, a fleshy, berrylike cone about ¼ in. long, bluish green, glaucous, ovoid to subglobose, skin thin and roughened somewhat by the scale remnants, flesh sweetish but resinous; seed solitary (rarely 2), ovoid, acute or obtuse at apex, rounded at base, somewhat grooved on 2 sides, lustrous, light to dark brown, about ³⁄₁₆ in. long.

Leaves. Usually at the ends of the twigs, ¹⁄₂₅–¹⁄₁₆ in. long, scalelike, opposite in 2–4 ranks, appressed, imbricate, ovate, acute, keeled, minutely denticulate or fringed on the margin, usually nonglandular but resinous and aromatic; on young shoots the awllike or acicular leaves are ¼–½ in. long, lanceolate, rigid, apex long and sharp pointed.

Twigs. Gray to reddish, scaly, aromatic, rather stiff.

Bark. Gray to reddish brown, reddish brown beneath, shredding into shaggy, longitudinal strips.

Wood. Streaked reddish brown, sapwood lighter colored, close-grained, hard, light, not strong, but durable in contact with the earth, specific gravity 0.59, somewhat aromatic.

Range. Mostly on limestone hills. In Texas, Arkansas, Oklahoma, and Missouri. The common juniper of central Texas. Southward and westward into Mexico and Guatemala.

Remarks. The genus name, *Juniperus*, is the classical name, and the species name, *ashei*, is in honor of William Willard Ashe (1872–1932), American botanist. Names used are Mountain Cedar, Cedar Brake, Texas Cedar, Sabino, Enebro, Tascate, Taxate, and Cedro. The wood is used for fuel, poles, posts, crossties, and small woodenware articles. The foliage is occasionally browsed by goats and deer, and the sweet fruit eaten by a number of species of birds and mammals, including the bobwhite quail, robin, Gambel's quail, cedar waxwing, curved-bill thrasher, gray fox, raccoon, and thirteen-lined ground squirrel. The tree is occasionally cultivated for ornament and is apparently resistant to the cedar-apple rust.

LILY FAMILY (Liliaceae)

Trecul Yucca

Yucca treculeana Carr. [H]

Field Identification. Tree 5–25 ft, with a simple trunk or with a few stout spreading branches at the top, crowned by large symmetrical heads of radiating sharp-pointed leaves. The plant sometimes occurs as a thicket-forming shrub.

Flowers. Maturing December–April, borne in a large dense, showy glabrous or puberulent panicle 1½–4 ft long; pedicels ½–3 in.; bracts ovate to lanceolate, often spinescent at apex, varying from 1 in. at base of pedicels to 1 ft at base of main stem, becoming dry, thin, and papery; flowers creamy white, rather globose, later expanding broadly, the 6 segments ovate to ovate-lanceolate, acute to acuminate at apex, waxy, brittle, thin, 1–2 in. long; stamens 6, filaments slightly papillose above, usually finely and shortly pubescent below, about as long as the pistil; pistil ¾–1⅓

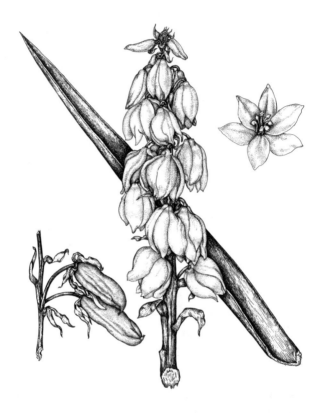

in. long, ovary slender and oblong-cylindric; style very short
(⅛–⅖ in.); stigmas 3, abruptly spreading, nearly horizontal at anthesis, deeply lobed.

Fruit. Capsule indehiscent, 2–4½ in. long, about 1 in. thick,
reddish brown or later black, oblong-cylindric, rather abruptly
contracted at the acute or acuminate apex, surfaces often with
fissures or deeply cleft, filaments and perianth often persisting,
heavy and thick-walled, 3-celled, flesh sweetish and succulent;
seeds numerous, flat, about 1/16 in. thick, ⅛–¼ in. broad, with a
narrow border to the rim.

Leaves. In large radiating clusters, bluish green, length 2½–4 ft,
1–3½ in. wide, usually straight, concavo-convex, apex acute to
short-acuminate, with a brown or black, short, sharp spine, margin entire, rigid, inner surface rather smooth, outer surface

scabrous to the touch; dead leaves hanging below the crown and long persistent.

Bark. Dark reddish brown, on older trunks ¼–½ in. thick, with shallow or deep irregular fissures. The intervening ridges broken into thin oblong plates with small appressed scales.

Wood. Light brown, spongy, fibrous, heavy, not easily cut.

Range. Well-drained hillsides, chaparral regions, or open flats near the Gulf of Mexico. From the shores of Matagorda Bay westward and southward along the coast to Brownsville. From San Antonio in Bexar County westward to the Rio Grande and Pecos River. In Mexico in Nuevo León, Tamaulipas, Durango, and Coahuila.

Remarks. The genus name, *Yucca*, is from a native Haitian name. The species name, *treculeana*, is in honor of A. A. L. Trecul (1818–1896), who in 1850 took the plant to France from Texas. Also known under the vernacular names of Spanish Dagger, Spanish Bayonet, Don Quixote Lance, Pita, Palma Pita, Palma de Dátiles, and Palma Loca. The plant is a handsome ornamental for use in central or coastal Texas or Louisiana and is sometimes grown in southern Europe. The leaves are very tough and were used in frontier days for making twine or rope. The blossoms were made into pickles or cooked like cabbage. The spines on the leaves are used by the Mexican people to jab the wound of a snake bite and induce bleeding. In this manner much of the poison is carried away. The Chihuahua Indians fermented the fruit of various species of *Yucca* to make an intoxicating beverage. The trunks are sometimes used for posts and the leaves for thatch in making huts. It is also reported that the seeds have purgative qualities.

Torrey Yucca

Yucca torreyi Shafer [H]

Field Identification. An arborescent plant 3–24 ft, with a simple or few-branched trunk. The crowded radiating leaves are usually untidy in appearance, this in part because of the persistent thatch of dead, reflexed leaves on the trunk below.

Flowers. Panicle densely flowered, 3–3½ ft long including the scape, extending above the leaves one fourth to one half of its length; branchlets of the panicle 20–35, erect to ascending, ridged and somewhat flattened; pedicels ¾–2 in. long, terete or nearly so, some curved; bracts variable in size, mostly short-acuminate

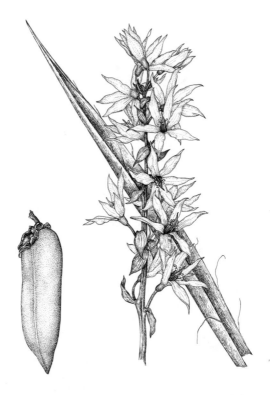

to acute at apex, those on lower part of scape ½–2 ft long, 1¾–2½ in. wide, those on upper parts of scape 4–7 in. long, those at base of pedicels small, narrowly ovate; flowers 1¾–4 in. long, perianth somewhat united at base, creamy white or tinged purplish, waxy, segments 6 (3 petals and 3 sepals), concave, apex pubescent, inner series sometimes shorter and broader; stamens 6, papillose to pubescent, rather stout, anthers ⅛–⅕ in. in length; pistil 1–1½ in., style ⅕–⅓ in., gradually broadened into the ovary; stigmas spreading, longer than broad, emarginate.

Fruit. Capsule 4–5½ in. long, 1¼–2 in. wide, dark brown to black, gradually narrowed toward the apex, which is abruptly acute or short-acuminate; surfaces with the primary divisions rather deep, secondary divisions less so, remnants of the perianth and filaments persistent at base; 3-celled; seeds numerous.

Leaves. Borne in a radiating head, dark yellowish green, straight, rigid, rarely curved, concavo-convex, but less so near base, gradually tapering from just above base to an acuminate apex bearing a rigid, sharp spine ¼–½ in. long, margin with curly to straight persistent fibers, surfaces usually scabrous, length of blade 2–4½ ft.

Range. In Texas from the Devil's River area westward, northwest into New Mexico and southwest into Mexico.

Remarks. The genus name, *Yucca*, is from the Haitian name. The species name, *torreyi*, is in honor of John Torrey (1796–1873), American botanist of Columbia University. The plant is closely related to the Trecul Yucca.

Thompson Yucca

Yucca thompsoniana Trel. [H]

Field Identification. A small tree 4–7½ ft, with a solitary trunk or with a few branches near the top. Leaves borne in a dense radiat-

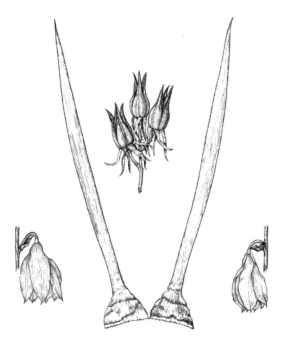

ing cluster 1–1½ ft long or wide. Trunk covered with dead reflexed leaves often to the ground.

Flowers. Sometimes appearing on young and stemless plants; panicle 2–3½ ft long, with about 25 branchlets that are erect or ascending to horizontal below, green to purplish, pubescent at first but glabrous later, somewhat angular; pedicels ½–⅝ in., rather slender; bracts numerous and variable in size, those at base of scape 4–6 in. long, those of the inflorescence proper 1½–2 in. long, those at base of pedicels about ½ in., shape of bracts from ovate to oblanceolate with acute or acuminate apices, margins entire, or on the larger ones corneous or intermittently denticulate, texture of bracts (especially the smaller ones of the pedicels) tending to become papery, crisp, and curling with age; flowers numerous, globose to campanulate, 1¼–2½ in. long, the 6 segments ovate to obovate, concave to flattened, thin, apex acute to short-acuminate, margins entire or toothed, white or greenish; stamens 6, ¾–1 in., pubescent above, anthers sagittate and less than ⅕ in. in length; pistil 1¼–1¾ in., ovary oblong-cylindric, greenish yellow, style slender, about ½ in. long, white, apex bearing 3 stigmas with thick rounded lobes.

Fruit. Abundant, persistent, reddish brown, length 1¼–2½ in., to ¾ in. wide, symmetrical, occasionally constricted, at apex abruptly narrowed with short, reflexed tips ¼–½ in. long, walls thin and strong, dehiscent the length of the primary fissures, carpels 3; remnants of the corolla segments long persistent.

Leaves. Borne in a radiating mass, yellowish green or bluish green to somewhat glaucous, 10–18 in. long, averaging ⅜–½ in. wide at the greatest width at about the center, gradually narrowed to a long acuminate apex terminating in a sharp, slender, fragile spine; gradually narrowed also to the base and becoming as narrow as ⅙ in. just above the base; leaves usually straight, or occasionally when falcate broader and shorter, surfaces scabrous, plano-convex, flattened, or becoming concavo-convex near the apex, thin and flexible, margins with numerous minute regular teeth.

Range. Rocky slopes and foothills at altitudes of 700–3,400 ft. In Texas in southeastern Val Verde, Terrell, and Brewster counties. In Mexico known from Chihuahua and Coahuila.

Remarks. The genus name, *Yucca*, is from the native Haitian name. The species name, *thompsoniana*, is in honor of the botanist C. H. Thompson.

WILLOW FAMILY (Salicaceae)

Black Poplar

Populus nigra var. *italica* Du Roi [H]

Field Identification. A cultivated medium to large tree with a very narrow erect habit of growth. Sometimes obtaining a height of as much as 90 ft. The bark, gray and smooth or deeply furrowed.

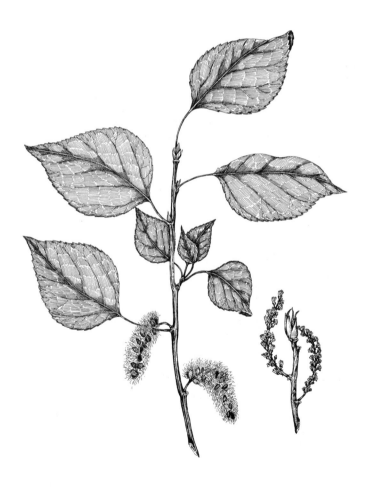

Flowers. Staminate catkins caducous, 2–3 in. long; stamens 20–30, under laciniate scales and with 2 bifid stigmas. Pistillate catkins separate, shorter and ascending, and also subtended by laciniate scales. All flowers with a cuplike disk. Pedicels slender.

Fruit. In fruit the catkins to 6 in. long; capsule 2–4 valved; seeds copiously hairy.

Leaves. Alternate, mostly as broad as long, triangular to ovate-triangular; about 4 in. long and 3 in. broad; margin with finely crenate-serrate teeth; apices gradually or abruptly acuminate; surfaces green and glabrous. Petioles slender, glandless or nearly so.

Twigs. Terete, glabrous, orange, but later gray. Winter buds with several or many scales, glabrous, more or less viscid but not resinous or balsamic.

Range. A native of Eurasia and often cultivated for ornament. Other varieties are known in cultivation.

Remarks. The genus name, *Populus*, is the classical name. The species name, *nigra*, means black but the usage is obscure. The variety name, *italica*, refers to its growth in Italy. Often planted as a slender accent tree in parks, along streets, or in cemeteries.

White Poplar

Populus alba L. [H]

Field Identification. Tree attaining a height of 100 ft, with a trunk diameter of 3–4 ft. Sometimes spreading by root suckers to form thickets in old fields or about abandoned dwelling sites. Recognized by the conspicuous white tomentose undersurface of the leaves.

Flowers. Borne in pendulous catkins, pistillate about 2 in., slender, stigmas 2, each deeply 2-parted; staminate 1½–4 in.; scales dentate, fringed with long hairs; stamens 6–10 (usually about 8).

Fruit. Capsule narrowly ovoid, ⅛–⅕ in. long, tomentose, 2-valved; seeds minute, numerous, with a tuft of long silky, white hair.

Leaves. Simple, alternate, rather variable, on vigorous shoots palmately 3–5-lobed, the lobes also coarsely toothed or with additional small lobes, base rounded to subcordate, blades 2⅓–5 in. long, upper surface dark green, lower surfaces conspicuously

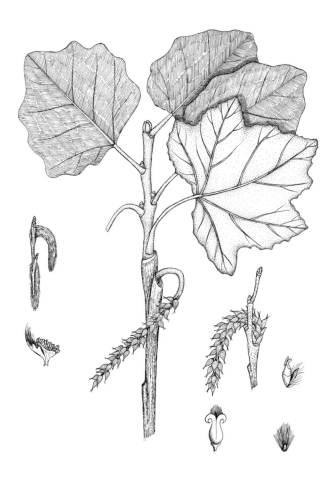

white tomentose; on older branches leaves often smaller, ovate to elliptic-oblong; margin sinuate-dentate; petioles terete, densely tomentose; young twigs and branches also white tomentose.

Bark. Greenish gray to white, usually smooth on branches or young trunks, toward the base of old trunks roughened into firm dark ridges.

Wood. Reddish to yellowish, sapwood nearly white, tough but light and soft.

Range. Adapted to many soil types, on dry, well-drained sites in the sun. Grown for ornament in Texas, New Mexico, Oklahoma,

Arkansas, Louisiana, and more or less throughout the United States. A native of central and southern Europe to western Siberia and central Asia.

Remarks. The genus name, *Populus,* is the ancient Latin name, and the species name, *alba,* refers to the white undersurface of the leaves. The tree is also known under the vernacular name of Abele. White Poplar has long been grown for ornament. It is very conspicuous because of the contrasting white and green leaf surfaces. However, the white undersurfaces catch soot and dust easily and become unsightly in some localities. The tree grows rapidly, transplants easily, prunes well, and has few insects or fungus pests, but is short-lived.

Great Plains Cottonwood

Populus sargentii Dode [H]

Field Identification. Tree attaining a height of 90 ft, a diameter of 6 ft. The branches erect and spreading to form a broad crown.

Flowers. In smooth staminate and pistillate catkins; staminate catkins 2–2½ in. long, scales light brown, roughened, apex fimbriate; disk broad, oblique, margin thickened, stamens 20–25, filaments short, anthers yellow; pistillate catkins 4–8 in.; disk cup-shaped, margin slightly lobed; stigmas laciniately 3–4 lobed, ovary subglobose.

Fruit. Capsule maturing June–August, about ⅖ in. long, oblong-ovoid, apex obtuse, three to four times longer than the pedicels; seeds oblong to obovoid, apex rounded, about 1/16 in. long.

Leaves. Simple, alternate, deciduous, ovate to broadly deltoid; apex mostly long-acuminate; base truncate or subcordate; margin crenate-serrate; leaves slightly hairy at first; when mature glabrous, shiny, light green to yellowish green, veins rather slender and delicate; blade length 3–3½ in., width 3½–4 in.; petiole slender, laterally flattened, 2–3½ in. long often with 2 small glands at the apex.

Twigs. Stout, glabrous, green to yellowish, somewhat angular or rounded, leaf scars rather large; buds ovoid, acute, resinous, scales puberulent and brownish.

Bark. Smooth on young trees and branches, pale gray, later with deep fissures, rounded ridges and irregular scales closely appressed.

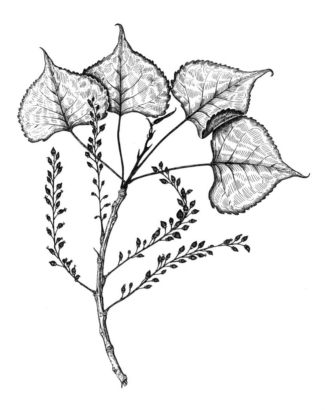

Range. It is known from Trans-Pecos Texas, the Texas Panhandle, western Oklahoma, New Mexico, Colorado, Utah, Nebraska, Wyoming, South Dakota, and Montana.

Remarks. The genus name, *Populus*, is the classical Latin name. The species name, *sargentii*, honors Charles Sprague Sargent (1841–1927), American dendrologist.

Some botanists consider the Great Plains Cottonwood to be a xerophytic western form of the Eastern Cottonwood (*P.deltoides*). However, it is usually smaller in stature, with glabrous and yellowish green leaves bearing coarser and fewer teeth, the flower pedicels shorter, and the fruit pointed more obtusely.

At one time *Populus sargentii* Dode was thought to hybridize with *Populus angustifolia* James to produce *Populus × acuminata* Rydb., but this is now accepted by some botanists as a species under the species name of *Populus acuminata* Rydb.

Texas Great Plains Cottonwood

Populus sargentii var. *texana* (Sarg.) Correll [H]

Field Identification. A species once described as Texas Cottonwood, *P. texana* Sarg., is now relegated as a variety under the
name of *P. sargentii* var. *texana* (Sarg.) Correll. It occurs over the
same range as the species. It is a tree attaining a height of 60 ft,
with a trunk sometimes to 3 ft in diameter and pendulous
branches. The twigs are yellow-brown, stout, glabrous, with glabrous, acuminate winter buds.

Flowers. The pistillate aments are borne on slender pedicels about
⅕ in. long. The fruit capsule is about ⅓ in. long; shape oblong-
ovoid; apex acute, deeply pitted, glabrous, thin-walled, 3-valved,
and disk slightly lobed.

Leaves. Alternate; length from 3–3¼ in. long and 2¼–2½ in.
wide; shape broadly ovate; apexes long-acuminate; margin coarsely
crenate-serrate below the middle, and entire above. The slender
petioles flattened and from 1½–2½ in. long. There may be an
abortive gland or so at the leaf base and petiole junction but often
they are absent. This character links the variety with *P. sargentii*
Dode, instead of with *P. fremontii* S. Wats and its variety *P. fre-*

montii var. *wislizenii* (Torr.) Wats. The first grows more frequently in the Texas Panhandle, and the others more westwardly along the Rio Grande and in the Trans-Pecos region.

Range. This species is common along streams in the eastern foothills of the Rocky Mountains, from 3,500–7,000 ft in Saskatchewan, and in the Dakotas, Wyoming, Nebraska, Kansas, Colorado, New Mexico, western Oklahoma, the Panhandle Plains area of western Oklahoma, and the Panhandle and Trans-Pecos region of western Texas.

Remarks. The genus name, *Populus*, is the classical Latin name. The species name, *sargentii*, honors Charles Sprague Sargent (1841–1927), American dendrologist and at one time director of the Arnold Arboretum. The variety name, *texana*, is for the state of Texas. The wood is used for fuel, posts, veneer, and baskets.

Eastern Cottonwood

Populus deltoides Marsh. [H]

Field Identification. Tree to 100 ft high and 8 ft in diameter. The trunk is often rather short, the branches massive, the top rounded, and the root system spreading and shallow.

Flowers. February–May, borne in separate staminate and pistillate catkins; staminate catkins densely flowered, 1½–2 in. long, ½–¾ in. wide, disk oblique and revolute; stamens 30–60, filaments short, anthers large and red; pistillate catkins at first 3–3½ in. long, loosely flowered; bracts brown, glabrous, apex fimbriate; disk ovoid, obtuse, enclosing about one third of ovary; ovary sessile, style short, stigmas 2–4, large, spreading, laciniately lobed.

Fruit. Ripening May–June, racemose, 8–12 in. long at maturity, capsules on slender pedicels, ⅛–⅖ in., ovoid to conical, acute, about ¼ in. long, 1-celled, 3–4-valved; seeds numerous, small, brown, oblong-obovoid, buoyant with cottony hairs when the capsule ruptures. The minimum seed-bearing age about 10 years and maximum about 125.

Leaves. Simple, alternate, deciduous, broadly deltoid-ovate, margin crenate-serrate, apex abruptly acute or acuminate, base truncate to heart shaped or abruptly cuneate, blades 3–7 in. long, about as broad; upper surface light green, glabrous, lustrous, main vein stout, yellow to reddish; lower surface paler and glabrous with primary veins conspicuous; petiole smooth and glabrous, flattened, stipules linear.

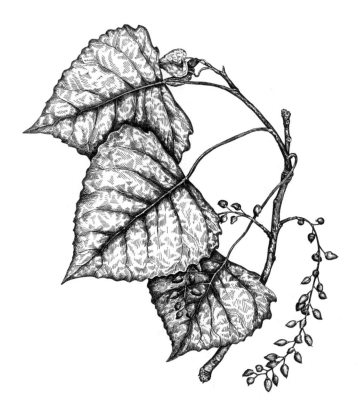

Twigs. Yellowish to brown or gray, stout, angular, lenticels prominent; buds ovoid, acute, resinous, brown, about ½ in. long or less, laterals much flattened; leaf scars triangular or lunate, with 3 bundle marks, pith star-shaped.

Bark. Thin and smooth on young branches or trunks, green to yellow; older trunks gray to almost black with flattened, confluent broad ridges broken into closely appressed scales.

Wood. Dark brown, sapwood white, weak, soft, weighing about 24 lb per cu ft, moderately weak in bending, weak in endwise compression, low in shock resistance, moderately easy to work with tools, takes paint well, easy to glue, warps and shrinks considerably, low in durability, below average in ability to stay in place, nails easily, does not split easily.

Range. Eastern Cottonwood is found in rich, moist soil, mostly along streams. It and its varieties occur over practically the entire

United States east of the Rocky Mountains. Texas, New Mexico, Oklahoma, Arkansas, and Louisiana; eastward to Florida and northward into Canada.

Remarks. The genus name, *Populus*, is the ancient name given by Pliny, and the species name, *deltoides*, refers to the triangular shape of the leaf. Other vernacular names are Carolina Poplar, Necklace Poplar, Water Poplar, Southern Cottonwood, Yellow Cottonwood, and Alamo. Alamo is the Spanish name for the tree, and was also the name given the famous Texas fort that was surrounded by the trees. "Remember the Alamo" was the battle slogan of the Texas-Mexico War. The tree is often planted for ornament and for erosion control in dune-fixing. The airborne cottony seeds are undesirable at fruiting season. The leaves flutter rapidly and make a rustling sound in the wind because of the flexible flattened petiole. The tree sprouts from the stumps and roots, is easily storm damaged, easily fire damaged when young, is much attacked by fungi, and grows rapidly. The foliage is known to be browsed by cattle, black-tailed deer, and cottontail. The seeds are eaten by rose-breasted grosbeak and evening grosbeak. The wood is used for paper pulp, cases and crates, tubs and pails, excelsior, veneer for plywood, musical instruments, dairy and poultry supplies, laundry appliances, and fuel.

Gulf Black Willow

Salix nigra Marsh. [H]

Field Identification. A rapidly growing tree sometimes attaining a height of 125 ft.

Flowers. April–May, dioecious, borne in many-flowered catkins preceding the leaves or with them; staminate catkins cylindrical, slender, 1–2 in. long; bracts obtuse, yellow, hairy below; stamens 3–7, filaments hairy below, anthers yellow; pistillate catkins 1½–3 in. long; bracts deciduous; pistil solitary, style short, the 2 stigmas thickened.

Fruit. May–June, borne on slender spreading pedicels, capsule light brown, conic-ovoid, sharp-pointed, glabrous, ¼–⅛ in. long, splitting into two valves; seeds minute, green, pilose with long hairs.

Leaves. Simple, alternate, deciduous, blades 3–6 in. long, ¼–¾ in. wide, narrowly lanceolate; apex long-attenuate and sometimes falcate; base rounded, acute; margin finely glandular-serrate;

green above and paler below, glabrous or puberulent along the veins, or pubescent when young; petiole short, puberulent; stipules variable, either large, persistent, semicordate, pointed, and foliaceous, or small, ovate, and deciduous.

Twigs. Slender, brittle, reddish brown.

Bark. Light brown to black, rough, deeply fissured, ridges dividing into thick shaggy scales, rich in tannin.

Wood. Light brown, soft, light, weak, not durable, weighing 27 lb per cu ft.

Range. In wet soil, Texas, Louisiana, Oklahoma, and Arkansas. Reaching its largest size on the banks of the Brazos, San Bernard, and Colorado rivers in Texas; east to North and South Carolina, north to New Brunswick, and west to North Dakota.

Remarks. The genus name, *Salix*, is the classical Latin name, and the species name, *nigra*, refers to the black bark. Vernacular names are Scythe-leaved Willow, Swamp Willow, and Pussy Willow. The bark was formerly used as a home remedy for fever ailments. The wood is used for artificial limbs, charcoal, toys, doors, fuel, cheap furniture, boxwood, and excelsior.

Western Black Willow

Salix nigra var. *vallicola* Dudley [H]

Field Identification. Western tree to 45 ft, and 3 ft in diameter.

Flowers. Dioecious, staminate catkins 1–2 in. long, cylindric; scales linear-oblanceolate, apex acute, yellow, with dense long soft hairs; stamens 3–6, filaments villose; pistillate catkins 2–3½ in. long at maturity, scales early deciduous; ovary conic, apex acuminate, pubescent to glabrous; stigmas 2, short and broad.

Fruit. Capsules spread well apart on mature catkins, pedicels ¹⁄₁₂–⅛ in. long; capsule body ⅕–¼ in. long, conic-ovoid to lanceolate, apex acute, reddish brown, pubescent at first but more glabrous later.

Leaves. Simple, alternate, deciduous, elliptic to lanceolate, some curved, long-acuminate at apex, base narrowly cuneate or attenuate, margin finely serrate, young with pale hairs, mature leaves glabrous and dull green on both sides, blade length 1½–3 in., width ¼–½ in., on young shoots considerably larger; petioles about ¼ in. long or less, pubescent to glabrous; stipules orbicular, base cordate, margin serrate, surface pubescent.

Twigs. Slender, yellow to orange or grayish, pubescent or glabrous when older.

Bark. On trunk dark gray to black, rather deeply furrowed, ridges breaking into thickish plates.

Wood. Reddish brown to pale brown, soft, weak, specific gravity 0.44.

Range. In clumps or patches along water courses at altitudes of 300–4,000 ft. In western Texas and New Mexico; west to California, north to Nevada and Utah, and south in Mexico to Chihuahua, Sonora, Sinaloa, and Baja California.

Remarks. The genus name, *Salix*, is the classical Latin name, and the species name, *nigra*, refers to the dark bark. The variety name, *vallicola*, means inhabitant of low places or valleys. Some authorities consider the tree to be a separate species instead of a variety of Black Willow and list it under the name of Gooding Willow, *S. goodingii* Ball. Leslie Newton Gooding was a botanist of the U.S. Department of Agriculture and collected the type specimen. However, the differences between the plants are so slight that a varietal name under *S. nigra* seems most fitting. The twigs of the variety are yellow to gray, whereas twigs of *S. nigra* are reddish brown; also, the leaves of the former are elliptic-lanceolate, the latter's narrow-lanceolate. Also known as the Dudley Willow. The young shoots are sometimes browsed by livestock and mule deer. A decoction of the leaves is reported as being used in Chihuahua for fevers.

Sand-bar Willow

Salix interior Rowlee [H]

Field Identification. A slender, upright shrub forming thickets by stolons, or a small tree to 30 ft.

Flowers. Dioecious, April–May on leafy twigs. Staminate and pistillate catkins slender, cylindric, linear, borne on different plants; staminate catkins terminal or axillary, dense, ¾–2 in. long, about ⅓–⅜ in. broad; stamens 2, exserted, filaments distinct, hairy at base; pistillate catkins loosely flowered, 2–3 in. long and about ¼ in. broad; scales light yellow, hairy, ovate to obovate, entire or erose; ovary short-stalked, oblong-cylindric,

silky-hairy when young, less hairy or glabrous later; stigmas 2, subsessile, lobed; young capsule with long white silky hairs.

Fruit. Capsule matures in April, sessile or short-peduncled, narrowly ovoid-conic, gradually narrowed to a blunt apex, ⅙–¼ in. long, brownish, glabrous or villous, 1-celled, splitting into 2·reflexed valves; seeds minute, attached to long white hairs, buoyant in the wind.

Leaves. Deciduous, alternate, blades 2–6 in. long, ⅛–⅓ in. wide, linear-lanceolate, sometimes falcate, thin, apex acuminate, base gradually narrowed into a short petiole, margin with remote, denticulate, glandular teeth, main vein prominent; upper surface dark green and glabrous or puberulent along the main vein; paler and pubescent beneath; petioles ⅛–³⁄₁₆ in., pubescent; stipules small or absent. Young leaves silky-hairy beneath.

Twigs. Slender, erect, green to brown or red, glabrous or puberulent and sometimes glaucescent.

Bark. Green to gray or brown, smooth; on older trunks furrowed and broken into closely appressed scales; lenticels sometimes large and abundant.

Wood. Soft, light, reddish brown, sapwood pale brown, weighing 31 lb per cu ft, little used except for fuel or charcoal.

Range. The species is found in alluvial soil along streams and lakes over a wide area; Texas and Louisiana coast, and north through Arkansas and Oklahoma to Canada and Alaska. Also in northern Mexico in the states of Nuevo León, Tamaulipas, and Coahuila.

Remarks. The genus name, *Salix*, is the classical Latin name, and the species name, *interior*, refers to the plant's inland distribution along water courses. It was formerly listed under the scientific names of *S. longifolia* Muehl. and *S. fluviatilis* Sarg. Known under the vernacular names of Riverbank Willow, Osier Willow, Shrub Willow, Long-leaf Willow, Narrow-leaf Willow, Red Willow, and White Willow.

Babylon Weeping Willow

Salix babylonica L. [H]

Field Identification. Cultivated tree attaining a height of 50 ft. The drooping twigs give the tree its name.

Flowers. April–May, catkins small, appearing on short lateral leafy branches; staminate catkins to 1⅝ in. long and ¼–⅓ in. wide on peduncles ⅜–⅝ in. long (pistillate catkins smaller); bracts ovate-lanceolate, yellowish, obtuse, deciduous; stamens 3–5, free, pubescent at base; style almost none.

Fruit. Capsule ovoid-conic, sessile or nearly so, glabrous, style almost absent, stigmas minute.

Leaves. Alternate, narrowly lanceolate, apex long-acuminate, base narrowed, margin serrulate, at first somewhat silky pubescent, glabrous with maturity, lower surface glaucous, blade length 3–7 in., width ¼–½ in., sometimes curling; stipules wanting or if present lanceolate and 1/12–⅓ in. long.

Twigs. Slender, glabrous, elongate, drooping, green at first, later yellowish or brownish.

Range. Grows best in damp sandy soils near water courses. In Texas, Arkansas, Oklahoma, and Louisiana; eastward to Florida, northward to Virginia and Connecticut, and westward to Michigan. A native of north China, cultivated throughout North America below an altitude of 3,500 ft.

Remarks. The genus name, *Salix*, is the classical name. The species name, *babylonica*, refers to its once-presumed west Asiatic origin, but it is a misnomer because the tree is a native of China.

The tree of the Biblical reference (Ps. 127: 1–2) is now known to be the willowlike Euphrates Poplar, *Populus euphratica* Oliv. Babylon Weeping Willow sometimes escapes cultivation by the distribution of its twigs. It is known also as the Garb Willow, Napoleon Willow, and Weeping Willow.

Coyote Willow

Salix exigua Nutt. [H]

Field Identification. Shrub with spreading stems to 12 ft tall, or sometimes a tree to 25 ft and 5–6 in. in trunk diameter. The branches spreading and forming a rounded crown.

Flowers. Appearing after the leaves on glabrous twigs 1–2 in. long, catkins terminal or axillary; staminate catkins ⅝–¾ in.; pistillate catkins ⅝–1⅝ in. Scales hoary-pubescent, varying from lanceolate to obovate with an acute or rounded apex; stamens 2, with the filaments hairy below; ovary sessile, villose, stigma bifid, sessile, style absent.

Fruit. Capsule ovoid-lanceolate, apex acuminate, glabrous or nearly so, ⅕ in. or less long, sessile or with pedicels shorter than the gland.

Leaves. Alternate, blade linear to lanceolate or oblanceolate, apex acuminate, some curved, base gradually narrowed, margin glandular-serrate, often entire below the middle, upper surface grayish green and glabrous, lower surface with white appressed hairs (or in some forms only puberulent), length 1½–4 in., ⅛–¼ in. wide (on young growth sometimes 4½ in. long and 1½ in. wide); stipules absent or minute; sessile or nearly so.

Twigs. Slender, glabrous, reddish brown to gray.

Bark. Grayish brown, thin, longitudinally fissured, older trunks more furrowed.

Range. Along streams in mountain woodlands or desert grasslands at altitudes of 4,000–7,000 ft. Oklahoma, western Texas, and New Mexico; westward to California and northward to British Columbia. In Mexico from Chihuahua to Baja California.

Remarks. The genus name, *Salix*, is the classical name. The species name, *exigua*, refers to the small leaves. Also known under the vernacular names of Basket Willow, Gray Willow, Sand-bar Willow, Narrow-leaf Willow, Slender Willow, and Acequia Willow.

Narrow-leaf Coyote Willow, *S. exigua* var. *stenophylla* (Rydb.)

Schneid., has very narrow leaves. It occurs in western Texas and New Mexico. Nevada Coyote Willow, *S. exigua* var. *nevadensis* (Wats.) Schneid., is segregated by having 2 glands on the glabrous ovary. From Arizona to Nevada.

Yew-leaf Willow

Salix taxifolia H. B. K. [h]

Field Identification. Large western shrub, or tree to 50 ft, and 18 in. in diameter. Branches short and divaricate, forming a broad open crown.

Flowers. Borne March–May. Catkins on leafy branches, terminal, or axillary, usually clustered, densely flowered, staminate and pistillate catkins separate; shape of catkins subglobose to cylindric-

oblong, ¼–½ in.; scales deciduous, yellowish, oblong or obovate, apex acute to rounded or apiculate, outer surface densely tomentose, inner surface glabrous or pubescent, margins ciliate; stamens 2, filaments free and pubescent below; ovary sessile or short-stalked, ovoid-conic, hairy; stigmas 2, deeply emarginate.

Fruit. Capsule sessile or short-stalked, about ¼ in., long, cylindric, ovate-conical, point acuminate, reddish brown, silky-hairy at first but more glabrate later; seeds numerous, small, hairy.

Leaves. Alternate, deciduous, linear-lanceolate or oblanceolate, graduated to apices, acute and mucronate, slightly curved, margin slightly revolute, obscurely and remotely denticulate above the middle or entire, soft white-hairy when young, later grayish green and finely pubescent above, lower surface paler and somewhat more hairy, blade length ⅓–1⅓ in., width 1/12–⅛ in.; leaves sessile, or petioles puberulent and less than 1/12 in.; stipules ovate, acute, minute, early deciduous.

Bark. Light gray to brown, on the trunk of mature trees ⅓–1 in. thick, fissures deep and irregularly longitudinal, with intervening broad, flat ridges breaking into small, close scales.

Twigs. Slender, reddish brown, densely tomentose at first but glabrous later except for roughened leaf scars; buds brown, 1/16–⅛ in. long, ovoid, puberulent.

Range. On creek banks and in canyons at altitudes of 3,000–6,000 ft. In Trans-Pecos Texas, southwestern New Mexico, and southern Arizona. In Mexico it is widespread, especially in Sonora, Chihuahua, Coahuila, and Baja California. Also in Guatemala.

Remarks. The genus name, *Salix*, is the classical Latin name. The species name, *taxifolia*, refers to the small, narrow, yewlike leaves. Also known in the Southwest and Mexico under the vernacular names of Sauz, Sauce, Jaray, Taray, Taray de Río, and Tarais. It is considered to be a good browse for livestock. The branches are used for brooms and the bark as a remedy for malaria by the Mexican Indians.

Coastal Plain Willow

Salix caroliniana Michx. [H]

Field Identification. Shrub or small tree to 30 ft, and 18 in. in diameter. Branches spreading or drooping to form an open, irregular crown. Closely related to Gulf Black Willow, *S. nigra* Marsh.,

and known to hybridize with it. However, Gulf Black Willow leaves are green beneath and Coastal Plain Willow leaves are very glaucous.

Flowers. May–June, buds single-scaled, expanding with the leaves; catkins terminal, slender, lax, narrow-cylindric, to 4 in. long; scales yellow, ovate to obovate, apex rounded or obtuse, densely villose-pubescent; glands of staminate flowers lobulate or forming a false disk; stamens 3–12, exserted, separate, filaments hairy at base, anthers yellow; gland of pistillate flower clasping the base of the pedicel; ovary stipitate, ovoid-conic, acute; style short, 2-lobed.

Fruit. Capsule ovoid-conic, ⅙–¼ in. long, granular-roughened, abruptly long-pointed, remnants of the 2 persistent stigmatic lobes almost sessile, base with pedicel to ¼ in.; seeds numerous, silky-hairy.

Leaves. Involute in the bud, simple, alternate, deciduous, length 2–7 in., width ⅜–1⅓ in., lanceolate to lanceolate-ovate, sometimes falcate, apex acuminate or acute, base gradually narrowed on young leaves, on older ones often rounded; upper surface bright green and glabrous; lower surface whitened or glaucous, somewhat puberulent when young, glabrous later, veins yellowish, delicate, margin finely serrate; petioles ⅛–½ in. long, densely hairy, glandless; stipules usually small on normal leaves, on vigorous shoots large (to ¾ in. wide), foliaceous, conspicuous, ovate to reniform, mostly serrate above the middle.

Twigs. Slender, yellowish to reddish brown or grayish, more or less pubescent, eventually glabrous; winter buds small, brown, lustrous.

Bark. Reddish brown to gray, ridges broad, fissures deep, conspicuously checkered, breaking into closely appressed scales.

Wood. Dark reddish brown, sapwood nearly white, light, soft, not strong.

Range. Mostly along gravelly banks and shores of streams or lakes or in low woods. Texas, western Arkansas, eastern Oklahoma, and Louisiana; east to Florida, north to Maryland, and west to Kansas.

Remarks. The genus name, *Salix*, is the classical Latin name, and the species name, *caroliniana*, refers to the states of Carolina. Also known under the vernacular names of Ward Willow and Carolina Willow. The scientific terminology of this willow has been very confused. The following names have been applied from time to time: *S. occidentalis* Bosc. *ex* Koch, *S. longipes* Shuttl., *S. nigra* var. *wardii* Bebb, *S. occidentalis* var. *longipes* (Anderss.) Bebb, *S. wardii* Bebb, *S. marginata* Wimm. *ex* Small, *S. amphibia* Small, *S. longipes* var. *venulosa* (Anderss.) Schneid., *S. longipes* var. *wardii* (Bebb) Schneid., *S. harbisonii* Schneid., *S. chapmanii* Small, and *S. floridana* Chapm.

GARRYA FAMILY (Garryaceae)

Mexican Silktassel

Garrya ovata Benth. [H]

Field Identification. Western evergreen shrub or small tree 2–18 ft, all parts densely pubescent with gray or brown curled hairs.

Flowers. Dioecious, catkins axillary; staminate catkins shorter than the pistillate, bracts small; calyx with 4 linear sepals; petals

absent; stamens 4, filaments distinct, anthers linear, ovary none;
pistillate catkins 1–3 in., bracts large and leaflike; calyx limb
abbreviated, stamens absent; styles 2, inwardly stigmatic, persistent on fruit; ovary 1-celled with 2 pendulous ovules.

Fruit. Drupe ⅙–⅓ in., sessile or with short pedicels, globose to
ovoid, bluish purple, sometimes drying brownish, eventually
glabrous, stigma persistent, flesh thin; seeds 1–2, subglobose
to short-oblong, one side more flattened than the other, ³⁄₁₆–¼
in. long.

Leaves. Persistent, blades 1–2½ in., opposite, leathery, variable in shape, either narrowly lanceolate to ovate, or oblong to oval or obovate, apex acute, obtuse, or rounded, usually mucronate, base broadly to narrowly cuneate or in some rounded, margin entire and sometimes irregularly thickened and muricate; young leaves densely curly-hairy on both sides; at maturity pale and densely curly-hairy beneath; becoming glabrous, or nearly so above and either dull or semilustrous, veins finely reticulate; petioles connate at base, ⅛–¾ in., at first densely curly-hairy but more glabrous later.

Twigs. Stout, 4-angled to terete later, densely curly-hairy, but eventually glabrous, reddish brown to gray; lenticels small, slitlike or elliptic.

Range. Rocky limestone hills and canyons of central Texas, and westward into the Trans-Pecos counties. In Mexico in Chihuahua, San Luis Potosí, and Puebla. The type specimens are from Guanajuato.

Remarks. The genus name, *Garrya*, is in honor of Nicholas Garry, secretary of the Hudson's Bay Company, and the species name *ovata*, refers to the ovate leaves. A variety known as the Lindheimer Silktassel, *G. ovata* var. *lindheimeri* Coult. & Evans, has been named as occurring in central and western Texas. However, the characters by which it is described—oblong or obovate, acute, nonthickened or muricate margined, and curly-haired leaves—do not appear distinct enough to warrant the segregation of the variety.

Wright Silktassel, *G. wrightii*, is a closely related, more glabrous species of extreme west Texas, New Mexico, and Arizona.

WALNUT FAMILY (Juglandaceae)

Eastern Black Walnut

Juglans nigra L. [H]

Field Identification. Tree to 125 ft with a rounded crown.

Flowers. May–June, staminate and pistillate flowers on same tree; staminate catkins 2–5 in. long, stout, stamens 20–30, sessile, calyx 6-lobed, lobes oval and pubescent; bracts triangular,

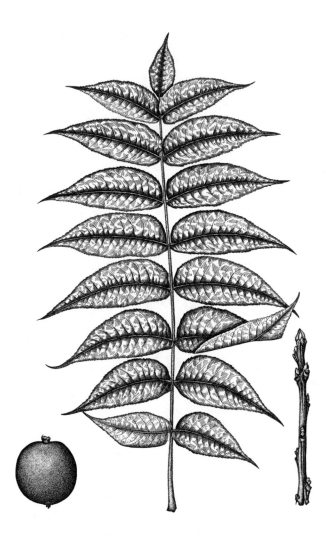

brown-tomentose; pistillate flowers in 2–5-flowered spikes, about ¼ in. long; stigmas 2, plumose, yellowish green; style short on a subglobose ovary; calyx lobes acute; ovate, green, pubescent.

Fruit. Ripening September–October, solitary or clustered, subglobose; husk yellowish green, thick, papillose, indehiscent, 1½–2½ in. in diameter; nutshell hard and bony; nut dark brown to black, compressed, corrugated, 4-lobed at base, oily, sweet, edible.

Leaves. Pinnately compound, 1–2 ft long, yellowish green, deciduous; petioles puberulent; leaflets 11–23, sessile or short-stalked, ovate-lanceolate, acute or acuminate, rounded or subcordate at base, inequilateral, serrate, glabrous above, pubescent below, 3–5 in. long, 1–2 in. wide.

Bark. Grayish brown, black, or reddish, fissures deep, ridges broad, rounded, and broken into close scales.

Wood. Very beautiful, dark rich brown, sapwood white, durable, strong, heavy, hard, close-grained, is easily worked, glues well, does not warp, shrink, or swell much, takes a good polish, weighs 38 lb per cu ft. The whitish sapwood is sometimes stained to match the color of the heartwood to bring a better price.

Range. Oklahoma, Arkansas, Louisiana, and Texas; east to Florida, north to Minnesota, New York, and Ontario; and west to Nebraska.

Remarks. The genus name, *Juglans*, is from the Latin *Jovis glans*, meaning "acorn [or any nut of similar shape] of Jove," and the species name, *nigra*, refers to the dark wood. The wood is used in making superior furniture, cabinets, veneers, musical instruments, interior finish, sewing machines, caskets, coffins, posts, railroad crossties, and fuel. Large amounts were used for gunstocks during the Civil War and World War I. Trees about 12 years old begin to bear nuts. Confections and cakes are made from the nuts, which were also a favorite with the American Indians. Squirrels are fond of the large nuts. The tree makes a fine ornamental because of its shape and beautiful large leaves. Black Walnut and English Walnut are known to hybridize. Eastern Black Walnut is sometimes planted in shelter belts and has been cultivated since 1686. It is a rapid grower and is usually found mixed with other hardwoods. Over 69 horticultural clones have been recognized by scholars.

Texas Black Walnut

Juglans microcarpa Berl. [H]

Field Identification. Strong-scented, many-stemmed shrub or small tree attaining a height of 30 ft, often with a number of trunks leaning from the base.

Flowers. Borne March–April in separate catkins on same tree. Staminate catkins from twigs of previous year, solitary, simple, long, slender, pendulous, pubescent at first, more glabrous later, 2–4 in. long; calyx short-stalked, greenish, puberulent, 3–6-lobed, lobes rounded; bracts densely hairy, ovate-lanceolate; stamens 20–30 in several rows; anthers almost sessile, yellow, connectives somewhat lobed; pistillate catkins solitary, or several together, at the end of branches of the current year, oblong, rufous-tomentose; calyx lobes usually 4, ovate and acute; bracts and bractlets laciniate; ovary inferior; stigmas spreading, plumose, greenish red.

Fruit. Borne solitarily, or several together, globose, ½–¾ in. in diameter; hull with persistent calyx remnants at apex, rusty-pubescent at first but more glabrous later, thin, indehiscent; nut subglobose or ovoid, deeply grooved longitudinally, 4-celled toward base, shell thick; kernel small, oily, sweet.

Leaves. Alternate, 9–12 in. long, odd-pinnate compound of 11–25 leaflets; the leaflets lanceolate to narrowly lanceolate, often scythe shaped; margin entire or serrate with appressed teeth; apex acuminate; base cuneate or rounded, inequilateral, petiolules short; surface pubescent when young, becoming glabrous later; light green; aromatic when crushed; petiole and rachis pubescent.

Twigs. Slender, orange reddish or gray, usually pubescent, lenticels pale, pith in plates.

Bark. Gray to dark brown, fissures deep.

Wood. Dark brown, sapwood white, heavy, hard, not strong.

Range. In valleys and rocky stream beds, Texas, Oklahoma, New Mexico, and northern Mexico. In Texas from the valley of the Colorado River west into the mountains of the Trans-Pecos, passing into the closely related Arizona Black Walnut in the far West.

Remarks. The genus name, *Juglans*, is from the Latin *Jovis glans*, meaning "acorn [or any nut of similar shape] of Jove," and the species name, *microcarpa*, refers to the small fruit. Vernacular names used are Dwarf Walnut, Little Walnut, Nogal, and Nogalillo.

The wood is used for cabinet work, furniture, paneling, and veneers. The tree is sometimes cultivated for ornament in the United States and in Europe. It is also used in shelter-belt planting and has some value as a wildlife food, especially for squirrels.

Pecan

Carya illinoensis(Wangh.) K. Koch [H]

Field Identification. Tree to 150 ft, with a broad rounded crown. The largest of all hickories.

Flowers. March–May, borne in staminate and pistillate catkins on same tree, subject to frost damage; staminate in slender, fascicled, sessile catkins 3–6 in. long; calyx 2–3-lobed, center lobe longer than lateral lobes; stamens 5–6, yellowish; pistillate catkins fewer, hairy, yellow, stigmas 2–4.

Fruit. Ripening September–October, in clusters of 2–10, persistent; husk thin, aromatic, splitting along its grooved sutures into 4 valves at maturity; nut oblong to ellipsoid, cylindric, acute, bony, smooth, reddish brown, irregularly marked with darker brown, 1½–3½ in. long; seed deeply 2-grooved, convoluted on surface.

Leaves. Alternate, deciduous, odd-pinnate compound, 9–20 in. long; leaflets 9–17, sessile or short-stalked, oblong-lanceolate, falcate, acuminate at apex, rounded to cuneate and inequilateral at base, doubly serrate on margin, 4–8 in. long, 1–2 in. wide; aromatic when crushed, dark green and glabrous above, paler and glabrous or pubescent beneath; rachis slender, glabrous or pubescent.

Twigs. Reddish brown, stout, pubescent, lenticels orange-brown.

Bark. Grayish brown to light brown under scales; ridges flattened, narrow, broken, scaly; fissures narrow, irregular.

Wood. Reddish brown, sapwood lighter, coarse-grained, heavy, hard, brittle, not strong, weighing 45 lb per cu ft, inferior to other hickories.

Range. Rich river-bottom soils. Texas, Oklahoma, Arkansas, and Louisiana; eastward to Alabama, and north to Kansas, Iowa, Indiana, and Tennessee.

Remarks. The genus name, *Carya*, is the ancient name for walnut, and the species name, *illinoensis*, refers to the state of Illinois, the tree at one time having been called Illinois Nut. It is widely planted as an ornamental and for its sweet edible nuts. The wood is not important commercially but is occasionally used for furniture, flooring, agricultural implements, and fuel. The nut is valuable to wildlife, being eaten by fox squirrel, gray squirrel, opossum, raccoon, peccary, and a number of species of birds. The bark and leaves are sometimes used medicinally as an astringent. Pecan is a rather rapid grower for a hickory and is long-lived but is subject to bark beetle attacks. It has been cultivated since 1766.

Mockernut Hickory

Carya tomentosa Nutt. [H]

Field Identification. Tree to 100 ft, with rather short limbs and a broad or oblong crown. A specimen has been reported from Turkey Run State Park, Indiana, with a circumference of 9 ft 6 in., a height of 146 ft, and a spread of 52 ft.

Flowers. April–May, borne in separate staminate or pistillate catkins; staminate catkins 3-branched, 4–5 in. long, yellowish green, hairy; bracts ovate to lanceolate, hairy, much longer than calyx lobes; stamens 4, with red, hairy anthers; pistillate in 2–5-flowered hairy spikes; bracts ovate and acute, longer than bractlets and calyx lobes; stigmas dark red.

Fruit. Ripening September–October, solitary or paired, very variable in size and shape, usually obovoid, globose, or ellipsoid, 1–3½ in. long, acute at apex, rounded or rarely with a short necklike base; hull dark reddish brown, woody, hairy or nearly glabrous with yellow resinous dots, 4-ribbed, dehiscent down the deep ribs to the middle or near the base, about ⅛–¼ in. thick; nut variable in shape, obovoid-oblong to globose or ovoid, rounded at base, acute or acuminate at apex, slightly flattened, noticeably or obscurely 4-ridged, brownish white or reddish, shell thick and hard; kernel dark brown, small, shiny, sweet, edible.

Leaves. Alternate, deciduous, 8–24 in. long, odd-pinnate compound of 5–9 (usually 7) leaflets; lateral leaflets sessile or nearly so, oblong to lanceolate or obovate, acute to acuminate at apex,

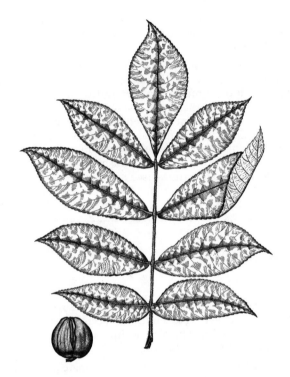

rounded or broadly cuneate at base and inequilateral, serrate on margin; shiny yellowish green above, paler beneath and clothed with brownish orange hairs, glandular and resinous, fragrant when crushed, 5–8 in. long, 2–5 in. wide, terminal leaflets and upper pairs generally larger than lower pairs; rachis and petiole glandular, hairy.

Twigs. Stout, grayish grown to reddish, hairy at first but more glabrous later; buds distinctively large and tomentose.

Bark. Gray, close and rough but never shaggy, ridges rounded and netted, separated by shallow fissures.

Wood. Dark brown, sapwood lighter, close-grained, heavy, hard, strong, tough, flexible, weighing 51 lb per cu ft.

Range. Texas, Louisiana, Arkansas, and Oklahoma; east to Florida, and north to Nebraska, Ontario, Iowa, Illinois, Michigan, and Maine.

Remarks. *Carya* is the ancient name for walnut, and the species name, *tomentosa*, refers to the tomentose hairs of the leaves. Vernacular names are Whiteheart Hickory, White Hickory, Red Hickory, Black Hickory, Whitebark Hickory, Hardback Hickory, Bigbud Hickory, Bullnut Hickory, and Fragrant Hickory. It is long-lived, is a rapid grower when young, will sprout from the stump, and is subject to insect damage. The foliage is occasionally browsed by white-tailed deer. The wood is important commercially and is used for vehicle parts, handles, fuel, and agricultural implements. The nut is sweet and edible but used in smaller quantities than other edible species.

Black Hickory

Carya texana Buckl. [H]

Field Identification. Tree attaining a height of 80 ft, with short, crooked branches forming a narrow crown.

Flowers. Borne in separate staminate and pistillate catkins, staminate catkins 2–3 in. long with acuminate bracts considerably

longer than the calyx lobes; stamens 4–5 with somewhat hairy anthers; pistillate catkins 1–2-flowered with red hair on all parts.

Fruit. Hull of nut 1¼–2 in. in diameter, puberulent, subglobose to obovoid, or sometimes with a short basal neck, splitting at sutures to the base with valves ½₂–⅙ in. thick; nut globose or obovoid, somewhat compressed, rounded at base, suddenly narrowed to an acute apex, 4-angled along upper part especially, reddish brown, reticulate veined, shell about ⅛ in. thick; kernel small, rounded, sweet.

Leaves. Alternate, deciduous, 8–12 in. long, odd-pinnate compound of 5–7 (usually 7) leaflets; leaflets sessile or nearly so, 4–6 in. long, lanceolate to oblanceolate or obovate, acuminate or acute at apex, cuneate and somewhat inequilateral at base, serrate on margin; dark green, shiny, and usually glabrous above; paler and rusty-pubescent below, especially when young, later becoming more glabrous; petioles rusty-hairy when young. The occurrence of rusty hairs and white scales on buds and young parts is a conspicuous feature.

Twigs. Rusty-pubescent and reddish brown at first, grayish brown and glabrous later.

Bark. Dark gray to black, ridges irregular, broken into deep fissures.

Wood. Brown, sapwood paler, hard, tough, brittle, used chiefly for fuel.

Range. The species, *texana*, and its variety, Arkansas Black Hickory, are distributed through east and south-central Texas and Louisiana; north to Oklahoma, Arkansas, Indiana, Illinois, Missouri, and Kansas.

Remarks. The genus name, *Carya*, is the ancient name for walnut, and the species name, *texana*, refers to the state of Texas. Some of the vernacular names for it are Buckley Hickory and Pignut Hickory. The thick shell makes the nut almost impossible to extract, but hogs sometimes crack them. Wood used for fuel.

BEECH FAMILY (Fagaceae)

Bur Oak

Quercus macrocarpa Michx. [H]

Field Identification. Tree to 150 ft, with heavy spreading limbs and a broad crown.

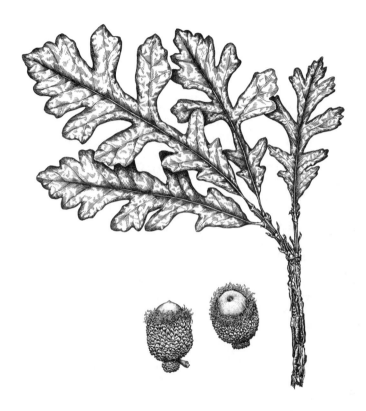

Flowers. Borne in staminate and pistillate catkins; staminate catkins 4–6 in. long, yellowish green; calyx deeply 4–6-lobed, hairy; pistillate flowers sessile or nearly so, solitary or a few together, involucral scales ovate, red, tomentose; stigmas red.

Fruit. Acorn very large, variable in size and shape, sessile or short-stalked, solitary or paired, ¾–2 in. long, ellipsoid to ovoid, apex pubescent; cup subglobose or hemispheric, thick, woody, tomentose, enclosing one-half to three-fourths of nut; scales imbricate, thick, upper scales with awnlike tips to produce a fringed border on the cup, giving a mossy appearance.

Leaves. Simple, alternate, deciduous, obovate-oblong, 5–9-lobed, lobes separated by very deep sinuses; terminal lobe usually largest and obovate with smaller lobes or coarse teeth, apex usually rounded; base cuneate from smaller lobes; blades 6–12 in. long, 3–6 in. wide; dark green, lustrous and glabrous above, paler and pubescent beneath; petioles stout, pubescent, ⅓–1 in.

Twigs. Light brown and pubescent, later becoming dark brown and glabrous, and sometimes with corky ridges; terminal buds reddish brown, pubescent, ovoid, obtuse, about ¼ in. long.

Bark. Light gray, or reddish brown, thick, deeply fissured and broken into irregular narrow flakes.

Wood. Dark or light brown, close-grained, heavy, hard, strong, tough, durable, weighing about 46 lb per cu ft.

Range. Not apparently at home on the Atlantic and Gulf Coast plains but on higher ground. Central and east Texas, Oklahoma, Arkansas, and Louisiana; east to Georgia, north to Nova Scotia, and west to Manitoba, Kansas, and Wyoming.

Remarks. The genus name, *Quercus*, is the ancient classical name, and the species name, *macrocarpa*, refers to the large acorn. Vernacular names are Mossycup Oak and Overcup Oak. The wood is similar to that of White Oak and is used for baskets, lumber, ties, fences, cabinets, ships, and fuel. The acorns are greedily eaten by squirrels and white-tailed deer, and young plants are browsed by livestock. A narrow-leaved and small-fruited variety of Bur Oak has been given the name of *Q. macrocarpa* var. *olivaeformis* Gray. A dwarf form of Bur Oak known as Bur Scrub Oak, *Q. macrocarpa* var. *depressa* (Nutt.) Engelm., is found in Minnesota, South Dakota, and Nebraska and has acorn cups about ⅖ in. wide, slightly fringed, innermost scales caudate-attenuate; acorns ovoid, about ⅖ in. long. It is usually 3–8 ft high with corky branches. However, many intermediate forms occur between it and the species.

Chinquapin Oak

Quercus muhlenbergii Engelm. [H]

Field Identification. Narrow, round-topped tree rarely over 60 ft.

Flowers. In separate staminate and pistillate catkins on the same tree; staminate catkins 3–4 in. long, hairy; calyx 5–6-lobed, yellow, hairy, ciliate, lanceolate; stamens 4–6, filaments exserted, pistillate catkins sessile, short, tomentose; calyx 5–6-lobed; stigmas red.

Fruit. Acorns mostly solitary or in pairs, sessile or short-peduncled, broadly ovoid, brown, shiny, ½–¾ in. long, enclosed about half its length in the cup; cup thin, bowl shaped, brown tomentose;

scales of cup appressed, obtuse to acute or cuspidate; kernel sweet, edible.

Leaves. Alternate, simple, deciduous, 4–6 in. long, 1–3½ in. wide, oblong to lanceolate or obovate, acute or acuminate at apex, cuneate to rounded or cordate at base; margin with coarse, large, acute, mucronate, often recurved teeth; dark green, lustrous, and glabrous above; paler gray, tomentulose, and conspicuously veined beneath; petiole slender, ½–1 in.

Twigs. Slender, hairy or glabrous, reddish brown to gray, terminal buds orange to reddish brown, ovoid, acute.

Bark. Light grayish brown, broken into narrow, loose plates.

Wood. Reddish brown, sapwood lighter, close-grained, durable, hard, heavy, strong, weighing 53 lb per cu ft.

Range. Well-drained uplands. Texas, Louisiana, Oklahoma, and Arkansas; east to Florida, north to Maine, and west to Ontario, Michigan, Wisconsin, and Nebraska. In Mexico in Coahuila and Nuevo León.

Bray Chinquapin Oak

Remarks. The genus name, *Quercus*, is the classical name of the oak tree, and the species name, *muhlenbergii*, is in honor of G. H. E. Muhlenberg (1753–1815), botanist and minister in Pennsylvania. Other vernacular names are Pin Oak, Shrub Oak, Scrub Oak, Yellow Oak, Chestnut Oak, Rock Oak, and Chinkapin Oak.

Chinquapin Oak sprouts from the stump, grows rather rapidly, and is fairly free of insects and disease. The wood is used for posts, ties, cooperage, furniture, and farm implements. Bray Chinquapin Oak, *Q. muhlenbergii* var. *brayi* (Small) Sarg., is somewhat similar and is found on the Edwards Plateau and into west Texas and south into Mexico. It has nuts sometimes to 1¼ in. long, and deeper cups to 1 in. in diameter. However, these differences are not distinct, and it is now considered by some botanists as only a form instead of a variety.

Post Oak

Quercus stellata Wangh. [H]

Field Identification. Shrub or tree to 75 ft, with stout limbs and a dense rounded head.

Flowers. Appearing with the leaves March–May, borne on the same tree in separate catkins; staminate in pendent catkins 2–4 in. long; calyx yellow, hairy, 5-lobed; lobes acute, laciniately segmented; stamens 4–6, anthers hairy; pistillate catkins short-stalked or sessile, inconspicuous; scales of involucre broadly ovate and hairy; stigmas red, short, enlarged.

Fruit. Ripening September–November. Acorns maturing the first season, sessile or short-stalked, borne solitary, in pairs, or clustered; acorn oval or ovoid-oblong, broad at base, ½–¾ in. long, striate, set in cup one-third to one-half its length; cup bowl-shaped, pale and often pubescent within, hoary-tomentose externally; scales of cup reddish brown, rounded or acute at apex, closely appressed.

Leaves. Simple, alternate, deciduous, oblong-obovate, blades 4–7 in. long, 3–4 in. wide, 5-lobed with deep rounded sinuses; lobes usually short and wide, obtuse or truncate at apex; middle lobes almost square and opposite, giving a crosslike appearance to the leaf; terminal lobe often 1–3-notched; base of leaf cuneate or rounded; dark green, rough or glabrous above, paler and tomentose beneath; leathery and thick; petioles short, usually ½–1 in., pubescent.

Twigs. Brown, stout, pubescent to tomentulose, or becoming glabrous later; buds ¹⁄₁₆–⅛ in. long, subglobose, brown.

Bark. Gray to reddish brown, thick, divided into irregular fissures with platelike scales.

Wood. Light to dark brown, durable, heavy, hard, close-grained, difficult to cure, weighing about 52 lb per cu ft.

Range. Post Oak is distributed in the Edwards Plateau of Texas, adjacent Oklahoma, and Arkansas; east to Florida, north to New England, and west to Iowa and Kansas.

Remarks. The genus name, *Quercus*, is the classical name; the species name, *stellata*, refers to the stellate hairs of the leaves and petioles. Vernacular names are Iron Oak, Cross Oak, Branch Oak, Rough Oak, and Box Oak. The wood is used for railroad crossties, fuel, fence posts, furniture, and lumber; the acorns are eaten by deer, javelina, and wild turkey.

Sand Post Oak

Quercus margaretta Ashe [H]

Field Identification. A low or moderate-sized shrub branched from the base, spreading by underground runners, especially in sandy soils. At one time described as a variety of Post Oak under the name of *Quercus stellata* var. *margaretta* (Ashe) Sarg. Also known to hybridize with Post Oak, *Quercus stellata* Wangh. and in contact areas, to produce an assemblage of forms sometimes given the specific name of *Quercus drummondii* Liebm. The vagueness of the latter is such that the name *Quercus margaretta* Ashe seems more acceptable. The following description is based on that of Cornelius H. Muller in *The Oaks of Texas* (1951).

Flowers. Staminate in aments 3–4 in. long; calyx hirsute, yellowish, with 5 segments laciniately cut. Pistillate catkins sessile or

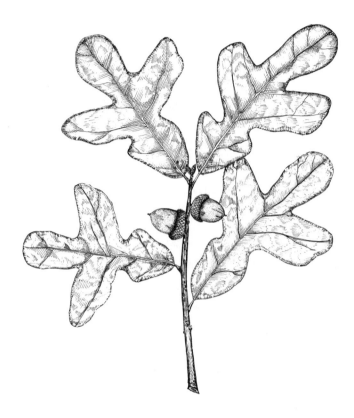

short-peduncled; scales of the involucre broadly ovate, hirsute; stigmas red.

Fruit. Annual, solitary or paired, subsessile or short-stalked. Cups ½–¾ in. broad, ¼–⅖ in. deep, deeply cup-shaped, bases rounded; scales oblong to ovate, the narrowed apices loosely appressed, densely short-pubescent. Acorns ⅖–⅗ in. long, ⅖–½ in. broad, ovoid, light brown, glabrous, about one-half of body included in cup.

Leaves. Deciduous, hard and membranous, 2–4⅞ in. long, 1¼–4 in. broad; shape obovate to oblong or elliptic; apices broadly rounded; base cuneate to rounded; blade 2–3-lobed on each side, sinuses deep, either broad or narrowed but rounded at the base; lobes rounded or clavate, simple or obscurely toothed or undulate; margins revolute; upper surface very sparsely sprinkled with minute stellate hairs or entirely glabrate, shiny green; lower surfaces from densely crisped-stellate-tomentose, becoming glabrate or more or less persistently pubescent, the lamina dull and somewhat glaucous; venation of 3–4 main lateral veins per side, and lesser ones between, branched toward the margins and variously connected; petioles ⅛–⅗ in. long, tomentose or glabrate.

Twigs. From ¹⁄₁₅–¹⁄₁₀ in. thick, fluted, glabrous and dull brown, or at least very sparsely spreading; lenticels very inconspicuous; buds ⅛–⅙ in. long, about ¹⁄₁₂ in. broad, reddish brown, from sparingly pubescent becoming glabrate. Stipules about ⅕ in. long, subulate, pubescent, promptly caducous, or sometimes persistent about the terminal buds.

Range. In low sandy soils in central and east Texas, east to the Atlantic and north to Virginia and eastern Oklahoma, the type from eastern North Carolina. In Texas in Angelina, Comanche, Dallas, Grayson, Grimes, Harris, Liberty, Polk, Nacogdoches, Rusk, Tarrant, and Wilson counties.

Remarks. The genus name, *Quercus*, is the ancient classical name of the oak. The species name, *margaretta*, is named for Margaret Henry Wilcox, the late Mrs. W. W. Ashe.

Drummond Post Oak

Quercus drummondii Liebm. [H]

Field Identification. Small or medium-sized trees.

Flowers. Borne in catkins, those of the staminate 2–2⅓ in. long, loosely flowered, sparsely villous. Pistillate catkins on short peduncles, or almost sessile, the subsessile involucres borne singly or in pairs.

Fruit. Acorns annual, solitary or paired, borne on short glabrous peduncles to ⅓ in. long or subsessile. Body of acorns ⅝–¾ in. long, about ⅓ in. broad; shape narrowly ovoid or elliptic, glabrous, and light brown, one-third to one-half of body included in cup.

Leaves. Simple, alternate, deciduous; texture thick and leathery; length to 4¾ in.; width to 3½ in.; shape obovate, deeply incised (one-half to two-thirds the distance to the midrib) by narrow or even closed sinuses, which are rarely rounded; lobes 2 or 3 on each side, oblong, rounded or truncate to clavate; upper surface with sparse stellate hairs, with maturity shiny and glabrate; lower surface villous or loosely tomentose with stellate hairs, at maturity persistently pubescent or finally glabrate; the midrib and veins with persistent pubescence. The lateral veins spreading, ir-

regular, and terminating into the lobes. Petioles about ½ in. long, at first stellate-pubescent, some persistently pubescent, others becoming glabrate.

Twigs. From 1/12 in. to 1/6 in. thick; color light brown, with spreading, stellate hairs; lenticels light and small at first, with age more prominent; buds 1/6–1/3 in. long; shape broadly or narrowly ovoid, obtuse or acute; color dull red or brown, glabrous, sparingly brown-pubescent near the apex.

Range. In deep sand belts of central Texas and eastward. In Austin, Bexar, Caldwell, Guadalupe, Medina, Robertson, Tarrant, and Wilson counties.

Remarks. The genus name, *Quercus*, is an ancient name, and the species name, *drummondii*, honors Thomas Drummond (1780–1835), Scotch botanical explorer. *Quercus drummondii* is separated from the closely related *Quercus margaretta* Ashe (*Quercus stellata* var. *margaretta* [Ashe] Sarg.) by the fact that the former is a tree of moderate size, and the latter is a shrub or small tree with running stolons. Also, *Quercus drummondii* has twigs about ⅛ in. in diameter and thick and leathery leaves with strongly revolute margins. *Quercus margaretta* has twigs usually about ¹⁄₁₂ in. in diameter, and the leaf margins are flat or slightly revolute.

Boynton Oak

Quercus boyntonii Beadle [H]

Field Identification. Trailing or erect shrubs with rhizomes in deep sand, from 8 in. to 10 ft tall or sometimes taller.

Flowers. Staminate catkins 1¼–2½ in. long, fulvous-glandular-

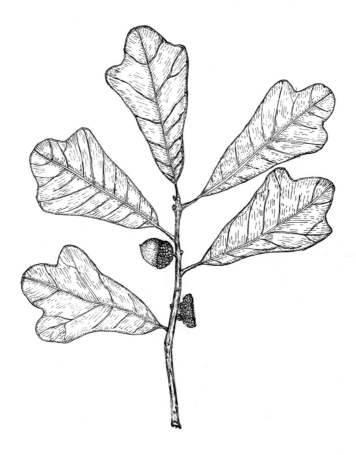

puberulent and stellate-pubescent, the puberulent anthers well exserted from the ciliate perianth. Pistillate catkins about ⅕ in. long, usually 3-flowered, subsessile, and densely fulvous-pubescent.

Fruit. Acorn annual, solitary or paired, on peduncles ½–⅖ in. long; acorn body ⅖–¾ in. long, ⅓–⅖ in. thick; shape broadly or narrowly ovoid, the ends broadly rounded; color brown and minutely puberulent, especially near the apex; about one-half to one-third included in the cup. Cups ⅖–½ in. broad; ⅕–⅖ in. high, deeply cup-shaped or more shallow, the scales densely fulvous or silvery-tomentulose, the bases moderately or markedly thickened, the thin apices closely appressed.

Leaves. Simple, alternate, deciduous or subevergreen, thin and rather soft; length 2–4 in. or more; width ¾–2½ in.; shape cuneate to oblanceolate or obovate to oblong, characteristically roundly 3-lobed at the broad apex or sometimes 5-lobed above the entire cuneate base; margins minutely revolute; upper surface shiny, when young sparsely glandular-puberulent and with scattered stellate hairs, finally glabrate or the stellate pubescence persistent especially about the midrib; lower surface dull, fulvous-glandular-puberulent and stellate-pubescent or the pubescence silvery; venation with 6–8 lateral veins to each side, irregularly branched, and reaching prominently into the lateral lobes, prominent beneath. Petioles ⅕–⅖ in. long, moderately slender, persistently pubescent like the twigs.

Twigs. About 1/15–⅛ in. thick, densely fulvous-tomentulose with a mixture of simple, appressed, glandular hairs and moderately spreading stellate hairs, the pubescence darkening and persisting through the second season. Buds 1/12–⅛ in. or more long; shape ovoid with apices acute or sometimes rounded, color russet, sparingly pubescent; stipules deciduous, ⅛–⅕ in. long, subulate, sparsely hairy.

Range. Locally abundant on deep sands in loblolly pine forests in east-central Texas, eastward to east Alabama.

Remarks. The genus name, *Quercus*, is the classical name. The species name, *boyntonii*, honors Frank Ellis Boynton (b. 1859), botanical collector for the Biltmore Herbarium, Biltmore, North Carolina, and superintendent of Biltmore estates to about 1935. It has also been listed under the name of *Quercus stellata* var. *boyntonii* (Beadle) Sarg.

The description of *Quercus boyntonii* Beadle was adapted from *Manual of the Vascular Plants of Texas* by Donovan Stewart Correll and Marshall Conring Johnston (1970).

Durand Oak

Quercus sinuata Walt. [H]

Field Identification. A tree attaining a height of 60 ft, with a trunk diameter of 30 in. The bark gray and flaky with broad, thin scales. This species has been referred to under the name of *Quercus durandii* Buckl. for many years, but it has been ascertained that the name *Quercus sinuata* Walt. has precedence as listed in Cornelius H. Muller's *The Oaks of Texas* (1951).

Flowers. Pistillate catkins about ⅕ in. long, usually 2-flowered on minutely stellate peduncles.

Fruit. Acorns solitary or paired on peduncles about ⅓ in. long, or

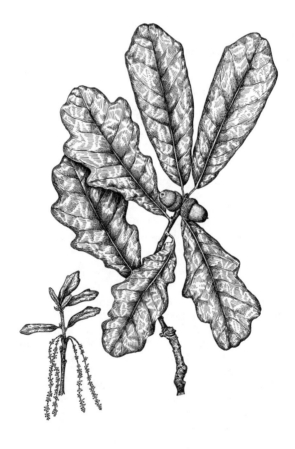

subsessile. Cups about ¾ in. broad and ⅓ in. high, saucer shaped or shallowly cup-shaped, flat or rounded at base, margin not enrolled; scales of cup narrowly ovate, only moderately thickened basally; apically loosely appressed, silvery-puberulent all over, the margins dark red. Acorns to ⅗ in. or more long or broad, elliptic to subrotund, glabrous except immediately above the apex, tan, one-fourth or less included in the cup.

Leaves. Simple, alternate, deciduous; texture firm; length to 5⅓ in.; width to 2½ in.; shape obovate to oblanceolate; apices broadly rounded; base cuneate or somewhat rounded; margin entire to regularly or irregularly sinuate teeth or lobes; margins minutely revolute; upper surface when young sparsely minute-stellate, with maturity glabrate and glossy green; lower surfaces noticeably whitened or less so later. Petioles to ⅓ in. long, somewhat stellate or glabrous.

Twigs. About 1/12–⅙ in. thick, when young sparsely stellate-pubescent; later glabrate and gray with minute lenticels.

Range. East Texas forests along rivers and eastward to South Carolina. Westward to the edge of the Edwards Plateau in Texas.

Remarks. The genus name, *Quercus*, is the ancient classical name. The species name, *sinuata*, refers to the leaf margins having regularly or irregularly sinuate teeth or lobes. Also, it has been listed as *Quercus austrina* Small and *Quercus durandii* var. *austrina* (Small) Palmer. Another vernacular name retained is Bastard Oak. In Central Texas on limestone soils and in northeast Mexico a variety has been named *Quercus sinuata* var. *breviloba* (Torr.) C. H. Mull.

Limestone Durand Oak

Quercus sinuata var. *breviloba* (Torr.) C. H. Mull. [H]

Field Identification. Straggling shrubs or small trees with gray flaking bark. This variety long has been listed under the name *Quercus durandii* var. *breviloba* (Torr.) Palmer, but it has been determined that the name of *Quercus sinuata* var. *breviloba* (Torr.) C. H. Mull. has precedence. (See Cornelius H. Muller, *The Oaks of Texas* [1951].)

Flowers. Staminate catkins to 3¼ in. long, finely and rather loosely flowered, tomentulose, the anthers moderately or only slightly exserted; pistillate catkins ⅛–⅓ in. long, 1–3-flowered, densely short-tomentose.

Fruit. Acorn annual, solitary or paired, subsessile or on a pubescent peduncle to ⅓ in. long; acorn cups to ½ in. broad and ⅓ in. high, goblet shaped or shallowly cup-shaped, base rounded or constricted; margins thin, smooth, simple; cup scales ovate, obtuse, the tomentose bases slightly or sharply keeled and thickened, the puberulent apices thin, closely appressed, dark reddish brown. Acorns to ⅝ in. long and ⅜ in. broad, ovoid to elliptic, glabrous, light brown, one-fourth enclosed in the cup.

Leaves. Simple, alternate, deciduous; texture thin to firm; to 3¼ in. long and 1½ in. broad, or often smaller; shape obovate to oblanceolate or oblong, usually broadest above the middle; apices broadly rounded; bases cuneate or obtuse or some gradually narrowed; margin entire to irregularly toothed or moderately lobed; upper surface glabrous and lustrous; lower surfaces duller, canescent with appressed, minute, stellate puberulence, or in shade forms green and only slightly puberulent or glabrous. Petioles ¹⁄₁₂–⅛ in. long, glabrous or pubescent like the twigs.

Twigs. Subterete or channeled, to ⅛ in. thick; color grayish-brown, glabrous or minutely stellate-tomentulose; lenticels minute; buds $\frac{1}{12}-\frac{1}{8}$ in. long, broadly ovoid, obtuse or acute, glabrous or sparsely pubescent, dark reddish brown or grayish brown; stipules rather promptly caducous, $\frac{1}{8}-\frac{1}{5}$ in. long, filiform-ligulate, pubescent.

Range. Wooded limestone hills of central Texas and northeast Mexico. The related species *Quercus sinuata* Walt. occurs in moist river bottoms of south and east Texas.

Remarks. The genus name, *Quercus*, is the ancient classical name. The species name, *sinuata*, refers to the sinuate leaf margins, and the variety name, *breviloba*, to the short leaf lobes.

Lacey Oak

Quercus glaucoides Mart. & Gal. [H]

Field Identification. Tree to 45 ft, and 1½ ft in diameter, with stout, erect, spreading branches, but sometimes only a clumpy shrub. Easily identified by the grayish green leaves that lend a rather smoky appearance when seen from a distance.

Flowers. Borne in spring in separate staminate and pistillate catkins; staminate catkins loosely flowered, $2-2\frac{1}{2}$ in. long; perianth deeply divided into 4 or 5 ovate lobes that are acuminate at the apex; stamens exserted, longer than the perianth lobes, anthers subglobose; pistillate catkins 1–3-flowered distally, $\frac{1}{5}-\frac{3}{5}$ in. long.

Fruit. Acorns borne annually, 1–3 in a cluster, sessile or short-peduncled, short-oblong, ovoid or ellipsoid, apex truncate or rounded, shiny chestnut brown, enclosed in cup one-fourth to one-half its length, or at the base only; cup stout, cup-shaped or saucer shaped, about $\frac{1}{4}-\frac{1}{2}$ in. wide, reddish brown, rather corky; scales closely appressed, apex rounded to obtuse, margin ciliate, tomentose, more glabrous later.

Leaves. Alternate, tardily deciduous, blades 2–5 in. long, $\frac{3}{4}-2$ in. wide, leathery, reticulate veined, upper surface conspicuously grayish green and glabrous; lower surface paler, glabrous to glaucous or pubescent on the veins; oblong, elliptic, or obovate, mostly shallowly sinuate, 2-lobed on each margin, apex rounded or occasionally 3-lobed; base rounded to cuneate or, rarely, cordate; petiole slender, glabrous or sparingly pubescent, $\frac{1}{4}-\frac{1}{3}$ in.; stipules caducous, about $\frac{1}{25}$ in. long, linear to subulate.

Twigs. Young twigs green to light brown, pubescent at first, gla-

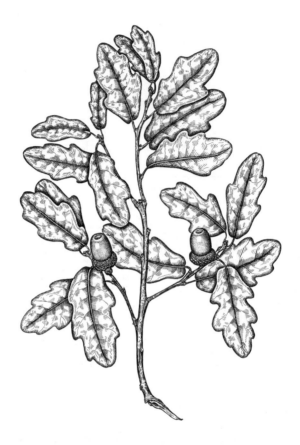

brous later; older ones gray, smooth, tight, marked with small, light, orbicular lenticels.

Bark. Gray, thick, broken into flat, narrow ridges and deep fissures.

Range. Rocky soils of bluffs and riverbanks, apparently confined to the limestone Edwards Plateau of Texas. In addition to the type locality, the Lacey Oak is also found in Real, Terrell, Edwards, Kimble, Uvalde, Menard, Bandera, Medina, and Kendall counties. Also in the mountains of Nuevo León, Tamaulipas, Coahuila, and San Luis Potosí, Mexico.

Remarks. The genus name, *Quercus*, is an ancient classical name, and the species name, *glaucoides*, refers to the paler glaucouslike lower leaf surface. The vernacular name is for Howard Lacey, who first collected it on his Kerrville ranch. Other vernacular names are Rock Oak, Canyon Oak, Mountain Oak, Smoky Oak, and Bastard Oak. The wood is occasionally used for fuel and posts. Lacey Oak is sometimes confused with Limestone Durand Oak, *Quercus sinuata* var. *breviloba* (Torr.) C. H. Mull., but the former has grayish green leaves as a distinguishing feature.

Shrub Live Oak

Quercus turbinella Greene [H]

Field Identification. Stiffly branched shrub or small tree sometimes attaining a height of 15 ft.

Flowers. Staminate catkins ¼–¾ in. long, yellowish green, bracts densely brown-tomentose, lobes rounded or obtuse, stamens exserted, anthers large, yellow, filaments short and densely hairy; pistillate catkins sessile or peduncled, very small, ⅛–¼ in. long, solitary or clustered, scales brown-tomentose.

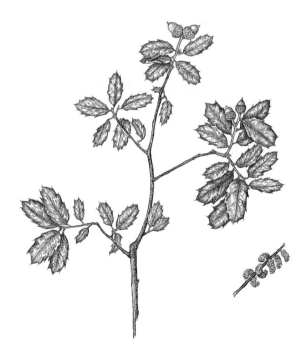

Fruit. Borne on tomentose peduncles ⅜–1¼ in., solitary or several at the distal end, acorn annual, length about ⅗ in. or less, width about ½ in., ovoid to short-oblong, light brown, pubescent at first, less so later, one-fourth to one-half included in the cup; cup shallowly cup-shaped, or turbinate, ⅓–½ in. broad, ⅙–¼ in. high, base rounded, scales ovate, closely appressed, reddish brown, densely tomentose to pubescent to semiglabrous, apex obtuse to rounded and thin, base thickened.

Leaves. Evergreen, stiff, thick, leathery, sometimes crinkled, broadly elliptic or ovate, blade length ⅖–1⅗ in., width ⅕–⅘ in., apex obtuse to acute or rounded, spinose, base subcordate or rounded, each margin coarsely 3–5-spinose-toothed, flattened or subrevolute and thickened (rarely entire), upper surface dull or semilustrous to glaucous, grayish green, lower surface densely stellate-tomentose, veins fairly prominent; petioles tomentose at first, but less so later, ¹⁄₂₅–⅙ in.

Twigs. Brownish gray, tomentulose to glabrate later, ¹⁄₂₅–⅕ in. thick, almost rounded or fluted, rather rigid; buds ovoid, ¹⁄₂₅–¹⁄₁₂ in. long, brown-tomentose; stipules persistent, ¹⁄₁₂–⅙ in., linear-filiform, hairy.

Range. In Trans-Pecos Texas, New Mexico, Arizona, California, southern Colorado, Utah, and Nevada. Usually at altitudes of 3,500–8,000 ft.

Remarks. The genus name, *Quercus*, is the ancient classical name, and the species name, *turbinella*, refers to the turbinate cup of the acorn. It is usually known as Scrub Oak locally and is very variable and comprises several races. Occasionally it resembles toothed forms of Gray Oak, *Q. grisea*.

Mohr Oak

Quercus mohriana Buckl. [H]

Field Identification. Usually a thicket-forming shrub, but sometimes a small, round-topped tree to 20 ft.

Flowers. Borne in separate staminate and pistillate catkins; staminate catkins ¾–1½ in. long, loosely flowered, from sparsely to densely hairy, anthers barely exserted, red; calyx hairy, divided into ovate lobes; pistillate catkins 1–3-flowered toward the apex, hairy, ¹⁄₁₂–⅓ in.; bracts and calyx lobes hairy.

Fruit. Acorns borne annually, solitary or 2–3, sessile or on densely pubescent peduncles ¼–¾ in. (usually about ⅜ in.); ovoid to ellipsoid or oblong; apex abruptly rounded and apiculate; young acorns with fascicled hairs, older ones brown and lustrous; length ⅓–⅗ in., width ¼–⅓ in., enclosed one-half to two-thirds of length in cup; cup turbinate or cup-shaped, ⅕–½ in. high and ⅓–¾ in. broad, color reddish brown and tomentose; margin thin and smooth; base flattened or rounded; scales closely appressed, ovate to oblong, thickened and more tomentose toward the cup base but smaller, thinner, and more glabrous toward the cup rim; apices elongate, obtuse or acute.

Leaves. Alternate, persistent, coriaceous, oblong to elliptic to lanceolate or obovate; margin entire or with a few large, coarse, apiculate teeth, sometimes with a few rounded lobes, the plane surface of the margin either undulate or flattened and slightly revolute; apex acute, rounded or acuminate; base rounded or cuneate, sometimes unequal sided; upper surface usually dark green and shiny, sparsely and minutely stellate-pubescent; lower surface usually densely gray or white-tomentose; blade length ¾−4 in., width ½−1½ in.; petiole ¹⁄₁₂−¼ in., tomentose; stipules caducous, subulate, about ⅛ in. long.

Twigs. Young parts brownish gray, tomentose, and fluted; older ones gray, smooth, and glabrous; buds reddish brown, smooth or pubescent.

Bark. Grayish brown, thin, pale, deeply furrowed.

Range. In dry, well-drained, preferably limestone soils of the West. In western central Texas; southwestern Oklahoma; and Coahuila, Mexico.

Remarks. The genus name, *Quercus*, is the classical name, and the species name, *mohriana*, refers to Charles Mohr (1824–1901), German-born druggist and botanist of Alabama. Vernacular names are Scrub Oak, Shin Oak, and Limestone Oak. Mohr Oak is known to hybridize with Post Oak, Harvard Oak, and Gray Oak when the contact is made. Gray Oak and Mohr Oak, especially, produce a very varied assemblage of hybrid forms. The wood of Mohr Oak, or its hybrids, has little value except as fuel or posts.

Havard Shin Oak

Quercus havardii Rydb. [H]

Field Identification. Low shrubs, hardly over 3 ft, forming thickets by underground rhizomes in deep sands. Rarely a small tree.

Flowers. Borne in separate staminate and pistillate catkins; staminate catkins pubescent, heavily flowered, ½−1½ in.; anthers pubescent, moderately exserted; pistillate catkins, ⅛−⅓ in., 1−5-flowered toward the apex.

Fruit. Acorn rather large, annual, very variable in size and shape, solitary or 2−3 in a cluster, sessile or short-peduncled, enclosed one-third to two-thirds in the cup, length ½−1 in., ½−¾ in. wide, ovoid to short-oblong, color chestnut brown, lustrous and glabrous or slightly glaucescent; cup deeply bowl shaped to goblet shaped, very variable in size, ½−1 in. broad and ⅖−½ in. high, base mostly rounded, margins either thin or thick; scales reddish brown,

pubescent, ovate-oblong, apex long-acuminate, blunt, thinner than the base.

Leaves. Alternate, deciduous, leathery, very variable in size and shape, blades ¾–4 in. long, ¾–1½ in. wide, oblong, elliptic, lanceolate, or oblanceolate, ovate or obovate; margin entire or variously undulate, coarsely toothed or lobed, sometimes margins falcate or asymmetrical, revolute or flattened; apices broadly rounded to obtuse or acute; base cuneate or rounded; upper surface bright green, lustrous, glabrous or with minute fascicled hairs; lower surface densely brown to gray-tomentose; petioles ¹⁄₁₂–¼ in., pubescent, about ⅕ in. long.

Twigs. Rounded or sulcate, young ones densely brownish yellow-tomentose, older twigs gray to reddish brown, glabrous or nearly so. Bark gray, smooth or scaly.

Range. Across the sandy plains of the lower Texas Panhandle area into eastern New Mexico.

Remarks. The genus name, *Quercus*, is the ancient name. The species name, *havardii*, honors the botanist Valery Havard (1846–1927). Vernacular names are Shinnery Oak, Sand Oak, Panhandle Shinnery, and Sand Scrub. Also known to hybridize with Mohr Oak and with Post Oak on the eastern contact of the species. The acorns and leaves of these hybrids vary greatly in size and shape. The acorn of Havard Oak has some value to wildlife, being eaten by peccary, prairie chicken, and bobwhite. It is reported to cause some stock poisoning.

Vasey Oak

Quercus pungens var. *vaseyana* (Buckl.) C. H. Muller [H]

Field Identification. Usually a shrub 1–5 ft, forming thickets over wide areas, or under favorable conditions a small tree to 20 ft.

Flowers. Staminate and pistillate catkins borne separately; staminate 1–1¼ in. long, loosely flowered, hairy; stamens exserted; calyx 4–5-lobed, lobes ovate, scarious, apex obtuse to rounded; pistillate 1–3-flowered on tomentose peduncles ⅛–⅕ in., subtended by ovate, pubescent scales shorter than the pubescent calyx, stigmas red, reflexed.

Fruit. Annual, solitary or in pairs, sessile or with peduncle ¹⁄₁₂–⅛ in.; acorns ellipsoid to oblong or subcylindric; light brown, shiny, and glabrous; one-fifth to one-third included in the cup, ½–¾ in. long, ¼–½ in. broad; cup saucer shaped or cup-shaped, thin, base rounded, puberulent within, ¼–½ in. broad, ⅛–⅙ in. high; scales closely appressed, ovate; apex glabrous or nearly so, thin, acute, reddish; base thickened and tomentose.

Leaves. Half-evergreen, alternate, coriaceous; oblong, obovate or lanceolate; margin with short, mucronate lobes, coarsely serrate to entire; apex acute, obtuse, or rounded; base cuneate to rounded; blade length ¾–2½ in., ½–¾ in. wide; upper surface grayish green to dark green, shiny, glabrous or nearly so; lower surface paler, densely pubescent or varying to glabrous, veins prominent; petiole pubescent at first, glabrous later, ¹⁄₂₅–¼ in.; stipules about ⅛ in., subulate, caducous, pubescent.

Twigs. Young slender, fluted, reddish brown to gray, tomentulose, later gray and glabrous; buds ¹⁄₂₅–⅛ in. long, ovoid to obovoid, reddish brown, pubescent or glabrous.

Bark. Grayish brown, rough, furrows deep, ridges scaly.

Range. Covering wide areas on dry limestone hills of central west Texas. Also in the Mexican states of Nuevo León, Tamaulipas, and Coahuila. In Texas in the counties of Edwards, Crockett, Kimble, Kinney, Kendall, Kerr, Menard, Pecos, Real, Schleicher, Sutton, Terrell, Uvalde, and Val Verde. The type was collected in Val Verde County.

Remarks. The genus name, *Quercus*, is the ancient classical name. The species name, *pungens*, means "prickly," referring to the mucronate teeth of the leaf, and the variety name, *vaseyana*, is in honor of the botanist G. R. Vasey, who made collections in Texas, New Mexico, and Arizona in 1881. Vernacular names are Scrub Oak and Shin Oak. Various species of ground squirrels eat the acorn. The wood is scarcely used except as fuel. This variety has been reported by some authors as *Q. vaseyana* Buckl. and *Q. undulata* var. *vaseyana* (Buckl.) Rydb.

Live Oak

Quercus virginiana Mill. [H]

Field Identification. Evergreen tree to 60 ft, with a wide-spreading crown and massive limbs close to the ground.

Flowers. Staminate and pistillate borne in separate catkins on same tree; staminate catkins hairy, 2–3 in. long; calyx yellow with 4–7 ovate lobes; stamens 6–12, filaments short, anthers hairy; pistillate catkins fewer, on pubescent peduncles ⅓ in. long; scales and calyx lobes hairy; stigmas 3, red.

Fruit. Acorn on peduncles ¼–4 in. long, in clusters of 3–5; nut ellipsoid-obovoid, brownish black, shiny, ⅓–½ in. long; enclosed about one-half its length in the cup; cup turbinate, light reddish brown, hoary-tomentose, scales of cup ovate, acute, thin, appressed.

Leaves. Simple, alternate, persistent, coriaceous, dark green and lustrous above, paler and glabrous to pubescent beneath; very variable in size and shape, 2–5 in. long, ½–2½ in. wide, oblong or elliptic or obovate; apex rounded or acute, base cuneate, rounded or cordate, margin entire and often revolute, sometimes sharply dentate, especially toward the apex; petioles about ¼ in. long, stout, glabrous or puberulent.

Twigs. Grayish brown, glabrous, slender, rigid; terminal buds ovate to subglobose, about ⅙ in. long, light brown; leaf scars half-moon shaped.

Bark. Dark brown to black (in some varieties gray), furrows narrow and interlacing, scales closely appressed, small.

Wood. Light brown, sapwood lighter, close-grained, tough, hard, strong, heavy, weighing about 59 lb per cu ft, difficult to work.

Range. This species is usually found in sandy loam but may also occur in heavier clays. In Texas, Oklahoma, and Louisiana. In Louisiana it reaches its largest size in the vicinity of New Orleans and the lower delta area. It extends eastward to Florida and north to Virginia.

Remarks. The genus name, *Quercus,* is the classical name, and the species name, *virginiana,* refers to the state of Virginia. The wood is used for hubs, cogs, shipbuilding, or any other purpose requiring a hard and strong wood. The tree is often planted in the southern states for ornament along avenues. It is comparatively free of insect pests and diseases and can stand considerable salinity, often growing close to the sea. The bark was formerly

much used in the production of tannin, and acorn oil was much used in cooking by the Indians. Live Oak seems to be susceptible to soil types and produces dwarf varieties and diverse leaf forms under certain conditions. The fruit seems to vary least in the varieties.

Scrub Live Oak

Quercus fusiformis Small [H]

Field Identification. A shrub or tree to 36 ft tall. Very similar in habit to *Q. virginiana* Mill. Although it appears distinct in the

western part of its distribution (beyond the Edwards Plateau area and into Mexico), on its eastern range it seems to pass into *Q. virginiana* with many intermediary variants.

Flowers. Staminate and pistillate flowers borne in separate catkins on the same tree; staminate catkins hairy, 2–3 in. long; calyx yellow with 4–7 ovate lobes; stamens 6–12, filaments short, anthers hairy; pistillate catkins fewer, on pubescent peduncles 1–3 in. long; scales and calyx lobes hairy; stigmas 3, red.

Fruit. Borne on peduncles ¾–2⅓ in. long, solitary or several together. The cups much constricted basally and flaring upward. Acorn elongate, fusiform or subfusiform, brown, shiny.

Leaves. Simple, alternate, evergreen; length ¾–2⅓ in. or more; width ⅓–1¼ in.; shape narrowly oblong; margins entire or toothed and strongly revolute.

Range. Limestone outcrops on the Coastal Plain uplands, abundant on the limestone hills west to the Pecos River and south along the east face of the mountains through Coahuila, Nuevo León, and Tamaulipas. The type from Kerr County.

Remarks. The genus name, *Quercus*, is the ancient Latin name. The species name, *fusiformis*, refers to the shape of the acorn. Some authors perfer to maintain it as a western, more shrubby variety of Live Oak under the name of *Quercus virginiana* var. *fusiformis* (Small) Sarg.

Bluejack Oak

Quercus incana Bartr. [H]

Field Identification. Shrub or tree to 35 ft, with stout crooked branches.

Flowers. In spring, in staminate and pistillate catkins; staminate catkins clustered, 2–3 in. long, hairy; calyx lobes 4–5, ovate, acute, red to yellowish green; stamens 4–5, yellow; anthers api-

culate; pistillate catkins on stout, tomentose, short peduncles; scales and calyx lobes of pistillate flowers tomentose, stigmas dark red.

Fruit. Maturing the second season, sessile or short-stalked, globose to ovoid, sometimes flattened, brown with grayish pubescence, often striate, about ½ in. long, set in a shallow cup one-third to one-half its length, kernel bitter; cup shallow, saucer shaped; scales imbricate, thin, ovate, tomentose, reddish brown.

Leaves. Alternate, simple, deciduous, entire (or, rarely, 3-dentate at the apex), oblong-lanceolate to elliptic, distinctly grayish green, densely tomentose beneath, smoother above, cuneate or rounded at base, acute or rounded at the apex, apiculate, 2–5 in. long, ½–1½ in. wide; petiole ¼–½ in. long, stout.

Twigs. Gray to dark brown, slender, smooth.

Bark. Grayish brown to black, broken into small blocklike plates.

Wood. Reddish brown, close-grained, hard, strong.

Range. Usually in dry sandy soils of east Texas, Louisiana, Oklahoma, and Arkansas; north and east to North Carolina and Virginia.

Remarks. The genus name, *Quercus*, is the ancient classical name, and the species name, *incana*, refers to the grayish green tomentum of the leaves. Vernacular names are Upland Willow Oak, High-ground Willow Oak, Sandjack Oak, Turkey Oak, and Cinnamon Oak. The trunk is generally too small to be of much value except for fuel or posts.

Blackjack Oak

Quercus marilandica Muenchh. [H]

Field Identification. Shrub, or round-topped symmetrical tree attaining a height of 60 ft and a diameter of 2 ft.

Flowers. With the leaves in spring, in staminate or pistillate catkins; staminate catkins clustered, loosely flowered, slender, hairy, yellowish green, 2–4 in. long; stamens 3–12, filaments filiform, anthers exserted; calyx thin, pubescent, reddish green, 4–5-lobed; pistillate flowers solitary or paired, ⅛–⅕ in. long, pubescent to glabrate, peduncles rusty-tomentose and short; styles recurved, stigmas red.

Fruit. Acorn ripening in 2 years, solitary or in pairs, sessile or on peduncles ⅛–⅖ in. long; light brown, enclosed one-third to two-thirds in cup, ⅗–⅘ in. long, ½–¾ in. wide, often striate, ovoid-oblong to subglobose, pubescent; cup thick, turbinate, ⅗–⅘ in. broad, bases rounded or suddenly constricted; scales of cup imbricate, loose, obtuse, ovate to oblong, thin.

Leaves. Simple, alternate, deciduous, stiff, coriaceous, broadly obovate to clavate, margin revolute; apex 3-lobed to entire or dentate, bristle-tipped, base rounded, cordate or cuneate; upper surface dark green, glossy and glabrous (or young leaves tomentose and hairy along the veins); lower surface semiglabrate or scurfy and yellow-hairy, veins conspicuous, length 3–7 in., width 2–5 in.; petioles ½–¾ in., stout, glabrous or pubescent; stipules caducous, ¼–⅓ in., glabrous or pubescent.

Twigs. Grayish brown, stout, stiff, densely tomentose at first, glabrous later; buds ⅙–⅓ in. long, ovoid to lanceolate, apex acute, reddish brown, slightly or densely tomentose.

Bark. Dark brown or black, broken into rough, blocklike plates.

Wood. Dark brown, sapwood lighter, heavy, hard, strong, weighing 46 lb per cu ft.

Range. Usually on dry, sandy, sterile soils. Central Texas, Oklahoma, and Arkansas; eastward through Louisiana to Florida, north to New York, and west to Minnesota, Michigan, Illinois, and Kansas.

Remarks. The genus name, *Quercus*, is of classical origin, and the species name, *marilandica*, refers to the state of Maryland. Also known by the vernacular names of Iron Oak, Black Oak, Jack Oak, Barren Oak, and Scrub Oak. The wood is used mostly for posts, fuel, and charcoal, and the acorns are sought by wild turkey and white-tailed deer.

Shumard Oak

Quercus shumardii Buckl. [H]

Field Identification. Tree attaining a height of 120 ft, with an open head and stout spreading branches. Leaves 5–9-lobed, usually 7-lobed, green and glabrous on both sides except for tufts of hairs in the axils of the veins beneath. Distinguished from Southern Red Oak by the smoothness and lobing, the Southern Red Oak having leaves irregularly lobed and densely pubescent beneath. Also, Southern Red Oak has much smaller acorns than Shumard Oak.

Flowers. Borne in spring on separate staminate and pistillate catkins; staminate catkins slender, 6–7 in. long, usually clustered; calyx lobes 4–5, hairy; stamens 4–12; pistillate flowers solitary or paired, peduncles pubescent; involucral scales ovate, pubescent, brown or greenish; stigmas red.

Fruit. Acorn sessile or short-stalked, solitary or paired, ovoid to oblong-ovoid, pubescent or glabrous, sometimes striate, ¾–1 in. long, ½–1 in. wide, set only at base in shallow, thick cups; cup covering one-fourth the length of acorn; scales appressed, imbricate, thin or tuberculate, acuminate.

Leaves. Simple, alternate, deciduous, obovate, or elliptic-oblong, cut into 7–9 more or less symmetrical lobes, lobes sometimes lobulate and bristle-tipped, sinuses broad and varying in depth. The leaves of upper and lower branches often vary considerably in the number and length of lobes. Upper surface dark green, glabrous and lustrous, lower surface paler and glabrous with tufts of axillary hairs; petioles glabrous, grayish brown.

Twigs. Grayish brown, glabrous; branches smooth.

Bark. Gray to reddish brown, smooth or broken into small tight interlacing ridges.

Wood. Light reddish brown, close-grained, hard, strong, weighing 57 lb per cu ft.

Range. Moist hillsides or bottomlands in clay soils. Central Texas, Oklahoma, and Arkansas; eastward through Louisiana to Florida, northward to Pennsylvania and west to Kansas.

Remarks. The genus name, *Quercus*, is the classical name, and the species name, *shumardii*, refers to Benjamin Franklin Shumard (1820–1869), state geologist of Texas. Vernacular names are Spotted Oak, Leopard Oak, and Spanish Oak. The wood is not commercially distinguished from that of the other Red Oaks and is used for veneer, cabinets, furniture, flooring, interior trim, and lumber.

It is a beautiful tree with a symmetrical leaf design and, being rather free from insects and diseases, could be more extensively cultivated for ornament.

Texas Oak

Quercus texana Buckl. [H]

Field Identification. Shrub or small tree rarely over 35 ft in height, with spreading branches. Confined mostly to the high dry uplands of central Texas. The leaves are small, averaging about 3½ in. long.

Flowers. In catkins borne separately on same tree; staminate catkins 1⅓–3½ in. long, loosely flowered, hairy; calyx hairy-fimbriate, divided into 4–5 acute lobes, shorter than the stamens, anthers glabrous; pistillate catkins with short tomentose peduncles, catkins 1½–3½ in. long, 1–3-flowered, involucral scales reddish brown, stigmas red.

Fruit. Acorn biennial, sessile or on short peduncles ¹⁄₁₂–⅓ in. long, solitary or paired, short-oblong or ovoid, ¼–¾ in. long (mostly about ½ in.), reddish brown, pubescent, often striate, narrowed or rounded at the apex or abruptly apiculate, rounded at the base, one-fourth to one-half included in the cup; cup turbinate, abruptly constricted at the base, reddish, densely pubescent, ⅜–½ in. high and wide; scales ovate, appressed, thin, pubescent, apex obtuse, rounded or truncate, margins darker brown and thin.

Leaves. Deciduous, turning red in autumn, 2½–5½ in. long, 2–3½ in. wide, ovate to obovate or rounded, margin with 3–7 (mostly 5) aristate lobes with intervening broad or rounded sinuses; terminal lobe often longest, entire or 2–3-lobed at the apex, acute; upper lateral lobes sometimes broad and entire or divided at the apex into lesser acuminate lobes; lower lateral lobes often much smaller (except when entire leaf is only 3-lobed); margin thin and slightly puberulent below along the veins, occasionally with tufts of hair in the vein angles; petioles ⅓–1½ in. long, slender, glabrous, reddish yellow; lenticels small and pale; buds ⅛–⅕ in. long, lanceolate-ovoid, acute, reddish brown, tomentose; young unfolding leaves densely pubescent and reddish.

Twigs. Slender, younger ones reddish brown, mostly glabrous; older ones gray and glabrous.

Bark. Dark gray to black with thick short ridges and platelike scales, fissures deep.

Range. Common on the dry uplands of central and west Texas (Edwards Plateau), but not known to occur beyond the Pecos River. Also in southern Oklahoma in the Arbuckle Mountains.

Remarks. The genus name, *Quercus*, is the classical name, and the species name, *texana*, refers to the state of Texas, its native habitat. The first specimen described in the literature was found on limestone hills near Austin. Also known under the names of Texas Red Oak, Rock Oak, Hill Oak, Spotted Oak, Red Oak, and Spanish Oak. The wood is used locally for fuel and posts, but the tree is generally too small for lumber.

ELM FAMILY (Ulmaceae)

Lindheimer Hackberry

Celtis lindheimeri K. Koch [H]

Field Identification. Tree to 40 ft, trunk 1–1½ ft in diameter. The stout spreading branches form a broad irregular head. Recognized by the decidedly grayish green leaves.

Flowers. Borne March–April on branches of the year, minute polygamo-dioecious or, rarely, monoecious, pedicels pubescent; staminate fascicled; pistillate solitary or few-flowered; calyx greenish yellow, deciduous, the 5 lobes oblong, scarious, apex narrowed and rounded; stamens inserted on the margin of a tomentose torus, filaments subulate, anthers ovoid; ovary ovoid, sessile, green; style short and sessile (rudimentary in the staminate flowers), lobes divergent and stigmatic within.

Fruit. Drupe maturing in September, persistent, peduncles ¼–⅔ in., tomentose; body subglobose, about ¼ in. in diameter, ellipsoid, reddish brown, shiny, flesh thin; seed a bony nutlet.

Leaves. Simple, alternate, blade length ¾–3 in., width ¾–2 in., blade ovate to lanceolate or ovate to oblong, apex acute to acuminate, base cordate or rounded, often asymmetrical, margin entire, or crenate-serrate on young growth, upper surface grayish green and scabrous, lower surface paler and conspicuously reticulate-veiny, clothed with white hairs when young, less so or almost glabrous at maturity, 3-veined; petioles ¼–½ in., densely villous-pubescent.

Twigs. Slender, gray, pubescent at first, glabrous later, lenticels numerous and rough.

Bark. Gray to brown, roughened by thick, wartlike excrescences and broken into narrow ridges and shallow fissures.

Wood. White to brownish, not strong or durable, of little commercial value, used occasionally for fuel.

Range. Rich bottomlands adjacent to limestone hills. The central Texas Edwards Plateau area—Austin, San Marcos, New Braunfels, Kerrville, and San Antonio.

Remarks. The genus name, *Celtis*, is the ancient classical name, and the species name, *lindheimeri*, in honor of Ferdinand Lindheimer (1801–1879), German botanist, who resided more than 30 years in Texas and gathered a large collection of plants. A vernacular name is Palo Blanco.

Sugar Hackberry

Celtis laevigata Willd. [H]

Field Identification. Tree attaining a height of 100 ft, with a spreading round-topped or oblong crown.

Flowers. In spring, monoecious-polygamous, small, inconspicuous, greenish, borne on slender glabrous pedicels; staminate fascicled; calyx 4–6-lobed (usually 5), lobes ovate-lanceolate, glabrous or pubescent; stamens 4–6; pistillate flowers solitary or 2 together, peduncled; ovary 1-celled, surmounted by 2 stigmas.

Fruit. Drupe ripening in late summer, pedicel ¼–½ in., subglobose-obovoid, orange-red to black, about ¼ in. in diameter, flesh thin and dry, sweetish; seed solitary, pale brown, roughened. Fruit pedicel often longer than the leaf petiole.

Leaves. Simple, alternate, deciduous, ovate-lanceolate, often falcate, long-acuminate at apex, rounded or wedge shaped and inequilateral at base, entire or a few teeth near apex, thin, light

green, and glabrous above, paler and smooth beneath, conspicuously 3-veined at base beneath, 2½–4 in. long, 1–2½ in. wide.

Twigs. Light green to reddish brown, somewhat divaricate, lustrous, glabrous or pubescent.

Bark. Pale gray, thin, smooth or cracked, with prominent warty excrescences.

Wood. Yellowish, close-grained, soft, weak, weighing 49 lb per cu ft.

Range. The species is found in Texas, Arkansas, Oklahoma, and Louisiana; east to Florida and north to Missouri, Kansas, Indiana, and Virginia. Also in Nuevo León, Mexico.

Remarks. *Celtis* is a name given by Pliny to a sweet-fruited African lotus. The species name, *laevigata*, means "smooth." The wood is used to a limited extent for furniture, flooring, crating, fuel, cooperage, and posts. The dry sweet fruit is eaten by at least 10 species of birds. The tree is often used for street planting in the lower South.

Texas Sugar Hackberry

This species presents a considerable number of local variations that have caused some botanists to name a number of varieties; other botanists feel that the distinctions are too slight. Some of these are as follows:

Texas Sugar Hackberry, *C. laevigata* var. *texana* (Scheele) Sarg., is scattered in Texas and extends over the Edwards Plateau limestone area to the west. It has leaves that are ovate-lanceolate, acuminate, mostly entire, rounded or cordate at the base, glabrous above and pubescent beneath with axillary hairs; fruit orange-red with pedicels longer than the petioles; branches gray to reddish brown and pubescent.

Uvalde Sugar Hackberry, *C. laevigata* var. *brachyphylla* Sarg., is a form with thicker and shorter leaves, found on the rocky banks of the Nueces River.

Scrub Sugar Hackberry, *C. laevigata* var. *anomala* Sarg., is a sandy-land shrub of Callahan County, having oblong-ovate, cordate leaves and dark purple, glaucous fruit.

Small Sugar Hackberry, *C. laevigata* var. *smallii* (Beadle) Sarg., is a small tree with sharply serrate, acuminate, somewhat smaller

Net-leaf Sugar Hackberry

Small Sugar Hackberry

leaves. It occurs from the Gulf Coast plain north to North Carolina and Tennessee.

Arizona Sugar Hackberry, *C. laevigata* var. *brevipes* Sarg., is an Arizona variety with ovate, mostly entire leaves 1½–2 in. long, yellow fruit, and glabrous reddish brown branchlets.

Some botanists consider Net-leaf Sugar Hackberry, *C. laevigata* var. *reticulata* (Torr.) L. Benson, a distinct species, but others feel that it has such close affinities it should be classed as a variety of the Sugar Hackberry with xerophytic tendencies. The flowers and fruit are similar except for more pubescence on the fruit pedicel. The leaves are smaller, broadly ovate, yellowish green, stiff, coriaceous, entire or serrate, conspicuously reticulate-veined beneath. The veins are pubescent beneath, and the leaf petiole is densely pubescent. As a tree it is rarely over 30 ft and quite often it is only a large shrub. Subsequently it may be found that Arizona Sugar Hackberry is a synonym of Net-leaf Sugar Hackberry. West Texas to California; north to Colorado, Utah, Washington, and Oklahoma; and south into Mexico. In Texas generally on limestone hills west of the Colorado River. Occasionally on shell banks near the Gulf as far east as Houston.

Common Hackberry

Celtis occidentalis L. [H]

Field Identification. Tree attaining a height of 120 ft, with a rounded crown. The gray bark bears corky warts and ridges.

Flowers. In spring, with the leaves, perfect or imperfect, small, green, borne in axillary, slender-peduncled fascicles, or solitary; staminate fascicles few-flowered; calyx 4–6-lobed, lobes linear-oblong; stamens 4–6 (mostly 5); no petals; pistillate flowers usually solitary or in pairs; ovary sessile, ovoid, with 2 hairy reflexed stigmas.

Fruit. Drupe variable in size and color, globose or subglobose to ovoid, orange-red turning dark purple, ¼–½ in. long, persistent; flesh thin, yellow, sweetish, edible; seed bony, light brown, smooth or somewhat pitted, pedicels longer than leaf petioles.

Leaves. Simple, alternate, deciduous, ovate to elliptic-ovate, often falcate, short acuminate or acute, oblique at base with one side rounded to cuneate and the other somewhat cordate, usually coarsely serrate but less so near the base, 3-nerved at base, light green and glabrous above (or rough in *C. occidentalis* var. *crassifolia*), paler green and soft-pubescent or glabrous beneath, blades

2¼−4 in. long, 1½−2 in. wide; petioles slender, glabrous, about ½ in. long. The leaves are broader, not as long taper-pointed, more serrate on margin, and drupes larger than corresponding parts of Sugar Hackberry.

Twigs. Green to reddish brown, slender, somewhat divaricate, glabrous or pubescent.

Bark. Gray to grayish brown, smooth except for wartlike protuberances.

Wood. Yellowish white, coarse-grained, heavy, soft, weak, weighing 45 lb per cu ft.

Range. Texas, western Oklahoma, Arkansas, and Louisiana; eastward to Georgia, north to Quebec, and west to Manitoba, North Dakota, Nebraska, and Kansas.

Remarks. *Celtis* was a name given by Pliny to a sweet-fruited lotus, and *occidentalis* means "western." Vernacular names are Nettle-tree, False-elm, Bastard-elm, Beaverwood, Juniper-tree, Rim-ash, Hoop-ash, and One-berry. The tree is drought resistant and often planted for shade in the South and for shelter-belt planting. The wood is occasionally used commercially for fuel, furniture, veneer, and agricultural implements. The fruit is known to be eaten by 25 species of birds, especially the gallinaceous birds. It was also eaten by the Indians.

Spiny Hackberry

Celtis pallida Torr. [H]

Field Identification. Spiny, spreading, densely branched evergreen shrub attaining a height of 18 ft.

Flowers. Axillary, inconspicuous, in 2-branched, 3–5-flowered cymes, pedicels about 1/12 in. long; flowers greenish white, polygamous or monoecious; corolla absent; calyx lobes 4 or 5; stamens as many as the calyx lobes; style absent; stigmas 2, each 2-cleft and spreading; ovary sessile, 1-celled.

Fruit. Drupe subglobose or ovoid, yellow or orange, thin fleshed, mealy, acid, edible, 1/5–1/3 in. in diameter; stone ovoid, oval or obovoid, reticulate, acute, about 1/4 in. long and 3/8 in. wide.

Leaves. Alternate, simple, small, 3-nerved, deep green, scabrous and puberulent, elliptic to oblong-ovate; rounded, acute or obtuse at the apex; oblique and somewhat semicordate at base; coarsely toothed on margin, or entire; blades 1/2–2 1/4 in. long, 1/2–1 in. wide; petioles pubescent, 1/16–3/16 in., or longer.

Bark. Mottled gray to reddish brown, rather smooth and tight, sometimes with long, stout, gray or brown spines. Bark only rough at base of very old trunks.

Twigs. Divaricate, flexuous, spreading, smooth, gray or reddish brown, glabrous or puberulent; with stipular spines 1/4–1 in., stout, straight, single or paired, often at ends of shoots; lenticels small, pale, and usually numerous.

Range. Central, western, and southern Texas, New Mexico, Arizona, and Mexico. In Mexico from Chihuahua to Baja California, and south to Oaxaca.

Remarks. The genus name, *Celtis*, is the classical name for a species of lotus, and the species name, *pallida*, refers to the paleness of the branches. Commonly used vernacular names in Texas and Mexico are Desert Hackberry, Chaparral, Granjeno, Granjeno Huasteco, Capul, and Garabata.

The Indians of the Southwest are reported to have ground the fruit and eaten it with fat or parched corn. It is reported that the larvae of the snout butterfly feed on the foliage. Spiny Hackberry is also considered a good honey plant. Many birds consume it, particularly the cactus wren, cardinal, pyrrholuxia, towhee, mockingbird, thrasher, scaled quail, Gambel's quail, and green jay. The raccoon, deer, and jackrabbit eat it occasionally. The wood is used for fence posts and fuel, and the plant is of some value in erosion control.

Slippery Elm

Ulmus rubra Muhl. [H]

Field Identification. Tree attaining a height of 75 ft, with spreading branches and a broad open head.

Flowers. February–April, before the leaves, borne in dense fascicles on short pedicels; perfect; no petals; calyx campanulate, green, hairy; calyx lobes 5–9, lanceolate and acute; stamens 5–9, with elongate yellow filaments and reddish purple anthers; pistil reddish, compressed, divided into a 2-celled ovary and 2 exserted, spreading, reddish purple stigmas.

Fruit. Ripening April–June. Samara short-stalked, green, oval to orbicular, apex entire or shallowly notched, ¼–¾ in. long; seed flattened with the surrounding wing reticulate-veined; seed area reddish brown and hairy; wing area glabrous. Minimum seed-bearing age of tree 15 years, optimum 25–125, and maximum 200 years. Good crops every 2–4 years and light crops intervening.

Leaves. Buds densely rusty-tomentose; leaves simple, alternate, deciduous, blades 4–8 in. long, 2–3 in. wide, obovate, ovate to oblong, acuminate at apex; rounded, cordate to cuneate, and in-equilateral at base; margin coarsely and sharply double-serrate; dark green and very rough above because of tiny pointed tubercles, also pubescent when young but later more glabrous; paler and soft-pubescent beneath, often with axillary hairs; petioles ⅓–½ in., stout; leaves fragrant when dry.

Twigs. Gray, stout, roughened and densely pubescent when young, more glabrous later.

Bark. Gray to reddish brown, ridges flattened, fissures shallow, inner bark mucilaginous and fragrant.

Wood. Reddish brown, tough, strong, heavy, hard, compact, durable, weighing 43 lb per cu ft.

Range. Texas, Oklahoma, Arkansas, and Louisiana; eastward to Florida, north to Maine and Quebec, and west to Ontario, Minnesota, Wisconsin, and Nebraska.

Remarks. *Ulmus* is the ancient Latin name for elm, and the species name, *rubra*, refers to the reddish wood. The older name *U. rubra* Muhl. has precedence over the name *U. fulva* Michx., as used in most books. Vernacular names are Rock Elm, Red Elm, Sweet Elm, Indian Elm, Moose Elm, Gray Elm, and Soft Elm. The wood is used for making posts, ties, sills, boats, hubs, agricultural implements, furniture, slack cooperage, veneer, and sporting goods. In frontier days the bark was often chewed as a thirst quencher. White-tailed deer, rabbit, porcupine, and moose browse the twigs and foliage. The tree is rather short-lived and subject to insect damage. It has been cultivated since 1830.

American Elm

Ulmus americana L. [H]

Field Identification. Much-loved and famous American tree, admired for graceful vaselike shape. Attaining a height of 120 ft, but

generally under 70 ft and often buttressed at base. Known to reach an age of 300 years or more.

Flowers. February–April, before the leaves, in axillary, 3–4-flowered (occasionally to 12) fascicles; pedicels slender, jointed, drooping, nearly sessile or to 1 in. long; individual flowers perfect, petals absent; calyx campanulate, red to green, lobes 7–9 and short; stamens 5–8, exserted, with slender filaments and red anthers; pistil pale green, compressed, composed of a 2-celled ovary and 2 inwardly spreading stigmatic styles.

Fruit. Ripening March–June. Samara about ½ in. long, red to green, oval-obovate, consisting of a central flattened seed surrounded by a membranous wing; wing reticulate-veiny, glabrous but ciliate on margin, a deep terminal incision reaching the nutlet. The minimum seed-bearing age is 15 years and the maximum 300 years. Good crops occur most years.

Leaves. Simple, alternate, deciduous, 4–6 in. long, 2–3 in. wide, oval, obovate or oblong, acute or abruptly acuminate at apex;

veins conspicuous to the serrations; somewhat cordate on one side at base and rounder or cuneate on the other side, giving an inequilateral shape; margin coarsely and doubly serrate, upper surface dark green and mostly smooth (occasionally scabrous on vigorous shoots); lower surface pubescent at first, but glabrate later; petioles ⅕–⅓ in., rather stout.

Twigs. Slender, varying shades of brown, pubescent at first, glabrous later.

Bark. Light to dark gray, ridges flattened and scaly, fissures deep.

Wood. Light to dark brown, sapwood whitish, coarse-grained, tough, heavy, hard, strong, weighing 40 lb per cu ft, difficult to split, durable, bends well, shrinks moderately, tends to warp and twist.

Range. Moist soils of bottomlands and upland flats. Texas, Oklahoma, Arkansas, and Louisiana; eastward to Georgia and Florida, northward to Newfoundland, and west to Ontario, North Dakota, Montana, and Nebraska.

Remarks. *Ulmus* is the ancient Latin name for elm, and the species name, *americana*, refers to its native home. Vernacular names are Rock Elm, Common Elm, Soft Elm, Swamp Elm, White Elm, and Water Elm. Known to the lumber trade as White Elm and makes up the greater part of elm lumber and logs. In most cases the trade does not distinguish between the elm species. A very desirable ornamental tree for street and park planting, attaining large size and much admired for the graceful upsweep of the branches. It is sometimes used for shelter-belt planting in the prairie states, but *U. pumila* is considered superior for that purpose. The wood is used for woodenware, vehicles, baskets, flooring, veneer, furniture, cooperage, cabinets, sporting goods, stock staves, boxes, crates, framework, agricultural implements, trunks, handles, toys, car construction, shipbuilding and boat building, and fuel. It is reported that the Indians used the wood for canoes and the bast fiber for ropes. The fruit is often eaten by gallinaceous birds, and the young twigs and leaves are browsed by white-tailed deer, opossum, and cottontail. In the northern part of its range it appears to be subject to the attack of the elm-leaf beetle, *Galerucella xanthomelaena,* and in some areas large numbers of trees are killed by the Dutch elm disease, caused by the fungus *Graphium ulmi,* and by phloem necrosis, caused by a virus. American Elm is distinguished from Slippery Elm by the former having leaves less scabrous above and the samara being ciliate on the margin.

Cedar Elm

Ulmus crassifolia Nutt. [H]

Field Identification. Tree attaining a height of 90 ft, with slender, somewhat drooping branches and a narrow or rounded crown. Twigs or branches often with lateral corky wings.

Flowers. Borne usually in July in small, 3–5-flowered fascicles; pedicels slender, ⅓–½ in.; calyx campanulate, hairy, red to green, 6–9-lobed, lobes hairy and acute; no petals; stamens 5–6, with slender filaments and reddish purple anthers; pistil green, flattened, pubescent, composed of a 2-celled ovary and 2 exserted spreading styles.

Fruit. Samara borne in late summer, small, ¼–½ in. long, oval-elliptic or oblong, green, flattened, pubescent; composed of a central seed surrounded by a wing that is deeply notched at apex and ciliate on margin.

Leaves. Simple, alternate, somewhat persistent, blades 1–2 in. long, ¾–1 in. wide, elliptic to ovate, acute or obtuse at apex, rounded or cuneate to oblique at base, doubly serrate on margin; dark green, stiff and very rough to the touch above, pubescent beneath; petiole about ⅓ in., stout, hairy.

Twigs. Reddish brown, pubescent, often with brown, thin, lateral, corky wings. The only other Texas elm with corky wings is the Winged Elm.

Bark. Brown to reddish, or gray, ridges flattened and broken into thin, loose scales.

Wood. Reddish brown, sapwood lighter, brittle, heavy, hard.

Range. Often in limestone soils. Texas, Oklahoma, Arkansas, and Louisiana; east to South Carolina, north to New York, and west to Kansas.

Remarks. *Ulmus* is the ancient Latin name, and *crassifolia* refers to the rough, thick leaves. Vernacular names are Scrub Elm, Lime Elm, Texas Elm, Basket Elm, Red Elm, and Southern Rock Elm. It is often planted as a shade tree, but the wood is considered inferior to other elms because of its brittle and knotty character. It is sometimes used for hubs, furniture, and posts.

Winged Elm

Ulmus alata Michx. [H]

Field Identification. Tree attaining a height of 60 ft, with slender branches and a rounded or oblong crown. Often with conspicuous corky wings on the twigs and branches.

Flowers. Before the leaves in spring, borne in few-flowered drooping fascicles on filiform pedicels; flowers perfect, petals absent; calyx campanulate, red to yellow, the 5 lobes obovate and rounded; stamens 5, with long, slender filaments and reddish anthers; pistil green, hairy, flattened, composed of a tomentose 2-celled ovary tipped by 2 spreading styles.

Fruit. Samara reddish or greenish, long-stipitate, ovate to elliptic or oblong, ¼–⅓ in. long; seed solitary, flattened, ovoid; wing flat, thin, narrow, prolonged into divergent, apically incurved beaks; seed and wing hairy, especially on margin; the reddish samaras giving the tree a reddish appearance when in fruit.

Leaves. Simple, alternate, deciduous, ovate-oblong to oblong-lanceolate, occasionally somewhat falcate, blades ½–3 in. long,

coarsely and doubly serrate on margin, acute or acuminate at apex, wedge shaped or subcordate at base, pale-pubescent or glabrous beneath, with axillary hairs and prominent veins; petioles about ⅓ in. long, stout, pubescent.

Twigs. Reddish brown, slender, pubescent at first, glabrous later, often with conspicuous, opposite, thin, corky wings. The only other elms having corky wings are the Cedar Elm, September Elm, and Rock Elm.

Bark. Reddish brown to gray, ridges flat with closely appressed scales, fissures irregular and shallow.

Wood. Brown, close-grained, compact, heavy, hard, difficult to split, weighing 46 lb per cu ft, not considered as strong as other elms.

Range. Texas, Oklahoma, Arkansas, and Louisiana; eastward to Florida, north to Virginia, and west through Ohio and Indiana to Kansas and Missouri.

Remarks. *Ulmus* is the ancient Latin name, and *alata* refers to the corky wings on the twigs. Vernacular names are Cork Elm, Water Elm, Wahoo Elm, Red Elm, and Witch Elm. The Winged Elm is a favorite shade and ornamental tree. It is easily transplanted, sprouts readily from seed, is a rapid grower, and is rather free of disease and insects. The wood is generally used for the same purposes as other elms, such as tool handles, vehicle parts, and agricultural implements. Formerly the bark was used in some localities for baling twine.

Siberian Elm

Ulmus pumila L. [H]

Field Identification. Graceful cultivated shrub or small tree with slender drooping branches.

Flowers. March–April, appearing with or before the leaves, axillary, inconspicuous, greenish, clustered, short-pediceled, perfect or rarely polygamous, petals absent; calyx campanulate, 4–5-lobed; stamens 4–5, with green to violet anthers; style 2-lobed, ovary flattened and 1-celled.

Fruit. Samara April–May, clustered, ¼–½ in. long and broad, rarely more; oval to obovate, composed of a central, dry, compressed nutlet surrounded by a wing that is thin, reticulate-veined, membranous, semitransparent, apex with a notch sometimes reaching one-third to one-half way to the nutlet; pedicel ¹⁄₂₅–⅛ in.

Leaves. Simple, deciduous, alternate, oval to ovate or elliptic, blade length 1–2 in., width ½–1 in., margin doubly serrate, apex acute, base cuneate or somewhat asymmetrical, leathery and firm; upper surface olive green to dark green, glabrous, veins impressed; lower surface paler and glabrous, or somewhat pubescent when young or with axillary tufts of hair; turning yellow in autumn; petiole glabrous or pubescent, ⅙–½ in., stipules caducous.

Twigs. Slender; when young brownish and pubescent; when older brown to gray and glabrous; bark of trunk gray to brownish.

Range. A native of Asia, extensively cultivated in the United States. In its typical form a small-leaved shrub or tree from Turkestan to Siberia, Mongolia, and north China.

Remarks. The genus name, *Ulmus*, is the ancient Latin name for elm, and the species name, *pumila*, refers to its shrubby habit in

some forms. Often wrongly called Chinese Elm, but that name should properly apply to *U. parvifolia* Jacq. Both the Siberian and the Chinese Elm are cultivated in the Gulf Coast states for ornament.

Varieties and hybrids include the following:

Weeping Siberian Elm, *U. pumila* var. *pendula* (Kirchn.) Rehd., has slender pendulous branches and is the form commonly cultivated.

Narrow Siberian Elm, *U. pumila* var. *arborea* Litvinov, is pyramidal in shape with pinnately branched shoots; leaves ovate to lanceolate, doubly serrate, lustrous, blades 1½–2¾ in., petioles pubescent. It apparently originated in Turkestan and came into cultivation about 1894.

Androssow Siberian Elm, *U. pumila* forma *androssowi* (Litv.) Rehd., is a cultivated form with a dense head and spreading corky branches that has been cultivated since 1934.

Siberian Elm is known to hybridize with Scotch Elm, *U. glabra* Huds., to produce *Ulmus* × *arbuscula* Wolf., a shrubby tree with elliptic to oblong leaves ¾–2¾ in. long, doubly serrate, and nearly equal at base. It originated in 1902.

The Siberian Elm is being extensively planted in the prairie-plains region in shelter belts and has some use as a game cover. It is rather drought resistant and seems to be less susceptible to the Dutch elm disease than the native elm species. The wood is hard, heavy, tough, rather difficult to split, and is used in China for agricultural implements, boat building, and wagon wheels. The inner bark was once made into coarse cloth.

Chinese Elm

Ulmus parvifolia Jacq. [H]

Field Identification. A cultivated, attractive, semievergreen tree, attaining a height of 45 ft or more, but usually smaller. The slender branches form a broad, rounded, open crown. Bark usually smooth, thin, and pale gray; young trees often marked with white blotches or circular, white bands; older trunks have irregular shallow fissures with thin small scales that exfoliate to expose an orange-red inner bark.

Flowers. Borne in August or September in axillary clusters on short pedicels, on twigs of the preceding season; bisexual or, more rarely, unisexual; corolla absent; calyx campanulate, the 4–5 lobes (or sometimes more) divided below the middle; stamens as many as the calyx lobes and opposite them, the filaments straight, long-exserted; ovary superior, 1-celled, 1-ovuled; styles 2.

Fruit. Samara flat, oval to ovate or elliptic, with a membranous wing surrounding the seed and notched at apex; from about ⅓ in. long and glabrous.

Leaves. Simple, alternate; texture subcoriaceous; shape elliptic to ovate; apices acute to obtusish; margin mostly simply serrate; base rounded to cuneate and only slightly unequal; length ¾–2½ in.; upper surface glabrous or somewhat roughened with minute papillae; lower surface glabrous or with scattered pale long hairs, but more pilose on the venation; color rather lustrous, olive green to dark green above, but somewhat paler beneath; venation with

8–10 straight, lateral veins to a side, each ending in a tooth; stipules linear-lanceolate, narrow at the base; petioles very short, ⅟₂₅–¼ in. long, pale-strigose.

Twigs. Slender, gray to brown, pubescent when young, more glabrous later.

Range. A native of China, Korea, and Japan. Cultivated in the Gulf Coast states, and occasionally escaping. In Houston, a considerable number cultivated on the grounds of the Town & Country shopping center on Katy Freeway.

Remarks. The genus name, *Ulmus*, is an ancient Latin name. The species name, *parvifolia*, refers to the small leaves. Closely related species have been described as *Ulmus sieboldii* Daveau, *Ulmus shirasawana* Daveau, and *Ulmus coreana* Nakai, but they differ little from *Ulmus parvifolia*.

MULBERRY FAMILY (Moraceae)

Common Paper Mulberry

Broussonetia papyrifera (L.) Vent. [H]

Field Identification. Small tree, rarely to 50 ft, with irregular spreading branches.

Flowers. Dioecious, staminate catkins peduncled, cylindric, pendulous, 2½–3½ in. long; no petals; stamens 4; calyx 4-lobed;

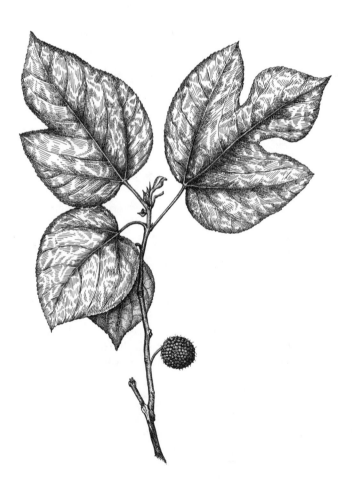

pistillate in globose heads with a tubular perianth; ovary stipitate, stigma filiform and slender.

Fruit. Globose, about ¾ in. across, a multiple fruit composed of many 1-seeded drupelets that are reddish orange and protrude from the persistent calyx.

Leaves. Alternate, deciduous, on long petiole, blades 3–8 in. long, ovate, margin coarsely dentate and often deeply lobed; apex acuminate; base cordate or rounded; rough above, conspicuously veined and velvety-pubescent beneath; stipules ovate-lanceolate, deciduous.

Twigs. Stout, hirsute, tomentose.

Bark. Smooth, tight, reticulate, green to yellow.

Wood. Coarse-grained, soft, light, easily worked.

Range. Texas, New Mexico, Oklahoma, Arkansas, and Louisiana; eastward to Florida, and northward to Missouri and New York. A native of Asia. Cultivated and escaping to grow wild in some areas in the United States.

Remarks. The genus, *Broussonetia*, is named in honor of Auguste Broussonet, a French naturalist, and the species name, *papyrifera*, refers to the use of the inner bark in papermaking. The inner bark is also used for making cloth in the tree's native home of Japan and China. The famous tapa cloth of the South Pacific islands is also made from the bark by macerating it and pounding it with a wooden mallet. It is often planted for ornament in the United States, being drought resistant and a rapid grower, and sprouting freely from the root. The fruit is also eaten by a number of species of birds.

Red Mulberry

Morus rubra L. [H]

Field Identification. Handsome tree to 70 ft, with a rather broad, spreading crown.

Flowers. With the leaves in spring, green; petals absent; staminate spikes cylindric, 2–3 in. long; stamens 4, green; filaments flattened; calyx with 4 ovate lobes; pistillate spikes about 1 in., cylindric, sessile; calyx 4-lobed; styles 2; ovary ovoid, flat, 2-celled, 1 cell generally atrophies.

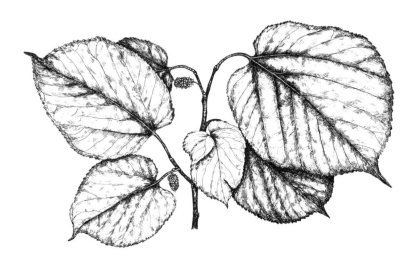

Fruit. Ripening May–August, a cylindric syncarp ¾–1¼ in. long, resembling a blackberry, red at first, becoming purplish black, juicy, edible; achene ovoid, acute, light brown, covered by the succulent calyx. Minimum seed-bearing age of the tree 10 years, optimum 30–85 years, maximum about 125 years.

Leaves. Simple, alternate, deciduous, 3–9 in. long, ovate or oval, or 3–7-lobed, doubly serrate, rough and glabrous above, soft-pubescent beneath, very veiny, acute or acuminate at apex, cordate or truncate at base, turning yellow in autumn; petiole 1–2 in.; stipules lanceolate and hairy. The lobing of the leaves varies considerably on different trees or even on the same tree; some are only serrate, while others have numerous lobes.

Bark. Dark brown to gray, ½–¾ in. thick, divided into irregular, elongate plates separating into appressed flakes.

Wood. Light orange, sapwood lighter, durable, close-grained, light, soft, weak, weighing about 45 lb per cu ft, used for boats, fencing, cooperage, and railroad crossties.

Range. Usually in rich moist soil. Does not grow well on thin, poor soil. Texas, Oklahoma, Arkansas, and Louisiana; eastward to Florida, north to Vermont, and west to Ontario, Wisconsin, Michigan, Minnesota, Nebraska, and Kansas.

Remarks. The genus name, *Morus*, is the classical name of the mulberry, and the species name, *rubra*, Latin for "red," has reference to the red, immature fruit. The fibrous bark was used by early Indians to make cloth. The fruit is known to be eaten by human beings, fox squirrels, and at least 21 kinds of birds. Although the fruit is sweet, it does not seem to be very much in demand for culinary uses. For fruit-bearing purposes the trees may be planted 20–40 ft apart. Trees should not be planted next to walks because the abundant ripe fruit mashes readily underfoot. Often planted for ornament and known in cultivation since 1629.

Black Mulberry

Morus nigra L. [H]

Field Identification. Cultivated shrub or tree attaining a height of 30 ft, or occasionally larger. The trunk is short and the wide-spreading branches form a broad, rounded, or irregularly shaped crown.

Flowers. Staminate flowers in cylindrical spikes ⅓–1 in., longer than the peduncles; stamens 4, inserted opposite the sepals under the ovary, filaments filiform; sepals 4; pistillate spikes cylindric-oval, ⅓–¾ in., shorter than the pubescent peduncles; sepals 4, lateral ones largest, sepals enclosing the fruit at maturity and becoming succulent; ovary sessile, 1-celled, style terminal and short, stigmas 2 and ascending.

Fruit. Syncarp dark red or black, fleshy, oval-oblong, ⅓–1 in. long, achenes included in calyx and tipped by persistent stigmas.

Leaves. Simple, alternate, deciduous, thin, ovate to oval, blades 1½–6 in. long, apex acute or short-acuminate, margin coarsely toothed or sometimes with one or more lobes, base rounded, cordate or semitruncate, upper surface dull dark green, usually rough and becoming glabrous, lower surface paler and sparingly pubescent on the veins to glabrous; young foliage pubescent; petioles usually shorter than the blade, one-fourth to one-half as long.

Twigs. Young ones green to brown and pubescent, older ones darker brown to gray or glabrous.

Range. Old gardens, roadsides, thickets, and waste grounds. Cultivated in Texas, Louisiana, Oklahoma, and Arkansas; eastward to Florida and north to New York. A native of western Asia.

Remarks. The genus name, *Morus*, is the classical Latin name of mulberry, and the species name, *nigra*, refers to the black color of the fruit. It is sometimes grown for fruit or for shade. Although

Black Mulberry is sometimes reported as being cultivated in the Southwest, many times incorrect identifications are made because of its close resemblance to a black-fruited race of White Mulberry, *M. alba* var. *tatarica* (L.) Ser.

White Mulberry

Morus alba L. [H]

Field Identification. An introduced tree to 40 ft, attaining a diameter of 3 ft.

Flowers. Staminate and pistillate catkins axillary, borne on the same tree or on different trees; staminate catkins ⅜–1 in., cylindric, slender, drooping; calyx 4-parted, lobes ovate; stamens 4, elastically expanding; pistillate catkins drooping, oblong or oval to subglobose, cylindric, ½–⅔ in. long, about ¼ in. in diameter; calyx 4-parted, lateral sepals largest, calyx greatly enlarging to envelop the achene at maturity; ovary sessile, 2-celled, 1 cell atrophies; styles 2, linear, stigmatic down the inner side.

Fruit. Borne June–August on slender, glabrous or pubescent peduncles ¼–⅔ in. long, pendent, subglobose to oval or oblong, white to pink (rarely black), ½–¾ in. long and about ¼ in. wide, sweet; fruit a syncarp, or an aggregation of ovate, compressed achenes, each covered by the succulent, thickened calyx, the whole fruit as a unit thus juicy and elongate.

Leaves. Alternate, deciduous, ovate to oval or asymmetrical, heart shaped, blades 2½–8 in. long, 1–4½ in. wide; margin with blunt, crenate teeth or often also 1–6-lobed, apex acute or short-acuminate; base semicordate, rounded or truncate, 3-veined; thin

and smooth; upper surface olive green, lustrous and glabrous, paler and glabrous beneath; petiole ½–1½ in., shorter than the blade, slender, glabrous or slightly pubescent.

Twigs. When young reddish brown, glabrous to slightly pubescent, when older slender, glabrous, gray.

Bark. Light to dark gray, broken into narrow furrows and irregular, often twisted, ridges.

Range. Escaping cultivation to roadsides, fields, and thickets. Naturalized Texas, Oklahoma, Arkansas, and Louisiana; north to Maine, and west to Minnesota and Wisconsin. Native home not positively known, either Europe or China, but most authorities cite an Asiatic origin. A cosmopolitan plant, known in nearly all parts of the world.

Remarks. The genus name, *Morus*, is the classical Latin name, and the species name, *alba*, refers to the white fruit. It is also known under the names of Silkworm Mulberry, Russian Mulberry, Morera, and Morea. The fruit is not as juicy as the native Red Mulberry and is somewhat smaller. It also seems to vary in sweetness, on some trees being very sweet and on others so insipid and dry as to be hardly edible. Although the fruit of the species is most commonly white or pink, some varieties produce red or black fruit. The fruit has some wildlife value, being eaten readily by a number of species of birds, opossums, and raccoon, as well as by poultry and hogs. The wood is hard and durable and is used for furniture, utensils, and boat building.

Texas Mulberry

Morus microphylla Buckl. [H]

Field Identification. Shrub, or sometimes a small, scraggy tree to 20 ft.

Flowers. Dioecious, small, green, inconspicuous, borne in amentlike spikes; staminate spikes on short pedicels, many-flowered, ½–¾ in. long; petals absent; calyx hairy, 4-lobed, lobes rounded, green to reddish; stamens 4, filaments filiform, anthers yellow with dark green connectives; pistillate sessile, drooping in short-oblong, few-flowered spikes rarely over ½ in. long; calyx hairy, 4-lobed, lobes thick, rounded, 2 larger than the others; ovary green and glabrous, 2-celled at first with one soon atrophying; stigmas 2, short, spreading.

Fruit. A syncarp (multiple fruit) ripening in May, subglobose or short-ovoid, red at first to black later, sweet or sour, with scant juice, edible. Syncarp composed of numerous small, 1-seeded drupes; drupes about ⅙ in. long, ovoid, rounded at ends, containing a thick-walled, crustaceous, brown nutlet; seed pendulous, ovoid, pointed, pale yellow.

Leaves. Simple, alternate, petioled, blades 1½–2½ in. long, ¾–1 in. wide; ovate to oval; margin coarsely serrate, sometimes 3–lobed; base truncate, rounded or semicordate; apex acute to short-acuminate; thin but firm; upper surface dull green, somewhat pubescent, tubercular roughened, veins inconspicuous; lower surface paler, glabrous to somewhat hairy, veins delicate-reticulate, 3-veined at base; petioles slender, pubescent, about ⅓–¾ in., stipules linear-lanceolate, somewhat falcate, apex acute, white-tomentose, about ½ in.

Twigs. Slender, white-hairy at first, glabrous later, light reddish brown to gray; lenticels small, round, pale.

Bark. Light gray or tinged with red, smooth, tight, shallowly furrowed and broken on the surface into narrow ridges and broad, flat fissures with slightly appressed scales.

Wood. Dark orange or brown, sapwood lighter, heavy, hard, elastic, close-grained, specific gravity 0.77.

Range. Texas, New Mexico, Arizona, and Mexico. In Texas generally west of the Colorado River on dry limestone hills. In Mexico in the states of Chihuahua to Durango.

Remarks. The genus name, *Morus*, is the classical name, and the species name, *microphylla*, refers to the small leaves. Vernacular names are Mexican Mulberry, Dwarf Mulberry, Wild Mulberry, Mountain Mulberry, Tzitzi, Hamdek-kiup, and Mora. The Indians or Arizona and New Mexico are reported to have grown the tree for its fruit and made bows from the wood. In Mexico the wood is used occasionally in carpentry. The fruit is rather small and dry but edible. It is consumed by a number of species of birds, including mockingbird, cardinal, mourning dove, Mearn's quail, scaled quail, and Gambel's quail and is sometimes browsed by the white-tailed deer. Texas Mulberry is easily distinguished from Red Mulberry by much smaller leaves and fruit. Texas Mulberry is generally found on dry, limestone soils. At one time the botanist E. L. Greene split the species into a number of segregates. However, most of these divisions are not constant in character, so the recent tendency is to regard them as geographical forms of the same species, *M. microphylla* Buckl.

Osage-orange

Maclura pomifera (Raf.) Schneid. [H]

Field Identification. Tree attaining a height of 60 ft, with a milky sap and bearing stout thorns.

Flowers. April–June, dioecious, green, staminate in long-peduncled axillary racemes, 1–1½ in. long; petals none; stamens 4, exserted; calyx 4-lobed; pistillate in globose, dense heads about 1 in. in diameter; calyx 4-lobed, thick, enclosing the ovary; ovary ovoid, compressed, 1-celled; style filiform, long, exserted.

Fruit. September–October, a syncarp, or aggregation of 1-seeded drupelets, globose, yellowish green, 4–5 in. in diameter; achenes surrounded by enlarged fleshy calyx; juice of fruit milky and acid.

Leaves. Deciduous, alternate, entire, broad-ovate to ovate-lanceolate, rounded or subcordate at base, or broadly cuneate, acuminate at apex, 3–6 in. long, tomentose at first, lustrous later, yellow in autumn, petioles ½–2 in., stipules triangular, small, early deciduous.

Bark. Brown to orange, deeply furrowed, ridges rounded and interlacing.

Wood. Bright orange or yellow, heavy, hard, durable, strong, weighing 48 lb per cu ft.

Range. Arkansas, Oklahoma, Louisiana, Missouri, and south into Texas. Well developed in the Oklahoma Red River Valley. Also escaping cultivation throughout eastern United States.

Remarks. The genus name, *Maclura*, is in memory of William Maclure, an early American geologist, and the species name, *pomifera*, means "fruit bearing." The name Bois d'Arc was given to it by the French, meaning "bow wood," with reference to the fact that the Osage Indians made bows from the wood. Vernacular names are Hedge-apple, Horse-apple, Mock-orange, and Yellow-wood. Yellow dye was formerly made from the root bark. Also the bark of the trunk was used for tanning leather. Squirrels feed on the little achenes buried in the pulpy fruit, and black-tail deer browse the leaves. The tree was formerly much planted in windbreaks or hedgerows and has been cultivated since 1818.

BARBERRY FAMILY (Berberidaceae)

Laredo Mahonia

Mahonia trifoliolata (Moric) Fedde [H]

Field Identification. Evergreen shrub to 10 ft, with stiff, spiny, hollylike, trifoliolate leaves.

Flowers. In racemes, on pedicels ⅓–¾ in.; yellow, perfect, corolla ⅜–½ in. across; sepals 6, petallike, greenish yellow, in 2 series, 3 long and 3 short, obovate; petals 6, in 2 series, outer 3 oval-obovate, concave, clawed, yellow with reddish streaks, inner 3 erect, ovate-oval; stamens 6, opposite the petals, filaments sensitive to touch, anthers opening by valves; pistil single, stigma circular, depressed.

Fruit. Berry ripening in June, on short peduncles ⅓–¾ in. long, obovate-oval, somewhat flattened, red, lustrous, aromatic, about ⅓ in. long, pulpy, acid; seeds 1 to several, crustaceous.

Leaves. Alternate, blades 2–4 in. long, trifoliolate; leaflets sessile, lanceolate to oblong or elliptic, apex acuminate-spiny, margin

3–7-lobed and spiny pointed, 1–2½ in. long, ½–1½ wide, thick, rigid, coriaceous, pale green, upper surface glabrous and reticulate–white-veined, lower surface paler and less prominently reticulate; petiole reddish green, glabrous, 1–3 in.

Twigs. Young shoots smooth and reddish green, older twigs gray to reddish brown.

Bark. On older stems gray to reddish brown, yellow within, broken into thin, small scales. Wood yellow.

Range. On dry, stony hillsides over most of Texas except in the east and southeast portions; west through New Mexico to Arizoña, and south into Mexico in the states of Chihuahua, Coahuila, Nuevo León, and San Luis Potosí.

Remarks. The genus name, *Mahonia*, is in honor of Bernard M'Mahon (1775–1816), and the species name, *trifoliolata*, refers to the trifoliolate leaves. Vernacular names are Wild Currant, Chaparral Berry, Agarita, Agrito, Algerita, Agrillo, and Palo Amarillo. The red, acid berries make excellent jellies and wine, and are gathered by threshing the thorny bush with a stick. The roasted seed has been reported as used for a coffee substitute. Birds eagerly devour the berries. In some areas the plant is used as a hedge, and the flowers are considered a good bee food. However, it is susceptible to black stem rust. A yellow dye is made from the wood and roots.

LAUREL FAMILY (Lauraceae)

Camphor-tree

Cinnamomum camphora Nees & Eberm. [H]

Field Identification. Handsome cultivated tree to 40 ft in height and to 2 ft in diameter, evergreen, dense, stout, round topped.

Flowers. Borne in axillary, slender-peduncled, green and glabrous panicles 1¾–3 in.; individual flower pedicels ⅛–¼ in.; glabrous; petals absent; perianth tube short, segments 5–6, early deciduous, leaving a truncate cup-shaped receptacle about ¼ in. long that is rugose, glabrous, and granular; stamens in 2–4 dissimilar groups, some rows gland-appendaged and some abortive; ovary 1-celled, with a slender style and minute stigma.

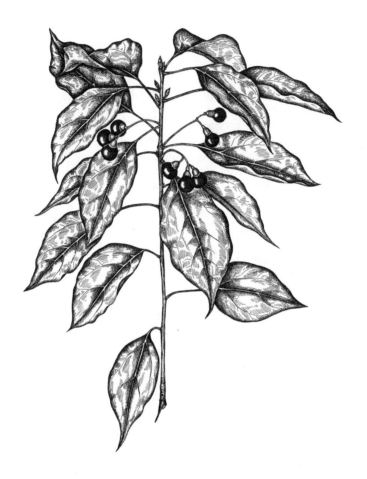

Fruit. Drupe solitary or a few together on the ends of the long, slender peduncles, globose, black, lustrous, fleshy, ¼–⅓ in. in diameter; seed solitary, globose, black, ridged around the center.

Leaves. Persistent, essentially alternate but often opposite, elliptic to ovate, apex acute to acuminate, base acute, blade length 1¼– 4½ in., width ¾–1½ in., margin entire and somewhat wavy on the plane surface, upper surface dark green, lustrous, and glabrous, veins yellowish green, lower surface paler and lightly glaucous, aromatic when bruised; petioles essentially glabrous, ¾–1½ in.

Twigs. Slender, elongate, green, and glabrous.

Bark. On young branches smooth, green to reddish brown or gray, on old trunks light to dark gray, broken into deep fissures and flattened, confluent, wider ridges.

Range. A native of Japan, China, and Malaya. Planted as an ornamental in Texas, Oklahoma, Arkansas, and Louisiana; east to Florida. Sometimes escaping cultivation. Often planted on the streets of Houston. Does well in cultivation in southern California.

Remarks. The genus name, *Cinnamomum*, is the ancient Greek name, and the species name, *camphora*, refers to the camphorous aromatic resin that the tree contains. The wood yields the camphor of commerce. The camphor is obtained by passing a current of steam through the chips, and the volatilized camphor is then condensed into crystals and oil. Later the crystals and oil are separated by filtration under pressure. About 30 lb of chips are required for 1 lb of camphor.

Common Spice-bush

Lindera benzoin (L.) Blume [H]

Field Identification. Stout, glabrous, aromatic shrub of damp woods. Attaining a height of 20 ft, with usually several stems from the base.

Flowers. Appearing before the leaves, polygamodioecious, yellow, fragrant, ¼–⅓ in. broad, in lateral, almost sessile, dense, umbel-like clusters of 3–6 flowers; involucre of 4 deciduous scales; petals absent; sepals 6, thin, obovate to elliptic, apex obtuse to retuse or truncate; staminate flowers with 9 stamens (in 3 series), some filaments glandular at base, anthers introrse, 2-celled and 2-valved; pistillate flowers with 12–18 rudimentary stamens in 2 forms (glandular and glandless); ovary globose, style slender and columnar.

Fruit. Ripening August–September, drupes solitary or in small clusters on pedicels 1/12–⅕ in., orbicular to obovoid, elongate, about ⅖ in. long, red, fleshy, spicy; 1-seeded, seeds light brown, speckled darker brown.

Leaves. Leaf buds scaly, leaves simple, alternate, deciduous, obovate to oval or elliptic, apex acute or short-acuminate, base acute or acuminate, margin entire, thin, bright green above, glaucous,

beneath glabrous, more rarely pubescent, blade length 2–4¾ in., width 1–2½ in.; petioles ³⁄₁₆–¾ in. Twigs often with 2 leaf sizes, much smaller ones sometimes at base of larger ones.

Twigs. Slender, glabrous, smooth, brittle, bark with corky lenticels, spicy to the taste.

Range. Sandy or peaty soils in low woods or swamps. Central Texas, Oklahoma, Arkansas, and Louisiana; eastward to Florida, north to Maine, and west to Ontario, Michigan, and Kansas.

Remarks. The genus name, *Lindera*, is for John Linder, a Swedish physician (1676–1723). The species name, *benzoin*, denotes its

Hairy Common Spice-bush

similarity in odor to that of the true balsamic resin of *Styrax benzoin*, an Asiatic tree. Vernacular names are Benjamin-bush, Spice-wood, Fever-bush, Snap-bush, and Wild Allspice. There are also a few varieties of Common Spice-bush, such as the Yellow-berry Common Spice-bush, *L. benzoin* var. *xanthocarpa* (Torr.) Rehd., which has yellow fruit, and the Hairy Common Spice-bush, *L. benzoin* var. *pubescens* (Palm. & Steyerm.) Rehd., which has pubescent and ciliate leaves and petioles. Some authorities list the Common Spice-bush under the scientific name of *Benzoin aestivale* (L.) Nees.

The leaves, twigs, bark, and fruit contain an aromatic oil that was made into a fragrant tea by the pioneers. The bark is aromatic, tonic, astringent, stimulant, and pleasant to chew. A substitute for allspice was once made from the dry, powdered drupes. Twenty-four species of birds are known to feed upon the fruit, also rabbit and white-tailed deer nibble the leaves.

JUNCO FAMILY (Koeberliniaceae)

Spiny Allthorn

Koeberlinia spinosa Zucc. [H]

Field Identification. Much-branched, usually leafless shrub or tree attaining a height of 24 ft and consisting of a tangled mass of stiff green spines.

Flowers. Borne on slender pedicels $\frac{1}{12}-\frac{1}{3}$ in. long in lateral racemes, each flower small, perfect, and about $\frac{1}{4}$ in. across; petals 4, greenish white, linear to oblong, apex obtuse or sometimes notched, longer than sepals; stamens 8, filaments flattened in the middle and somewhat petaloid, anthers large, sagittate, and deciduous; ovary 2–5 united carpels, styles united; calyx of 4 ovate, deciduous sepals about $\frac{1}{25}$ in. long. In some flowers it is difficult to distinguish between the petals and petaloid stamens with deciduous anthers.

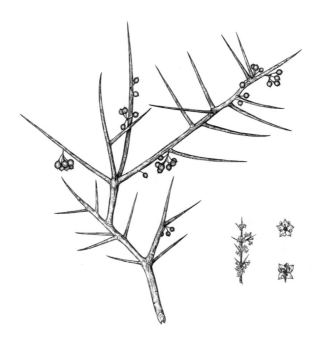

Fruit. Borne in clusters about 1 in. long, peduncles clavate and about ⅓ in. long; berry black, subglobose, apiculate, 3/16–¼ in. in diameter, fleshy, 2-celled; seeds 1–4, about ⅛ in. long, curled, wrinkled, and striate.

Leaves. Alternate, consisting of minute scales that are early-deciduous, thus leaving the plant barren most of the year.

Twigs. Green, smooth, stout, stiff, divaricate, all ending in large, sharp thorns.

Bark. Smooth, green to brown or gray on young trunks, older with small scales and shallow fissures.

Wood. Black or brown, hard, resinous, close-grained, with a specific gravity of 1.12, emitting a disagreeable odor when burned.

Range. Arid places in western and southwestern Texas; west through New Mexico to Arizona, and south into Mexico in Sonora to Tamaulipas and Hidalgo.

Remarks. The genus name, *Koeberlinia*, is in honor of C. L. Koeberlin, German clergyman and amateur botanist. The species name, *spinosa*, refers to the abundant spines. Common names for the plant are Junco, Corona de Cristo, and Crucifixion Thorn. Scaled quail have been seen to eat the fruit, as has the jackrabbit. The plant is perhaps of some value in erosion control. It is a perfect example of adjustment to desert conditions, with the green thorns and twigs carrying on the photosynthetic process. Being thicket forming, it presents an impenetrable green mass of thorns to any intruder.

WITCH HAZEL FAMILY (Hamamelidaceae)

American Sweetgum

Liquidambar styraciflua L. [H]

Field Identification. Large tree, attaining a height of 150 ft, with palmately lobed, serrate, alternate leaves. The branches and twigs are corky winged, or wingless on some trees.

Flowers. March–May, monoecious, very small, greenish; perianth none; staminate flowers in terminal, erect, tomentose racemes 2–3 in. long; stamens numerous, set among tiny scales, filaments slender and short; pistillate flowers in axillary, globose, long-

peduncled, drooping heads; styles 2, inwardly stigmatic, sterile stamens 4.

Fruit. September–November, persistent, globular, spinose, lustrous, 1–1½ in. in diameter, long-peduncled, resulting from the aggregation of the many 2-celled ovaries that are tipped by the 2-beaked or hornlike styles; ovules many, but maturing only 1–2 flat-winged seeds, the rest abortive, light brown; good seed crops every three years, light years in between.

Leaves. Simple, alternate, deciduous, petioled, broader than long, blades 3–9 in. wide, with 3–7 acuminate lobes; lobes oblong-triangular, glandular-serrate; slightly cordate or truncate at base; glabrous and glossy above, pubescent along the veins beneath, aromatic when bruised; petioles 2–4¾ in., slender, stipules falling away early.

Twigs. At first with rusty-red tomentum, later glabrous and with wide corky wings, or some trees without wings.

Bark. Very rough, deeply furrowed, ridges rounded, brown to gray.

Wood. Fine-grained, fairly hard, not strong, heartwood reddish brown, takes a high polish, sapwood white or pinkish, weighing about 37 lb per cu ft.

Range. Usually in low bottomland woods. In east Texas, Oklahoma, Arkansas, and Louisiana; eastward to Florida, north to New York and Connecticut, and west to Illinois and Missouri; also in mountains of Mexico.

Remarks. The genus name, *Liquidambar*, refers to the amber-colored liquid sap, and the species name, *styraciflua*, is from *styraci* ("storax") and *flua* ("fluidus"). Vernacular names are White Gum, Alligator-tree, Opossum-tree, Red Gum, Bilsted, Stain-walnut, Gum-wood, California Red Gum, and Star-leaf Gum. Medicinally the tree is known as "copalm balsam," and the resinous gum is used extensively in Mexico and Europe, especially as a substitute for storax. Various ointments and syrups are prepared from it and are used in the treatment of dysentery and diarrhea. The gum is sometimes chewed by children. It is also used as a perfuming agent in soap and as an adhesive. It is reported as excellent for healing wounds. The reddish brown wood is used for flooring, furniture, veneers, woodenware, general construction, boxes, crossties, barrels, sewing machines, cabinets, molding, vehicle parts, conveyors, musical instruments, tobacco boxes, and other articles. At least 25 species of birds, as well as the gray squirrel and Eastern chipmunk, are known to feed upon the fruit. The autumn foliage is conspicuous because of its beautiful color variations of red and yellow. It has been cultivated since 1681 and is highly ornamental. It is rapid growing, long-lived, and relatively free from insects and disease damage. Perhaps it could be used more extensively in reforestation projects because of its rapid growth in cutover lands.

SYCAMORE FAMILY (Platanaceae)

American Plane-tree (Sycamore)

Platanus occidentalis L. [H]

Field Identification. Tree attaining a height of 170 ft, with reddish brown bark that scales off to expose the white, smooth, new bark.

Flowers. April–May, monoecious, the separate heads globose and peduncled; staminate head red, with 3–8 short-filamented stamens accompanied by tiny, club-shaped scales; pistillate heads solitary, green at first, brown when mature, composed of angular ovaries set among tiny scales; ovary linear, 1-celled; style elongate, threadlike; carpels mingled with staminodia.

Fruit. Ripe September–October, borne on peduncles 3–6 in. long, usually solitary, persistent, globose, 1–1½ in. in diameter, light brown; achenes numerous, obovoid, small, leathery, obtuse at the apex, hairy at base, 1-seeded.

Leaves. Simple, alternate, deciduous, thin, broadly ovate, 4–12 in. across; margin usually set with 5 short, sinuate, acuminate lobes with large teeth between; truncate or heart shaped at the base; bright green above, paler and densely pubescent along the veins beneath; stipules sheathing, conspicuous, toothed, 1–1½ in.; petiole stout, woolly, shorter than the blade, 3–5 in.

Twigs. Slender, shiny, tomentose at first, glabrous later, orange-brown to gray.

Bark. Reddish brown, scaling off in thin plates to expose the conspicuous white, or greenish, new bark.

Wood. Light brown, rather weak, close-grained, hard, weighing 33 lb per cu ft, difficult to work.

Range. In rich bottomland soils, mostly along streams. Texas, Oklahoma, Arkansas, and Louisiana; east to Florida, and north to Maine, Minnesota, Nebraska, and Ontario.

Remarks. The genus name, *Platanus*, is the classical name of the plane-tree, and the species name, *occidentalis*, means "western." Vernacular names are Button-wood, Buttonball-tree, and Water-beech. The wood is used for crates, interior finishing, furniture, cooperage, rollers, butcher blocks, and tobacco boxes. It attains the largest size of any deciduous tree in the United States and is often planted for ornament. It is slow growing, but long-lived, and old trees are often hollow with decay. It was first cultivated in 1640. The seeds are eaten by a number of species of birds and sometimes by muskrat.

Smooth American Plane-tree

Smooth American Plane-tree, *P. occidentalis* var. *glabrata* (Fern.) Sarg., is a variety with less numerous and more angular teeth to the leaves. It occurs in Texas on limestone soils from the Colorado River westward to the Devils River and the Rio Grande. Also in Coahuila and Nuevo León, Mexico.

ROSE FAMILY (Rosaceae)

Genus *Crataegus*

The *Crataegus* Problem

The genus *Crataegus* with its numerous variations and hybrids represents a very difficult taxonomic complex. One of the difficulties appears to be in the separation of the so-called successful hybrid misfits from the normal, well-distributed, sexual, diploid species. To make the matter more complicated, many of the non-hybrid good species cannot be determined with certainty by any one set of parts or characters. It is evident that too many species have been described. Most of the 1,100 specific names given during the last 25 years were applied by authors C. S. Sargent, W. W. Ashe, and C. D. Beadle. Many of these have been, and more probably will be, reduced to synonymy as a better knowledge of the group is achieved.

Faced with the very difficult problem of choosing the tree and shrub species of the southwestern United States, the author has turned to Dr. Ernest J. Palmer of Webb City, Missouri, for advice. Dr. Palmer is the leading authority on this group and has done much to clarify many problems concerning its species. He has studied the group closely for more than thirty years and has contributed a monographic treatment in the 1950 edition of *Gray's Manual of Botany* by M. L. Fernald. Dr. Palmer has graciously provided a list of those southwestern species which he considers to be valid and also has contributed a key to both the series and the species.

Using these keys and list as a basis of approach, the author has carefully reviewed all the original descriptions of Palmer, Sargent, Ashe, and Beadle. This was supplemented by inspection of all the type material available at the Missouri Botanical Garden, the New York Botanical Garden, the Smithsonian Institution, and the Arnold Arboretum. Although five years were spent in the study of this complex group, the author makes no claim to having clarified all the problems concerning the southwestern species. The last word has certainly not been said, and the material presented is only broadly interpreted. Changes and corrections will undoubtedly have to be made when the species become better known.

The key is in two parts: a Key to the Series of *Crataegus* and a Key to the Species under the Series. In the Key to the Series, the characters of the series are outlined in contrasting pairs of statements or, occasionally, groups of three contrasting statements. Always choose the statement that most closely describes the plant you have to identify. For example, first compare the two statements designated as (a). If the first (a) is the one that seems to apply to the plant in question, then choose between the two (b) characters. It will be noted that the first (b) requires a further choice between (c) and (c), whereas the second (b) leads to the number and name of a series. Whenever a sequence of choices leads to the name of a series, turn to the Key to the Species under the Series and proceed in the same manner.

The reader will note that both the series and the species sections of the following keys refer to all the species of *Crataegus* in Texas and adjacent states. However, only the central Texas species are marked H in the species key.

Key to the Series of *Crataegus*

(a) Veins of the leaves running to the sinuses as well as to the points of the lobes
  (b) Leaves thin but firm, early deciduous; fruit ⅛–⅕ in. thick; nutlets 3–5; native species
    (c) Leaves mostly 1¼–1⅞ in. wide, ovate or deltoid in outline; flowers opening in May; fruit with deciduous calyx exposing tips of nutlets .... 1. **Cordatae** Beadle
    (c) Leaves mostly ⅝–1½ in. wide, narrowly obovate to deltoid in outline; flowers opening in March or April; fruit with persistent calyx .... 2. **Microcarpae** Loud.
  (b) Leaves thick, persistent until late in the season; fruit ⅜–¼ in. thick; introduced species .... 3. **Oxyacanthae** Loud.
(a) Veins of the leaves running only to the points of the lobes
  (d) Fruit red or yellow or remaining green at maturity; thorns usually long and slender, to 1¾–2½ in. long, or rarely thornless.
    (e) Flowers single or 2–5 in simple clusters; stamens 20–25
      (f) Leaves mostly 1⅜–2½ in. long; petioles slender, ⅜–⅝ in. long; sepals not foliaceous, entire or serrate; fruit ½–¾ in. thick, becoming mellow or succulent, edible;

arborescent shrubs or small trees in wet or swampy
ground .... 5. **Aestivales** Sarg.
  (f) Leaves mostly ⅝–1¼ in. long; petioles stout, ⅛–⅕ in.
    long; sepals foliaceous, pectinate or deeply glandular-
    serrate; fruit ⅜–⅞ in. thick, remaining firm or hard,
    scarcely edible; slender shrubs 1½–6 ft tall, in dry or
    sandy ground .... 6. **Parvifoliae** Loud.
(e) Flowers more numerous, usually 5–20 in simple or compound cymes or corymbs; stamens 5–20
  (g) Flowers opening in late March through April according
    to latitude; nutlets plane on ventral surfaces
    (h) Foliage and inflorescence glandular, usually conspic-
      uously so
      (i) Leaves mostly narrowly obovate or spatulate, broad-
        est above the middle except at the ends of branchlets
        where sometimes broadly oval or suborbicular; fruit
        red or orange-red, becoming mellow; arborescent
        shrubs or small trees .... 7. **Flavae** Loud.
      (i) Leaves mostly ovate, oblong-ovate, or rhombic in
        outline, broadest at or below the middle, gradually
        or abruptly narrowed at base, usually lobed, espe-
        cially at the ends of branchlets; fruit bronze-green or
        dull red, remaining firm or hard; shrubs usually less
        than 9 ft tall .... 8. **Intricatae** Sarg.
    (h) Foliage and inflorescence eglandular, or if slightly
      glandular, the glands small and soon deciduous
      (j) Leaves mostly narrowly obovate, cuneate or oblong-
        obovate, unlobed or very obscurely lobed except at
        the ends of branchlets, where sometimes broadly
        obovate to oval or suborbicular
        (k) Leaves thick or firm, glossy above in most spe-
          cies; fruit remaining hard and often green at ma-
          turity; nutlets 1–3 (or rarely 2–5 in a few species)
          .... 10. **Crus-galli** Loud.
        (k) Leaves thin to firm, not coriaceous, dull green
          above; fruit becoming soft or mellow; nutlets
          usually 3–5
          (l) Leaves relatively thin, the veins obscure, mostly
            1¾–2½ in. long, quite variable in shape, often
            oblong-obovate or rhombic, unlobed or slightly
            lobed except at the ends of branchlets where
            broadly oval or ovate and more deeply lobed;
            fruit ¼–⁷⁄₁₆ in. thick; bark thin, exfoliating from
            orange-brown inner bark ...... 9. **Virides** Beadle

(l) Leaves firm, more uniform in shape, mostly oblong-obovate, unlobed or with small shallow lobes above the middle; veins distinctly impressed above, mostly 1¼−2 in. long; fruit usually ⅜−⅝ in. thick; bark gray, thick, slightly scaly or ridged . . . . 11. **Punctatae** Loud.

(j) Leaves mostly oblong-ovate to rhombic, or broadly ovate to suborbicular at the ends of branchlets, all sharply lobed; New Mexico . . . . 12. **Rotundifoliae** Egglest.

(j) Leaves mostly ovate or deltoid in outline, broadest below the middle, often rounded, truncate, or subcordate at base; Arkansas and eastward, except some species in 16 and 19

(m) Sepals entire or serrate, not pectinate or deeply glandular-serrate; filaments as long or nearly as long as the petals; nutlets 3−5, usually less than 5

(n) Leaves thin, glabrous except for short pilose hairs above while young; stamens about 10; fruit less than ⁷⁄₁₆ in. thick, becoming succulent . . . . 13. **Tenuifoliae** Sarg.

(n) Leaves firm or thick; fruit usually ⁷⁄₁₆ in. or more thick, remaining firm or hard

(o) Young leaves scabrate with sparse hairs above, becoming glabrous; fruiting calyx small and sessile . . . . 14. **Silvicolae** Beadle

(o) Young leaves glabrous above, glabrous or rarely pubescent beneath; fruiting calyx elevated and usually prominent . . . . 15. **Pruinosae** Sarg.

(m) Sepals conspicuously glandular-serrate or pectinate; filaments distinctly shorter than the petals; nutlets usually 5

(p) Foliage and inflorescence pubescent; flowers ¾−⅞ in. wide; fruit pubescent at least while young, ripening in August or early September . . . . 16. **Molles** Sarg.

(p) Foliage and inflorescence glabrous; flowers ¾−1 in. wide; fruit glabrous, ripening in October. . . . . 17. **Dilatatae** Sarg.

(d) Fruit blue or black at maturity; thorns short and stout, usually less than ¾ in. long

(q) Leaves mostly abruptly pointed or rounded at the apex,

lustrous above; fruit blue at maturity (except in rare form), glaucous; eastern Texas and eastward . . . . 4. **Brevispinae** Beadle

(q) Leaves mostly acute or acuminate at the apex, dull green above; fruit turning from purple to black, lustrous but not glaucous; New Mexico and westward . . . . 18. **Douglasianae** Egglest.

(q) Flowers opening late, April or May according to latitude; nutlets pitted on ventral surfaces . . . . 19. **Macracanthae** Loud.

Key to the Species under the Series

1. **Cordatae** (only one species in this area) . . . . 1. *C. phaenopyrum*
2. **Microcarpae**
   a. Leaves mostly broadly ovate in outline, often as broad or broader than long, deeply incised, rounded to cordate at base; anthers red; fruit oblong . . . . 2. *C. marshallii*
   a. Leaves mostly narrowly obovate or spatulate, unlobed or nearly so except at the ends of branchlets, cuneate or attenuate at base; anthers pale yellow; fruit subglobose . . . . 3. *C. spathulata*
3. **Oxyacanthae** (only one species in this area) . . 4. *C. monogyna*
4. **Brevispinae** (only one species in this area) . . . . 5. *C. brachyacantha*
5. **Aestivales**
   a. Pubescence on the under surface of the leaves rusty brown, mainly along the veins; fruit ripening in May . . . . 6. *C. opaca (typical)*
   a. Pubescence on the under surface of the leaves gray, mainly in the axils of the veins; fruit ripening in June . . . . 6a. *C. opaca* var. *dormanae*
6. **Parvifoliae** (only one species in this area) . . . . 7. *C. uniflora*
7. **Flavae** (only one species in this area) . . . . 8. *C. pearsonii*
8. **Intricatae**
   a. Foliage and inflorescence glabrous or essentially so
      b. Leaves mostly 1⅝–2½ in. long, 1–2 in. wide; flowers ⅝–¾ in. wide.
         c. Fruit remaining dry and hard; sepals glandular-serrate
            d. Terminal leaves often ovate and deeply lobed near the base; fruit remaining green or yellowish green
               e. Anthers white or pale yellow (rarely pink) . . . . 9. *C. intricata* var. *straminea*
               e. Anthers pink or red (rarely white); fruit subglobose

or short-oblong; nutlets 2–4, usually 2–3 . . . .
. . . . 9a. *C. neobushii*
  d. Terminal leaves usually oblong-ovate or broadly ellip-
    tic, not deeply lobed; fruit becoming dull red
    f. Fruit subglobose; nutlets 3–5 . . . . . . 10. *C. buckleyi*
    f. Fruit obovoid or oblong; nutlets 2–5, usually less
      than 5 . . . . 11. *C. rubella*
  c. Fruit becoming mellow or juicy; sepals entire or finely
    glandular-serrate . . . . 12. *C. padifolia* var. *incarnata*
  b. Leaves mostly 1–1⅝ in. wide; flowers ½–⅝ in. wide . . . . . .
    . . . . 13. *C. pagensis*
a. Foliage and inflorescence pubescent, at least while young;
  young leaves and inflorescence sparsely pilose, becoming glabrous or nearly so; stamens about 20; anthers red; fruit usually less than ⁷⁄₁₆ in. thick, glabrous.
  g. Leaves mostly 1⅝–2 in. long, 1¼–1⅝ in. wide; flowers
    mostly 6–12 in corymb; fruit subglobose, about ⁷⁄₁₆ in.
    thick, orange-colored; arborescent shrub or small tree . . . . .
    . . . . 16. *C. harveyana*
  g. Leaves mostly ¾–1⅝ in. long and wide; flowers mostly
    3–8 in corymb; fruit oblong or pyriform, about ⅓ in. thick,
    dull red; widely branching shrub 3–6 ft tall . . . .
    . . . . 14. *C. ouachitensis*
a. Foliage and inflorescence pubescent throughout the season;
  stamens about 10; anthers cream-white or pale yellow; fruit
  pubescent while young . . . . 15. *C. biltmoreana*
9. **Virides**
  a. Mature leaves and inflorescence glabrous or essentially so
    (except in variety of no. 17)
    b. Leaves firm but comparatively thin at maturity, dull green
      above; nutlets normally 5
      c. Leaves variable in shape, mostly oblong-ovate or oblong-
        elliptic, glabrous (except in variety); anthers pale yellow
        or rarely pink . . . . 17. *C. viridis*
      c. Leaves more uniform in shape, mostly ovate or oblong-
        ovate, pubescent above as they unfold, soon glabrous;
        anthers pink . . . . 22. *C. sutherlandensis* [H]
    b. Leaves thick or subcoriaceous at maturity, glossy above,
      nutlets 3–5
      d. Leaves mostly 2–2¾ in. long; terminal leaves broadly
        ovate and sharply lobed; fruit ¼–⁷⁄₁₆ in. thick . . . .
        . . . . 18. *C. nitida*
      d. Leaves mostly 1⅝–2½ in. long; terminal leaves broadly
        ovate to suborbicular; fruit about ⅓ in. thick . . . .
        . . . . 23. *C. glabriuscula* forma *desertorum* [H]

 a. Foliage and inflorescence conspicuously pubescent while
young, the leaves more or less pubescent throughout the
season

  e. Mature leaves comparatively thin; flowers mostly 8–15 in
corymb; fruit subglobose

   f. Leaves pubescent beneath throughout the season; flowers
½–⅝ in. wide .... *C. viridis* var. *velutina*

   f. Leaves strongly pubescent while young, becoming nearly
glabrous; flowers about ¾ in. wide ...... 19. *C. anamesa*

  e. Mature leaves thick or subcoriaceous, pubescent while
young, becoming glabrous and glossy above and slightly
hairy along the veins beneath

   g. Flowers ¾ in. or more wide, mostly 10–20 in corymb;
sepals narrowly lanceolate, long-acuminate ....
.... 20. *C. stenosepala*

   g. Flowers ⅝–¾ in. wide, mostly 5–15 in corymb; sepals
lanceolate or deltoid-lanceolate, broad based

    h. Leaves mostly 1¼–1¾ in. long; fruit subglobose or
ovoid, orange-red, becoming mellow ....
.... 21. *C. poliophylla*

    h. Leaves mostly 1–1¼ in. long; fruit subglobose, dull
red, remaining hard and dry .... 24. *C. amicalis*

10. **Crus-galli**

 a. Foliage and inflorescence glabrous or essentially so, except in
no. 30 and in var. of no. 32, in which the young leaves are
more or less pubescent

  b. Mature leaves thick or subcoriaceous and glossy above (except sometimes in shade)

   c. Leaves mostly obovate or spatulate, distinctly longer
than broad, broadest above the middle, except sometimes
at the ends of branchlets

    d. Serration of the leaves sharp with acute teeth; fruit
usually ⅓–½ in. thick; nutlets 1–3, usually 1 or 2

     e. Terminal shoot leaves unlobed or rarely very ob-
scurely lobed; flowers ⁷⁄₁₆–⅝ in. wide; stamens about
10 (except in var. *leptophylla*) ...25. *C. crus-galli* [H]

     e. Terminal shoot leaves often slightly lobed; flowers
about ¾ in. wide; nutlets usually 2 .... 26. *C. bushii*

    d. Serration of the leaves shallow or crenate; fruit ¼–⅖
in. thick; nutlets usually 2 ....
.... 34 and 34a. *C. pyracanthoides* vars.

   c. Leaves broader, mostly broadly obovate, oblong-obovate
or oval, only slightly longer than broad or often as broad
as long at the ends of shoots

f. Young leaves quite glabrous; terminal shoot leaves usually broadly ovate to suborbicular
  g. Flowers ½–⅝ in. wide; fruit ⁷⁄₁₆ in. or less thick; nutlets usually 3; terminal leaves broadly ovate or oblong-ovate, sometimes slightly lobed toward the base .... 27. *C. palmeri*
  g. Flowers ⅝–¾ in. wide; fruit ⁷⁄₁₆–½ in. thick (or smaller in varieties); terminal leaves broadly oval or suborbicular, often with several small shallow lobes .... 29. *C. reverchonii* [H]
  g. Flowers about ½ in. wide; corymbs glabrous; stamens 10, anthers red or pink; fruit ellipsoidal; leaves oblong .... 29a. *C. cherokeensis*
f. Young leaves sometimes slightly villous, soon glabrous (except in var. of no. 32 where they are permanently pubescent)
  h. Leaves mostly obovate or oblong-obovate; terminal leaves incisely lobed; flowers usually 8–15 in lax corymbs
    i. Leaves sharply and deeply serrate; terminal shoot leaves mostly oval with 2–3 pairs of small shallow lobes; stamens about 10; fruit ⁷⁄₁₆–½ in. thick, dull red; nutlets 2–3 .... 32. *C. regalis*
    i. Leaves with sharp but shallow serrations; terminal leaves mostly elliptic, sometimes slightly lobed toward the apex; flowers about ¾ in. wide; stamens about 10; fruit about ⁷⁄₁₆ in. thick, bright orange or orange-red; nutlets usually 3 .... 30. *C. mohrii*
  h. Terminal shoot leaves broad-obovate to elliptic, glabrous at maturity; unlobed but deeply and irregularly serrate; flowers mostly 5–6 in compact corymbs; stamens 20, anthers pink .... 36. *C. sublobulata*
  h. Terminal shoot leaves ovate to oval or obovate, pale villose below at maturity .... 36a. *C warneri*
b. Mature leaves comparatively thin, not subcoriaceous, yellowish green, slightly lustrous but not glossy above
  j. Leaves mostly elliptic or oblong-obovate, longer than wide except sometimes at the ends of shoots, the veins obscure; fruit subglobose or slightly obovoid, dull red at maturity .... 28. *C. acutifolia*
  j. Leaves mostly broadly obovate or rhombic, nearly or sometimes quite as broad as long, the veins slightly impressed above; fruit oblong, green or yellowish flushed

with red at maturity .... 33. *C. sabineana*
a. Foliage and inflorescence pubescent while young and usually
   throughout the season
   k. Leaves mostly obovate or oblong-obovate, broadest above
      the middle except sometimes at the ends of shoots
      l. Fruit 7/16 in. or less thick, remaining dry and hard
         m. Flowers 7/16–5/8 in. wide; fruit red or orange at matu-
            rity, not lustrous
            n. Flowers mostly 4–5 in compact corymbs; stamens
               about 20; anthers pale yellow ....
               .... 38. *C. berberifolia*
            n. Flowers mostly 8–12 in loose corymbs; stamens
               about 10; anthers usually pink, rarely white ....
               .... 39. *C. engelmannii*
      l. Fruit 1/2–3/4 in. thick, becoming mellow or succulent;
         flowers 5/8–3/4 in. wide .... 31. *C. palliata*
   k. Leaves broader, mostly oblong-obovate, oval or elliptic,
      usually broadest about the middle
a. Leaves pubescent beneath throughout the season; flowers
   flattish, not noticeably cup-shaped
   o. Leaves mostly broadly obovate or oval, those at the ends of
      shoots similar but larger and relatively broader; sepals en-
      tire or minutely serrate; anthers yellow
      p. Flowers about 5/8 in. wide; stamens about 20; fruit sub-
         globose or short-oblong .... 40. *C. subpilosa*
      p. Flowers about 3/4 in. wide; stamens about 10; fruit ovoid
         .... 32a. *C. regalis* var. *paradoxa*
   o. Leaves mostly rhombic or oval, those at the ends of shoots
      broadly oval to suborbicular; sepals conspicuously
      glandular-serrate; anthers pink or red ..... 41. *C. tracyi* [H]
a. Leaves slightly pubescent on both sides while young, becoming glabrous at maturity, flowers cup-shaped ... 30. *C. mohrii*

11. **Punctatae**
   a. Leaves mostly obovate or oblong-obovate, or at the ends of
      shoots elliptic or oval; flowers 5–12 in villose corymbs
      b. Flowers mostly 5–8 in corymbs; usually less than 3/4 in.
         wide; stamens 10–20, usually 10–15; anthers white or pale
         yellow .... 42. *C. collina*
      b. Flowers mostly 8–12 in corymbs, usually 3/4 in. or more
         wide; stamens about 20; anthers pink or rose ....
         .... 44. *C. verruculosa*
   a. Leaves mostly broadly oval or ovate; flowers mostly 8–15 in
      glabrous corymbs .... 43. *C. fastosa*
   a. Leaves oval to obovate, acute or acuminate at apex; fruit
      often rather longer than broad, bright canary yellow; flowers

in broad 7–8-flowered, slightly villose corymbs ....
.... 43a. *C. brazoria*

12. Rotundifoliae

    a. Leaves elliptic, oval or suborbicular, usually slightly lobed, more or less pubescent while young; fruit about 7/16 in. thick, dark red or rarely dull yellow at maturity ....
.... 45. *C. chrysocarpa*

    a. Leaves mostly ovate or obovate, glabrous; fruit about 1/3 in. thick, orange-red or reddish orange at maturity ....
.... 46. *C. erythropoda*

13. Tenuifoliae (only one species in this area) ....
.... 47. *C. macrosperma*

14. Silvicolae (only one species in this area) ....
.... 48. *C. iracunda* var. *silvicola*

15. Pruinosae

    a. Flowers 1/2–3/4 in. wide; fruit 7/16–5/8 in. thick with prominent elevated calyx

        b. Leaves of flowering spurs mostly 1–1¾ in. wide; terminal shoot leaves larger, ovate or deltoid, sharply lobed

            c. Leaves mostly abruptly narrowed or rounded at the base; fruit usually pruinose .... 49. *C. pruinosa*

            c. Leaves mostly rounded, truncate or subcordate at base; fruit not pruinose

        b. Leaves of flowering spurs mostly 1–1⅜ in. wide, the terminal lobe often conspicuously elongate especially at the ends of shoots .... 51. *C. gattingeri*

            d. Leaves with shallow or obscure lobes, mostly rounded or abruptly narrowed at base; fruit with a narrow slightly elevated calyx .... 51a. *C. disjuncta*

        b. Leaves of flowering spurs mostly 1⅜–1¾ in. wide; terminal shoot leaves sometimes as broad as long or broader, the terminal lobe not conspicuously elongate

            e. Leaves glabrous or essentially so from the first ....
.... 50. *C. mackenzii*

            e. Leaves short villose above while young, and pubescent along the veins beneath throughout the season ....
.... 50a. *C. mackenzii* var. *aspera*

    a. Flowers 3/4–1 in. wide; fruit 5/8–3/4 in. thick, subglobose or depressed-globose, often wider than long, with a broad, slightly elevated, calyx .... 53. *C. platycarpa*

16. Molles

    a. Leaves of flowering spurs mostly oval or ovate, rounded at base; terminal shoot leaves broadly ovate, often truncate or subcordate at base

        b. Fruit bright red at maturity

c. Leaves longer than broad except rarely at the ends of shoots
   d. Mature leaves firm but comparatively thin; flowers numerous, to 15–20 in corymb
      e. Fruit ripening in August or September; flesh succulent and edible; nutlets 4–5, usually 5 . . . . 54. *C. mollis*
      e. Fruit ripening in October; flesh dry and mealy; nutlets 3–5 . . . . 57. *C. limaria*
   d. Mature leaves thick or subcoriaceous; flowers mostly 5–12 in corymb
      f. Leaves bluish green; flowers mostly 5–12 in compound corymbs; stamens about 20 . . . . 60. *C. lanuginosa*
      f. Leaves dull yellowish green; flowers mostly 5–8 in simple corymbs . . . . 64. *C. greggiana* [H]
c. Leaves often as broad as long, comparatively small; terminal shoot leaves sometimes broader than long . . . . 62. *C. brachyphylla*
b. Fruit bright yellow at maturity . . . . 63. *C. viburnifolia*
a. Leaves of flowering spurs mostly elliptic or oblong-ovate, noticeably longer than broad, gradually or abruptly narrowed at base; terminal shoot leaves broader, usually rounded or rarely truncate at base; fruit red at maturity; sepals glandular-serrate
  b. Stamens 10 or less; nutlets 3–5 . . . . 56. *C. noelensis*
  b. Stamens about 20; nutlets 4–5, usually 5, except in no. 58
   c. Mature leaves thick; sepals foliaceous, deeply glandular-serrate; anthers large, dark red; fruit with thick mellow flesh, edible . . . . 55. *C. texana*
   c. Mature leaves relatively thin; sepals not foliaceous, more or less glandular-serrate; fruit with thin dry or mealy flesh, scarcely edible
     d. Anthers white or pale yellow; sepals laciniately glandular-serrate; nutlets 3–5 . . . . 58. *C. invisa*
     d. Anthers pink or rose, or sometimes white in no. 59; nutlets 4–5, usually 5
      e. Flowers about 1 in. wide; sepals glandular-serrate; fruit bright red or crimson and lustrous at maturity . . . . 59. *C. dispessa*
      e. Flowers about ¾ in. wide; sepals sparingly and irregularly glandular-serrate; fruit dull dark red at maturity . . . . 61. *C. dallasiana*
17. **Dilatatae** (only one species in this area) . . . . 66. *C. coccinioides*

18. **Douglasianae** (only one species in this area) ....
.... 67. *C. rivularis* [H]
19. **Macracanthae**
  a. Leaves relatively large, those of the flowering spurs mostly
    2–4 in. long, 1¾–3¼ in. wide; flowers mostly 8–20 in loose
    compound corymbs
    b. Mature leaves dull yellowish green above; anthers pink or
      rarely pale yellow in variety; arborescent shrubs or small
      trees to 18–24 ft .... 68. *C. calpodendron*
    b. Mature leaves bright green, glossy above; anthers pale
      yellow; diffuse shrubs 6–9 ft tall .... 70. *C. carrollensis*
  a. Leaves relatively small, those of the flowering spurs mostly
    1–1¾ in. long, ¾–1¼ in. wide; flowers mostly 5–8 in com-
    pact corymbs; low branching shrubs 3–4½ ft ....
    .... 69. *C. thermopegaea*

Sutherland Hawthorn

Crataegus sutherlandensis Sarg.–Series **Virides** (9) [H]

Field Identification. Slender tree attaining a height of 15 ft. Bark
dark gray, breaking into long, thin, oblong flakes to expose the
reddish brown inner bark. The branches spreading, smooth and
gray.

Flowers. Opening in March in lax 7–10-flowered corymbs, the
pedicels slender and glabrous; calyx tube narrow-obconic, glabrous,
the 5 sepals slender, acuminate, often laciniately divided near the
base into glandular teeth, glabrous on the outer surface, villose-
pubescent inwardly; stamens 20, anthers faintly tinged with pink;
styles 5; petals 5, white, rounded, entire corolla about ¾ in.
across.

Fruit. Maturing September–October, subglobose, base often truncate, orange-red, about ⅓ in. in diameter, calyx prominent, the 5
sepals erect or spreading and a narrow deep cavity; nutlets 5, apex
rounded, base acute, obscurely grooved on dorsal side, ⅕–¼ in.
long, ⅛–⅙ in. wide.

Leaves. Simple, alternate, deciduous, the young ones coated with
pale pubescence, maturing when the flowers open and then thin,
upper surface dull yellowish green and glabrous, lower slightly
paler, blades 1¼–1½ in. long, ¾–1 in. wide, midrib thin; blades
ovate, apex acute, base gradually or abruptly narrowed and
concave-cuneate, margin serrate with straight or incurved acumi-

nate teeth; petioles slender, at first villose, later glabrous, ⅓–⅗ in.; leaves on young shoots irregularly divided into short wide lateral lobes, 1½–2 in. long.

Twigs. Slender, slightly divaricate, green to orange, sparingly hairy at first, older ones reddish brown to gray and glabrous, set with occasional straight slender spines to 2 in. long.

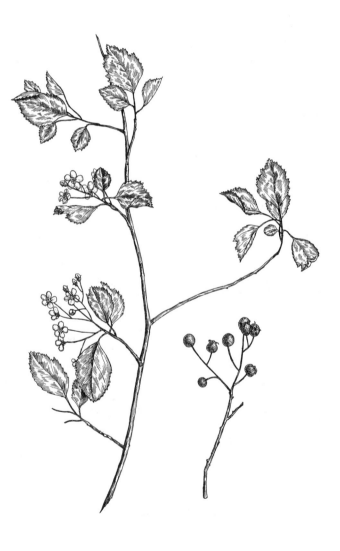

Spiny Sutherland Hawthorn

Range. The species is found in south-central Texas, in Wilson County, on the Cibolo River near Sutherland Springs.

Remarks. The genus name, *Crataegus*, is an ancient name and refers to the hard wood. The species name, *sutherlandensis*, is named for Sutherland Springs, where this species was discovered. Spiny Sutherland Hawthorn, *C. sutherlandensis* var. *spinescens* Sarg., differs by the rather smaller leaves more pubescent early in the season, often with tufts of white axillary hairs, and spines larger and more numerous. It is a shrub or small tree to 15 ft, forming thickets of slender stems covered with dark scaly bark separating into narrow scales and of slender zigzag twigs armed with many slender straight spines 1¼–2½ in. Found in the same range as the species.

Smooth Western Hawthorn

Crataegus glabriuscula forma *desertorum* Sarg. – Series **Virides** (9)
[H]

Field Identification. Shrub to 9 ft. Bark on the branches thin, pale, and flaky.

Flowers. Appearing in April in small glabrous, 4–5-flowered corymbs; petals 5, white, oval to obovate; calyx broad-obconic, slightly villose, with the 5 sepals slender, acuminate, obscurely serrate, externally glabrous, inwardly villose; stamens 20, anthers pale yellow; styles 4–5.

Fruit. Maturing in October, orange-red, subglobose, ⅙–⅕ in. in diameter, flesh dry and thin; calyx lobes with 5 sepals erect or spreading, with a wide shallow cavity in the bottom; nutlets 4–5, rounded and rather broader at apex than at base, dorsally only slightly grooved, about ⅙ in. long, ⅒–⅛ in. wide.

Leaves. Simple, alternate, deciduous, young with shiny white hairs, mature leaves thin, upper surface yellowish green and slightly roughened above by short white hairs, lower surface pale and glabrous or slightly villose toward the base of the prominent midrib below, with 3–4 pairs of primary veins extending to the points of the lobes, or 3-nerved from the base, ovate to slightly obovate or suborbicular, apex acute, acuminate, or rounded, base gradually or abruptly narrowed and cuneate, margin finely double-serrate usually above the middle, with blunt glandular teeth, and often divided into short acute lobes, 5⁄8–7⁄8 in. long, 3⁄8–5⁄8 in. wide; leaves on young shoots ovate, base broad and rounded, apex acute, often deeply lobed, 3⁄4–1 in. long and wide.

Twigs. Slender, usually divaricate, at first reddish brown and slightly villose, later pale gray, armed with numerous thorns that are slender, straight or slightly curved, brown to gray, 1–2 in. long.

Range. In the rocky bed of a creek usually dry, but flooded during a few hours two or three times a year, near Uvalde.

Remarks. The genus name, *Crataegus*, is the ancient name referring to the hard wood. The variety name, *glabriuscula*, means "somewhat smooth," and the form name, *desertorum*, is for its dry habitat. The following comments concerning it were made by Charles Sprague Sargent in 1922: "In its unusually zigzag branches, numerous long slender spines and minute fruit this is perhaps the most distinct hawthorn of the Virides group. The fact that it inhabits a region of rare rainfall where the soil in which it grows is only thoroughly wet two or three times in the year would be remarkable for any species of *Crataegus*; it is most remarkable for a species of this group, for the Virides, growing usually in low ground, are moisture loving plants. It is unfortunate that E. J. Palmer has been able to find only a single plant." Since Sargent wrote his comments the plant has been relegated to the status of a form only, under *C. glabriuscula*, instead of a species listed as *C. desertorum* Sarg.

Cock's-spur Hawthorn

Crataegus crus-galli L.–Series **Crus-galli** (10) [H]

Field Identification. Shrub or tree to 30 ft, and 6–12 in. in diameter. The branches are stout, rigid, horizontal or drooping, forming a round-topped or broadly depressed crown.

Flowers. Opening May–June after the leaves, in lax, many-flowered, glabrous corymbs; pedicels slender and glabrous, corolla ½–⅗ in. broad, petals 5, white, reflexed after anthesis; calyx tube narrow and obconic, glabrous, sepals 5, ⅛–⅕ in. long, linear-lanceolate, entire or glandular-serrate; stamens 10, anthers pink or white; styles 2, hairy at the base.

Fruit. Maturing in October, persistent over winter, short-oblong to subglobose or ovoid (occasionally slightly 5-angled), dull red, ⅓–½ in. long, with a terminal depression, flesh thin and dry; nutlets 2 (rarely 1 or 3), ridged dorsally, ends rounded, about ¼ in. long.

Leaves. Simple, alternate, deciduous, thick and leathery at maturity, mostly obovate to oblanceolate, apex obtuse to rounded or acute, base gradually cuneate, margin sharply and minutely

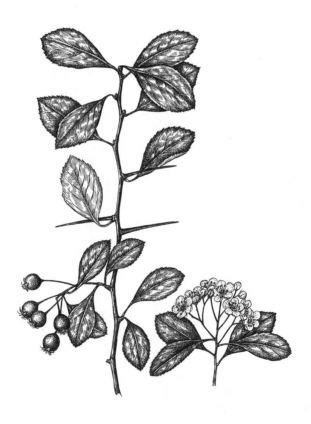

toothed above the middle, teeth often glandular; upper surface dark green and lustrous, lower surface paler and reticulate-veined, blade length ⅗–4 in., width ½–1⅓ in., turning yellow, orange, or red in the fall; petiole ½–¾ in. long, stout, winged above; leaves on young shoots often longer and apex acute or acuminate.

Twigs. Stout, reddish brown to gray, glabrous, armed with sharp, straight or slightly curved spines 2–8 in. long, sometimes with lateral spines; bark of trunk dark brown to gray, breaking into small scales with irregular, moderately deep fissures.

Wood. Heavy, hard, fine-grained, suitable for tool handles.

Range. Fence rows, woods, and thickets. The species and varieties are widespread. East Texas, Oklahoma, Arkansas, and Louisiana; east to Georgia, north to Michigan, Kansas, and southern Quebec, and west to Ontario.

Remarks. The genus name, *Crataegus*, is the classical Greek name for hawthorn. The species name, *crus-galli*, refers to the long thorns that resemble the spurs of a fowl. Cock's-spur Hawthorn is very desirable for cultivation because of the rounded crown, shiny leaves, and conspicuous flowers. It is perhaps the most widely planted hawthorn in the United States and Europe.

Reverchon Hawthorn

Crataegus reverchonii Sarg.—Series **Crus-galli** (10) [H]

Field Identification. Shrub 3–9 ft, usually with many stems from the base, or occasionally a small thorny tree to 26 ft.

Flowers. April–May, borne in slender-pediceled, compact, glabrous, few-flowered corymbs; each flower about ⅓ in. in diameter; petals 5, white, rounded; calyx tube narrowly obconic, 5-lobed, lobes slender, apices acuminate with a small red gland, margins entire or obscurely serrate; stamens 10–15, styles 3–5, usually 5.

Fruit. Maturing in September on drooping few-flowered corymbs, with slender pedicels; subglobose, some slightly broader than long, light scarlet, shiny, marked by occasional large dots, about ⅓ in. in diameter; flesh sweet, juicy, yellow, thick; nutlets usually 4, dorsally and prominently ridged, about ¼ in. in diameter; calyx lobes slender and deciduous.

Leaves. Simple, alternate, deciduous, oval to obovate, margin finely crenate-serrate with gland-tipped teeth above the base; at

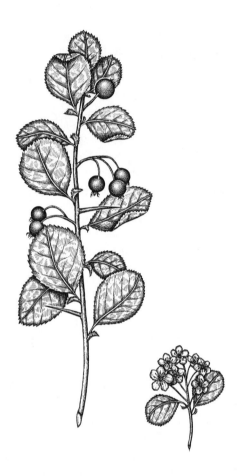

first yellowish green and mostly glabrous above, lower surface
slightly hairy on the midrib and veins; mature leaves leathery,
dark green and shiny above, lower surface paler; blade length
1¼–1½ in., width ¾–1 in.; midrib stout, yellow, primary veins
5–6 pairs; petioles stout, about ⅓ in., grooved, wing-margined
almost to the base; stipules minute, linear, reddish later, falling
early; leaves on vigorous shoots rounded, less often ovate or elliptic, margin coarsely serrate or slightly lobed, about 1½ in. in diameter, petioles short-glandular, broad winged.

Twigs. Erect, divaricate, glabrous, lustrous, orange-brown to reddish brown, lenticels small, pale, and numerous; older twigs gray,

armed with spines 1½–3 in. long (occasionally to 5 in.), slender, nearly straight, lustrous, reddish brown or purple.

Range. Southwestern Oklahoma, Arkansas, northern (Dallas County) and central Texas, Missouri, and eastern Kansas.

Remarks. The genus name, *Crataegus*, is the classical name of the hawthorn, and the species name, *reverchonii*, honors Julien Reverchon (1837–1905), a Texas plant collector of French birth. Charles Sprague Sargent remarks that the Reverchon Hawthorn is one of the most typical species of the Crus-galli group.

Tracy Hawthorn

Crataegus tracyi Ashe–Series **Crus-galli** (10) [H]

Field Identification. Bushy tree rarely more than 12–15 ft, with a trunk 8–12 in. in diameter, the branches erect and spreading.

Flowers. Opening late in April, about ⅝ in. in diameter, on villose pedicels ¼–½ in., in compact, mostly 7–10-flowered villose corymbs, their bracts and bractlets linear-obovate, glandular-serrate; calyx tube broadly obconic, glabrous or with occasional hairs near the base, the lobes gradually narrowed from a wide base, glandular-serrate, sometimes laciniate near the acuminate apex, glabrous on the outer surface, villose on the inner surface; petals 5, white, rounded to obovate; stamens 10–15, usually 10; anthers pink; styles 2–3.

Fruit. Ripening in September or early October, on erect nearly glabrous or villose pedicels, short-oblong to ellipsoid, orange-red, about ⅓ in. long, the calyx much enlarged; flesh thin, dry, and mealy, yellowish green; nutlets 2–3, rounded at apex, ridged on the back with a low broad rounded ridge, about ¼ in. long.

Leaves. Simple, alternate, deciduous, obovate to oval, rhombic or suborbicular; rounded, acute or acuminate or abruptly short pointed at apex, concave-cuneate at base, sharply serrate to below the middle with straight, acuminate, glandular teeth; dark green, lustrous and scabrate above, pale yellowish green below, blades 1–1⅓ in. long, ½–1 in. wide, with a thin midrib and prominent primary veins; petioles slender, wing-margined at apex, villose early in the spring, becoming glabrous later, about ¼ in. long.

Twigs. Slender and nearly straight, the young ones covered with long scattered pale hairs, becoming dull brown or reddish and glabrous, eventually gray.

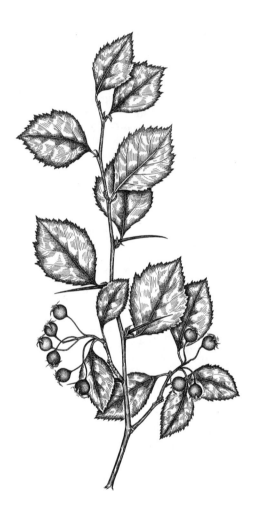

Range. Rocky banks of streams of the Texas Edwards Plateau area and westward. In Kendall, Comal, Bandera, Edwards, Callahan, Brown, Brewster, and Jeff Davis counties.

Remarks. The genus name, *Crataegus*, is the classical name for hawthorn. The species name, *tracyi*, is in honor of C. Tracy, a Texas botanist who collected the type. The description cited is based on C. S. Sargent's original one of *C. montigava*, which is now considered a synonym of *C. tracyi* Ashe.

Gregg Hawthorn

Crataegus greggiana Egglest.—Series **Molles** (16) [H]

Field Identification. Shrub 9–12 ft, with a stem covered with thin scaly bark.

Flowers. Opening early in April, about ⅜ in. in diameter on slender villose pedicels in small, compact, 5–7-flowered corymbs, densely villose like the narrow obconic calyx tube, calyx lobes slender, acuminate, entire or minutely and irregularly glandular-serrate, pubescent on the outer surface, densely villose on the inner surface, deciduous from the ripe fruit; stamens 5–10, anthers yellow; styles 3–5.

Fruit. Ripening early in October on more or less densely villose erect pedicels in small clusters, globose, bright red, ⅜–½ in. in diameter, slightly pubescent with a ring of white hairs surrounding the slightly enlarged calyx (or hairless in some forms), com-

posed of a short tube and a deep narrow cavity pointed in the bottom, flesh dry and thick; nutlets 3–5, gradually narrowed and rounded at the ends, slightly ridged on the back, ⅙–⅕ in. long and ⅛–⅙ in. wide, the broad, conspicuous hypostyle extending to below the middle.

Leaves. Ovate, acute and short-pointed at apex, concave-cuneate at base, on weak shoots slightly lobed, more deeply so on leading shoots; the lobes short, acuminate, usually occurring only above the middle, with deep double serrations, often extending nearly to the leaflet base; the teeth slender, acuminate, gland-tipped; expanding blades covered above with short pale hairs; pale and villose below, especially along the midrib and primary veins; mature blades thin, dark dull green and scabrate on the upper surface, pale and nearly glabrous on the lower surface; blades 1½–2 in. long and 1¼–1½ in. wide, with a slender, slightly villose pale yellow midrib and primary veins; petioles slender, slightly wing-margined at the apex by the decurrent base of the blade, thickly covered early in the season with matted pale hairs, becoming pubescent, ¼–⅗ in. in length; stipules large, foliaceous, coarsely and sharply serrate.

Twigs. Slender, nearly straight, covered when elongating with matted pale hairs, light orange-brown and slightly hairy at the end of the first season, ashy gray and glabrous the following year, armed with numerous straight gray spines 1¼–2 in. long.

Range. In Texas in Uvalde, Menard, Real, and Kerr counties; southward into Coahuila and Nuevo León, Mexico.

Remarks. The genus name, *Crataegus*, is the classical name of the hawthorn, and the species name, *greggiana*, honors Josiah Gregg (1806–1850), early American botanical explorer of the West. This species has also been listed in the literature as *C. uvaldensis* Sarg.

River Hawthorn

Crataegus rivularis Nutt.–Series **Douglasianae** (18) [H]

Field Identification. Small western tree 9–20 ft, with erect, ascending branches forming a narrow, open head.

Flowers. Opening in May, borne in compact, glabrous corymbs on long, slender pedicels; corolla about ½ in. in diameter, petals 5, white, rounded; calyx tube broadly obconic, slightly hairy at first but glabrous later, 5-lobed; lobes slender, entire or minutely glan-

dular, glabrous externally, hairy within, sometimes reddish; stamens 10–20, anthers rose colored; styles usually 5.

Fruit. Ripening in September, corymbs drooping, few-fruited, long-pediceled; fruit body short-oblong, ends full and rounded, dark red to almost black, lustrous, usually dotted white, length ⅓–½ in.; flesh yellow, thin, dry, mealy; nutlets 3–5, about ¼ in. long, apices narrowed or rounded, dorsally ridged, ventral cavities broad and shallow; calyx persistent, rather closely appressed, outer surface reddish and some slightly hairy below.

Leaves. Simple, alternate, deciduous, lanceolate to narrowly oblong-obovate or elliptic, apices acute or abruptly acuminate, base gradually narrowed and cuneate to concave, entire, margin irregularly and crenately serrate above, with glandular teeth, rarely lobed; young leaves reddish and pale-hairy; mature leaves rather dull green, thin, smooth and glabrous above, paler and yellowish green beneath, blade length 1½–2 in.; about ¾ in. wide, some twice as long as wide; midrib yellow, slender, primary veins obscure and 3–4 pairs; petiole about ½ in. long, slender, slightly winged above, hairy at first but reddish and glabrous later; young leaves almost round, coarsely toothed, some slightly incised-lobed, leathery, often to 3 in. long and 2 in. wide, petiole broadly winged.

Twigs. Slender, reddish brown, lustrous, glabrous, lenticels numerous and pale, spineless, or spines straight, slender, blackish, ¼–1¼ in. long, bark on older stems or trunk dark brown and scaly.

Range. At altitudes of 3,000–8,500 ft, borders of streams. Arizona, New Mexico, and northwestern Texas; northward to Idaho and Wyoming.

Remarks. The genus name, *Crataegus*, is the classical name for the hawthorn, and the species name, *rivularis*, refers to its preference for the moist banks of small rivulets or streams.

Black Cherry

Prunus serotina Ehrh. [H]

Field Identification. Tree to 100 ft, with oval-oblong or lanceolate leaves that are finely callous-serrate on the margin.

Flowers. March–June, racemes in spring with immature but nearly expanded leaves; individual flowers white, about ¼ in. in diameter, borne on slender pedicels; petals 5, obovate; stamens numerous, in 3 ranks; stigmas flattened; calyx tube shaped like saucer, the lobes short, ovate-oblong, acute.

Fruit. Ripening June–October, drupe borne in racemes, skin thin, black when mature, juicy, bittersweet, ⅓–½ in. in diameter; stone oblong-ovoid, about ⅓ in. long. The commercial seed-bearing age is about 10 years, with 25–75 the most prolific and 100 the maximum. Good crops are borne almost annually.

Leaves. Simple, alternate, finely callous-serrate, apex acuminate, base cuneate, oval-oblong or oblong-lanceolate, firm, dark green and lustrous above, glabrous or hairy on midrib beneath, blades 2–6 in. long, 1–2 in. broad, with one or more red glands at base, tasting of hydrocyanic acid.

Bark. Reddish brown, gray, or white, striped horizontally with gray to black lenticels, smooth when young, broken into small plates later, bitter to the taste.

Wood. Rich reddish brown, sapwood whitish or light brown, heavy, moderately hard, strong, bends well, shock resistance high, works well, finishes smoothly, glues well, seasons well, shrinks moderately, moderately free from checking and warping, weighing about 36 lb per cu ft, taking a beautiful polish.

Escarpment Black Cherry

Range. Texas, Oklahoma, Arkansas, and Louisiana; eastward to Florida, north to Nova Scotia, west to North Dakota, Nebraska, and Kansas; and southward in Mexico.

Remarks. *Prunus* is the ancient classical name, and the species name, *serotina*, means "late-flowering." It is also known under the vernacular names of Mountain Black Cherry and Rum Cherry. The bark is used medicinally as a cough remedy. The fruit is used as a basic flavoring extract and is also eaten raw by man. It is eaten by a wide variety of wildlife, including 33 birds, raccoon, opossum, squirrel, bear, and rabbit. The foliage is considered to be poisonous to livestock. The wood is used for furniture, cabinet-making, printer's blocks, veneer, patterns, panels, interior trim, handles, woodenware, toys, and scientific instruments. The tree has been cultivated for ornament since 1629.

Escarpment Black Cherry, *P. serotina* var. *eximia* (Small) Little, has flowers 35–60 on the rachis, pedicels ⅛–⅕ in. (or ⅙–¼ in. in fruit); the 5 petals ⅒–⅙ in. long or wide; calyx segments 1/25–1/15 in. long; drupe about ⅜ in. across; leaves 2–3½ in. long, 1¼–1¾ in. wide, margin with 4–6 teeth every ⅜ in., surfaces glabrous or some with axillary red tufts of hairs; petioles ⅝–¾ in.

(to 1¼ in. sometimes). In Texas in the valley of the Colorado River, in San Saba and Burnet counties; south to Comal and Medina counties; west to the south fork of the Llano River in Kimble County and to the west fork of the Nueces River in Kinney County.

Common Choke Cherry

Prunus virginiana L. [H]

Field Identification. Large shrub or small tree to 30 ft, with erect or horizontal branches.

Flowers. April–July, in short, dense, cylindric racemes 3–6 in. long; flowers ¼–⅓ in. in diameter, borne on slender, glabrous pedicels from the axils of early-deciduous bracts; corolla small, white, 5-merous; petals rounded, short-clawed; filaments glabrous; style thick, short, with orbicular stigmas; calyx tube 5-lobed, lobes short, obtuse at apex, glandular-laciniate on the margin.

Fruit. Ripening July–September, cherry ¼–⅓ in. thick, globose, lustrous, dark red, scarlet, or nearly black; skin thick, flesh juicy, acidulous and astringent, barely edible; stone oblong-ovoid, one suture ridged, and the other suture acute. Good crops are borne almost annually.

Leaves. Alternate, simple, deciduous, thin, blades ¾–4 in. long, ½–2 in. wide, oval to oblong or obovate, abruptly acuminate or acute at the apex, rounded to cuneate or somewhat cordate at the base, sharply serrate on the margin, dark green and lustrous above, paler on the lower surface, sometimes pubescent on veins, turning yellow in autumn, strong odor when crushed; petioles slender, ½–1 in., 2 glands at the apex.

Twigs. Reddish brown to orange-brown, glabrous, slender, lenticels pale.

Bark. Dark gray to brown or blackish; old trees somewhat irregularly fissured into small scales with paler excrescences, smoother and tighter when young, inner bark ill-scented.

Wood. Light brown, sapwood lighter, close-grained, moderately strong, hard, heavy, weighing 36 lb per cu ft.

Range. The species and its varieties rather widespread. Texas, New Mexico, Oklahoma, Arkansas, and Louisiana; eastward to Georgia, northward to Maine and Newfoundland, and west to British Columbia, Washington, Oregon, and California.

Remarks. The genus name, *Prunus*, is the classical name, and the species name, *virginiana*, refers to the state of Virginia. Vernacular names are Wild Black Cherry, Cabinet Cherry, Rum Cherry, Whiskey Cherry, Black Chokeberry, California Chokeberry, Eastern Chokeberry, Eastern Choke Cherry, Western Choke Cherry, and Caupulin. The tree is sometimes planted for ornament and for erosion control. It has been in cultivation since 1724. It has a tendency to form thickets of considerable extent from root sprouts. The fruit, used to make jellies and jams, is eaten raw by at least 40 species of birds and browsed by black bear and cottontail. The bark is sometimes used as a flavoring agent in cough syrup.

Oklahoma Plum

Prunus gracilis Engelm. & Gray [H]

Field Identification. Straggling thicket-forming shrub 1–15 ft.

Flowers. Opening in March, usually before the leaves, borne in sessile lateral umbels, 2–4 in a cluster; pedicels slender, pubescent, ⅓–⅖ in. long; corolla ¼–⅓ in. broad; petals 5, white, rounded, imbricate, spreading, inserted in the throat of the hypanthium; stamens numerous, inserted with the petals, filaments filiform and distinct; ovary sessile, 1-celled, ovules 2 and side by side, pendulous; style simple and terminal; calyx with 5 imbricate sepals that are spreading, deciduous, ovate to ovate-lanceolate, obtuse to acute, entire or denticulate, and finely pubescent.

Fruit. Drupe maturing June–August, subglobose or ovoid to somewhat pointed at the ends, to ⅝ in. in diameter, usually red with a slight bloom, pulpy; stone oval, indehiscent, obtuse at ends, bony, nearly smooth, slightly flattened; seed with membranous testa.

Leaves. Simple, alternate or fascicled, deciduous, length 1–2 in., elliptic to oval or ovate, margin finely and sharply serrate with appressed teeth, apex acute or obtuse, base gradually narrowed, thickish, upper surface slightly pubescent to glabrous when mature, lower surface reticulate-veined and densely pubescent; winter buds with imbricate scales; petioles short, pubescent, glandless.

Twigs. Slender, slightly divaricate, soft-pubescent, reddish brown, later gray and glabrous.

Range. On dry sandy soils in the sun. North Texas, Oklahoma, and western Arkansas, to Tennessee and Kansas.

Remarks. The genus name, *Prunus*, is the ancient Latin name, and the species name, *gracilis*, refers to the slender branches. The plant was introduced into cultivation in 1916. It is susceptible to black knot, a fungus disease, on the limbs and twigs. The fruit is edible but not of particularly good quality. Also known as the Sour Plum.

Chickasaw Plum

Prunus angustifolia Marsh. [H]

Field Identification. Twiggy shrub forming dense thickets, or a short-trunked, irregularly branched tree to 25 ft.

Flowers. March–April, in lateral 2–4-flowered umbels borne before the leaves on slender, glabrous pedicels ¼–½ in.; corolla white, about ⅓ in. across; petals 5, obovate, rounded at apex, somewhat clawed at base; calyx tube campanulate, glabrous, 5-lobed; lobes ovate, obtuse, ciliate, pubescent within; stamens usually 15–20, filaments free with oval anthers; ovary 1-celled.

Fruit. May–July, drupe globose, ½–¾ in. in diameter, red or yellow, dotted yellow, lustrous, little bloom if any, skin thin with juicy, edible, subacid flesh; stone ovoid to oblong, about ½ in. long, rounded, somewhat grooved on the dorsal suture, rugose and turgid.

Leaves. Alternate, simple, deciduous, 1–2 in. long, ⅓–⅔ in. wide, lanceolate or oblong-lanceolate, acuminate to acute and apiculate

at the apex, rounded or broadly cuneate at the base, troughlike, glabrous and lustrous green above, paler and glabrous or pubescent beneath, sharply serrate with small glandular teeth; petioles slender, glabrous or puberulent, ¼–½ in. long, glandless or with 2 red glands near the apex.

Twigs. Reddish brown, lustrous, hairy at first but glabrous later, slender, zigzag, often with spinescent spurlike lateral divisions; lenticels horizontal, orange.

Bark. Reddish brown to dark gray, scales thin and appressed; lenticels horizontal and prominent.

Wood. Reddish brown, sapwood lighter, rather soft, not strong, fairly heavy, weighing 43 lb per cu ft.

Range. Thought to be originally native in Texas and Oklahoma but now rather rare in a wild state. Arkansas and Louisiana; eastward to Florida, northward to New Jersey, and west to Illinois.

Remarks. The genus name, *Prunus*, is the classical name for the European plum, and the species name, *angustifolia*, refers to the narrow foliage. Called Mountain Cherry in some localities. Seldom found in a wild state but most often around dwellings. It is sometimes used in shelter-belt planting.

Mexican Plum

Prunus mexicana Wats. [H]

Field Identification. Shrub or small tree to 25 ft, with an irregular open crown.

Flowers. White, ¾–1 in. in diameter, borne on slender glabrous pedicels in 2–4-flowered umbels; petals 5, ovate-oblong, rounded,

narrowed into a claw, entire or crenulate, pubescent, much longer than the calyx lobes; stamens 15–20; style elongate, ovary 1-celled; calyx tube obconic, puberulent on the exterior, tomentose within, 5-lobed; lobes ovate to oblong, entire or serrate, ciliate and glandular on the margin, about as long as the tube.

Fruit. Drupe subglobose to short-oblong, dark purplish red with a bloom, 1¼–1⅓ in. in diameter; flesh juicy, of varying palatability; stone ovoid to oval, dorsal edge ridged, ventral edge grooved, smooth, turgid.

Leaves. Alternate, simple, deciduous, thickish, blades 1¾–3½ in. long, 1–2 in. wide, ovate to elliptic or obovate, abruptly acuminate at the apex; cuneate or rounded at the base; singly or doubly serrate with apiculate teeth; upper surface yellowish green, glabrous, shiny, hairy below especially on the veins; prominently reticulate-veined both above and below; petioles stout, pubescent, hardly over ⅗ in. long, glandular at the apex.

Twigs. Slender, stiff, glabrous, or pubescent early, shiny, grayish brown.

Bark. Gray to black, exfoliating in platelike scales when young, when older rough and deeply furrowed.

Range. Texas, Louisiana, Arkansas, and Oklahoma; north to Missouri, Tennessee, and Kentucky, and southward into northeastern Mexico.

Remarks. The genus name, *Prunus*, is the ancient classical name for a plum of Europe, and the species name, *mexicana*, refers to this species' southwestern distribution. It is sometimes known as Big-tree Plum because it is treelike and does not sucker to form thickets. It is rather drought resistant and has been used as a grafting stock.

Peach

Prunus persica Batsch [H]

Field Identification. Tree attaining a height of 24 ft, with a rounded crown and spreading branches.

Flowers. Usually expanding before the leaves March–May, subsessile, solitary or 2 together, fragrant, perfect, 1–2 in. across; petals 5, pink, spreading, rounded; calyx with the 5 sepals externally pubescent; stamens 20–30, filaments usually colored like the petals, exserted, slender, distinct; ovary tomentulose, 1-celled

and sessile, the 2 ovules pendulous; pistil solitary with a simple terminal style.

Fruit. Drupe maturing July–October, subglobose, grooved on one side, velvety-tomentose, 2–3⅓ in. in diameter, fleshy, separating in halves at the sutures; stone elliptic to ovoid-elliptic, usually pointed at distal end, deeply pitted and furrowed, very hard; fruit of escaped trees usually harder and smaller.

Leaves. Numerous, conduplicate in the bud, almond-scented, impregnated with prussic acid, simple, alternate, some appearing clustered, elliptic-lanceolate to oblong-lanceolate, broadest at the middle or slightly above the middle, 3–6 in. long, apex long-acuminate, base varying from acute to acuminate or broad-cuneate, margin serrate or serrulate, surfaces glabrous and lustrous, bright green, thin; petioles glandular, ⅜–⅝ in.

Range. A native of China but extensively cultivated from Texas eastward to Florida and northward to New York and southern

Ontario. Sometimes escaped from cultivation in the southeastern United States.

Remarks. The genus name, *Prunus*, is the classical Latin name of a plum of Europe. The species name, *persica*, means "Persian" and is also an old generic name for peach. The genus name of *Amygdalus* L. is used by some authors.

Common Pear

Pyrus communis L. [H]

Field Identification. Tree generally pyramidal and upright, living to an old age. Attaining a height of 75 ft and 2–3 ft in diameter. The branches are stiff, upright, and sometimes thorny.

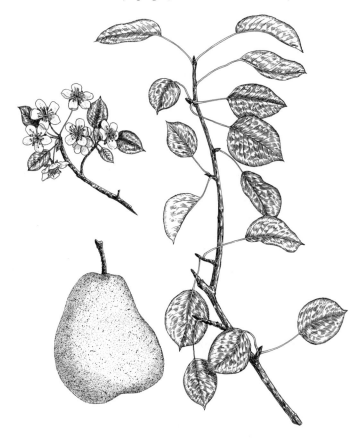

Flowers. March–May, with or before the leaves; cymes simple, terminal, 4–12-flowered, borne on short twigs of the preceding year; pedicels ½–2 in., pubescent at first, glabrous later; corolla white or pink, 1–2 in. broad, 5-petaled, petals broad-oblong, rounded, short-clawed; stamens numerous, exserted; anthers yellow, small, 2-celled, sacs longitudinally dehiscent; styles 5, distinct to the base, stigma small, ovules 2 in each cavity, cavities as many as the styles; disk cushionlike; calyx urn-shaped, the 5 acute lobes about as long as the tube.

Fruit. Ripening July–October, pome tapering to the base, in the wild form about 2 in. long, much longer in cultivated forms, yellow to reddish, flesh with abundant grit cells; seeds small, smooth, brown to black, endosperm none, cotyledons fleshy, the pome consisting of the thickened calyx tube and receptacle enclosing the carpels.

Leaves. Simple, alternate, deciduous, usually on short lateral spurs, ovate to elliptic or obovate, margin finely serrate to entire, apex acute or acuminate, sometimes abruptly so, base usually rounded, blade length 1½–4 in., young leaves downy and ciliate, mature leaves lustrous, dark green to olive green above, lower surface paler, both sides glabrous or nearly so; petioles 1¼–3 in., as long as the blades or longer.

Twigs. Somewhat pubescent at first, glabrous later, reddish brown to gray or black.

Wood. Reddish brown, hard, fine-grained, 51 lb per cu ft.

Range. Common Pear is a native of Europe and Asia and escapes cultivation in some areas of the Southwest and elsewhere in North America. It is often cultivated in Texas, Oklahoma, Arkansas, and Louisiana.

Remarks. The genus name, *Pyrus*, is the classical name for the pear tree, and the species name, *communis*, means "common." The tree is sometimes used for shelter-belt planting and for wildlife food.

Prairie Crab-apple

Pyrus ioensis (Wood) Bailey [H]

Field Identification. Tree attaining a height of 28 ft and a trunk diameter of 18 in., the numerous rigid, crooked branches forming a rounded spreading crown.

Flowers. Borne April–June, fragrant, in 2–5-flowered clusters on very hairy pedicels 1–1½ in.; calyx lobes 5, lanceolate-acuminate, longer than the tube, densely white-tomentose; petals 5, white or pink, about ½ in. wide, obovate, base narrowed into a slender claw; stamens numerous, shorter than the petals; styles 5, joined below and white-hairy.

Fruit. Maturing September–October, peduncles ¾–1½ in. long, globose, somewhat depressed, apical and basal depressions shallow, greenish to yellow, sometimes with minute yellow dots, surface waxy and greasy to the touch, length ¾–1¼ in., width ¾–1½ in., flesh sour and astringent.

Leaves. Simple, alternate or clustered, deciduous, length and width variable on weak and vigorous shoots, blades 1½–5 in. long, ¾–4 in. wide, elliptic to oblong or obovate-oblong, apex acute or obtuse to rounded, base cuneate or rounded, margin singly or doubly crenate-serrate, or on some deeply lobed as well; at maturity coriaceous, dark green, lustrous and glabrous above, lower surface varying from almost glabrous to densely white-tomentose, turning yellow in autumn; petioles slender, at first with hoary-white tomentum, becoming pubescent or glabrous later.

Twigs. Reddish brown to gray, densely tomentose at first but with age less so, finally glabrous, lenticels small and pale; twigs often set with numerous short lateral shoots bearing thorns terminally; winter buds small, obtuse, pubescent.

Bark. Reddish brown to dark gray, about ⅓ in. thick, scales small, narrow, persistent.

Range. In Texas, Oklahoma, Arkansas, and Louisiana; eastward to Alabama and north to Minnesota.

Remarks. The genus name, *Pyrus*, is the classical name for the pear tree, and the species name, *ioensis*, refers to the state of Iowa where it was first described. Other vernacular names are Iowa Crab, Prairie Crab, and Western Crab-apple. The flesh of this crab-apple is sour and inedible but is sometimes used for making vinegar. It has been cultivated for ornament since 1885. It is of considerable value as food for wildlife, the fruit known to be eaten by at least 20 species of birds and mammals, including bobwhite quail, ruffed grouse, ring-necked pheasant, gray and red fox, skunk, opossum, raccoon, cottontail, woodchuck, red squirrel, and fox squirrel.

Narrow-leaf Firethorn

Pyracantha angustifolia (Franch.) Schneid. [H]

Field Identification. Cultivated, half-evergreen shrub with diffusely spreading, irregular, spiny branches, or sometimes a tree to 20 ft. Occasionally almost prostrate in form.

Flowers. April–May, corymbs axillary, pubescent, many-flowered, ½–3 in. broad; calyx 5-lobed, lobes short, about 1/16 in. long, broadly obtuse to acute, white-hairy; margins thin and whitened, glandular or glandless, ciliate; corolla about ⅜ in. across, white, 5-petaled; petals spreading, suborbicular, narrowed to a broad base; stamens exserted, numerous, spreading, filaments white, anthers yellow; carpels 5, spreading, free on the ventral side, on the dorsal side partially connate with the calyx tube.

Fruit. Pomes persistent in the winter, numerous, red to orange, ⅕–⅜ in. across, depressed-globose, fleshy, calyx remnants persistent; seeds 5, about ⅛ in. long, black, lustrous, 2 surfaces plane, dorsal surface rounded, one end rounded, the other abruptly apiculate-pointed.

Leaves. Simple, alternate, or somewhat clustered on short, lateral, spinescent branches, half-evergreen, leathery, oval-oblong to oblanceolate, apex obtuse to rounded or notched, base cuneate,

margin entire, length ½–1¾ in.; upper surface dark green, shiny, apparently smooth (but often with scattered, white, cobwebby hairs under magnification); lower surface much paler, glabrous, or with a few white hairs along the main vein, obscurely reticulate-veined; petioles ¹⁄₁₆–¼ in., pubescent to glabrous; stipules minute, caducous, buds small and pubescent.

Twigs. Green to grayish with dense, fine pubescence; secondary twigs almost at right angles, and usually short and spiniferous; spines straight, ⅛–½ in. long, often pubescent at the base with apex reddish brown and more glabrous.

Range. Cultivated in gardens in Texas, Louisiana, Arkansas, Oklahoma, and elsewhere, sometimes escaping. Hardy as far north as Massachusetts. A native of southwest China.

Remarks. The genus name, *Pyracantha*, is from the Greek words *pyr* ("fire") and *akanthos* ("thorn"), alluding to the bright red fruit. The species name, *angustifolia*, refers to the narrow leaves. The plant is often cultivated for ornament. Robin and cedar waxwing, as well as other birds, eagerly devour the fruit. Other closely related species, such as the Scarlet Firethorn, *P. coccinea* Roem., with crenate, more glabrous leaves, are also cultivated extensively. The Narrow-leaf Firethorn is propagated by seeds, layers, or cuttings or ripened wood under glass. It was introduced into cultivation about 1895.

Loquat

Eriobotrya japonica Lindl. [H]

Field Identification. Evergreen tree often planted for ornament in the warmer parts of the United States. Persistent in abandoned gardens for many years. Attains a height of 25 ft with an open but rather rounded crown.

Flowers. August–November, fragrant, borne in terminal woolly panicles 4–7½ in. long, buds with conspicuous rusty-woolly tomentum, flowers about ½ in. across; calyx lobes 5, ⅛–¼ in. long, acute, densely rusty-woolly; petals 5, white, oval to suborbicular, short-clawed; stamens 20; styles 2–5, connate below, ovary inferior, 2–5-celled, cells 2-ovuled.

Fruit. In spring, pome edible, small, pear-shaped or spherical, yellow, 1½–3 in. long, endocarp thin; seeds large, ovoid, solitary or a few.

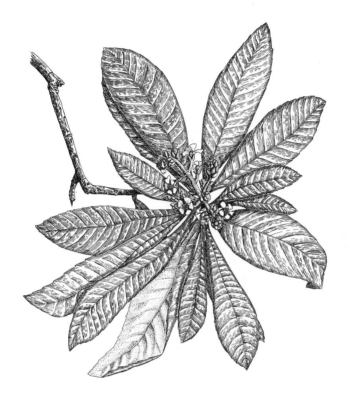

Leaves. Simple, alternate, sessile or very short-petioled, crowded terminally and whorled to give a rosettelike appearance; rather stiff and firm, large and ornamental, 4–12 in. long, oval to oblong or obovate, margin with remote slender teeth but entire toward the base; upper surface with veins deeply impressed, dark green, lustrous, at maturity glabrous; lower surface much paler and densely feltlike with rusty tomentum.

Twigs. Stout, green to brown, densely woolly-tomentose, when older brown to dark gray and glabrous; leaf scars large, half-round, bundle scars 3.

Range. A native of China and Japan, much planted for ornament in Texas, Louisiana, and other Gulf states. Grown as a pot plant in the North.

Remarks. The genus name, *Eriobotrya*, is the Greek word for "woolly cluster," referring to the hairy panicles. The species name, *japonica*, is for Japan, its original home. It is also known as

Japanese-plum and China-plum. The fruit may be eaten raw or prepared as jelly, jam, pies, and preserves. It has an agreeable acid flavor.

The tree may be propagated by seeds, and trees are planted in orchards 20–24 ft apart. Individual trees are often planted in gardens for the ornamental leaves. For best results in fruit yield, improved varieties are bud-grafted on seedling stock. *E. japonica* var. *variegata* Hort. is a variety with variegated white, pale green, or dark green leaves.

True Mountain Mahogany

Cercocarpus montanus Raf. [H]

Field Identification. Western shrub or small tree to 12 ft, with upright or spreading branches. The present taxonomical treatment follows that of Floyd L. Martin, "A Revision of *Cercocarpus*," *Brittonia* 7 (March 1950): 91–111.

Flowers. Often crowded on short spurlike branchlets, solitary or fascicled; pedicels to ⅛ in., to ⅓ in. long in fruit; floral tube ⅕–⅓ in. long, elongate, cylindrical, spreading-villous or appressed-silky, usually somewhat enlarged below, and at apex abruptly widened into a campanulate deciduous limb; sepals 5, ⅛–⅕ in. wide; corolla absent; stamens 22–44, filaments distinct, inserted in 2–3 rows, anthers hairy, emarginate at both ends, affixed dorsally above the base; pistil solitary, inserted in the bottom of the floral tube; ovary cylindric-fusiform, sessile; style terminal, elongate, exserted, silky-plumose; ovules solitary, ascending, affixed above the middle.

Fruit. Length ⅓–⅖ in., appressed silky-hairy, cylindric-fusiform, about one-third exserted from the floral tube at maturity; tail 1¾–2½ in. long, densely spreading, silky-plumose, testa membranaceous, seed cylindric; cotyledons linear, elongate, hypocotyl very short.

Leaves. Simple, alternate, or somewhat fascicled on short spurlike branchlets, blade ovate to oval or obovate (in some varieties lanceolate, oblanceolate, or elliptic), apex acute to rounded, base usually cuneate, margin usually with coarse ovate to triangular teeth but sometimes entire, length ⅝–1¼ in., to ¾ in. wide; thin but firm, upper surface green to grayish green, lower surface lighter and varying from glabrous to short-villous or rather densely appressed-silky; lateral veins 3–6, parallel or somewhat curved

toward the margins, prominent to less noticeable; petiole to ⅓ in. long; stipules adnate to petiole at base, lanceolate to ovate, acute, brown, scarious.

Twigs. Rather stout, rigid, terete, roughened by leaf scars, often with short lateral spurs, gray to brown, pubescent, later roughened and fissured on old branches or trunk; wood hard and dark colored.

Range. Dry rocky bluffs or mountainsides at altitudes of 3,500–9,000 ft. In New Mexico in the Zuni, Jemez, Sandia, and Sangre de Cristo mountains; west to Arizona and northward to Wyoming and South Dakota.

Remarks. The genus name, *Cercocarpus*, refers to the long tail of the fruit. The species name, *montanus*, is for the mountainous habitat.

Silver Mountain Mahogany, *C. montanus* var. *argenteus* (Rydb.) F. L. Martin, is a shrub 4–15 ft, with ascending branches; flowers June–July, floral tube 1⁄5–1⁄8 in. long (in fruit to 2⁄5 in. long), appressed-silky; calyx limb 1⁄8–2⁄5 in. wide; pedicel 1⁄25 in. or less in length in flower (in fruit 1⁄8–1⁄6 in. long); leaves oblanceolate, narrowly obovate, to narrowly elliptic; margin set with short, broad, triangular teeth that are apiculate or entire, length 3⁄4–1½ in., width 3⁄8–3⁄4 in., surfaces white, appressed-silky, rarely sparsely villous or nearly glabrate, veins 5–6. In New Mexico and Texas. In Texas in Hutcheson, Randall, Lubbock, Presidio, Brewster, Pecos, Edwards, Kimble, Real, and Uvalde counties. In New Mexico in Sandoval, Santa Fe, San Miguel, Lincoln, and Otero counties. Rocky hillsides, canyons, mountains at altitudes of 4,000–8,500 ft. (Listed elsewhere as *C. argenteus* Rydb.)

Shaggy Mountain Mahogany, *C. montanus* var. *paucidentatus* (Wats.) F. L. Martin, is a shrub 3–15 ft; flowers May–November, floral tube 1⁄8–1⁄4 in. long (in fruit 1⁄8–1⁄3 in. long), spreading-villous or appressed-silky; calyx limb 1⁄12–1⁄5 in. wide; pedicel very short in flower, in fruit 1⁄12–1⁄6 in. long; tail of fruit 5⁄8–2 in. long; leaves lanceolate, oblanceolate, or narrowly obovate, margin entire or with 3–5 short teeth at apex, short-villous, appressed-silky, or glabrate, lateral veins 3–5 (rarely 6), length 3⁄8–3⁄4 in. (rarely to 1¼ in.), width 1⁄4–1⁄3 in. In Arizona, New Mexico, Texas, and Mexico. In New Mexico south to the Mexican border. In Texas in El Paso and Jeff Davis counties. In Mexico in Sonora, Chihuahua, Coahuila, San Luis Potosí, and Hidalgo. Rocky hills at altitudes of 4,500–8,500 ft.

The following names have been used for this plant in the literature: *C. breviflorus* A. Gray, *C. paucidentatus* (Wats.) Britt., *C. eximius* (C. K. Schneid.) Rydb., *C. parvifolius* Nutt. var. *paucidentatus* Wats., *C. parvifolius* Nutt. var. *breviflorus* Cov.

LEGUME FAMILY (Leguminosae)
Subfamily Mimosoideae

Black-brush Acacia

Acacia rigidula Benth. [H]

Field Identification. Stiff, thorny shrub with many stems from the base, attaining a height of 15 ft. Often forming impenetrable thickets in west and southwest Texas.

Flowers. Heads April–May, axillary, white or light yellow, fragrant, arranged in oblong and densely flowered spikes; individual flowers small, sessile, calyx 4–5-toothed, corolla of 4–5 petals, stamens numerous, exserted, distinct.

Fruit. Legume 2–3½ in. long, ³⁄₁₆–¼ in. wide, linear, often falcate, apex acuminate, base attenuate and stipitate, constricted between the seeds, flattened, reddish brown to black, striate and puberulent, 2-valved and dehiscent; seeds about ¼ in. long, ends rounded or obtuse, lustrous, dark green to brown, compressed.

Leaves. Bipinnate, rachis grooved and somewhat hairy, about ³⁄₈–1 in. long, pinnae 1–2 pairs, leaflets 2–4 pairs (or, rarely, 5 pairs), ¹⁄₆–½ in. long and ¼–⅓ in. wide, sessile or nearly so, elliptic to oblong, oblique, apex rounded and mucronate or sometimes notched, base unsymmetric, firm; surface lustrous, dark green, glabrous, nerves conspicuous.

Twigs. Divaricate, gray to reddish, glabrous, thorns usually paired at the nodes, straight or slightly curved, slender, pale, ⅓–1 in. long.

Bark. Light to dark gray, smooth, tight.

Range. Widespread over Texas in areas west and southwest of the Guadalupe River. Collected by the author in Bexar, Val Verde, and Brewster counties. In Mexico in the states of Tamaulipas, Nuevo León, Chihuahua, San Luis Potosí, and Jalisco.

Remarks. The genus name, *Acacia*, is an old word meaning "a hard, sharp point," with reference to the spinescent stipules. The species name, *rigidula*, refers to the stiff or rigid branches. Vernacular names used are Chaparro Prieto, Catclaw, and Gavia. The plant has good possibilities for use as an ornamental in dry and sandy or limestone areas. It could be used also as an erosion-control plant, and the flowers are a source of honey.

This plant is sometimes listed under the name of *A. amentacea* DC. However, the latter is a closely related species of central Mexico, with a more pubescent petiole and pinnae with only 2 pairs of leaflets.

Mescat Acacia

Acacia constricta Benth. [H]

Field Identification. Spiny shrub to 18 ft, the slender spines in pairs at the nodes.

Flowers. Flowering date variable, borne on slender, puberulent peduncles ¾–1¾ in. long, flowers small, sessile, yellow, fragrant, in dense heads, ¼–⅓ in. in diameter; calyx campanulate, 4–5-lobed, lobes ciliate; petals 4–5, yellow, united into a tube below, 1⁄12–⅛ in. long; stamens numerous (30–40), exserted, filaments yellow and about ⅙ in. long, anthers yellow; ovary stalked.

Fruit. July–September, legume linear, slender, falcate or straight, 2–4¾ in. long, 1⁄12–⅙ in. wide, somewhat constricted between the seeds; apex acute or mucronate; base narrowed and stipelike; surface reddish brown to black, glabrous, glandular or nonglandular, 2-valved, readily dehiscent; seeds in one row, lenticular, about ⅕ in. long and 1⁄12 in. broad, black or mottled gray, smooth, germination about 45 percent.

Leaves. Alternate, or appearing clustered at the nodes, rachis pubescent, 1–2 in. long, bipinnate; pinnae 3–9 pairs (usually 3–7 pairs), petiole gland-bearing; leaflets 6–16 pairs (usually 6–12 pairs), oblong to linear, obtuse, thick, apparently nerveless, glabrous or puberulent, 1/16–1/6 in. long, 1/25–1/12 in. wide, somewhat viscid or nonviscid.

Twigs. Reddish brown to dark brown or black, pubescent or glabrous, sometimes glandular; spines in pairs at the nodes, 1/4–1 1/2 in. long, straight or slightly curved, slender, sharp, white to ashy or brown. Plant sometimes spineless or nearly so.

Bark. Dark brown to black or reddish, smooth or roughened by small scales.

Range. In Texas, New Mexico, Arizona, and Mexico. Generally in dry and sandy or caliche soils at altitudes of 1,500–6,500 ft. Scattered along the Rio Grande drainage in west Texas, but mostly west of the Pecos River and beyond. Abundant in southern New Mexico and Arizona. In Mexico in the states of Sonora, Tamaulipas, Puebla, Zacatecas, Chihuahua, and San Luis Potosí.

Remarks. The genus name, *Acacia*, means "a hard, sharp point," referring to the spinescent stipules of some species. The species name, *constricta*, refers to the constricted legume. Vernacular names are White-thorn Acacia, All-thorn Acacia, Huisache, Gigantillo, Vara Prieta, Chaparro Prieto, and Largancillo.

Spineless Mescat Acacia, *A. constricta* var. *paucispina* Woot. & Standl., a variety with very few or no thorns and with leaves that are less glandular and somewhat larger in size, is found at higher elevations. The plant is usually taller.

Viscid Acacia, *A. vernicosa* Standl., is a closely related species with 1–4 pairs of pinnae, each bearing 3–9 pairs of leaflets, characterized by being very sticky-viscid and glandular. The legume is usually less than 2½ in. long and is also sticky-viscid. The calyx is glandular-dentate and not ciliate as is the Mescat Acacia. However, where the Viscid and Mescat Acacia occur together, intermediate forms between the two are found.

The seeds of Mescat Acacia serve as food for various species of birds including the Gambel's and Mearns's quail. Jackrabbits occasionally nibble the foliage. Cattle eat the unpalatable legumes when nothing else is available. The Indians of Arizona and New Mexico made a coarse meal known as "pinole" out of the legumes. The flowers are an important source of desert honey.

Huisachillo

Acacia tortuosa (L.) Willd. [H]

Field Identification. Usually a spiny, spreading shrub, with numerous stems from the base. More rarely a small tree to 20 ft, and 5–6 in. in diameter, with an irregular crown.

Flowers. In spring, the heads borne on solitary or clustered puberulent peduncles ⅓–1 in. long; bracts 2, minute, hairy; flower heads yellow, fragrant, globose, ¼–⅜ in. in diameter; calyx mi-

nute, shorter than the corolla, 5-lobed, lobes puberulent; corolla 5-parted, puberulent; stamens numerous, exserted, distinct, twice as long as the corolla; ovary pubescent.

Fruit. Legume 2¾–5 in. long, about ¼ in. wide, elongate, linear, almost round but slightly compressed, somewhat constricted between the seeds, dark reddish brown to black, velvety-pubescent, tardily dehiscent, somewhat pulpy; seeds in one row, about ¼ in. long, obovoid, compressed, dark reddish brown, shiny.

Leaves. Bipinnate, rachis slender and puberulent, short-petiolate, usually less than 1¼ in. long; pinnae 2–5 pairs (usually 3 or 4); leaflets 10–15 pairs, each leaflet linear to oblong, somewhat curved, apex mucronulate, base subsessile, surface light green and glabrous, ¹⁄₂₅–⅙ in. long.

Twigs. Reddish brown or gray, slender, somewhat angled, glabrous or pubescent; lenticels numerous and minute; spines ¼–¾ in. long, terete, puberulent to glabrous.

Bark. Dark brown to black, deeply furrowed.

Range. Widespread in Texas, Mexico, the West Indies, South America, and the Galápagos Islands. In Texas from the valley of the Cibolo River to Eagle Pass on the Rio Grande. In Mexico in the states of Nuevo León, Chihuahua, Durango, Hidalgo, Puebla, Colima, and San Luis Potosí.

Remarks. The genus name, *Acacia*, means "sharp-pointed" and refers to the spinescent stipules. The species name, *tortuosa*, refers to the twisted branches. It has also been known under the name of Schaffner Acacia, *Acacia schaffneri* (S. Wats.) Hermann, for Wilhelm Schaffner, pharmaceutical dentist from Darmstadt. It is also known as Huisache Chino. It resembles Sweet Acacia, *A. farnesiana*, somewhat, but the legume of the former is much narrower and elongate.

Sweet Acacia

Acacia farnesiana (L.) Willd. [H]

Field Identification. Shrub with many stems from the base, or a thorny tree to 30 ft, and 18 in. in diameter. With either a flat top in coastal specimens, or round-topped with pendulous branches.

Flowers. February–March, very fragrant, solitary, or 2–5 heads together on puberulent peduncles 1–1½ in. long; bracts 2, minute; heads about ⅔ in. in diameter; stamens numerous, yellow, with distinct filaments (about 20), much longer than the corolla; corolla tubular-funnelform, shallowly 5-lobed, lobes as high as broad, about ¹⁄₁₂ in. long; calyx about half as long as corolla lobes, somewhat hairy; ovary short-stipitate and hairy, style filiform.

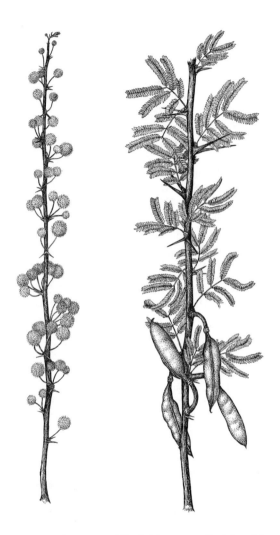

Fruit. Legume persistent, tardily dehiscent, cylindric, oblong, thick, woody, stout, straight or curved, 2–3 in. long, ½–⅔ in. broad, short-pointed, reddish brown to purple or black, partitions thin and papery, pulp pithy; seeds in solitary compartments, transverse, ovoid, brown, shining, flattened on one side, about ¼ in. long, peduncles stout and short.

Leaves. Pinnately compound, alternate, deciduous, 1–4 in. long; pinnae 2–8 pairs; leaflets 10–25 pairs, linear, apex acute, obtuse,

or with a minute mucro, base inequilateral, length about ½₂–
¼ in., width about ½₅ in., sessile or short-petioled, bright green
and glabrous or puberulent.

Twigs. Ascending, pendulous or horizontal, slender, terete, striate,
angled, glabrous or puberulent, armed with paired, straight, rigid,
stipular spines to 1½₂ in. long.

Wood. Reddish brown, sapwood paler, hard, heavy, durable, close-
grained, specific gravity 0.83.

Range. Cultivated in tropical and semitropical regions of both
hemispheres. In Texas and Louisiana; eastward to Florida, northward in New Mexico and Arizona, southward on the Texas coast
through Mexico, through Central America and northern South
America to Guiana.

Remarks. The genus name, *Acacia*, refers to the hard, sharp spinescent stipules of some species. The species name, *farnesiana*,
honors Cardinal Odoardo Farnese (1573–1626) of Rome. This species was the first introduced to his gardens in 1611. Our species is
cultivated in France under the name of Cassie, but is usually
known in Texas as Huisache; however, because of confusion with
other acacias, it seems best to apply the name of Sweet Acacia.
Vernacular names in the United States and Latin America are
Acacia-catclaw, Honey-ball, Opopanax, Yellow-opopanax, Popinach, Hinsach, Binorama, Vinorama, Huisache (from the Nahuatl
huitz-axin), Guisache Yondino, Guisache, Huisache de la Semilla,
Huixachin, Uisatsin, Xkantiriz, Matitas, Finisache, Bihi, Espiño,
Aroma, Zubin, Zubin-ché, Gabia, Gavia, Subin, Aroma Amarilla,
Espiño Blanco, Cacheto de aroma, Cuji Cimmarón, Pelá, Uña de
Cabra, and Espinillo.

   Sweet Acacia is commonly cultivated as a garden ornamental in
tropical countries. The wood is used for many purposes, including
posts, agricultural instruments, and woodenware articles. It is
considered a good winter forage plant and a desirable honey plant
in semiarid areas, being resistant to drought and heat. The bark
and fruit are used for tanning, dyeing, and ink making. Glue from
the young pods is used to mend pottery.

Berlandier Acacia

Acacia berlandieri Benth. [H]

Field Identification. Spreading shrub, with many stems from the
base, or sometimes a small tree to 15 ft. The gray to white branches
are thornless or nearly so.

Flowers. Blooming November–March, in heads on axillary, solitary or clustered, pubescent peduncles arranged in racemes; the heads white, dense, fragrant, globose, or short-spicate, ⅜ in. or more in diameter; calyx 5-lobed, pubescent, lobes valvate; corolla 5-parted, pubescent; stamens numerous, exserted, distinct, anthers small; ovary densely white-hairy.

Fruit. Legume matures June–July, 4–6 in. long, ½–1 in. wide, linear to oblong, flat, thin, firm, straight or somewhat curved, apex obtuse or apiculate, base stipitate, margins somewhat thickened, surface whitish when young, velvety-tomentose when older, valves dehiscent; seeds 5–10, about ⅜ in. long and broad, one margin straighter than the other, compressed, dark brown, lustrous.

Leaves. Delicate and almost fernlike in appearance, bipinnate, 4–6 in. long; pinnae 5–9 pairs (sometimes to 18 pairs); leaflets 30–50 pairs (sometimes to 90 pairs); leaflets ⅙–¼ in. long, linear to oblong, oblique, acute, prominently nerved, at first tomentose but more glabrate later; petiolar gland sessile; stipules small, early deciduous.

Twigs. Gray to white, tomentose when young, when older glabrous, unarmed or prickly.

Bark. Gray, older stems with shallow fissures and broad, flat ridges.

Range. In sandy or limestone soils from the Nueces River valley westward and southward into Mexico. Abundant along the lower Rio Grande drainage. In Mexico in the states of Nuevo León, Tamaulipas, Querétaro, and Veracruz.

Remarks. The genus name, *Acacia*, refers to the spinescent stipules of some species, and the species name, *berlandieri*, is for Luis Berlandier, a Belgian botanist who explored the United States–Mexico boundary for the Mexican government in 1828. Vernacular names are Thornless Catclaw, Mimosa Catclaw, Round-flowered Catclaw, Guajillo, Huajilla, and Matoral. This species is a very famous honey plant, producing a clear, white, excellent-flavored honey. The wood is sometimes used for fuel locally or for making handles and small woodenware articles. It is a desirable plant for cultivation both as a specimen plant or hedge plant in the areas suited to it. The fernlike leaves and globose white flower heads are very attractive. It can be propagated by seeds or by young seedlings that come up at the base of the old plant, but these are deep-rooted and hard to transplant.

Catclaw Acacia

Acacia greggii Gray [H]

Field Identification. Thorny, thicket-forming shrub or small tree to 30 ft, and 1 ft in diameter. The numerous slender, spreading, thorny branches are almost impenetrable.

Flowers. Usually April–October; spikes 1¼–2½ in. long, about ½ in. in diameter, dense, oblong, creamy yellow, fragrant, peduncle usually about one-half the length of the spike, sometimes a number of spikes clustered together at the ends of the twigs; calyx green, about 1⁄12 in. long (half as long as the petals), obscurely 5-toothed, puberulent on the outer surface; petals 5,

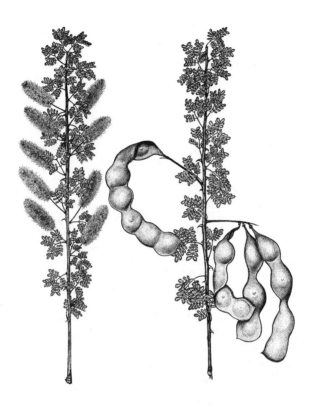

⅛−⅙ in. long, greenish, yellowish, and hairy on the margins; stamens numerous, exserted, about ¼ in. long, filaments pale yellow; ovary long-stalked, hairy.

Fruit. Persistent from July through the winter, legume 2−5½ in. long, ½−¾ in. wide, compressed, straight, curved, or often curling and contorted, constricted between the seeds, apex acute or rounded, sometimes mucronulate, base obliquely narrowed into a short stalk, margins thickened, light brown or reddish, reticulate-veined, valves thin and membranous; seeds dark brown, shiny, almost orbicular, compressed, ¼−⅓ in. long, germination about 60 percent.

Leaves. Bipinnate, 1−3 in. long; pinnae short-stalked, 1−3 pairs, petiole with a minute brown gland near the middle; leaflets 3−7 (usually 3−5) pairs, obovate to oblong; apex rounded, obtuse or truncate, apiculate; base unequally contracted into a short petiolule; blade surface 2–3-nerved, lightly reticulate-veined, pubescent, length ⅙–¼ in.

Twigs. Pale brown to reddish or gray, pubescent or glabrous; spines ⅛–¼ in. long, dark brown or gray, stout, recurved, flat at base, infrastipular.

Bark. Gray to black, about ⅛ in. thick, furrowed, the surface separating into small thin scales on older trunks.

Wood. Brown to reddish, sapwood light yellow, close-grained, hard, heavy, strong, durable.

Range. At altitudes of 1,000–5,000 ft, on dry gravelly mesas, sides of canyons, and banks of arroyos. In west Texas there are two more or less disjunct ranges. The more southerly of these extends southward from Bexar County to Willacy County; the other from Taylor County southwestward, with heavy concentration in the Big Bend area. Also in New Mexico, Arizona, and Colorado; north to Nevada and Utah, west to California, and south into the Mexican states of Coahuila, Chihuahua, Sonora, and Baja California.

Remarks. The genus name, *Acacia*, means "hard-pointed" and refers to the spinescent stipules of some of the species. The species name, *greggii*, honors Josiah Gregg (1806–1850), early botanist who collected in the Southwest and northern Mexico. Vernacular names used are Devil Claws, Texas Mimosa, Paradise Flower, Gregg Acacia, Long-flowered Acacia, Huajilla, Chaparral, Gatuña, and Uña de Gato.

Catclaw Acacia often grows in almost impenetrable thickets, furnishing shelter for various birds and mammals. The seeds are eaten by scaled quail, and the leaves are nibbled by jackrabbit when other food is scarce. The wood is used for fuel, small household articles, and singletrees. Cattle browse on the young foliage when grass is scarce, but it is not palatable. The plant apparently stands heavy grazing well and is drought resistant. The fragrant yellow flowers furnish an excellent bee food, and honey from it is light yellow and of good flavor. From the legumes the Indians of west Texas, New Mexico, and Arizona made a meal known as "pinole," which was eaten in the form of mush or cakes. It is also reported that the lac insect, *Tachardia lacca* Kerr., feeds on the sap and exudes the substance from its body. This substance is used as commercial lac. However, the infestation does not appear to be abundant enough to make the gathering of the lac commercially profitable on Catclaw Acacia.

Wright Acacia

Acacia wrightii Benth. [H]

Field Identification. Spiny shrub, or sometimes a tree attaining a height of 30 ft, and to 1 ft in diameter. The glabrous, spreading branches form a wide irregular-shaped crown.

Flowers. March–May, or at odd times after rains, in cylindric spikes ¾–1½ in. long, which are sometimes interrupted; peduncles slender, glabrous or pubescent, solitary or clustered; individual flower pedicels slender, subtended by minute caducous bracts; calyx minutely 5-toothed, pubescent on the outer surface; petals spatulate, slightly united at base, margin ciliate; stamens exserted, about ¼ in. long; ovary hairy, long-stalked.

Fruit. Ripe June–September, legume often abundant and conspicuous, borne on peduncles ¾–2 in. long; legume 2–4 in. long, 1–1¼ in. wide; margin thick, straight or irregularly contracted or

irregularly curved; apex rounded and usually short-pointed; base round or oblique and short-stipitate; valves much flattened, papery, thin, finely reticulate-veined, glabrous; seeds compressed, narrow-obovoid, light brown, sometimes marked with oval depressions, length about ¼ in.

Leaves. Solitary or fascicled, 1–2 in. long, petiole and rachis pubescent, petiole ¼–1⅓ in. long, sometimes with a solitary gland near the apex; pinnae 1–3 pairs, each pinna with 2–6 pairs of leaflets obovate to oblong, apex obliquely rounded to obtuse or retuse, often apiculate; base sessile or short-petiolulate; length ¼–⅚ in.; surface 2–3-nerved and reticulate-veined, glabrous or pubescent, paler green on the lower surface.

Twigs. Gray to brown or yellowish, mostly glabrous and somewhat striately angled; spineless, or armed with brown, recurved, flattened, sharp-pointed infrastipular spines about ¼ in. long.

Bark. Rather thin, gray to brown, divided into broad ridges and shallow fissures, the ridges separating into thin, narrow scales on old trunks.

Wood. Pale brown to reddish brown, sapwood white to yellow, close-grained, heavy, hard.

Range. On dry, rocky, prairie soils. In Texas from the valley of the Guadalupe River westward. Assuming tree habit and of greatest abundance in the vicinity of Brackettville, Uvalde, Sabinal, and Montell. In Mexico in Sonora, Tamaulipas, and Nuevo León.

Remarks. The genus name, *Acacia*, refers to the sharp, pointed spinescent stipules of some species. The species name, *wrightii*, is in honor of Charles Wright, who collected plants in Texas 1847–1848 while with the military forces at western forts. Wright Acacia can be transplanted or grown from seed and makes an excellent ornamental tree in the drier areas of the state. A few horticultural varieties have been developed. The legume is borne abundantly and is conspicuous. The spikes of yellow flowers make a good bee food, and the wood is sometimes used for fuel and posts. Vernacular names are Tree Catclaw, Texas Catclaw, Uña de Gato, and Negra. Wright Acacia can be distinguished from Catclaw Acacia, *A. greggii*, by the wider legume and leaflets that are twice as large.

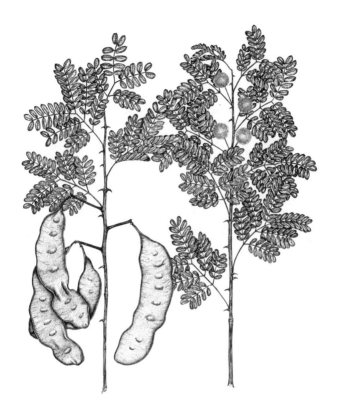

Roemer Acacia

Acacia roemeriana Scheele [H]

Field Identification. Prickly, round-topped shrub with many spreading branches. More rarely a small tree to 15 ft or more, with a maximum trunk diameter to 16 in.

Flowers. Heads mostly axillary; borne on slender, glabrous peduncles ⅓–1⅓ in. long; flowers white to pale greenish yellow, ¼–½ in. in diameter; calyx small, 5-lobed; corolla 5-lobed; stamens numerous, exserted, distinct, anthers small; ovary stalked.

Fruit. Legume oblong to linear, 2–5 in. long, ¾–1¼ in. broad, straight or somewhat curved, compressed, leathery, margin entire to lobed or constricted, apex obtuse, base rounded to cuneate and stipitate, surface red or pink at maturity, glabrous and prominently nerved on the edge of the valves.

Leaves. Bipinnate, 1⅓−4 in. long, pinnae 1−3 pairs, leaflets 3−8 pairs, each leaflet ⅓−⅗ in. long, oblong to oval or cuneate, oblique, obtuse to retuse and often apiculate, glabrous or nearly so, veins prominent beneath.

Twigs. Gray to brown, smooth, with short curved prickles.

Bark. Gray to brown, smooth on young trunks, breaking into thin, small scales on old trunks.

Range. In dry, limestone soil, or on gravelly bluffs or banks. From the valley of the Colorado River south and west to El Paso County. The type specimen was collected at Austin. Abundant in the vicinity of New Braunfels, San Antonio, Langtry, and Del Rio. To altitudes of 4,500 ft in the foothills of the Chisos Mountains in Brewster County. In the lower Rio Grande Valley in Cameron and Hidalgo counties. Also in southern New Mexico near Carlsbad, and in Mexico in the states of Coahuila, Chihuahua, and Baja California.

Remarks. The genus name, *Acacia*, refers to the sharp-pointed, spinescent stipules of some species. The species name, *roemeriana*, honors Ferdinand Roemer, a German geologist and naturalist who collected specimens 1845−1847 in the vicinity of New Braunfels. Vernacular names for the plant are Round-flowered Acacia and Round-flowered Catclaw. It is sometimes planted for ornament and is an important source of honey.

Silk-tree Albizia

Albizia julibrissin (Willd.) Durazz. [H]

Field Identification. Cultivated tree attaining a height of 40 ft, with a flat top and widely spreading branches, often broader than high.

Flowers. May−August, on the upper ends of the branches, in axillary, tassellike, capitate clusters on slender, pubescent peduncles ½−2 in. long; heads 1½−2 in. broad, flowers perfect; stamens numerous, conspicuous, long-exserted, filamentous, 1−1½ in. long, pink distally, whitish proximally, united at base; pistils considerably longer than stamens, style white or pink, filiform, stigma minute, ovary short-stalked; corolla tubular, greenish, pubescent, ⅛−¼ in. long, 5-lobed, lobes oblong or ovate, obtuse or acute; calyx tubular, 1/12−⅛ in. long, shallowly 5-lobed, pubescent.

Fruit. Legume on a pubescent peduncle 1−2½ in. long, oblong to linear, 5−8 in. long, ¾−1 in. wide, margin straight or wavy, apex

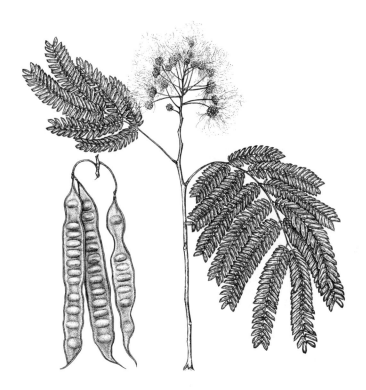

gradually or abruptly narrowed into a long, spinose point, base cuneate; valves thin, flattened, papery, yellowish brown, not separating on margin, without partitions between the seeds; seeds brown, lustrous, flattened, rounded or obtuse at the ends, about ¼ in. long, averaging 11,000 seeds per lb, one-fourth to one-third germinating.

Leaves. Alternate, deciduous, twice-pinnately compound, 10–15 in. long; rachis green to brown, smooth or striate, pubescent, often glandular near the base; pinnae 2–6 in. long, 5–12 pairs, rachilla pubescent; leaflets 8–30 pairs per pinna, sessile or nearly so, ¼–⅜ in. long, oblong, slightly falcate, oblique; margin entire, ciliate, straighter on one side than the other; apex half-rounded and mucronulate; base truncate or rounded, attached to the rachilla on one side; main vein parallel to and close to the margin on one side; glabrous to puberulent.

Twigs. Green to brown or gray, somewhat angular or rounded, glabrous, lenticels small but numerous.

Bark. Smooth, tight, blotched gray, sometimes brownish on young trunks or limbs.

Range. A native of Asia, cultivated from Washington, D.C., Philadelphia, and Indianapolis; from Maryland south to Florida and west into Texas. Commonly planted on the streets of Houston and other Gulf Coast cities.

Remarks. The genus, *Albizia*, was named after F. Degli Albizzi, an Italian nobleman and naturalist. The tree is often called Mimosa in the southern states. Silk-tree was first introduced into cultivation in 1745 and is considered a top ornamental for the South, being somewhat drought resistant and fairly free from disease and insects. However, it has been reported that specimens in Georgia and the Carolinas have been very susceptible to the killing attacks of the root fungus *Fusorium perniciosum*. The tree does not seem to escape cultivation and reproduce readily. The seeds may furnish a limited amount of food for birds, squirrels, and other wildlife. The wood is used for cabinetmaking in its native Asiatic home.

Gregg Lead-tree

Leucaena greggii Wats. [H]

Field Identification. Unarmed shrub or small tree attaining a height of 20 ft, with a trunk diameter of 3–5 in.

Flowers. Borne on slender, pubescent, solitary or clustered peduncles 1–3 in. long; involucre of 2–3 lobed bracts; flowers small, white, dense, sessile, in globose heads ¾–1 in. in diameter; calyx tube minutely 5-toothed, glabrous except for the pubescent teeth; petals 5, longer than the calyx, narrowly spatulate, glabrous or pubescent, each about ⅕ in. long; stamens 10, free, exserted, about ⅓ in. long; filaments filiform, anthers oblong, versatile; ovary stipitate, style slender, stigma minute and terminal.

Fruit. Legume narrowly linear, flattened, 6–8 in. long, ⅓–½ in. wide, apex with a subulate beak ½–2 in. long, base narrowed into a short, stout stipe, cinereous-pubescent when young, at maturity glabrous, margins narrow and thickened; valves impressed between the seeds, seeds compressed and transverse.

Leaves. Bipinnate, 5–9 in. long and broad, rachis with a solitary, subcylindric gland between each pair of pinnae; pinnae 10–18, short-stalked; leaflets 15–30 pairs, lanceolate to linear, often somewhat falcate, apex acute or acuminate, base rounded on

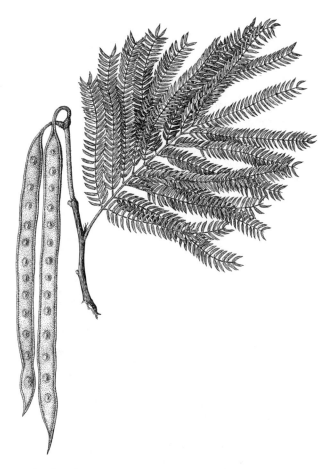

proximal side, almost straight on the distal side; grayish green, puberulent to glabrous, midvein nearly central and lateral veins obscure, sessile or short-petiolulate, blade length ¼–⅓ in., width about ⅛ in.; petioles pubescent, ¾–1⅓ in. long; stipules persistent, rigid, acuminate, ⅓–½ in. long.

Twigs. Reddish brown, stout, somewhat divaricate, pubescent at first, later glabrous, lenticels pale and numerous.

Bark. Dark brown, with low ridges that break into small, appressed scales on old trunks.

Wood. Reddish brown, sapwood paler, close-grained, heavy, hard, specific gravity 0.92.

Range. Dry, well-drained soil on the edges of rocky ravines. In Texas confined to a limited area from the upper San Saba to the Devils River. Southward into Chihuahua, Coahuila, and Nuevo León, Mexico.

Remarks. The genus name, *Leucaena*, refers to the white flowers of several species, and the species name, *greggii*, is in honor of Josiah Gregg (1806–1850). The Gregg Lead-tree is generally too small to be of much value for wood.

Golden-ball Lead-tree

Leucaena retusa Benth. [H]

Field Identification. Shrub or small tree to 25 ft, and 8 in. in diameter.

Flowers. April–October, borne on stout, single or fascicled, axillary peduncles, 1½–3 in. long and subtended by 2 villous bracts; bracts ⅙–¼ in. long, apex subulate; flower heads yellow, globose, dense, ¾–1¼ in. in diameter; calyx tubular, minutely 5-toothed, membranous, ¹⁄₁₂–⅛ in. long; petals 5, free, narrowly oblong, barely longer than the calyx; stamens 10, distinct, free, exserted, ¼–⅓ in. long; filaments filiform, anthers glabrous and oblong; ovary stipitate, style slender, stigma minute and terminal.

Fruit. Generally mature in August, solitary or clustered, borne on stout puberulent peduncles 1½–5 in. long; pods 3–10 in. long, ⅓–½ in. wide, stipitate, narrowly linear, flattened, somewhat constricted on the thickened margin, apex acute or acuminate, base cuneate; rigid, thin, papery, glabrous; light to dark brown; seeds numerous, obliquely transverse, compressed, about ⅓ in. long and ¼ in. wide; seed coat thin, crustaceous, brown and lustrous.

Leaves. Alternate, bipinnate, stipellate, 3–8 in. long, 4–5 in. wide, petiole and rachis slender; pinnae 2–5 pairs (usually 3 or 4), long-stalked and distant; leaflets 3–8 pairs (usually 3–6 per pinna), short-stalked; oblong to elliptic, or the upper obovate, basally asymmetric; apex rounded or obtuse to retuse, mucronulate; base rounded or cuneate; margin entire; length ⅓–1 in., width ⅓–½ in.; surface glabrous or pubescent, reticulate-veined, bluish green, thin; glands usually solitary and elevated, borne between the pinnae or leaflets; stipules ovate to lanceolate, subulate-tipped, ⅖–⅗ in. long.

Twigs. Slender, grooved, brown to reddish, pubescent or puberulous, lenticels numerous and oval.

Bark. Light gray to brown, broken into small thin scales on old trunks, smooth on young branches.

Range. Mostly on dry, well-drained, rocky, limestone soils in central Texas and the Trans-Pecos area. Also in New Mexico and Mexico.

Remarks. The genus name, *Leucaena*, refers to the white flowers of some species, and the species name, *retusa*, refers to rounded, sometimes concave-tipped, leaflets. It is apparently not abundant enough to warrant the application of other vernacular names except Mimosa and Wahoo-tree. Much browsed by cattle. Worthy of cultivation in the central and west Texas limestone areas because of the attractive flowers, fruit, and leaves.

Honey Mesquite

Prosopis glandulosa Torr. [H]

Field Identification. Thorny shrub or small tree to 30 ft with crooked drooping branches and a rounded crown. Trunk usually dividing into branches a short distance above the ground and often leaning. Root system radially spreading and deep.

Flowers. May–September, perfect, borne in axillary yellowish-green, cylindric, pedunculate, spikelike racemes; calyx bell-shaped, minute, 5-lobed, with lobes triangular; corolla greenish white, small, with 5 linear petals that are erect, pubescent within, and much longer than the calyx tube; stamens 10, exserted, with filiform filaments and oblong anthers; ovary stipitate, pubescent; style filiform; stigma small.

Fruit. August–September, legumes in loose clusters 4–9 in. long, terete or somewhat flattened, glabrous, linear, straight or curved,

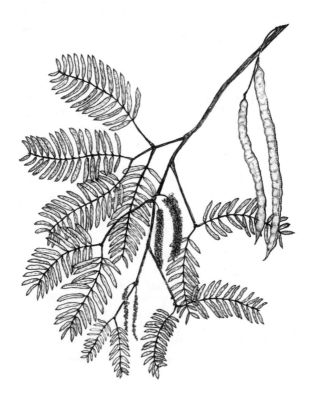

Torrey Mesquite

somewhat constricted between the seeds, indehiscent; seeds oblong, compressed, shiny, brown, set in spongy tissue.

Leaves. Alternate, deciduous, long-petioled, bipinnately compound of 2 (rarely 3 or 4) pairs of pinnae; with 12–20 pairs of leaflets; leaflets smooth, dark green, linear, acute or obtuse at apex, about 2 in. long and ¼ in. wide.

Twigs. Zigzag, armed with stout straight spines to 2 in. long, or sometimes spineless.

Bark. Rough, reddish brown, with shallow fissures and thick scales.

Remarks. The genus name, *Prosopis*, is the old Greek name for burdock. The species name, *glandulosa*, is for the glandular anther connectives of the flowers. Mesquite is often shrubby, forming thickets in dry areas and taking over grasslands rapidly. It readily sprouts from the stump, is very deep rooted, and is not easily damaged by disease or insects. The wood is reddish brown, heavy, hard, durable, close-grained, and the sapwood yellow. It is used for charcoal, fuel, furniture, building blocks, crossties, and posts and is often the only wood available in regions in which it grows. Mesquite foliage and pods are eaten by livestock, and the seeds pass through the digestive tracts and grow where they fall. This fact has been responsible for much of its rapid distribution. The seeds are also considered an important wildlife food, being eaten by Gambel's quail, scaled quail, white-winged dove, rock squirrel, ground squirrel, coyote, skunk, jackrabbit, and white-tailed and mule deer. Mesquite beans played an important part in the diet of the southwestern Indian. The legumes contain as much as 30 percent sugar, and meal known as "pinole" was prepared from them and made into bread. Fermentation of the meal also produced an intoxicating beverage. Exudation of gum from the branches and trunk offers possibilities as a substitute for gum arabic and is used locally to make candy. Honey Mesquite also produces a black dye and a cement for mending pottery.

Torrey Mesquite, *Prosopis glandulosa* var. *torreyana* (L. Benson) M. C. Johnston, has leaflets from ⅖–1⅕ in. long, about 5–8 times as long as broad, with 8–20 (average 10–15) pairs of pinna. Common in the Trans-Pecos region. Also occurring along the Rio Grande, and then along the Gulf in the vicinity of Corpus Christi. Also in the Mexican states of Nuevo León, Coahuila, Chihuahua, and Sonora. In New Mexico and Arizona.

Subfamily Caesalpinioideae

Common Honey-locust

Gleditsia triacanthos L. [H]

Field Identification. Tree to 100 ft, with a thorny trunk and branches and a loose, open crown.

Flowers. May–June, perfect or imperfect, borne in axillary, dense, green racemes; racemes of the staminate flowers often clustered, pubescent, 2–5 in. long; calyx campanulate; lobes of calyx 5, elliptic-lanceolate, spreading, hairy, acute; petals 4–5, longer than calyx lobes, erect, oval, white; stamens 10, inserted on the calyx tube, anthers green, pistil rudimentary or absent in the staminate flower; pistillate racemes 2–3 in. long, slender, few-flowered, usu-

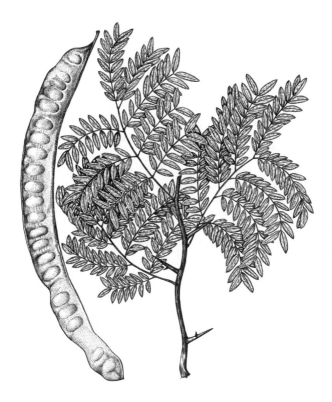

ally solitary; pistil tomentose, ovary almost sessile, style short, stigma oblique, ovules 2 or many; stamens much smaller and abortive in pistillate flower.

Fruit. Ripening September–October, legume 6–18 in. long, ½–1½ in. wide, borne on short peduncles, usually in twos or threes, dark brown, shiny, flattened, often twisted, falcate or straight, coriaceous, pulp succulent and sweetish between the seeds, occasional sterile legumes are seedless and pulpless, some trees with rather small legumes, others with large legumes, and some with a mixture of small, intermediate, and large; seeds about ⅓ in. long, oval, hard, compressed. The minimum commercial seed-bearing age is 10 years and the maximum 100 years.

Leaves. Alternate, deciduous, once- or twice-pinnate (the twice-pinnate usually on more vigorous shoots), 5–10 in. long; pinnae 4–8 pairs; leaflets 14–30, alternate or opposite, almost sessile, ¾–2 in. long, ½–1 in. wide, oblong-lanceolate, rounded or acute at apex, cuneate or rounded or inequilateral at base, crenulate or entire on margin, dark green and lustrous above, paler and often pubescent beneath; rachis and petioles pubescent.

Twigs. Greenish or reddish brown, lustrous, stout, armed with solitary or 3-branched thorns that are rigid, sharp, straight, shiny, purplish brown.

Bark. Grayish brown to black, on older trees with fissures deep and narrow, separating into scaly ridges, often bearing heavy simple to multibranched thorns.

Wood. Brown to reddish, sapwood yellowish, coarse-grained, strong in bending and end compression, stiff, highly shock resistant, tools well, splits rather easy, shrinks little, does not glue satisfactorily, rather hard, moderately durable, weighing 42 lb per cu ft.

Range. In moist fertile soil. Texas, Oklahoma, Arkansas, and Louisiana; eastward to Florida, northward to Pennsylvania and New York, and west to Nebraska.

Remarks. The genus name, *Gleditsia*, is a contraction and is in honor of Johann Gottlieb Gleditsch, an eighteenth-century German botanist. The species name, *triacanthos*, refers to the commonly 3-branched thorns. Other vernacular names are Honey-shucks, Sweet Locust, Thorn-tree, Thorny Locust, Three-thorned-acacia, and Sweet-bean. It has been known in cultivation since 1700 and is often planted for ornament, particularly the thornless form. The tree has few diseases or insect pests. The wood is used for farm implements, fuel, lumber, posts, vehicles, furniture, and railroad crossties. The flowers are reported to be a good bee food, and the Indians ate the fleshy sweet pulp of the young pods, older pods turning bitter. The pods are also eaten by cattle, white-tailed deer, gray squirrel, and cottontail.

Texas Paloverde

Cercidium texanum Gray [H]

Field Identification. Spiny, green-barked shrub or small tree to 25 ft. Usually with a short crooked or leaning trunk, or with semiprostrate lower branches.

Flowers. Borne in clusters or short racemes; pedicels solitary, reddish, pubescent, ¼–½ in. long; corolla yellow, of 5 imbricate petals, each about ½ in. long, ovate to elliptic, apex acute to obtuse

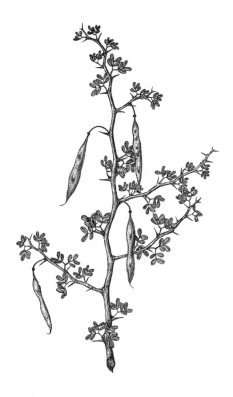

or rounded, margin frilled and crisped. One petal abruptly contracted into a long claw at base and spotted red; stamens 10, filaments distinct, red, glabrous; anthers yellow, opening lengthwise; pistils equaling or slightly exceeding the stamens, filiform, hairy; calyx valvate, sepals 5, linear to oblong, puberulent to pubescent, reflexed.

Fruit. Legume 1–2½ in. long, about ¼ in. wide, flattened, apex long-apiculate, margin straight or somewhat constricted between the seeds; surfaces light brown, at first finely hairy but later glabrate; seeds usually 1–4, about ¼ in. long, dark brown, shiny, flattened, short-oblong, ends rounded.

Leaves. Early deciduous, leaving bare twigs and branches; leaves twice-pinnately compound, ½–¾ in. long; petiole puberulent, about ¼ in. long; leaflets 1–3 pairs (usually 1 or 2 pairs per pinna); blades very short-petioluled or sessile, short-oblong or narrowly obovate, somewhat broader toward the rounded apex, ⅛–¼ in. long, grayish green with closely appressed pubescence.

Twigs. Grayish green or dark green, zigzag, very thorny, smooth, finely grooved, densely appressed pubescence, later more glabrous; spines white to green or pale brown, straight or slightly recurved, sharp, pubescent or glabrous, ¼–½ in. long.

Bark. Thin, smooth, light or dark green.

Range. Usually on limestone soils of flats or gentle slopes. Abundant in the vicinity of Brackettville, Del Rio, and Langtry. In Mexico in Nuevo León, Tamaulipas, and Coahuila.

Remarks. The genus name, *Cercidium*, is from the Greek *kerkidion* ("a weaver's comb"), to which the fruit has a fancied resemblance. The species name, *texanum*, is for the state of Texas.

Texas Paloverde is closely related to Border Paloverde, *C. macrum* I. M. Johnston. Generally Texas Paloverde has fewer pinnae on the average and a hairy ovary, but intermediate forms between the two are found where the ranges overlap in the lower Rio Grande area.

Border Paloverde

Cercidium macrum I. M. Johnst. [H]

Field Identification. Green-barked spiny tree attaining a height of 25 ft, its branches crooked and sometimes close to the ground and horizontal.

Flowers. Borne in short racemes ¾–1¼ in. long; pedicels ⅛–½ in. long, puberulent to glabrous; corolla yellow, petals 5, ovate or elliptic, apex obtuse, margin crisped; one petal spotted red, long-clawed, larger than the other petals; stamens 10, filaments distinct and hairy toward the base; pistil elongate, glabrous, calyx of 5 sepals, lanceolate or oblong, glabrous or nearly so, ⅛–³⁄₁₆ in. long, reflexed.

Fruit. Pedicels ½–1½ in. long, legume 1–2½ in. long, ¼–½ in. wide, flattened, apex abruptly obtuse or acute to slender-mucronulate, margin straight or slightly undulate, dark brown, glabrous at maturity; seeds 1–5, flattened, shiny, dark brown, oval or short-oblong, with ends rounded.

Leaves. Often early deciduous or releafing after rains, twice-pinnate, ¾–1 in. long; petioles puberulent to glabrous, about ¼ in. long; leaflets usually 2 or 3 pairs (more rarely 1 pair per pinna);

blades oblong, apex mostly rounded or some semitruncate and slightly notched, base narrowed, margin entire, surfaces olive green to dark green, ⅛–¼ in. long, young ones minutely puberulent, later glabrous; petiolules very short, about ¹⁄₂₅ in. long.

Twigs. Zigzag, young ones light green, eventually dark green or dark brown on older branches, smooth, finely grooved; spines averaging about ¼ in. long, green to brown or black, slender, sharp, straight or slightly curved.

Bark. Thin, smooth, dark green to brown on old trunks.

Range. Either on sandy loams or clay soils. Valley of the lower Rio Grande; Cameron, Willacy and Hidalgo counties in Texas; and in adjacent Mexico.

Remarks. The genus name, *Cercidium*, is from Greek, *kerkidion* ("a weaver's comb"), to which the fruit has a fancied resemblance. The species name, *macrum*, means "large," but the application is obscure.

Border Paloverde is closely related to Texas Paloverde, *C. texanum* Gray, which grows in the Del Rio area. However, the latter has a hairy pistil, more pubescent leaves and twigs, and usually fewer leaflets (1 or 2 pairs) on the average. These characters are not always clearly distinguishable, especially where the two ranges approach each other and overlap.

Jerusalem-thorn

Parkinsonia aculeata L. [H]

Field Identification. Green-barked, thorny shrub or tree to 36 ft. Branches slender, spiny, spreading, often pendulous to form a rounded head.

Flowers. Fragrant, borne in spring or throughout the summer, especially after rains. Racemes 5–6 in. long, axillary, solitary or fascicled, pedicels ⅓–½ in. long; petals 5, imbricate in the bud, yellow, about ½ in. long, spreading, oval, clawed at the base, margin erose or entire; one petal larger than the others and bearing a gland at base, becoming red-dotted or orange with age; stamens 10, shorter than the petals, filaments distinct and hairy below,

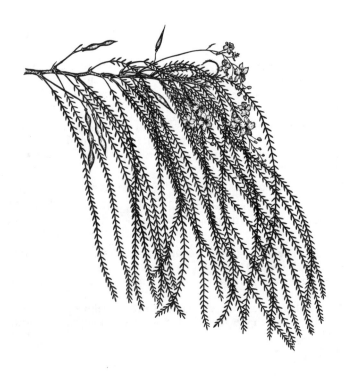

anthers yellow to reddish, opening lengthwise; ovary pubescent; calyx glabrous or nearly so, tube short, lobes oblong and reflexed, longer than the tube.

Fruit. On pedicels ½–¾ in. long; a linear legume, 2–4 in. long, brown to orange or reddish, puberulent or glabrous, leathery, ends attenuate, constricted between the seeds, swollen portions almost terete, constrictions flattened; seeds 1–8, about ⅓ in. long, oblong, seed coat green to brown.

Leaves. Bipinnate or, rarely, pinnate, petioles short, alternate or fascicled, linear, 8–16 in. long, rachis flat and winged; leaflets numerous (25–30 pairs), remote, linear to oblanceolate, about ⅓ in. long or less, inequilateral, dropping away early and leaving the persistent, flat, naked, photosynthetic rachis, petiolules slender; stipules spinescent; rachis terminating with a weak spine.

Twigs. Somewhat divaricate, green to yellowish, puberulent to glabrous; later gray to brown or orange; spines green, brown or black, to 1 in. long.

Bark. Thin, smooth, green, later brown to reddish with small scales on old trunks.

Wood. Light brown to yellow, hard, heavy, close-grained, specific gravity 0.61.

Range. Usually in moist sandy soils, but resistant to saline situations. In the southern half of Texas; west through New Mexico to Arizona and southward through Mexico to northern South America. Probably an escape from cultivation in California, Florida, and the West Indies.

Remarks. The genus name, *Parkinsonia*, refers to John Parkinson, an English botanical author. The species name, *aculeata*, refers to the spines. Other vernacular names are Horsebean, Cloth-of-Gold, Crown-of-thorns, Barbados Fence Flowers, Paloverde, Lluvia de Oro, Cambrón, Espilla, Espinillo, Espinillo de España, Junco, Junco Marion, Palo de Rayo, Flor de Rayo, Yabo, Calentano, Espiño Real de España, Acacia de Aguijote, Guichi-belle, Mesquite Extranjero, Guacopano, Retama de Cerda, and Retama. A grove of trees is known as a "retamal" by the Mexican people. The tree is a rapid grower and is generally free of diseases and insects. It is often grown for ornament and hedges. The wood is occasionally used as fuel and was formerly used for papermaking. An infusion of the leaves is used in tropical America as a febrifuge, for diabetes, for epilepsy, and as a sudorific and abortifacient. The leaves and pods are eaten by horses, cattle, and deer, particularly in times of stress. The Indians formerly pounded the seeds into flour to make bread. The flowers are sometimes important as a bee food.

Paradise Poinciana

Caesalpinia gilliesii Wall. *ex* Hook. [H]

Field Identification. Shrub or small tree rarely over 8 ft. Branches green, light brown or reddish, glandular-pubescent, malodorous.

Flowers. Blooming most of the summer, borne in terminal, showy, open racemes; flowers ¾–1½ in. in diameter, solitary; pedicels ½–1½ in., yellowish and densely brown-glandular, some glands stalked; sepals larger than the petals, yellow, one noticeably incurved and hooded, imbricate, oblong-elliptic, somewhat narrower than the inner obovate or oval petals; petals 1–1½ in. long; stamens 10, conspicuously red, curved, long-exserted; stigma small, discoid.

Fruit. Pod maturing at lower part of racemes as flowers open at apex, hence flowers and mature fruit often found on the same plant; pedicels stout, ¾–1½ in. long, often with stalked glands; pod flat, oblong-oblanceolate, somewhat falcate or straight, apex acuminate or abruptly acute; light tan or reddish brown when mature, 2–3½ in. long, ½–¾ in. wide; at dehiscence seeds ejected forcibly and fly out a considerable distance.

Leaves. Bipinnate, 3–5 in. long; primary pinnae of 6–12 pairs, each about ¾–1 in. long; leaflets 5–9 pairs per pinna, each leaflet ⅛–³⁄₁₆ in. long; oblong, apex rounded or obtuse, base asymmetrical; petiole, petiolules, and rachis glabrous or nearly so.

Stems. All parts of plant malodorous; older stems green, tan, or reddish, glandular-pubescent; younger twigs thickly brown-glandular, some glands stalked.

Range. A native of Argentina, escaping cultivation and growing in a wild state in west Texas, New Mexico, and Arizona; also in Florida. Southward in Mexico.

Remarks. The genus name, *Caesalpinia*, was named for Andreas Caesalpinus, chief physician to Pope Clement VIII. The species name, *gilliesii*, is for its discoverer, John Gillies (1747–1836). Another vernacular name is Bird-of-paradise.

Subfamily Papilionoideae

Eastern Redbud

Cercis canadensis L. [H]

Field Identification. Shrub or small tree to 40 ft, trunk usually straight, branching usually 5–9 ft from the ground, top broadly rounded or flattened. Distinctly ornamental in spring with small, clustered rose-purple flowers covering the bare branches before the leaves.

Flowers. March–May, before the leaves, in clusters of 2–8, on pedicels ¼–¾ in. long; flowers ¼–⅖ in. long, perfect, imperfectly papilionaceous, rose-purple, petals 5, standard smaller than the wings; keel petals not united, large; stamens 10, shorter than the petals; ovary pubescent, short, stipitate, style curved; calyx campanulate, 5-toothed.

Fruit. September–October, persistent on the branches, often abundant, peduncles divaricate and reflexed, ⅓–⅗ in. long; le-

gume 2−4 in. long, about ½ in. wide or less, tapering at both ends, flat, leathery, reddish brown, upper suture with a somewhat winged margin; valves 2, thin, reticulate-veined; seeds several, oblong, flattened, ⅙−⅓ in. long.

Leaves. Simple, alternate, deciduous, 2−6 in. long, 1¼−6 in. broad, ovate to cordate or reniform, apex usually abruptly obtuse or acute, base cordate or subtruncate, margin entire, palmately 7−9-veined; upper surface dull green and glabrous; lower surface paler and glabrous or somewhat hairy along the veins, membranous at first but firm (not coriaceous) later; petioles 1¼−5 in. long, essentially glabrous, stipules caducous.

Twigs. Slender, glabrous, somewhat divaricate, brown to gray, when young lustrous, when older dull.

Bark. Reddish brown to gray, thin and smooth when young, older ones with elongate fissures separating long, narrow plates with small scales, lenticels numerous.

Wood. Reddish brown, sapwood yellowish, close-grained, hard, weak, weighing 30 lb per cu ft.

Range. Eastern Redbud is found in rich soil along streams or in bottomlands from central Texas, Oklahoma, Arkansas, and Louisiana; eastward to Florida, northward to Connecticut and Ontario, and west to Michigan, Missouri, Nebraska, and Kansas.

Remarks. The genus name, *Cercis*, is the ancient name of the closely related Judas-tree of Europe and Asia. According to tradition, Judas hung himself from a branch of the tree. The species name, *canadensis*, literally means "of Canada," where it is rather uncommon. Or perhaps the Linnean name refers to northeastern North America before political boundaries were set up. The tree is a very handsome ornamental and has been in cultivation since 1641. It is reported that the acid flowers are sometimes pickled for use in salad, and in Mexico they are fried. Redbud bark has some medicinal value. In the form of a fluid extract it is an active astringent and is used in the treatment of dysentery. The seeds are eaten by a number of species of birds, and the foliage browsed by the white-tailed deer. Eastern Redbud also has some value as a source of honey.

A number of varieties and horticultural forms are cultivated as follows: White Eastern Redbud, *C. canadensis* forma *alba* Rehd., has white flowers; Double Eastern Redbud, *C. canadensis* forma *plena* Sudw., has some stamens changed to petals; Smooth Eastern Redbud, *C. canadensis* forma *glabrifolia* Fern., has glabrous leaves; and Hairy Eastern Redbud, *C. canadensis* var. *pubescens* Pursh, has more or less pubescent leaves.

Two native varieties of Texas, Oklahoma, and Mexico are Texas Redbud, *C. canadensis* var. *texensis* (S. Wats.) Hopkins, and Mexican Redbud, *C. canadensis* var. *mexicana* (Rose) Hopkins.

Both the Texas and Mexican varieties differ from the Eastern Redbud by having conspicuously shiny and stiffly coriaceous leaves (leaves of the Eastern Redbud are dull green and not distinctly coriaceous). The leaf shapes of the species and the 2 varieties are rather similar, varying from cordate with an acute apex to reniform or rounded with the apex obtuse or emarginate.

The Texas and Mexican varieties are separated from each other on the dubious characters of the amount of hairs present on various parts. Texas Redbud has pedicels, young branchlets, and leaves glabrous or nearly so. Mexican Redbud has pedicels and young branchlets densely woolly-tomentose and leaves slightly so. These distinctions are so close that some botanists consider the Mexican Redbud to be only a hairy form of the Texas Redbud, instead of a distinct variety of the Eastern Redbud. However,

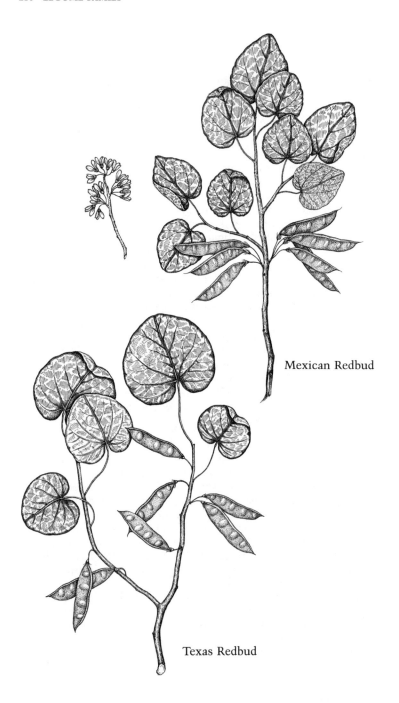

Mexican Redbud

Texas Redbud

since forms closely resembling *C. canadensis* var. *mexicana* have been found in northeast Texas, it is more likely that the latter is derived from *C. canadensis*.

Texas Redbud has been collected on limestone areas in Texas in Val Verde, Kerr, Austin, Comal, Erath, Brown, Dallas, and Hood counties. It is known in Oklahoma near Turner Falls Park in the Arbuckle Mountains, in Platt National Park at Antelope Springs, and in Mexico in Nuevo León and Tamaulipas.

Mexican Redbud has been collected on limestone areas in Texas in Brown, Dallas, Terrell, Nolan, Brewster, and Austin counties. It is the prevalent form in Trans-Pecos Texas and occurs in Mexico in Coahuila, Nuevo León, and San Luis Potosí.

Anacacho Bauhinia

Bauhinia congesta Britt. & Rose [H]

Field Identification. Western shrub or small tree, leaves bifoliate, each leaflet sessile, oblique.

Flowers. Borne March–April, racemes 1–2½ in. long, showy, pedicels ¼–½ in. long, densely short-hairy; flowers ¾–1 in. across when open; calyx to ½ in. long, tubular at first, splitting into 3–5 linear segments with short subulate teeth, densely hairy; petals 5, white, oblong to elliptic, apex obtuse to rounded, base gradually or abruptly long-clawed; style elongate, linear, stigma small and capitate; a single stamen elongate and fertile, the balance much shorter and apparently sterile, all very hairy at the base.

Fruit. Borne August–September. Legume on a peduncle ¼–¾ in. long, oblong to linear, length 1¼–3½ in., width ¼–⅜ in., base cuneate or narrowed gradually, apex abruptly long- or short-pointed, the point sometimes curved, flattened, or twisted, glabrous, dark brown at maturity, dehiscent into 2 valves, 1–4-seeded; seeds black, oval to short-oblong, flattened, ¼–⁵⁄₁₆ in. long.

Leaves. Alternate, divided to the base into 2 leaflets, occasionally simple, entire or bifid, leaflets ⅜–1¼ in. long, ¼–⅞ in. wide, sessile, asymmetrical, inner margin straighter than the outer, margins calloused and slightly wavy; apices rounded, upper surface dull green to semilustrous with scattered short, stiff hairs, later almost glabrous; lower surface varying from very fine- to brown-tomentose; especially on the palmate veins; veinlets reticulate; stipel about ¹⁄₂₅ in. long, tomentose; sometimes with 1 or 2 glands at the base of the tomentose petiole, which is ¼–⅝ in. long.

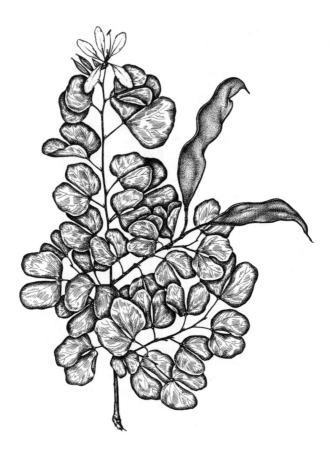

Twigs. Slender, at first finely but densely brown-tomentose with short, stiff, curved hairs, later becoming brown to gray and glabrous; lenticels small, pale, scattered.

Range. Known in Texas only from the Anacacho Hills west of Uvalde. Type specimen examined from the United States National Herbarium, Edward Palmer, No. 285, north of Monclova, Coahuila, Mexico.

Remarks. The genus name, *Bauhinia*, honors John and Caspar Bauhin, sixteenth-century herbalists, and the species name, *congesta*, refers to the crowded flowers.

Black Locust

Robinia pseudo-acacia L. [H]

Field Identification. Spiny tree attaining a height of 100 ft, with a trunk diameter of 30 in. Rapid-growing trees, reaching maturity in 30–40 years.

Flowers. May–June, attractive, fragrant, in loose, pendent racemes 4–5 in. long; individual flowers perfect, bonnet shaped, about 1 in. long; corolla white, petals 5; standard petal obcordate, rounded, a yellow blotch often on inner surface; wing petals 2, free; keel petals incurved, obtuse, united below; stamens 10, in 2 groups, 9 united and one free, the group forming a tube; pistil superior, ovary oblong, style hairy and reflexed, stigma small; ovules nu-

merous; calyx 5-lobed, lower lobe longest and acuminate; pedicels about ½ in. long.

Fruit. A legume, ripe September–October; brown, flattened, oblong-linear, straight or slightly curved, 2–5 in. long, about ½ in. wide, 2-valved, persistent; peduncle short and thick; seeds 4–8, hard, flat, brown mottled, kidney shaped, seed dispersed September–April from the persistent legume.

Leaves. Pinnately compound, alternate, deciduous, 8–14 in. long; leaflets 7–19, each one ½–2 in. long and ½–1 in. wide, sessile or short-stalked; rounded at both ends or sometimes wedge shaped at base; ovate-oblong or oval, entire, mature leaves bluish green and glabrous above, usually paler and glabrous except on veins beneath; young leaves silvery-hairy, mature leaves turning yellow in autumn; stipules becoming straight or slightly curved spines; leaves folding on dark days or in the evenings.

Twigs. Stout, zigzag, brittle, greenish brown, glabrous, somewhat angular, stipules modified into sharp spines.

Bark. Gray to reddish brown, ½–1½ in. thick, rough, ridged, deeply furrowed, sometimes twisted, inner bark pale yellow, thorns paired and scattered.

Wood. Greenish yellow or light brown, sapwood white and narrow, durable, hard, heavy, strong, stiff, close-grained, weighing about 45 lb per cu ft, resists shock and decay, shows little shrinkage, but is difficult to hand-tool.

Range. Prefers deep, well-drained calcareous soil, probably originally native to the high lands of the Piedmont Plateau and Appalachian Mountains. Georgia; west to Oklahoma and Arkansas and northeast to New York. In other areas probably introduced and escaped from cultivation. Not native to Texas but persistent along fence rows, abandoned fields, and old home sites. Now commonly distributed by nurserymen in the Gulf Coast states.

Remarks. The genus name, *Robinia*, is in honor of Jean and Vespasian Robin, herbalists to Henry IV of France, and the species name, *pseudo-acacia* ("false acacia"), refers to its resemblance to an acacia. Other vernacular names are White Locust, Yellow Locust, Red Locust, Red-flowering Locust, Green Locust, Honey Locust, Silver Locust, Post Locust, Pea-flower Locust, Silver-chain, and False-acacia Locust. The wood is highly resistant to decay.

New Mexico Locust

Robinia neomexicana Gray [H]

Field Identification. Spiny shrub or tree to 24 ft, with a trunk to 4 in. in diameter. Thicket-forming plant, sprouting freely from stumps and roots.

Flowers. April–August in axils of the leaves of the current year; racemes, large, showy, pendent, 2–4 in. long, all parts pubescent or glandular-hispid, the hairs straight and glanduliferous; calyx slightly 2-lipped, tube campanulate, ⅓–⅖ in. long, the teeth triangular; corolla rose-colored, ⅘–1 in. long, papilionaceous; standard large and rounded, reflexed; stamens 10 (9 united into a tube, the other free); style elongate.

Fruit. Legume maturing September–October, 2–4 in. long, ⅜–⅖ in. wide, flat, thin, glandular-hispid, reticulate, thickened on one edge, 2-valved, 3–8-seeded.

Leaves. Alternate, deciduous, odd-pinnate compound of 13–21 leaflets, blades elliptic-lanceolate, apex obtuse to rounded and

mucronate, margin entire, length ⅜–1½ in., finely strigillose on both sides.

Twigs. Young ones puberulent and glandular, older ones reddish brown to gray and more glabrous; prickles straight or subrecurved, sharp, and stout.

Range. Generally in moist soil along streams in the sun. At altitudes of 4,000–8,500 ft in the conifer belt. Trans-Pecos Texas; west through New Mexico and Arizona, north to Colorado, Utah, and Nevada.

Remarks. The genus name, *Robinia*, is in honor of Jean Robin (1550–1629) and his son Vespasian Robin (1579–1662), herbalists to kings of France. The species name, *neomexicana*, refers to the state of New Mexico where it grows. It is sometimes known under the name of Uña de Gato. It is reported to be used as a remedy for rheumatism by the Hopi Indians. The tree is valuable for erosion control. It is an important browse for goats and is sometimes eaten by cattle and horses. It is also eaten by Gambel's quail, mountain sheep, mule deer, black-tailed deer, chipmunk, and porcupine. The tree has been planted for ornament in the United States and Europe since 1881.

Texas Kidneywood

Eysenhardtia texana Scheele [H]

Field Identification. Irregularly shaped shrub usually less than 8 ft, growing on calcareous soils. Parts unpleasantly scented when bruised.

Flowers. Mostly in May, or intermittently after rains; racemes terminal, 1¼–4½ in. long; bracts ovate-lanceolate, brown, pubescent, ⅟₂₅–⅟₁₂ in. long, calyx about ⅟₁₂ in. long, hairy, glandular, unequally lobed, anterior lobes longer than posterior, split more deeply on the posterior side, apex obtuse or acute, lobes less than ⅟₂₅ in. long; petals 5, inserted on the hypanthium, white, nearly equal, distinct, concave, membranous, much longer than the calyx, standard petal somewhat broader and rounded to slightly emarginate; style slender, ⅟₁₂–⅛ in. long, pubescent, slightly hooked at the apex, bearing a reddish brown, stout gland (these stipellike structures referred to by some authors as small apiculate pustules); stigma large and capitate; ovary sessile with 2–4 ovules; stamens 10, 9 of them united half their length, the other free.

Fruit. Maturing in September, indehiscent, on pedicels 1/25 in. long or less, pod linear-oblong, 1/5–1/3 in. long, 1/25–1/8 in. wide, thickened, green to brown, glabrous, glandular-punctate, upwardly falcate and ascending; seed about 1/8 in. long, lanceolate to obovoid, brown, smooth, thickened, hilum near the distal end, germination about 50 percent.

Leaves. Alternate, odd-pinnate compound, rachis grooved and glandular, leaves 1¼–2⅓ in. long; leaflets 15–31, 1/5–3/8 in. long, oblong, margin entire, apex rounded or notched, base rounded or obcordate; upper surface dull green, puberulent, obscurely reticulate; lower surface paler, puberulent, and minutely punctate; stipules 1/12–1/8 in. long, brown, subulate; stipels subulate, persistent, less than 1/25 in. long.

Stems. Slender, younger ones appressed-hairy; older gray and smooth, broken into thin, elongate plates later.

Range. On dry hills and in canyons, central and southwestern Texas. The type locality is at New Braunfels. Specimens have been collected by the author at Langtry, Kerrville, and Waring. Also known from Coahuila and Tamaulipas, Mexico.

Remarks. The genus name, *Eysenhardtia*, honors Karl Wilhelm Eysenhardt (1794–1825), professor of botany at the University of Königsberg. The species name, *texana*, refers to the state of Texas, its natural habitat. It is also known as Rock Brush in the Texas Hill Country. The name Kidneywood is derived from the fact that closely related species are used in the treatment of renal disorders. The wood has been used to make dyes and is fluorescent in water.

A plant once described as *E. angustifolia* Pennell is now thought to be only a form of *E. texana* with larger leaves. It occurs mostly west of the Pecos River in Texas.

Mescal-bean Sophora

Sophora secundiflora (Ortega) Lag. [H]

Field Identification. Evergreen shrub, or sometimes a tree to 35 ft, with a narrow top, upright branches, and velvety twigs.

Flowers. With the young leaves March–April; racemes densely flowered, terminal, 2–4¾ in. long, showy, violet, fragrant; pedicels ¼–⅖ in. long, subtended by subulate bracts about ½ in. long; calyx campanulate, ⅓–⅖ in. long, oblique, the 2 upper teeth almost united throughout, the lower 3 teeth triangular to ovate; corolla bonnet shaped, violet; standard petal erect, broad, suborbicular to ovate, crisped, notched, ⅗–⅔ in. long, somewhat spotted at the base within; wing and keel petals oblong to obovate; stamens 10; ovary white-hairy.

Fruit. Pod in September, on pedicels ¼–1 in. long, woody, hard, oblong, terete, densely brown-pubescent, somewhat constricted between the seeds, apex abruptly prolonged by persistent style remnants, indehiscent, 1–5 in. long, about ¾ in. wide, walls about ¼ in. thick; seeds red, 1–8 (usually 3 or 4), about ½ in. long, globose to oblong, often flattened at one end, hard, bony; hilum small, pale, and about ⅛ in. long.

Leaves. Odd-pinnate compound, 4–6 in. long, rachis grooved above; leaflets 5–13 (usually 5–9), persistent, elliptic-oblong or oval; apex rounded or obtuse, notched or mucronulate; base gradually narrowed; margin entire; upper surface lustrous, leathery, reticulate, dark green, hairy when young but glabrous later; lower

surface paler, glabrous or puberulent; 1–2½ in. long, ½–1½ in. wide; petioles stout, puberulent, sometimes leaflets sessile or nearly so.

Twigs. With fine velvety tomentum at first, later becoming glabrous, or nearly so, green to orange-brown.

Bark. Dark gray to black, broken into shallow fissures with narrow flattened ridges and thin scales.

Wood. Heartwood orange to red; sapwood yellow, hard, heavy, close-grained, specific gravity about 0.98, said to yield a yellow dye, otherwise of no commercial value.

Range. Usually on limestone soils in central, southern, and western Texas, New Mexico, and northern Mexico. In Texas from the shores of Matagorda Bay, almost at sea level, west into the Chisos and Davis mountains to altitudes of 5,000 ft. Frequent on the limestone hills around Austin. In Mexico from Nuevo León to San Luis Potosí.

Remarks. The genus name, *Sophora*, is from the Arabic name *Sophero*, and the species name, *secundiflora*, refers to the one-sided inflorescence. Other vernacular names are Texas Mountain-laurel, Frigolito, Frijollito, Frijolillo, Coral Bean, Big-drunk Bean, and Colorín.

Although called Mountain-laurel in Texas, this plant is not a member of the Laurel family (Lauraceae). However, neither is the so-called Mountain-laurel of the eastern states, which is *Kalmia latifolia*, a heath. The true laurel, or Poet's Laurel, *Laurus nobilis*, is a native of Asia and south Europe. American representatives of the true Laurel family native to the Southwest are the Red Bay, *Persea borbonia*, and the Sassafras, *Sassafras albidum*.

The persistent, shiny leaves of Mescal-bean give a lustrous effect when seen in mass at a distance. The beautiful violet flowers are very fragrant, in fact, offensively so to some people. A volatile liquid alkaloid, sophorine, which is identical with cytisine, exists in many species of *Sophora*, including *S. secundiflora*, *S. tomentosa*, and *S. sericea*. Other sophoras, including *S. angustifolia*, *S. alopecuroides*, and *S. pachycarpa*, contain the alkaloids matrine and sophocarpine.

The narcotic properties of the red seeds of Mescal-bean Sophora were well known to the Indians. A powder from them, in very small amounts, was mixed with the beverage mescal to produce intoxication, delirium, excitement, and finally a long sleep. The seeds are poisonous to both humans and livestock. They were frequently used as a trade article by the Indians in the form of necklaces. The red seeds of *Erythrina herbacea* were also used for this purpose, and the two plants are often confused. But *Erythrina* has 3 leaflets only, and the pod is dehiscent at maturity. Mescal-bean is rather difficult to transplant, but transplanting can be done if sufficient calcium is in the soil. The shrub is rather slow growing.

Texas Sophora

Sophora affinis Torr. & Gray [H]

Field Identification. A shrub or small tree to 25 ft, with spreading branches and a rounded head.

Flowers. In June, arranged in simple axillary racemes 2–6 in. long; pedicels slender, finely tomentose, about ½ in. long, subtended by small deciduous bracts; corolla bonnet shaped, about ½ in. long, pink to white, somewhat fragrant; petals short-clawed, standard large, nearly orbicular, somewhat notched, reflexed, ⅜–⅝ in. long; wing and keel petals ovate to oblong and auricu-

late at base; stamens 10; ovary hairy and stipitate, stigma capitate; calyx campanulate, short, about ¼ in. long, abruptly narrowed at the base, obscurely 5-toothed with teeth triangular to ovate, somewhat pubescent.

Fruit. Fruiting peduncle 2−4 in. long; legume ½−3½ in. long, abruptly constricted between the seeds, terete, black, often hairy, especially on the strictures, coriaceous, indehiscent, tipped with the prolonged style remnants, flesh thin, persistent; seeds 1−8 (mostly 4−8), ovoid or oval, seed coat brown. Constrictions between the seeds give the pod a beadlike appearance.

Leaves. Alternate, odd-pinnate compound, deciduous; rachis lightly tomentose, 3–9 in. long, leaflets 9–19 (usually 13–15); leaflets elliptical or oval, margin entire; apex obtuse, acute, retuse, or mucronulate; base rounded or cuneate, contracted into short stout petiolules ⅛–¹⁄₁₆ in. long; upper surface dark green to yellowish green, lustrous, glabrous or slightly hairy; lower surface slightly paler and pubescent; thin and soft; ¾–1½ in. long, about ½ in. wide; young leaves hoary-pubescent.

Twigs. Slender, green to brown or streaked with lighter brown, nearly glabrous or puberulent, somewhat divaricate, somewhat swollen at the nodes.

Bark. Gray to reddish brown, broken into small, thin, oblong scales.

Wood. Light red, sapwood yellow, heavy, strong, and hard.

Range. Usually on limestone soils of northwestern Louisiana and southwestern Oklahoma, down through central Texas. Occurs at Dallas, Kerrville, Austin, and San Antonio. Often in small groves on hillsides or along streams.

Remarks. The genus name, *Sophora*, is from the Arabic word *Sophero*, which was applied to some tree of the same family, and the species name, *affinis*, means "related to." Another vernacular name is Eve's Necklace. The plant could be more extensively cultivated for ornament.

CALTROP FAMILY (Zygophyllaceae)

Texas Porlieria

Porlieria angustifolia (Engelm.) Gray [H]

Field Identification. Shrub or tree to 21 ft, often in clumps, scrubby, compact, stiff, evergreen, the branches thick and stubby.

Flowers. Terminal, clustered or solitary, violet or purple, ⅓–¾ in. across, fragrant, attractive; petals 5, short-clawed, elliptic, apex often notched; sepals 5, shorter than petals, suborbicular, concave; stamens 10, as long as the petals, with scalelike appendages at the base; anthers yellow; ovary densely villous, 2–5-celled.

Fruit. Capsule heart-shaped, mostly 2-lobed, somewhat winged on margin, apex abruptly attenuate-apiculate, surface reticulate,

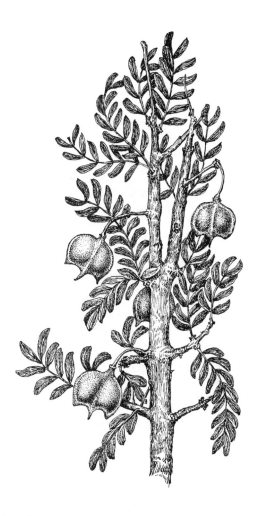

⅓–⅔ in. broad; seeds 2 (sometimes 1 or 3), beanlike, large, shiny, red, yellow, or orange.

Leaves. Often half-folded in the heat of the day, opposite or alternate, abruptly pinnate, rachis pubescent, composed of 4–8 pairs of leaflets; leaflets sessile or nearly so, about ⅔ in. long or less, entire, linear to oblong, leathery, lustrous, reticulate, dark green, acute and apiculate at the apex, oblique at the base, persistent; stipules persistent, somewhat spiniferous.

Twigs. Short, stout, stiff, knotty, and gray.

Bark. Gray to black, broken into rough scales on old trunks and branches.

Range. From central through western and southwestern Texas; Mexico, Coahuila to Tamaulipas.

Remarks. The genus name, *Porlieria*, is in honor of Porlier de Baxamar, Spanish patron of botany. The species name, *angustifolia*, refers to the narrow leaflets. Vernacular names for the plant are Soap-bush, Guayacán, and Guajacum. Texas Porlieria has possibilities as an ornamental. It is a good honey plant, and the wood is used for fence posts in some localities. The bark of the roots is sold in the Mexican markets as a soap for washing woolens. Extracts of the root are used to treat rheumatism and venereal disease, and they are also used as a sudorific.

RUE FAMILY (Rutaceae)

Trifoliate Orange

Citrus trifoliata L. [H]

Field Identification. Green, aromatic, spiny tree to 30 ft, with stiff, flattened branches.

Flowers. Borne on the bare branches of old wood in spring, axillary, subsessile, white, spreading, 1½–2 in. across, perfect; petals 5, flat, thin, oblong-obovate to spatulate, at first imbricate but later spreading, base clawed, much longer than the sepals; sepals ovate-elliptic; stamens 8–10 free; ovary pubescent, 6–8-celled, ovules in 2 rows; style stout and short.

Fruit. Berry September–October, yellow, aromatic, densely downy, globose, 1½–2 in. across; pulp thin, acid, rather sour; seeds numerous, large, taking up the greater part of the berry, ¼–½ in. long, flattened, obovate, rounded at one end and acute at the other, white to brown, smooth, often ridged or grooved on one side.

Leaves. Trifoliate, about 3½ in. long or less; petiole broadly winged, ⅓–1 in. long or less; leaflets 3, aromatic, elliptic, oblong, oval, or obovate; margin crenate-toothed; apex obtuse, rounded or emarginate; base often cuneate or rounded (in lateral leaflets often asymmetrical); sessile or very short-petioled; terminal leaflet

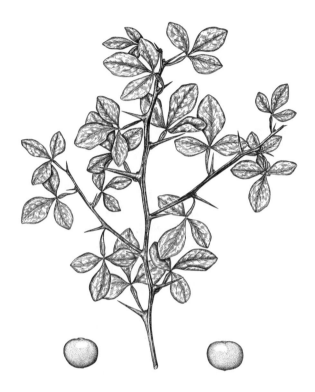

1–2½ in. long, laterals usually smaller; olive green, glabrous, with pellucid dots above; lower surface paler, glabrous or puberulent along the veins.

Twigs. Dark green, glabrous, divaricate, conspicuously flattened at the nodes to flare out into heavy, green, sharp, flattened spines ⅓–2¾ in. long.

Bark. Green or streaked brown, smooth, often with thorns.

Range. Frequently planted for ornament and hedges from Texas to Florida, escaping cultivation in some areas. Hardy as far north as Washington, D.C. Native of China and Korea. Often planted for ornament in Japan.

Remarks. The genus name, *Citrus*, is from the Greek and was given by Pliny the Elder (A.D. 23–79), a Roman naturalist. The species name, *trifoliata*, is for the trifoliate leaves. Some authors use the name of *Poncirus trifoliata* (L.) Raf. *Poncirus* is from the

French word *poncire*, a kind of citrus. Some vernacular names are
Bitter Orange and Limoncito. Oil from the fruit has a rancid flavor, and the pulp is aromatic.

Common Hop-tree

Ptelea trifoliata L. [H]

Field Identification. Usually a rounded shrub, but occasionally a
small tree to 25 ft. Leaves divided into 3 leaflets that are very
unpleasantly scented. This is an extremely variable species in
form and habit of growth and in the size and shape of the leaflets.
Numerous varieties, forms, and species have been segregated by
various authors. The entire genus *Ptelea* should be revised.

Flowers. March–July, polygamous, in terminal cymes; flowers
small, borne on slender pedicels ¼–1½ in. long; calyx lobes 4–5,
obtuse, pubescent; petals 4–5, greenish white, oblong, somewhat
puberulent, exceeding the calyx lobes; stamens 4–5, alternating
with the petals, filaments hairy, anthers ovoid; pistillate flowers
with a raised pistil and abortive anthers; style short, sometimes
dotted with glands, stigma 2–3-lobed, ovary puberulous.

Fruit. Ripening August–September, samaras borne in drooping
clusters on slender reflexed pedicels; reticulate-veined, membranous, compressed, thin, waferlike, suborbicular or obovate,
¾–1 in. across, persistent in winter, unpleasantly scented, 2–
3-celled; seeds 2–3, oblong-ovoid, acute, leathery, reddish brown,
about ⅓ in. long.

Leaves. Alternate or opposite, trifoliate; leaflets sessile or nearly
so, entire or finely serrulate, ovate-oblong, acute or acuminate,
wedge shaped at base with lateral leaflets often oblique, more or
less pubescent and glandular below (in *P. trifoliata* var. *mollis*
densely woolly beneath), darker green and lustrous above, unpleasantly scented, 4–6 in. long, 2–4 in. wide; petiole stout, base
swollen, pubescent.

Twigs. Slender, green, yellowish or reddish brown, pubescent, unpleasantly scented when bruised.

Bark. Thin, smooth, light to dark gray or brown, numerous excrescences, bitter to the taste.

Wood. Yellowish brown, close-grained, hard, heavy, weighing
about 51 lb per cu ft.

Root. Taste bitter, pungent, slightly acid, aromatic.

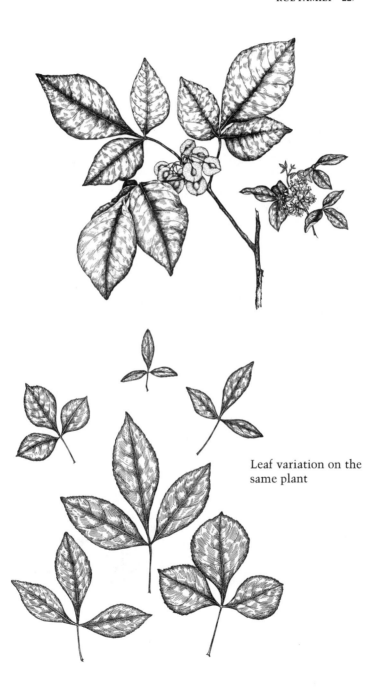

Leaf variation on the same plant

Baldwin Hop-tree

Range. Common Hop-tree, with its many varieties and closely related species, is distributed over a rather wide territory, growing in various types of soil; Texas, Louisiana, Arkansas, Oklahoma, and New Mexico; eastward to Florida, westward into Arizona and California, northward into Colorado, Utah, Nebraska, Minnesota, Michigan, Illinois, and continuing on east to Ontario, New York, and Quebec.

Remarks. The genus name, *Ptelea*, is the classical name for the elm. The species name, *trifoliata*, refers to the three leaflets. Vernacular names are Three-leaf Hop-tree, Shrubby-trefoil, Swamp

Dogwood, Wafer-ash, Skunk-bush, Potatochip-tree, Quinine-tree, Ague-bark, Pickaway-anise, Prairie-grub, Cola de Zorillo, and Wingseed. All parts of the plant emit a disagreeable odor. The fruit was once used as a substitute for hops in beer brewing.

A tincture of the root bark is occasionally used medicinally in tropical countries as a remedy for dyspepsia and as a mild tonic. Some western physicians used it as a bitter stomachic. It contains the alkaloid berberine. The plant also has some value as food for wild game. It is occasionally planted for ornament and is used in shelter-belt planting. It was first introduced into cultivation in 1724.

Baldwin Hop-tree, *P. baldwinii* Torr., has somewhat larger flowers in smaller corymbs; fruit ⅜–⅝ in. across and apiculate; leaves 1–2½ in. long, narrowly elliptic-ovate or oblong-ovate, pubescent beneath; branches dark brown. It occurs from central and southern Texas to New Mexico, Colorado, Utah, northern California, and Arizona; also in Mexico.

Hercules-club

Zanthoxylum clava-herculis L. [H]

Field Identification. Small tree with a broad, rounded crown, easily recognized by the corky-based prickles on the trunk and branches.

Flowers. Dioecious, greenish white, in large terminal cymes; petals 4–5, oblong-ovate, obtuse, ⅛–¼ in. long, stamens 4–5, filaments slender and exserted, longer than the petals; pistils 2–3, styles short, with a 2-lobed stigma; calyx of 4–5 ovate or ovate-lanceolate, obtuse sepals.

Fruit. Follicles 2–5 together, globose-obovoid, brownish, rough, pitted, apiculate, ⅙–¼ in. long, 2-valved; seed solitary, wrinkled, black, shining, persistent outside of follicle after dehiscence.

Leaves. Alternate, 5–15 in. long, odd-pinnate compound of 5–19 leaflets, ½–4½ in. long, subsessile, sometimes falcate, ovate or ovate-lanceolate, acute or acuminate at apex, somewhat oblique and cuneate at base, crenate-serrulate, leathery, glabrous, lustrous above and more or less hairy below, spicy and dotted with pellucid glands, bitter-aromatic, stinging the mouth when chewed; petioles somewhat spiny, stout, hairy or glabrous.

Twigs. Brown to gray, stout, hairy at first, glabrous later, often somewhat glandular, spinescent.

Wood. Light brown or yellow, light, soft, close-grained, weighing 31 lb per cu ft.

Bark. Light gray, thin, covered with conspicuous, conelike corky tubercles.

Range. Texas, Louisiana, Oklahoma, and Arkansas; eastward to Florida and northward to Virginia.

Remarks. The genus name, *Zanthoxylum*, comes from an erroneous rendering of the Greek word *xanthos* ("yellow") plus *xylon* ("wood"); the species name, *clava-herculis*, means "club of Hercules" and refers to the trunk's thorny character. Vernacular names are Toothache, Sea Ash, Pepperwood, Prickly Yellowwood, Yellow Prickly-ash, Tongue-bush, Rabbit Gum, Wild Orange, Sting Tongue, Tear Blanket, Pillenterry, and Wait-a-bit. It is sometimes used as a treatment for rheumatism. It has also been used as a gastrointestinal stimulant in treating flatulence and diarrhea and as a masticatory in toothache, but at present it is little used. A number of species of birds eat the fruit.

Texas Hercules-club

Zanthoxylum hirsutum Buckl. [H]

Field Identification. Thorny shrub 3–15 ft, aromatic in all parts.

Flowers. Borne in early spring, dioecious, in cymes ⅓–2 in. long, 1–1½ in. wide; pedicels ¹⁄₁₂–⅛ in. long; sepals 5, minute, linear to subulate, acute; petals 5, greenish, elliptic, concave, about ¹⁄₁₂ in. long; stamens 5, exserted on filiform filaments about as long as the petals or shorter, but shorter than the anthers, wanting or rudimentary in the pistillate flowers; pistils 2–3, ovary sessile, style short, stigma entire or slightly 2-lobed.

Fruit. Capsule borne in clusters ⅓–2 in. long on red, pubescent pedicels ¼–½ in., body of fruit subglobose, asymmetrical, dotted with glands, apiculate, green at first, reddish brown later, about ¼ in. long, splitting into valves; seed black, shiny, obliquely ovoid, persistent to one valve.

Leaves. Odd-pinnate compound, 1½–2½ in. long (more rarely to 4 in.); rachis red, pubescent, bearing reddish brown, straight, sharp thorns to ¼ in. long; leaflets 3–7 (usually 5), ½–1½ in. long, elliptic to oblong or oval, leathery, aromatic, dotted with glands, especially on the margin, crinkled, crenate, apex obtuse, base cuneate, lustrous above, dull beneath; lateral leaflets short-petioluled or sessile, the petiolule of the terminal leaflet longer.

Twigs. Young ones greenish, pubescent; older ones gray and armed with stout, straight, gray or brown spines to ½ in. long.

Bark. Smooth, mottled light to dark gray; spines straight, or slightly curved, to 1 in. long, not built up on conspicuous corky bases as in *Z. clava-herculis*.

Range. On sandy or gravelly soil of central west Texas. Sandy areas south of San Antonio, also between Utopia and Tarpley. Reported from Arkansas.

Remarks. The genus name, *Zanthoxylum*, comes from an erroneous rendering of the Greek word *xanthos* ("yellow") plus *xylon* ("wood"). The species name, *hirsutum*, refers to the hirsute twigs and leaves. It has also been listed under the names of *Z. carolinianum* var. *fruticosum* Gray and *Z. clava-herculis* L. var. *fruticosum* Gray.

QUASSIA FAMILY (Simarubaceae)

Tree-of-heaven

Ailanthus altissima (Mill.) Swingle [H]

Field Identification. Cultivated tree attaining a height of 100 ft, and a diameter of 3 ft. Handsome and rapid-growing with a symmetrical open head and stout branches.

Flowers. April–May, borne in clusters of 1–5 in large, loose, terminal panicles 6–12 in.; pedicels subtended by small bracts or none; staminate and pistillate panicles on different plants or polygamous; flowers small, ⅕–⅓ in. across, yellowish green; stami-

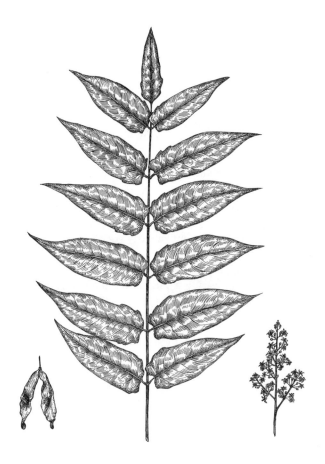

nate flowers unpleasantly scented; calyx regular, sepals 5, valvate in the bud, oval to oblong, spreading, ⅛–⅙ in. long, villous near the base, inserted at the base of the small 10-lobed disk; stamens 10 (in perfect flowers), staminate flowers with or without a rudimentary pistil; pistillate flowers smaller than staminate with 2 or 3 imperfect stamens or none; ovary deeply 2–5-cleft, the lobes flat and cuneate, ovules solitary in each cavity.

Fruit. September–October, in persistent clusters of 1–5, samara linear-elliptic; ½–1½ in. long; flattened, thin, membranous, veiny, dry, twisted at the apex, sometimes curved, notched on one side, brownish red, the single flattened seed in the center, albumin thin.

Leaves. Alternate, deciduous, odd-pinnate compound, length 8 in.–2½ ft, rachis pubescent or glabrous, unpleasantly odorous when bruised; leaflets 11–41; petiolules ⅛–⅓ in., pubescent or glabrous, leaflets ovate to oblong or lanceolate, sometimes asymmetrical, apex acute or acuminate, base cordate or truncate and often oblique, margin entire except for 2–4 coarse, glandular teeth at the base, length 2–5 in., upper surface dull dark green, glabrous or slightly hairy, lower surface paler and glabrous or with a few hairs on the veins; petiole swollen at base.

Twigs. Coarse, blunt, yellowish orange or brown, younger ones pubescent, older ones glabrous, leaf scars large and conspicuous, pith reddish.

Bark. Pale grayish brown, fissures shallow.

Wood. Pale yellowish brown, medium hard, not durable, weak, coarse, open-grained, said to make fairly good fuel, and sometimes used in cabinet work.

Range. A native of China, cultivated for ornament in the United States and sometimes escaping cultivation in our area. Very hardy, seemingly growing well under adverse conditions of dust, smoke, and poor soil. Often found in waste places, trash heaps, vacant lots, cracks of pavement, crowded against buildings, and other situations. Does best on light, moist soils. In Texas, New Mexico, Oklahoma, Arkansas, and Louisiana; east to Florida and north to Massachusetts. Also cultivated westward throughout the interior to the Pacific coast.

Remarks. The genus name, *Ailanthus*, is from a Chinese name, *Ailanto*, meaning "tree of heaven" and referring to its height. The species name, *altissima*, means "very tall." Vernacular names for the tree are Copal, Tree-of-the-Gods, Chinese Sumac, Heavenward-tree, False Varnish-tree, and Devil's Walkingstick.

The tree was introduced into the United States from China by William Hamilton in 1784. It is a very rapid grower, spreads freely from suckers and by seed, is rather free of insects, but is easily storm damaged. It was once used in erosion control work in the dune areas of the Black Sea and was planted for timber in New Zealand. The seeds are known to be eaten by a number of birds, including the pine grosbeak and crossbill, and occasionally browsed by white-tailed deer. The tree is sometimes planted in China as a host to a species of silkworm, *Attacus cynthia*, which produces a coarse, inferior silk.

MAHOGANY FAMILY (Meliaceae)

China-berry

Melia azedarach L. [H]

Field Identification. Tree to 45 ft; rounded crown; twice-compound leaves sometimes 2 ft long.

Flowers. March–May, panicles 4–6 in., loose, open, fragrant, showy, individual flowers about ½ in. across; sepals 5–6, lobes acute; petals 5–6, purplish, oblanceolate to narrow-oblong, obtuse; staminal tube with 10–12 stamens and sagittate anthers; ovary 5-celled, style elongate, stigma 3–6-lobed.

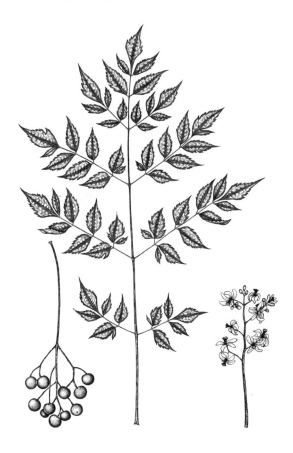

Fruit. Ripening September–October, persistent, drupe ½–¾ in. in diameter, subglobose, coriaceous, fleshy, translucent, smooth, yellow, indehiscent, borne in conspicuous drooping clusters; stone ridged, seeds 3–5, smooth, black, ellipsoid, asymmetrical, acute or obtuse at ends, dispersed by birds or mammals.

Leaves. Large, alternate, deciduous, twice-compound, to 25 in., long-petioled; leaflets numerous, ovate-elliptic, serrate or lobed, some entire, acute at apex, 1¼–2 in. long, mostly glabrous.

Wood. Color variegated, durable, somewhat brittle.

Range. A native of Asia, introduced into the United States as an ornamental, and escaping to grow wild over a wide area. Texas; east to Florida, and north to Oklahoma, Arkansas, and North Carolina.

Remarks. The genus name, *Melia*, is an old Greek name. The species name, *azedarach*, is from a Persian word meaning "noble tree." Vernacular names are China-tree, Bead-tree, Indian-lilac, and Pride-of-India. The fruit is eaten by birds and swine, but if fermented it sometimes has a toxic effect. The fruit pulp is also used as an insect repellent and vermifuge. In some countries the hard seeds are made into rosaries. The wood was formerly used in cabinet work. China-berry grows rapidly, is rather free of insects, but cannot stand excessive droughts or much cold below zero. It is desirable as a shade tree and was formerly much planted in the South. The northern limit of hardiness is probably Virginia. Besides the species, there occurs an umbrella-shaped variety known as the Texas Umbrella China-berry, *M. azedarach* forma *umbraculiformis* Berckm., which was reported to be found by botanists originally near the San Jacinto battlefield in Harris County.

EUPHORBIA FAMILY (Euphorbiaceae)

Castor-bean

Ricinus communis L. [H]

Field Identification. Mostly a stout, large herb to 15 ft in temperate regions, but in the tropics to 40 ft, soft-woody.

Flowers. In stout, pyramidal, terminal panicles on jointed peduncles, flowers monoecious, greenish, numerous, small, petals absent; pistillate flowers disposed above the staminate; staminate

short-pediceled, calyx of 3–5 sepals that are valvate, oval, concave, reflexed, and purplish; stamens numerous and crowded, filaments much-branched; pistillate flowers long-pediceled, calyx
caducous, sepals narrowly lanceolate; styles 3, red, plumose,
linear, each branch 2-cleft, united at base; ovary 3-sided and
rounded, 3-celled and 3-ovuled.

Fruit. Maturing August–September, capsule ½–1 in. in diameter,
glaucous, subglobose or 3-lobed, usually soft-spiny or sometimes
smooth, suddenly dehiscent into three 2-valved carpels, 1 seed in
each carpel; seeds variously colored, lustrous, smooth, black to
gray or brown and mottled, seed coat crustaceous, endosperm
white, highly oily, sweetish to the taste, easily becoming rancid,
caruncle large.

Leaves. Alternate, conspicuously large, blades ⅓–1½ ft broad,
nearly orbicular in outline, palmately 6–11-lobed, the lobes acute

or acuminate, also irregularly serrate, smooth, glabrous or glaucous on both sides, petioles stout, very variable, but commonly approximating blade length.

Stems. Of vigorous growth, erect, usually branching, hollow, smooth, glaucous, green to reddish or purplish.

Range. Cultivated and escaped to waste places, old fields, abandoned home sites; Texas and Louisiana; eastward to Florida and northward to New Jersey; also in southern California and southward to tropical America. Considered by some authorities as a native of Africa, by others as from India. Now grown on a commerical scale in some of the Gulf states.

Remarks. The genus name, *Ricinus*, is the classical name of the tick, which the seed resembles in shape. The species name, *communis*, means "common." Other common names are Castor-oil plant and Palma Christi. The plant is not subject to attack by insects or disease. The large, colorful foliage is useful as a screen and for tropical effects. Propagation is generally practiced by planting the seeds in pots in fall and then planting out in May. The seeds yield the castor oil of commerce. The oil is known in French as *huile de ricin*, in German as *Castarol*, in Italian as *olio di ricino*, and in Spanish as *aceite de castor*. The oil is reported in legend as keeping away moles and malaria.

Chinese Tallow-tree

Sapium sebiferum (L.) Roxb. [H]

Field Identification. Small cultivated tree with a rounded crown, attaining a height of 30 ft.

Flowers. Male and female together on a yellowish green terminal spike, the pistillate below the staminate; calyx of staminate flowers 2–3-lobed, the lobes imbricate; petals absent; stamens 2–3, filaments free, anthers opening lengthwise; pistillate calyx of 2–3 sepals; ovary 1–3-celled, styles 2–3.

Fruit. Capsule 3-lobed, lobes rounded externally and flattened against each other, ⅓–½ in. in diameter, dehiscent by the valves of the capsule falling away to expose the 3 white seeds; seed solitary, crustaceous.

Leaves. Alternate or, rarely, opposite, entire, rhombic-ovate, ·
abruptly long-acuminate, base broadly cuneate, 1–3½ in. long, 1–3 in. broad, widest across the middle, deep green and glabrous

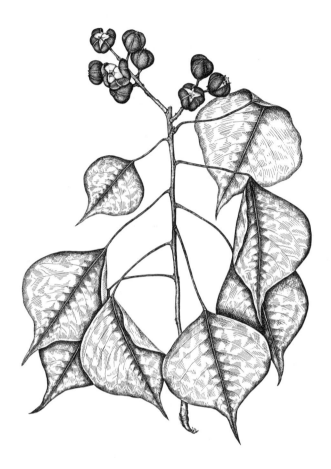

above, paler below, turning deep red in winter; petiole slender, usually shorter than the blade, 2 glands at the apex.

Twigs. Young twigs slender and green, older grayish brown and marked with numerous small lenticels.

Bark. Brownish gray, broken into appressed ridges, fissures shallow.

Range. Cultivated for ornament and sometimes escaping. Texas, Oklahoma, Arkansas, and Louisiana; eastward to Florida, along the Atlantic coast to South Carolina. A native of China.

Remarks. The genus name, *Sapium*, was given by Pliny to a resinous pine, and the species name, *sebiferum*, refers to the vegetable tallow, or wax, of the fruit. Another vernacular name is Vegetable Tallow-tree. The milky sap is poisonous, but the tree is cultivated in China for the wax of the seed covering, which is used for soap, candles, and cloth-dressing. The wax was formerly imported into the United States, but mineral waxes have almost entirely taken its place. The tree is easily propagated by seeds and cuttings and is attractive with white seeds and red leaves in the fall.

SUMAC FAMILY (Anacardiaceae)

American Smoke-tree

Cotinus obovatus Raf. [H]

Field Identification. Tree with slender, spreading branches attaining a height of 35 ft, with a diameter of 12–14 in. Most often only a straggling shrub.

Flowers. April–May, regular, dioecious or rarely polygamo-dioecious, greenish yellow, borne in loose, few-flowered terminal panicles 5–6 in. long and 2½–3 in. broad; pedicels slender, becoming conspicuously glandular-villose and purplish; subtending bracts linear or spatulate; corolla about ⅛ in. across, petals 5, oblong, acute, crisped, deciduous, about twice as long as the calyx lobes and alternate with them; calyx lobes 5, persistent, ovate-lanceolate, obtuse, disk at the base; stamens 5, inserted under the disk, included within the corolla, shorter than the petals and alternate with them, abortive or absent in the pistillate flower; ovary 1-celled, sessile, obovoid, oblique, compressed, rudimentary in the staminate flower; styles 3, short and spreading, stigmas large.

Fruit. Drupelets ⅛–¼ in. long, peduncles 2–3 in. long, slender pedicels 1½–2 in. long, conspicuously purple or brown glandular-hairy; fruit body kidney shaped or oblong-oblique, flattened, glabrous, veiny, pale brown, style remnants persistent; skin thin, dry, chartaceous; stone thick and bony.

Leaves. Simple, alternate, deciduous, most abundant distally on the twigs, 1½–6 in. long, 2–3½ in. wide, elliptic-oval or obovate; apex rounded, obtuse, or slightly emarginate; base broadly cuneate or rounded; margin entire or somewhat undulate, surface olive green and glabrous to puberulent above, paler and pubescent below, veins conspicuous; petiole ¼–2 in., yellowish green to red-

dish, glabrous or pubescent, blade of leaf sometimes slightly decurrent on petiole.

Twigs. Slender, young ones green to reddish or purple, lenticels small, abundant, pale; older ones gray, smooth, leaf scars large and conspicuous.

Bark. Gray to black, roughly breaking into thin, oblong, small scales.

Wood. Orange to yellow, sapwood cream-white, coarse-grained, soft, light, weighing about 40 lb per cu ft.

Range. On rocky limestone hills of Texas, Oklahoma, Arkansas, Missouri, Alabama, Tennessee, and Kentucky. Nowhere very abundant or widespread. In Texas mostly on rocky banks of the upper Guadalupe and Medina rivers. In Kendall, Kerr, and Bandera counties. Near Kerrville; between Utopia and Tarpley; also at Spanish Pass.

Remarks. The genus name, *Cotinus*, is the classical name for the Wild Olive, and the species name, *obovatus*, refers to the leaf shape.

The wood yields a yellow dye and was much used for that purpose during the Civil War period. The wood is very durable in contact with the soil and is used for fence posts. The tree easily sprouts from the stump. The brilliant orange and red colors of the leaves in autumn make it a worthwhile ornamental, but the purple flower pedicels, which give it the name of Smoke-tree, are not as showy as those of the European Smoke-tree, *C. coggygria* Scop. American Smoke-tree has obovate, larger, thinner, basally cuneate leaves, a less showy fruiting pedicel, and lacks the white leaf margins of the European Smoke-tree. However, the two resemble each other closely and are somewhat difficult to distinguish under cultivation.

Texas Pistache

Pistacia texana Swingle [H]

Field Identification. Large shrub or small tree, with a number of trunks from the base. Attaining a height of 15–30 ft, with a spread of 15–30 ft or, rarely, to 36 ft. The larger trunks 8–10 in., rarely 12–14 in., in diameter. Forming compact rounded clumps. Young foliage in spring a beautiful red.

Flowers. Pistillate with or before the new leaves, loosely paniculate, glabrous, 1½–2¾ in. long; flowers small, subtended by a small reddish ciliate bract and 2 bractlets; perianth absent; ovary ovate or subglobose; styles 3, 2 shorter ones with 2-lobed stigmas, the longer one with a 3-lobed stigma; staminate in compact panicles ¾–1½ in. long, more crowded than the pistillate, the subtending bracts reddish, anthers very evident, reddish yellow.

Fruit. Oval to lens-shaped, reddish brown, finally glaucescent, ⅕–¼ in. long, ⅙–⅕ in. broad, 1⁄15–⅛ in. thick.

Leaves. Persistent, odd-pinnate compound, 2–4 in. long, 1–2½ in. broad, petiole ⅖–⅗ in., or sometimes ⅘ in. on staminate trees, flattened and very narrowly winged; rachis very narrowly winged, puberulent above; leaflets 4–9 pairs (usually 5–8 pairs), opposite or subopposite, thin, reticulate-veined, ⅓–1 in. long, ⅕–⅓ in. broad, young leaves reddish, lanceolate, acute, at maturity leaves

broadly rounded, spatulate or nearly so, apex mucronate, base deltoid or subcuneiform; lateral leaflets usually somewhat falcate and inequilateral; midrib near the twig side, upper surface dark green and sparingly pubescent along the midrib, lower surface pale green and glabrous, margin entire; lateral leaflets almost sessile, terminal leaflet with a petiolule ⅙–¼ in. long.

Twigs. Slender, slightly pubescent, at first reddish, later brown to gray; buds small, puberulent, ⅟₁₅–⅟₁₀ in. long.

Wood. Heartwood yellowish brown, sapwood pale yellowish, tough, strong, compact, fine-grained, weighing 60 lb per cu ft.

Range. In rocky limestone stream beds or on limestone cliffs, sometimes in alluvial soils. Along the Pecos River near its junction with the Rio Grande in southwestern Texas and adjacent Mexico. Type locality near Hinojose Spring, Rio Grande Valley, near the mouth of the Pecos River, about 20 miles west of Comstock in Val Verde County.

Remarks. The genus name, *Pistacia*, is from the Greek *pistake* or *pistakia* ("pistache") and ultimately from the ancient Persian *pistah* ("pistache nut"). The species name, *texana*, refers to the state of Texas. This plant has been confused with the closely related *P. mexicana* H. B. K. of Mexico. Walter T. Swingle gave the following comparison: "This new species, *Pistacia texana*, differs from *P. mexicana* H. B. K. in having smaller leaves with fewer leaflets (4–9, usually 5–8 pairs, instead of 8–18, usually 12–16 pairs), which are more or less spatulate, broader and more obtuse at the tip, not so markedly mucronate and more or less curved. The young twigs more or less pubescent and have smaller and less pubescent flower-buds and bracts than in *P. mexicana*. The mature fruits of *P. texana* are dark reddish brown, slightly glaucescent rather than glaucous and purplish black, as in *P. mexicana*. The trunks of the trees of *P. texana* are much branched near the ground, while *P. mexicana* often (perhaps always) has a single trunk. The smaller branches are rough grayish brown whereas those of *P. mexicana* are smooth and often light brownish gray, almost silvery."

The tree has possibilities as an ornamental because of its dark, evergreen mature foliage and red new foliage in spring. It is highly intolerant of shade and self-prunes very rapidly.

Skunk-bush Sumac

Rhus aromatica Ait. var. *flabelliformis* Shinners [H]

Field Identification. An offensively scented shrub with slender, spreading, crooked branches, attaining a height of 12 ft.

Flowers. March–April, numerous, small, borne before the leaves in terminal spikes; bracts ⅟₂₅–⅟₁₂ in. long, triangular, margin ciliate, upper surface glabrous, lower surface pubescent; individual flower pedicels ⅟₁₂–⅛ in. long; sepals 5, persistent, triangular-lanceolate to oblong, apex obtuse to rounded, margin ciliate, glabrous, ⅟₂₅–⅟₁₂ in. long, less than ⅟₂₅ in. broad; petals 5, greenish white, obovate or oblong, obtuse, glabrous above, somewhat hairy beneath, ⅟₁₂–⅛ in. long, anthers oval, less than ⅟₂₅ in. long, stamens 5, filaments as long as the sepals; pistil short, stigmas short.

Fruit. Drupe August–September, persistent, ⅕–¼ in. long, red, subglobose, with glandular or simple short hairs; seed lenticular, about ⅕ in. long or less, broader than long, somewhat roughened.

Leaves. Strongly pungent when crushed, alternate, deciduous, trifoliate, ¾–2 in. long; leaflets cuneate, obovate, oval, or spatulate;

firm, sessile or nearly so, dark green and glabrous above, paler and pubescent beneath; terminal leaflet cuneate, larger than the others, 3-lobed with smaller lobes or crenate-toothed, apex obtuse or rounded, base cuneate, about ¾ in. long; lateral leaflets smaller than the terminal, obovate to oval, about ⅜ in. long, also 3-lobed, but often much less so; petiole ¼–⅓ in., pubescent, reddish. Leaves brilliantly colored in autumn.

Twigs. Slender, gray to reddish brown, puberulent at first, glabrous later.

Range. Often in limestone outcrops. Central, northern, western, and southwestern Texas, New Mexico, Arizona, and California. In Mexico in Nuevo León, Chihuahua, Coahuila, Tamaulipas, Durango, Puebla, Hidalgo, San Luis Potosí, and Colima.

Remarks. The genus name, *Rhus*, is the ancient Latin name, and the variety name, *flabelliformis*, refers to the fan-shaped leaves. This plant was formerly known under the name of *R. trilobata*

Nutt., but the name has been changed. Other vernacular names are Ill-scented Sumac, Three-leaf Sumac, Lemonade Sumac, Squaw-bush, Quail-bush, Agrillo, and Lemita. The acid fruit is eaten, and a cooling drink is made by steeping it in water. The slender twigs are mixed with willow in basket weaving by the Indians, and they also produce a yellow dye. The fruit is known to be eaten by 25 species of birds, especially the gallinaceous birds such as various species of quail, grouse, prairie chicken, sage hen, and pheasant. It is browsed by mountain sheep and more rarely by deer. Its value for livestock browse seems to vary according to locality.

Evergreen Sumac

Rhus sempervirens Scheele [H]

Field Identification. Western evergreen shrub to 12 ft, forming rounded clumps. Branches spreading and often the lower ones touching the ground.

Flowers. Appearing irregularly during the summer after rains, borne in terminal or axillary thyrsoid panicles 3/4–2 in. long, shorter than the leaves; panicles subtended by persistent bracts that are ovate, acute to rounded at the apex, 1/25–1/12 in. long, upper surface glabrous or nearly so, lower surface hairy, margin ciliate; sepals 5, oval, ovate or triangular, obtuse at apex, about 1/12 in. long, glabrous above and somewhat hairy beneath, the ciliate marginal hairs simple or glandular; petals 5, white or greenish, oblong-ovate to obovate, obtuse at apex, base obtuse or truncate, 1/8–1/6 in. long and 1/12 in. broad, glabrous above and hairy beneath; stamens 5, filaments as long as the sepals with anthers about 1/25 in. long and broad; pistil with a slightly lobed stigma.

Fruit. Maturing usually by September, subglobose, lenticular, oblique, 1/3–2/5 in. long, covered with red hairs that are simple and glandular; seed lenticular, broader than long, smooth.

Leaves. Alternate, evergreen, 2–5½ in. long, odd-pinnate compound of 5–9 leaflets on a softly pubescent rachis, oblong, oval, ovate, or lanceolate, apex acute, base cuneate, margin entire or subrevolute, leathery; upper surface dark green, lustrous, and glabrous to puberulent; lower surface paler dull green with simple or glandular hairs; lateral leaflets ½–1½ in. long, 3/8–3/4 in. broad, petiolules about 1/12 in. long; segments of rachis between leaflets 1/4–½ in. long; terminal leaflet 3/4–1½ in. long, 3/8–3/4 in. wide,

long-petiolulate; petioles about ⅝ in. long. Leaves turning red, yellow, or brown in autumn.

Twigs. Brown to gray, slender, stiff, young puberulent, older glabrous.

Bark. Gray to brown, rough with small loose scales.

Range. In central and western Texas, New Mexico, and Mexico. On rocky hillsides, cliffs, and slopes at altitudes of 2,000–7,500 ft. In Mexico in the states of Nuevo León, Coahuila, Chihuahua, San Luis Potosí, Zacatecas, Durango, and Hidalgo.

Remarks. The genus name, *Rhus*, is the ancient Latin name, and the species name, *sempervirens*, refers to the evergreen habit. It has also been listed by some authors under the name of *R. virens* Lindh. Vernacular names in English, Spanish, and Indian dialects are Tobacco Sumac, Capulín, Lambrisco, Lantrioco, Ayume, Kinnikinnick, and Tamaichia. Tamaichia was the name given by the

Comanche Indians, who gathered the leaves in the fall, sun-cured them, and mixed them with tobacco for smoking. It is also reported that the leaves were used in domestic medicine for relieving asthma. The acid, red fruit steeped in water makes a cooling drink. The red fruit and evergreen, lustrous leaves suit the plant for use in horticulture.

A closely related species of Arizona is *R. choriophylla* Woot. & Standl., which has longer, more glabrous leaves and axillary inflorescence. However, some authors feel that it is only a geographical variation of *R. sempervirens*.

Flame-leaf Sumac

Rhus copallina L. [H]

Field Identification. Slender-branched shrub or small tree to 25 ft.

Flowers. Polygamo-dioecious, about ⅛ in. across, borne in a densely pubescent, terminal thyrse about 4¾ in. long and 4 in. broad; pedicels about 1⁄12 in. long, pubescent; bracts very small, lanceolate, about 1⁄12 in. long; sepals 5, deltoid, pubescent, glandular-ciliate, 1⁄12–⅛ in. long, about 1⁄25 in. broad; stamens 5, anthers lanceolate; pistil 1, sessile, ovary pubescent, stigmas 3, styles 3; disk annular. Petals greenish white, 1⁄12–1⁄10 in. long, 1⁄25 in. broad, glabrous externally, a few hairs on the inner side, margin ciliate and glandular, deciduous.

Fruit. In compact panicles, erect or drooping, persistent; drupe subglobose, flattened, red, glandular-hairy, ⅛–⅙ in. in diameter; seeds solitary, smooth.

Leaves. Deciduous, alternate, pinnate, 5–12 in. long, rachis pubescent, broadly winged; leaflets 7–17, subsessile, inequilateral,

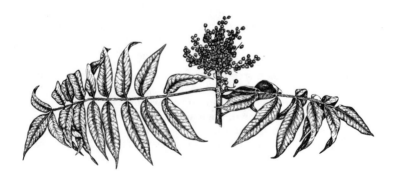

elliptic or ovate to lanceolate, acute or acuminate at the apex, asymmetrical and obtuse, or rounded to subcuneate at the base, entire or few-toothed, lustrous, glabrous to pubescent above, hairy and glandular beneath; lateral leaflets sessile, 1–3½ in. long, ½–1¼ in. broad, terminal leaflet petiolulate or sessile.

Twigs. Green to reddish brown, pubescent at first, glabrous later; lenticels dark.

Bark. Thick, greenish brown, excrescences circular, scales thin.

Wood. Light brown to greenish, coarse-grained, soft, weighing 32 lb per cu ft, sometimes used for small posts.

Range. Moist soil in shade or sun. Texas, Oklahoma, Arkansas, and Louisiana; eastward to Georgia, northward to New Hampshire, and west to Michigan and Missouri.

Remarks. The genus name, *Rhus*, is the ancient Latin name, and the species name, *copallina*, means "copal gum." Vernacular names for this plant are Mountain Sumac, Smooth Sumac, Black Sumac, Shining Sumac, Dwarf Sumac, Upland Sumac, and Winged Sumac.

The bark and leaves contain tannin and are used in the tanning industry. The crushed acrid fruit of this and other species was added to drinking water by the Indians to make it more palatable.

According to stomach records, the fruit has been eaten by at least 20 species of birds, and white-tailed deer occasionally browse it. It is propagated by seed. It is conspicuous in fall because of the brilliant red leaves.

Flame-leaf Sumac is generally replaced in central Texas by the Prairie Flame-leaf Sumac, *R. copallina* L. var. *lanceolata* Gray, which has narrower and more falcate leaves, larger clusters of fruit, and a more treelike rounded form. It is thought that the two may hybridize in their overlapping areas.

White Flame-leaf Sumac, *R. copallina* var. *leucantha* (Jacq.) DC., is a variety with white flowers found near New Braunfels.

A variety with 5–13 broader, oblong to narrow-ovate leaflets has been described from Oklahoma, Texas, Arkansas, and Louisiana as *R. copallina* L. var. *latifolia* Engl., but other authors have relegated it to the status of a synonym of the species.

Prairie Flame-leaf Sumac

Rhus copallina L. var. *lanceolata* Gray [H]

Field Identification. Clumpy shrub or small tree to 30 ft, with a rounded top.

Flowers. Borne in terminal panicles 4–6 in. long and 2–3 in. wide, peduncle pubescent, secondary pedicels about ⅙ in. long or flowers almost sessile; individual flowers yellowish green to white, about ⅛ in. long; bracts deciduous, ovate, ½₅–¹⁄₁₂ in. long, apex rounded, glabrous above, hairy below, margin ciliate; sepals 5, erect, ovate-triangular, acute or obtuse, ½₅–¹⁄₁₂ in. long, glabrous above, hairy beneath, margin ciliate with glandular or simple hairs; petals 5, yellowish green to white, about ⅛ in. long and

$\frac{1}{25}$ in. wide, oblong-ovate, obtuse, reflexed, smooth above, hairy beneath, margin ciliate; stamens 5, exserted, filaments elongate; anthers lanceolate, yellow, conspicuous, about $\frac{1}{25}$ in. long and wide; ovary 1-celled, stigmas 3, styles 3.

Fruit. In terminal showy panicles, drupe about $\frac{3}{16}$ in. long, subglobose, flattened, dark red, glandular-hairy, the stigma persisting; seeds about $\frac{1}{8}$ in. long and $\frac{1}{12}$ in. broad, smooth, oval to obovate.

Leaves. Alternate, 5–9 in. long, odd-pinnate compound of 9–21 leaflets; rachis between the leaflets narrowly winged, green to reddish, pubescent; leaflets sessile or short-petioluled, 1–3 in. long, $\frac{1}{4}$–$\frac{1}{2}$ in. wide, lanceolate to linear, falcate, apex acuminate, base cuneate or rounded, asymmetrical, margin entire or with coarse teeth, thin, subrevolute; upper surface dark green, lustrous, glabrous; lower surface duller, paler, pubescent or glandular-hairy, veins rather conspicuous; petiole 1–1½ in. long.

Twigs. Slender, all young parts hairy, green to red; older twigs gray, glabrous, lenticels small.

Bark. Gray to brown, smooth when young, with small scales when older, excrescences lenticular, numerous, horizontal.

Range. Usually on dry and rocky soil of the Texas Edwards Plateau area; north into Oklahoma, northwest into New Mexico, and south into Mexico. In Mexico in the states of Coahuila, Puebla, and Tamaulipas.

Remarks. The genus name, *Rhus*, is the ancient Latin name; the species name, *copallina*, means "gum copal," and the variety name, *lanceolata*, refers to the lanceolate-shaped leaflets. Vernacular names are Lance-leaf Sumac, Tree Sumac, Limestone Sumac, Mountain Sumac, Black Sumac, and Prairie Shining Sumac.

Prairie Flame-leaf Sumac is considered by some authorities to be a distinct species instead of a variety of the Flame-leaf Sumac, *R. copallina*. However, later classification takes into account the considerable variation of the Flame-leaf Sumac and has assigned the Prairie Flame-leaf Sumac as a variety of it. The Prairie Flame-leaf Sumac, in its most typical form, seems most abundant on the dry, stony hills of central and west Texas. It has longer panicles of flowers and larger fruit than the Flame-leaf Sumac. The leaflets tend to be narrower, entire or remotely serrate, and falcate, and the wing of the rachis narrower. The habit approaches that of a small rounded tree instead of a straggling shrub.

The leaves of both the Flame-leaf and Prairie Flame-leaf Sumac contain considerable amounts of tannin and have been used as a substitute for oak bark in tanning leather. The acrid drupes, when crushed in water, produce a cooling drink known as "Sumac-ade" or "Rhus-ade." The drupes also produce a black dye for woolen goods. Because of the brilliant fall coloring of its red, purple, and orange leaves, Prairie Flame-leaf Sumac is being adapted to horticulture.

It has considerable wildlife value, the drupe being eaten particularly by the gallinaceous birds, such as various species of quail, grouse, prairie chicken, and ring-necked pheasant. It is also browsed by white-tailed deer and mule deer.

Smooth Sumac

Rhus glabra L. [H]

Field Identification. Thicket-forming shrub or small tree attaining a height of 20 ft. Leaves pinnate, bearing 11–31 elliptic or lanceolate, sharply serrate leaflets.

Flowers. June–August, in a terminal thyrse, 5–9 in. long; bracts narrowly lanceolate, about ⅟₂₅ in. long; calyx of 5 lanceolate sepals, each about ⅟₁₂ in. long; petals 5, white, spreading, lanceolate, ⅙ in. long or less; stamens 5; pistil 1, ovary 1-seeded, stigmas 3.

Fruit. Ripening September–October, drupe subglobose, about ⅙ in. long, covered with short, red-velvety hairs; 1-seeded, stone smooth, seed dispersed by birds and mammals.

Leaves. Alternate, pinnately compound, 11–31 leaflets that are elliptic, lanceolate, oblong, or ovate, acuminate at the apex; rounded, subcordate, cuneate, or oblique at the base, sharply serrate, usually dark green above, lighter to conspicuously white beneath; lateral ones sessile or almost so, 2½–4¾ in. long, ½–1¼ in. broad; terminal leaf sessile or petiolulate, 2–3¾ in. long, ½–1½ in. broad.

Wood. Orange, soft, brittle.

Range. In moist, rich soil. Texas, New Mexico, Oklahoma, Arkansas, and Louisiana; eastward to Florida, northward to Quebec, and westward to British Columbia, Washington, Oregon, Utah, Colorado, and Missouri.

Remarks. The genus name, *Rhus*, is the ancient Latin name, and the species name, *glabra*, refers to the plant's smoothness. Vernacular names are Scarlet Sumac, Red Sumac, White Sumac, Shoe-make, Vinegar-tree, Senhalanac, Pennsylvania Sumac, Up-

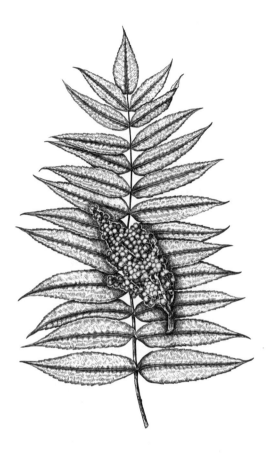

land Sumac, and Sleek Sumac. The leaves are reported to have been mixed with tobacco and smoked. The twigs, leaves, and roots contain tannin and were used for staining and dyeing. The Indians used the plant in many ways. The crushed acid fruits were added to water to freshen it. Various concoctions of the bark, twigs, leaves, and flowers were used medicinally to act as astringents, to stop bleeding, and to treat renal disorders.

Smooth Sumac is now used extensively for ornament. Its red clusters of fruit and long graceful leaves that turn brilliant colors in the autumn are its attractive features. It should be more extensively cultivated for ornament. Records show that the date of earliest cultivation was 1620. It is occasionally planted for erosion control and used for shelter-belt planting in the prairie states. Thirty-two species of birds are known to feed on it. Wild turkey, bobwhite, cottontail, and white-tailed deer eat it eagerly.

Little-leaf Sumac

Rhus microphylla Engelm. [H]

Field Identification. Clump-forming, intricately branched shrub attaining a height of 15 ft. Branches crooked, stiff, almost spinescent.

Flowers. Borne in dense, crowded, stiff, compound spikes before the leaves appear, spikes ½–2 in. long and broad, bracts hardly over ⅟25 in. long and slightly broader, somewhat glandular-hairy, ciliate, persistent; pedicels about ⅟25 in. long or shorter; flowers about 3⁄16 in. across, bracteolate; sepals 5, rounded to deltoid, concave, acute, ciliate, glabrous, about ⅟25 in. long; petals 5, imbricate, greenish white, rounded to ovate, ciliate, glabrous on one side, hairy on the other; stamens 5, filaments exceeding the sepals; anthers about ⅟25 in. long or less; disk ⅟25–⅟12 in. broad, lobed; styles united or nearly so.

Fruit. Drupe May–July, subglobose to ovoid, reddish orange, glandular-hairy, ⅕–¼ in. long, 1-celled.

Leaves. Small, deciduous, odd-pinnate compound, ½–1½ in. long, composed of 5–9 leaflets with a winged rachis; petiole about ⅛ in. long, leaflets oblong, elliptic, obovate or ovate, sessile; apex obtuse, acute, often mucronate; base cuneate, somewhat asymmetrical; margin entire, slightly revolute; thin, dull green and hairy above, somewhat paler and hairy beneath; lateral leaflets 3⁄16–3⁄8 in. long, ⅟12–⅙ in. broad; terminal leaflet 3⁄16–5⁄8 in. long, ⅛–⅙ in. broad.

Twigs. Almost spinescent, stiff, crooked, roughened, puberulent at first to glabrous later, lenticels prominent.

Bark. Dark gray to black, smooth when young, broken into small scales with age.

Range. On dry, rocky hillsides or gravelly mesas at altitudes of 2,000–6,000 ft. In Texas, New Mexico, and Arizona. Widespread in the western half of Texas. Also in the Mexican states of Chihuahua, Sonora, Coahuila, Durango, Nuevo León, San Luis Potosí, Zacatecas, and Baja California.

Remarks. The genus name, *Rhus*, is the old Latin name, and the species name, *microphylla*, refers to the small leaves. Vernacular

names are Winged Sumac, Small-leaf Sumac, Correosa, Agrito, and Agrillo. The reddish orange, hairy drupe is edible but sour. It is eaten by a few species of ground squirrels and chipmunks. The leaves are rather poor browse for livestock, but are sometimes browsed by mule deer and Sonora deer.

HOLLY FAMILY (Aquifoliaceae)

Yaupon Holly

Ilex vomitoria Ait. [H]

Field Identification. An evergreen, thicket-forming shrub with many stems from the base, or a tree to 25 ft, and a diameter of 1 ft. The crown is low, dense, and rounded.

Flowers. April–May on branchlets of the previous year, solitary or fascicled in the leaf axils, polygamo-dioecious, pedicels slender, 1/25–1/6 in. long; staminate glabrous, 2–3-flowered; pistillate puberulent, 1–2-flowered; calyx lobes 4–5, glabrous, ovate or rounded, obtuse, about 1/25 in. long; corolla white, petals 4–5, united at base, elliptic-oblong, 1/12–1/8 in. long, about 1/12 in. wide; stamens 4–5, almost as long as the petals, anthers oblong and cordate; staminodia of the pistillate flowers shorter than the petals; ovary ovoid, 1/25–1/12 in. long, 1–4-celled, stigma flattened and capitate.

Fruit. Often in abundance, drupe shiny red, semitranslucent, subglobose, about 1/4 in. long, often crowned by the persistent stigma, nutlets usually 4, to 1/6 in. long, obtuse, prominently ribbed.

Leaves. Evergreen, simple, alternate, elliptic-oblong to oval, margin crenate and teeth minutely mucronulate, apex obtuse or rounded and sometimes minutely emarginate and mucronulate, base obtuse or rounded, thick, and coriaceous; upper surface dark lustrous green and glabrous, veins obscure; lower surface paler, glabrous or with a few hairs on veins; petioles 1/25–1/4 in. long, grooved, glabrous or puberulent. Leaves vary considerably in size and shape on different plants.

Twigs. Gray to brown, terete, stout, rigid, crooked, short, glabrous or puberulent; winter buds minute, obtuse, scales brown.

Bark. Averaging 1/16–1/8 in. thick, brownish to mottled gray or almost black, tight, smooth except for lenticels, or on old trunks eventually breaking into thin, small scales.

Wood. White, heavy, hard, strong, close-grained, weighing about 46 lb per cu ft, sometimes used for turnery, inlay work, or woodenware.

Range. Low moist woods, mostly near the coast. Texas, Oklahoma, Arkansas, and Louisiana. Evidently reaching its largest size in the east Texas bottomlands. Eastward to Florida and northward to Virginia.

Remarks. The genus name, *Ilex*, is the ancient name for the Holly Oak, and the species name, *vomitoria*, refers to its use as a medicine. Local names in use are Cassena, Cassine, Cassio-berry-bush, Evergreen Cassena, Yapon, Yopan, Youpon, Emetic Holly, Evergreen Holly, South-sea-tea, Carolina-tea, Appalachian-tea, Yopon del Indio, Chocolate del Indio, Indian Blackdrink, Christmas-berry.

The fruit is known to be eaten by at least 7 species of birds. In regions where it grows it is often used as a holiday decoration. Although yellow-fruited plants have been given variety names from time to time, they do not apparently reproduce true to color and are therefore to be regarded only as unstable forms.

American Holly

Ilex opaca Ait. [H]

Field Identification. An evergreen tree to 70 ft, with short, crooked branches and a rounded or pyramidal crown.

Flowers. April–June, in short-stalked, axillary, cymose clusters; polygamo-dioecious, staminate in 3–9-flowered cymes, small, white, petals 4–6; stamens 4–6, alternating with the petals; pistillate flowers solitary or 2–3 together; ovary 4–8-celled, style

short with broad stigmas; pistil rudimentary in the staminate flowers; calyx 4–6-lobed, lobes acute, ciliate; peduncles with 2 bracts.

Fruit. Maturing November–December, spherical or ellipsoid, mostly red, more rarely yellow or orange, ¼–½ in. long, nutlets prominently ribbed.

Leaves. Variable in shape, size, and spines, simple, alternate, persistent, ovate to oblong or oval, flattened, keeled or twisted, stiff and coriaceous, margins wavy, set with sharp, stiff, flat or divaricate spines, sometimes spineless; apex acute, spinose; base cuneate or rounded; upper surface dark to light green, lustrous or dull, paler and glabrous to somewhat puberulent beneath, length 2–4 in., width 1–1½ in.; petioles short, stout, grooved, sometimes puberulent; stipules minute, deltoid, acute.

Twigs. Stout, green to light brown or gray, glabrous or puberulent.

Bark. Light or dark gray, often roughened by small protuberances.

Wood. White or brownish, tough, close-grained, shock resistance high, works with tools well, shrinks considerably, checks or warps badly unless properly seasoned, not durable under exposure, rather heavy, specific gravity when dry about 0.61. It is used for cabinets, interior finish, novelties, handles, fixtures, and scientific instruments.

Range. Texas, Oklahoma, Arkansas, and Louisiana; eastward to Florida, north to Massachusetts and New York, and westward through Pennsylvania, Ohio, Indiana, and Illinois to Missouri.

Remarks. The genus name, *Ilex*, is the old name for Holly Oak, and the species name, *opaca*, refers to the dull green leaf. Vernacular names are Yule Holly, Christmas Holly, and White Holly. The foliage and fruit are often used for holiday decorations and are sometimes browsed by cattle. At least 18 species of birds eat the fruit.

Possum-haw Holly

Ilex decidua Walt. [H]

Field Identification. Usually a shrub with a spreading open crown, but sometimes a tree to 30 ft, with an inclined trunk to 10 in. in diameter.

Flowers. Borne March–May with the leaves, polygamo-dioecious, solitary or fascicled, borne on slender pedicels; pedicels of stami-

nate flowers to ½ in. long, those of the pistillate flower generally shorter than the staminate; petals 4–6, white, united at the base, oblong to elliptic, ⅛–⅙ in. long; calyx lobes 4–6, lobes ovate to triangular, acute or obtuse, entire to denticulate, sometimes ciliolate; stamens 4–6, anthers oblong and cordate, fertile stamens as long as the petals or shorter; staminodia of pistillate flowers shorter than the petals; ovary ovoid, about 1/12 in. long, 4-celled, stigma large, capitate, and sessile.

Fruit. Ripe in early autumn, persistent on branches most of the winter after leaves are shed, drupe globose or depressed-globose, orange-red, ¼–⅓ in. in diameter, solitary or 2–3 together; nutlets usually 4, crustaceous, ovate or lunate, longitudinally ribbed, up to ⅕ in. long.

Leaves. Simple, deciduous, alternate or often fascicled on short lateral spurs, obovate to spatulate or oblong, margin crenate-serrate with gland-tipped teeth; apex acute to obtuse, rounded or emarginate; base cuneate or attenuate, membranous at first but firm later; upper surface dark green and glabrous or with a few hairs, main vein impressed; lower surface paler and glabrous or pubescent on ribs, blade length 2–3 in., width ½–1½ in.; petiole slender, grooved, glabrous to densely puberulent, length ¹⁄₁₂–½ in.; stipules filiform, deciduous.

Twigs. Elongate, slender, often with many short, spurlike lateral twigs, light to dark gray, glabrous or puberulent, lightly lenticellate, leaf scars lunate, buds small and obtuse.

Bark. Smooth, thin, mottled gray to brown, sometimes with numerous warty protuberances.

Wood. White, close-grained, weighing 46 lb per cu ft, of no commercial value.

Range. In rich, moist soil, usually along streams or in swamps. Texas, Louisiana, Oklahoma, and Arkansas; eastward to Florida, and northward to Tennessee, Kentucky, Indiana, Illinois, Kansas, and Missouri.

Remarks. The genus name, *Ilex*, is the ancient name of the Holly Oak, and the species name, *decidua*, refers to the autumn-shed leaves. Local names are Deciduous Holly, Meadow Holly, Prairie Holly, Welk Holly, Bearberry, and Winterberry. It is occasionally planted for ornament and is attractive in winter because of the persistent orange-red drupes. It is sometimes mistaken for a hawthorn in fruit, and possums are fond of it, hence the name, Possum-haw. At least 9 species of birds are known to feed upon the fruit, including the bobwhite quail.

MAPLE FAMILY (Aceraceae)

Box-elder Maple

Acer negundo L. [H]

Field Identification. Tree attaining a height of 75 ft, with a broad rounded crown.

Flowers. March–May, dioecious, small, greenish, drooping, on slender stalks; staminate in fascicles 1–2 in. long; no petals; stamens 4–6, exserted, filaments hairy with linear anthers; calyx campanulate, hairy, 5-lobed; pistillate flowers in narrow racemes; ovary pubescent, style separating into 2 elongate, stigmatic lobes; calyx of pistillate flower narrowly 5-lobed.

Fruit. Ripening August–October, borne in early summer in drooping clusters 6–8 in. long; samara double, greenish, minutely pubescent or glabrous, 1–2 in. long; wings divergent to about 90°, straight or falcate, thin and reticulate; seeds at base of wings, solitary, smooth, reddish brown, about ½ in. long.

Leaves. Deciduous, opposite, 6–15 in. long, odd-pinnate compound of 3–7 (sometimes 9) leaflets; leaflets short-stalked, 2–4 in. long, 1½–3 in. wide, ovate-elliptic or oval-obovate; margin irregularly serrate or lobed, mostly above the middle; acute or acuminate at apex; rounded, cuneate or cordate at the base, sometimes unsymmetrical; light green, glabrous or slightly pubescent above, paler and pubescent beneath, especially in axils of veins; petioles glabrous.

Twigs. Slender, smooth, shiny, green to purplish green.

Bark. Young bark green, smooth, thin, later pale gray to brown, divided into narrow rounded ridges with short scales and shallow fissures.

Wood. Whitish, light, soft, not strong, close-grained, weighing 27 lb per cu ft.

Range. Texas, Oklahoma, Arkansas, and Louisiana; eastward to Florida, northward to New Brunswick, and west to Ontario, Michigan, Minnesota, and Nebraska.

Remarks. The genus name, *Acer*, is from an old Celt word, and the application of the species name, *negundo*, is obscure. The synonyms *Negundo aceroides* Moench and *Rulac negundo* (L.) A. S. Hitchcock are also used by some writers. Vernacular names are Maple-ash, Ashleaf Maple, Water-ash, Sugar Maple, Red River Maple, Black Maple, and Manitoba Maple. The tree is easily transplanted when young, grows rapidly, is short-lived, and is easily damaged by rot, insects, storm, and fire. It is widely planted as a quick-growing ornamental tree and has been extensively used in shelter-belt planting in the prairie states. The wood is used for paper pulp, cooperage, woodenware, interior finish, and cheap furniture. The seeds are eaten by many species of birds and squirrels. It is occasionally tapped for its sugary sap, which is inferior to that of Sugar Maple.

BUCKEYE FAMILY (Hippocastanaceae)

Texas Buckeye

Aesculus arguta Buckl. [H]

Field Identification. Usually a shrub, but under favorable conditions a tree to 35 ft. The branches are stout and the crown is rounded to oblong.

Flowers. Inflorescence a dense, yellow panicle, borne after the leaves, 4–8 in. long, 2–3½ in. broad, primary peduncle of panicle densely brown-tomentose, secondary racemes ¾–½ in. long, 3–15-flowered, tomentose; individual flower pedicels ⅛–¼ in., densely tomentose; calyx campanulate, ⅕–¼ in. long, brown-tomentose, 4–5-lobed above, lobes imbricate in the bud, lobes unequal, apices obtuse to rounded or truncate; petals 4, pale yellow, some reddish at the base, ⅓–¾ in. long, upright, parallel, clawed, thin, deciduous, densely hairy, margin ciliate; upper pair oval to broadly oblong; lateral pair elongate, oblong to spatulate, long-clawed, apex rounded to truncate or notched; disk hypogynous, annular, depressed; stamens 7–8, inserted on the disk, long-

exserted, upcurved, unequal, filiform, hairy, longer than the petals; anthers yellow, ellipsoid, introrse, 2-celled, opening longitudinally; style 1, slender, elongate, curved; stigma terminal and entire; ovary 3-celled, sessile, cells often 1-ovuled by abortion.

Fruit. Maturing May–June, peduncles stout, hairy at first, glabrate later; capsule ¾–1¾ in. in diameter, subglobose to obovoid or asymmetrically lobed, armed with stout warts or prickles or occasionally smooth, light brown, dehiscent into 2–3 valves at maturity; seeds usually solitary and rounded, if 2, usually flattened by pressure, coriaceous, smooth, lustrous, brown, ⅝–¾ in. in diameter.

Leaves. Deciduous, opposite, palmate compound of 7–9 leaflets (often 7), sessile or nearly so, narrowly elliptic to lanceolate, or, more rarely, obovate, apex long-acuminate (less often broader and abruptly acuminate), base attenuate to narrowly cuneate, margin finely serrate or occasionally incised above the middle, blade length 2½–5 in., width ½–2 in.; upper surface olive green, lustrous, a few fine hairs mostly along the veins; lower surface paler and more pubescent; petioles slender, 3–5 in., grooved, woolly-hairy.

Bark. Gray to black; fissures narrow, short, and irregular; ridges broken into small short, rough scales.

Twigs. Tough, stout, terete, the young ones green and glabrous to somewhat hairy, the older ones gray to reddish brown, lenticels small; leaf scars lunate or horseshoe shaped, fibrovascular marks 3–6.

Range. Texas Buckeye is found on limestone or granite soils in the Edwards Plateau area of Texas, north to southern Oklahoma, and in Missouri.

Remarks. The genus name, *Aesculus*, is the old name for a European mast-bearing tree, and the species name, *arguta*, means "sharp-toothed," perhaps referring to the foliage. Texas Buckeye is closely related to Ohio Buckeye, *A. glabra* Willd., and at one time was listed as a variety of it under the name of *A. glabra* var. *arguta* (Buckl.) Robinson. Although listed only as a shrub in most literature, Texas Buckeye becomes a tree to 35 ft in height and 18 in. in diameter on the Texas Edwards Plateau. The leaves and flower parts of Texas Buckeye appear to be only lightly pubescent on some specimens and heavily tomentose on others.

Red Buckeye

Aesculus pavia L. [H]

Field Identification. Shrub with an inclined stem or, more rarely, a tree attaining a height of 28 ft and a diameter of 10 in. The crown is usually dense and the branches short, crooked, and ascending.

Flowers. March–May, panicles narrow to ovoid, erect, pubescent, 4–8 in. long; pedicels slender, ¼–½ in., flowers single to numerous, red, ¾–1½ in. long; calyx tubular, ⅜–⅝ in. long, dark red, tube about five times as long as the rounded lobes; petals 4, red, connivent, ⅝–1 in. long, oblong to obovate, apex rounded, base narrowed into a claw, limbs of the 2 superior petals shorter than the 2 lateral pairs; stamens about equaling the longest petals, exserted, usually 8 in number, filaments filiform and villous below; ovary sessile, villous, 3-celled (or by abortion fewer), style slender.

Fruit. Capsule 1–2 in. in diameter, subglobose or obovoid, light brown, smooth but finely pitted, dehiscent into 2–3 valves; seeds

1–3, rounded, or flattened by pressure against each other, lustrous, light to dark brown, about 1 in. in diameter.

Leaves. Deciduous, opposite, palmate compound of 5 leaflets (rarely 3 or 7), leaflets oblong to elliptic or oval to obovate, apex acute to short-acuminate, base gradually narrowed, margin coarsely serrate, leaflet length 3–6 in., width 1–1½ in., firm; upper surface lustrous, dark green, glabrous except a few hairs on the veins; lower surface paler, almost glabrous to densely tomentose; petiole nearly glabrous or with varying degree of hairiness, red, 3–7 in.

Bark. Gray to brown, smooth on young branches, on old trunks roughened into short plates that flake off in small, thin scales.

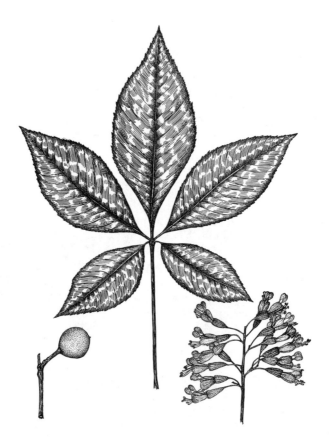

Yellow Woolly Buckeye

Twigs. Green to gray or brown, crooked, stout, smooth; lenticels pale brown to orange; leaf scars large and conspicuous, with 3 fibrovascular bundles.

Range. Mostly along streams of the coastal plains. East and central Texas to the Edwards Plateau, Oklahoma, and Arkansas; eastward through Louisiana to Florida, north to southern Illinois, and west to southeast Missouri.

Remarks. The genus name, *Aesculus,* is the ancient name for an old mast-bearing tree, and the species name, *pavia,* honors Peter Paaw (d. 1617) of Leiden. Some vernacular names in use for the plant are Scarlet Buckeye, Woolly Buckeye, Firecracker Plant, and Fish-poison−bush. A variety with more hairy leaves and yellow flowers has been named Yellow Woolly Buckeye, *Aesculus pavia* var. *flavescens* (Sarg.) Correll. It appears to be more common on the Edwards Plateau of central Texas. It is reported that the powdered bark is used in domestic medicine for toothache and ulcers, the roots are used for washing clothes, and the crushed fruit is used for fish poison.

SOAPBERRY FAMILY (Sapindaceae)

Western Soapberry

Sapindus saponaria L. var. *drummondii* (H. & A.) L. Benson [H]

Field Identification. Tree attaining a height of 50 ft, with a diameter of 1–2 ft. The branches are usually erect to form a rounded crown.

Flowers. May–June, in large, showy panicles 5–10 in. long and 5–6 in. wide; perianth about ½₅ in. across; petals 4–5, obovate, rounded, white; sepals 4–5, acute, concave, ciliate on margin, shorter than the petals; stamens usually 8, inserted on the disk; style single, slender, with a 2–4-lobed stigma; ovary 3-lobed and 3-celled, each cell containing 1 ovule.

Fruit. September–October, globular, fleshy, from white to yellowish or blackish, translucent, persistent and shriveled; seed 1,

obovoid, dark brown, the other 2 seeds seeming to atrophy.

Leaves. Short-petiolate, deciduous, alternate, 5–18 in. long, abruptly pinnate; leaflets 4–11 pairs, 1½–4 in. long, ½–¾ in. wide, falcate, lanceolate, acuminate at the apex, asymmetrical at base, veiny, yellowish green, glabrous above, soft pubescent or glabrous beneath.

Bark. Gray to reddish, divided into narrow plates that break into small reddish scales.

Twigs. Yellowish green to gray, pubescent to glabrous, lenticels small.

Wood. Light brown or yellowish, close-grained, hard, strong, weighing 51 lb per cu ft.

Range. In moist soils along streams; Texas, New Mexico, Arizona, Oklahoma, and Arkansas; eastward into Louisiana, north to Missouri and Kansas, and south into Mexico.

Remarks. The genus name, *Sapindus*, is from *sapo* ("soap") and *Indus* ("Indies") referring to the fact that some of the West Indies species are used for soap. The species name, *saponaria*, also refers to the saponaceous character of the fruit. The variety name, *drummondii*, is in honor of Thomas Drummond. Vernacular names are Amole de Bolita, Tehuistle, Palo Blanco, Jaboncillo, Wild China-tree, and Indian Soap-plant.

The fruit of this tree and related species contains the poisonous substance saponin, which produces a good lather in water. It is used in Mexico as a laundry soap. The fruit is also used medicinally as a remedy for renal disorders, rheumatism, and fevers. Buttons and necklaces are made from the seeds. The wood is of little value except for making baskets and frames and as fuel. Soapberry makes a desirable shade tree and could be more extensively planted for ornament. It has been cultivated since 1900 and is sometimes used for shelter-belt planting.

Mexican-buckeye

Ungnadia speciosa Endl. [H]

Field Identification. Western shrub or tree to 30 ft, and 10 in. in trunk diameter. Branches small and upright to spreading with an irregularly shaped crown.

Flowers. Borne in pubescent fascicles in spring, appearing with the leaves, or just before them; polygamous and irregular, about

1 in. across, fragrant; petals usually 4 or occasionally 5, rose-colored, deciduous, obovate, erect, clawed, margin crenulate, somewhat tomentose, with a tuft of fleshy hairs; disk 1-sided, oblique, tongue shaped, connate with the ovary base; calyx campanulate, 5-lobed, lobes oblong-lanceolate; stamens 7–10, unequal, exserted, inserted on edge of disk, filaments filiform and pink, anthers oblong and red; ovary ovoid, stipitate, hairy, 3-celled, rudimentary in the staminate flower, ovules 2; style subulate, elongate, filiform, slightly upcurved; stigma terminal, minute.

Fruit. Capsule stipitate, broad-ovoid, crowned by the style remnants, about 2 in. broad, leathery, roughened, reddish brown, 3-celled and 3-valved, dehiscent in October while still on the trees, but hardly opening wide enough to release the large seeds;

seeds usually solitary because of the abortion of the others, about ½ in. in diameter, round, smooth, shining, black or brown, hilum scar broad.

Leaves. Odd-pinnate compound, alternate, deciduous, 5–12 in. long, leaflets 5–7 (rarely 3), ovate to lanceolate, apex acuminate, base rounded or cuneate, margin crenate-serrate, 3–5 in. long, 1½–2 in. wide, rather leathery, upper surface dark green, lustrous and glabrous, lower surface paler and pubescent to glabrous; petiole 2–6 in.; petiolule of terminal leaflet ¼–1 in.; lateral leaflets sessile or very short-petioluled.

Twigs. Buds imbricate, ovate to almost globose, leaf scars large and obcordate, twigs slender, terete, brown to orange and pubescent at first, later reddish brown and glabrous.

Bark. Mottled gray to brown, thin, tight, smooth, broken into shallow fissures on old trunks.

Wood. Reddish brown, sapwood lighter, brittle, soft, close-grained.

Range. Usually in limestone soils of stream banks, moist canyons, or on bluffs. In Texas, New Mexico, and Mexico. In Texas of greatest abundance west of the Brazos River. A few trees found as far east as Harris County. In Mexico in the states of Nuevo León, Coahuila, and Chihuahua.

Remarks. The genus name, *Ungnadia*, is in honor of Baron Ungnad, ambassador of Emperor Rudolph II. The species name, *speciosa*, means showy, with reference to the flowers. Also known under the vernacular names of Monillo, Texas-buckeye, Spanish-buckeye, New Mexican-buckeye, False-buckeye, and Canyon-buckeye. The tree should be grown more for ornament, being very beautiful in the spring. The flowers resemble redbud or peach blossoms at a distance. It is also a source of honey. The sweet seeds are poisonous to human beings. Seemingly a few may be eaten with impunity, but a number cause stomach disturbances. The leaves and fruit may also cause some minor poisoning to livestock, but they are seldom browsed except in times of stress. Children in west Texas sometimes use the round seeds for marbles.

Goldenrain-tree

Koelreuteria paniculata Laxm. [H]

Field Identification. A cultivated, deciduous, ornamental tree to 30 ft with a rounded crown. Conspicuous by the large panicles of

yellow flowers in summer, followed later by the reddish brown, bladderlike fruit capsule. Leaves usually pinnate compound.

Flowers. Borne July–August in wide terminal panicles to 18 in. long, polygamous. Flowers numerous, about ½ in. long, irregular; calyx of 5 unequal lobes; petals 3–4, lanceolate, strongly reflexed, clawed, with 2 upturned appendages at the cordate base; disk crenate above, between petals and stamens; stamens 8 or fewer, filaments long, distinct; ovary superior, usually 3-celled, each cell 2-ovuled; style 3-parted.

Fruit. Capsule 1½–2 in. long, inflated; the 3 loculicidally dehiscent valves with papery walls, ovoid-oblong in shape, narrowed into a mucronate apex. The rounded seeds black.

Leaves. Alternate, to 14 in. long, pinnate or sometimes bipinnate; leaflets 7–15; shape ovate to oblong-ovate, 1–3¼ in. long; margins coarsely and irregularly crenate-serrate, sometimes incisely lobed or pinnatisect; upper surface dark green and glabrous; lower surface paler and pubescent or glabrous on veins. Winter buds small with 2 outer scales.

Range. Native to China, Korea, and Japan. Often cultivated for ornament.

Remarks. The genus name, *Koelreuteria*, honors Joseph G. Koelreuter (1733–1806), professor of natural history at Karlsruhe. The species name, *paniculata*, refers to the panicled flowers. Some vernacular names are China-tree, Varnish-tree, Pride-of-India. It is not to be confused with the China-berry-tree (*Melia azedarach*), which also bears some of the same vernacular names. Goldenrain-tree was introduced into cultivation in 1763.

BUCKTHORN FAMILY (Rhamnaceae)

Texas Colubrina

Colubrina texensis (Torr. & Gray) Gray [H]

Field Identification. Thicket-forming shrub rarely over 15 ft, with light gray divaricate twigs.

Flowers. April–May, borne in axillary, subsessile clusters; perfect, tomentose, greenish yellow, less than ⅓ in. across; petals 5, hooded and clawed; calyx 5-lobed, persistent on the fruit, lobes triangular-ovate; stamens 5, inserted below the disk, opposite the petals, filaments filiform; ovary 3-celled, immersed in the disk, styles 3, stigma obtuse.

Fruit. Pedicels recurved, ¼–⅓ in. long, drupes borne at the twig nodes, ovate to subglobose, tomentose at first, later glabrous, dry, crustaceous, brown or black, about ⅓ in. in diameter, style persistent to form a beak, separating into 2–3 nutlets; seeds one in each partition, about 3/16 in. long, rounded on the back, angled on the other 2 surfaces, dark brown, shiny, smooth.

Leaves. Simple, alternate or clustered, grayish green, blades ½–1 in. long, ovate, obovate or elliptic, densely hairy at first and glabrous later; 3-nerved, margin denticulate and ciliate; apex rounded, sometimes apiculate; base cuneate, rounded, truncate or subcordate; petioles ⅛–⅜ in. or less, hairy, reddish.

Twigs. Slender, ashy gray, noticeably divergent, scarcely spiniferous, densely white-tomentose at first but glabrous later.

Bark. Gray, smooth, close, cracked into small, short scales later.

Range. Central, western, and southwestern Texas and New Mexico; Mexico in the states of Nuevo León, Coahuila, and Tamaulipas.

Remarks. The genus name, *Colubrina*, is from *coluber* ("a serpent"), perhaps for the twisting, divaricate branches or for the sinuate grooves on the stems of some species. The species name, *texensis*, refers to the state of Texas. A vernacular name is Hogplum. The dark brown or black drupes are persistent.

Bluewood Condalia

Condalia hookeri M. C. Johnst. [H]

Field Identification. Thicket-forming spinescent shrub or tree to 30 ft, with a diameter of 8 in. The branches are rigid and divaricate.

Flowers. Solitary, or 2–4 in axillary clusters, sessile, or on short pedicels about ¹⁄₁₆ in. long; calyx ¹⁄₁₆–⅛ in. broad, glabrous or nearly so; sepals 5, green, spreading, triangular, acute, persistent; disk fleshy, flat, somewhat 5-angled; petals absent; stamens 5, shorter than the sepals, incurved, inserted on the disk margin; ovary superior, 1-celled, or sometimes imperfectly 2–3-celled, styles stout and short, stigma 3-lobed.

Fruit. Ripening at intervals during the summer, drupe black at maturity, shiny, smooth, subglobose, somewhat flattened at apex, ⅕–⅓ in. in diameter, thin-skinned, fleshy, sweet, juice purple; seed solitary, ovoid to globose, flattened, acute at one end and truncate at the other, light brown, crustaceous, about ⅛ in. long.

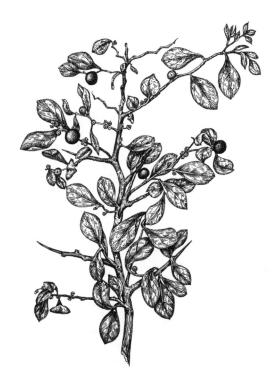

Leaves. Alternate, or fascicled on short, spinescent branches, obovate to broadly spatulate, margin entire, apex rounded to retuse or truncate and mucronate, base attenuate or cuneate, leathery, ⅓–1½ in. long, ⅓–½ in. wide; light green and lustrous, pubescent at first, glabrous later, paler beneath, midrib prominent, subsessile or short-petioled.

Twigs. Divaricate, ending in slender, reddish or gray thorns, green to brown or gray, finely velvety-pubescent at first but glabrous later.

Bark. Smooth, pale gray to brown or reddish on branches and young trunks. Old trunks with narrow, flat ridges, deep furrows, and breaking into small, thin scales.

Wood. Light red, sapwood yellow, close-grained, heavy, hard, dense, specific gravity 1.20.

Range. Dry soil, central, southern, and western Texas. On the Texas coast from Matagorda County to Cameron County, frequent along the lower Rio Grande. In central Texas in greatest abundance on the limestone plateau area and west to the Pecos River. Less common west of the Pecos and north into the Texas Panhandle. Also in Mexico in Nuevo León and Tamaulipas.

Remarks. The genus name, *Condalia*, is in honor of Antonio Condal, Spanish physician of the eighteenth century, and the species name, *hookeri*, is for Joseph Dalton Hooker (1817–1911) of England. Some vernacular names are Brazil, Logwood, Purple Haw, Capulín, Capul Negro, and Chaparral. The wood yields a blue dye and is sometimes used for fuel. The flower pollen serves as bee food. The black fruit makes good jelly, but it is difficult to gather because of the thorns. Birds eagerly devour the fruit. The bushes often form impenetrable thickets.

Green Condalia

Condalia viridis I. M. Johnst. [H]

Field Identification. Shrub 3–9 ft, with spreading spinescent branches.

Flowers. Axillary, solitary or paired, glabrous, 5-merous; hypanthium disklike, glabrous, about ⅟₁₅ in. in diameter; 5 lobes triangular, about ⅟₁₅ in. long, half-crested within and above; petals absent; stamens ⅟₂₅–⅟₁₅ in. long, affixed within and below the calyx bowl; ovary glabrous, stigma rather obscurely 2-lobed.

Fruit. Drupe black, globose, about ⅕ in. long; seed ellipsoid, slightly less than ⅕ in. long.

Leaves. Bright green, oblanceolate to oblong-obovate, blades ⅙–¾ in. long, ¹⁄₁₂–¼ in. wide; somewhat wider above the middle, gradually attenuated toward the base into a petiole ¹⁄₂₅–¹⁄₁₂ in., apex obtuse to rounded and mucronulate, midrib slender, lateral veins 2–3 and easily seen; surfaces bright green, glabrous; young leaves sparsely pubescent to glabrous later; stipules about ¹⁄₂₅ in. long, triangular, persistent, margin ciliate.

Twigs. Young ones minutely hispid, at maturity glabrous, bark grayish.

Range. Green Condalia is found along gravelly washes or dry stream beds. In Texas in Val Verde and Hudspeth counties. In Brewster County between Burro Mesa and the Chisos Mountains. In Mexico in Chihuahua.

Remarks. The genus name, *Condalia*, is in honor of Antonio Condal, Spanish physician of the eighteenth century. The species name, *viridis*, refers to the bright green leaves.

Reed's Green Condalia, *C. viridis* Johnston var. *reedii* Cory, is a variety described as differing from the species in being (on the average) twice as tall, having twice its spread, and bearing leaves about twice as large. The type locality is along the Frio River, Garner State Park, Uvalde County, at altitudes of 1,500–1,600 ft.

Lote-bush Condalia

Ziziphus obtusifolia (T. & G.) Gray [H]

Field Identification. Stiff, spiny, much-branched shrub with grayish green grooved twigs.

Flowers. Inconspicuous, in clustered umbels; pedicels ½₅–¹⁄₁₂ in. long, pubescent or villous; corolla small, green, 5-parted; petals 5, hooded and clawed, shorter than the sepals; sepals 5, triangular, acute, soft-hairy; stamens 5, inserted on the edge of the disk opposite the petals; filaments subulate with anther sacs opening lengthwise; style partly 2-cleft with a basal 2–3-celled ovary immersed in a flattened, obscurely 5-lobed disk.

Fruit. In June, drupe globular, ¹⁄₃–²⁄₅ in. in diameter, black, fleshy, not palatable; stone solitary, hard, with a thin, membranous testa.

Leaves. Alternate, green, thin, firm, glabrous or puberulent, blades ½–1¼ in. long, elliptic, ovate, or narrowly oblong; apex obtuse, acute, retuse or occasionally emarginate; margin entire to coarsely serrate; base narrowed and 3-veined; petioles one-third to one-fourth as long as the blade.

Twigs. Divaricate, grayish green, grooved, glaucous; spines stout, straight or nearly so, green or brown, to 3 in. long.

Bark. Smooth, light or dark gray.

Range. Widespread in central, southern, and western Texas. At altitudes of 5,000 ft in the Chisos Mountains in Brewster County to almost sea level at the mouth of the Rio Grande in Cameron County. On the central Texas limestone plateau. Also in Arizona, New Mexico, and northern Mexico.

Remarks. The genus name, *Ziziphus*, is from an ancient Greek name derived from the Persian *zizafun*. The species name, *obtusifolia*, is for the obtusely pointed leaves. Other names used at one time are *Ziziphus lycioides* Gray and *Condalia lycioides* (Gray) Weberb. Vernacular names are Texas Buckthorn, Chaparral, Chaparro Prieto, and Abrojo. The mealy drupe is edible but not tasty. It is eaten by gray fox, raccoon, and various birds. The roots are used as a soap substitute and as a treatment for sores and wounds of domestic animals.

Common Jujube

Ziziphus jujuba Lam. [H]

Field Identification. Tree to 50 ft, with a diameter of 10 in. The short trunk supports slender ascending branches forming a rounded head.

Flowers. Borne March–May in the axils of the leaves, solitary or a few together on glabrous pedicels ¹⁄₁₆–³⁄₁₆ in. long; flowers perfect,

¹⁄₁₆–⅛ in. across, yellowish green; calyx campanulate, spreading, 5-lobed, lobes ovate-triangular, acute, keeled within; petals 5, hooded, clawed, ¹⁄₂₅–¹⁄₁₂ in. long, much smaller than the sepals and alternating with them; stamens 5, as long as the petals or shorter and opposite to them; ovary 2–4-loculed, style 2-parted.

Fruit. Ripe July–November, slender-pediceled, drupe very variable in size and shape, subglobose to oblong, ½–1 in. long, green at first, turning yellowish, reddish brown, or black at maturity, pulp yellow, sweet, shriveling later, acidulous; 1–3-celled; seeds usually 2, deeply furrowed, oblong, reddish brown to gray, apices pointed, about ¾ in. long.

Leaves. Alternate on short thickened spurlike twigs, often somewhat fascicled, ovate to oblong or lanceolate; apex obtuse; base rounded or broadly cuneate, sometimes inequilateral; margin shallowly toothed, some teeth minutely mucronulate; distinctly 3-nerved at base; upper surface dark waxy green and glabrous; lower surface paler and the 3 nerves more conspicuous, glabrous to pubescent, stipules spinescent.

Twigs. Stout, green to gray or black, some nodes thickened, lateral branchlets thickened and leaves often fascicled on them. Spine-like stipules ⅛–¾ in. long, straight or curved.

Bark. Mottled gray or black, smooth on younger branches, on older branches and trunks roughly furrowed and peeling in loose shaggy strips.

Range. Grows on most soils, except very heavy clays or swampy ground. Considered to be a native of Syria. Widely distributed in the warmer parts of Europe, south Asia, Africa, and Australia. Cultivated in North America in Florida, California, and the Gulf Coast states. First introduced into America from Europe by Robert Chisholm in 1837 and planted in Beaufort, North Carolina.

Remarks. The genus name, *Ziziphus*, is from an ancient Greek name derived from the Persian *zizafun*. The species name, *jujuba*, is the French common name, derived from the Arabic. The tree is also known as the Chinese Date. It is popular with the Chinese and as many as 400 varieties have been cultivated by them. The fruit exhibits great variety in shape, size, and color, sometimes becoming as large as a hen egg. It is processed with sugar and honey and is sold in Chinese shops.

In India the wood is used for fuel and small timber, and the leaves for cattle fodder and as food for the Tasar silkworm and lac insect. In Europe it has long been used as a table dessert and dry winter sweetmeat. The Common Jujube has also been used in shelter-belt planting and for wildlife food. *Z. jujuba* var. *inermis* is a thornless variety.

Humboldt Coyotillo

Karwinskia humboldtiana (R. & S.) Zucc. [H]

Field Identification. Shrub or small tree attaining a height of 24 ft.

Flowers. In axillary, sessile or short-pedunculate, few-flowered cymes ⅓–½ in. long, persistent, perfect; petals 5, hooded, clawed; calyx of 5 sepals, glabrous, about ⅛ in. broad, sepals triangular, acute, keeled within; stamens 5, inserted on the edge of a disk, longer than the petals, filaments subulate; styles united except at apex, stigmas obtuse, ovary immersed by the disk and 2–3-celled.

Fruit. In October, peduncle one-third to one-half as long as the drupe, subglobose, brown to black at maturity, apiculate, ¼–⅜ in. long; stone solitary, ovoid, smooth, grooved on one side, about ¼ in. long, poisonous.

Leaves. Opposite or nearly so, ovate, elliptic or oblong; apex acute, obtuse or mucronate; base cuneate or rounded, ¾–1¾ in. long, ½–¾ in. wide, margin entire or undulate, dark lustrous green above, firm, glabrous or puberulent, paler beneath, conspic-uously pinnate-veined and marked with black spots and longitudi-nal marking on veins and young twigs; petioles slender, 1–3 in.

Twigs. Gray to reddish brown, smooth, glabrous or puberulent; lenticels abundant, white, oval to oblong.

Bark. Gray, smooth, tight.

Wood. Hard, strong, tough, but of no commercial value.

Range. Dry plains and prairies in the western and southwestern parts of Texas. Abundant near the mouth of the Pecos River and near the mouth of the Rio Grande in Cameron County. In Mexico in the states of Tamaulipas, Veracruz, Yucatán, Oaxaca, and Baja California, and south into Central America.

Remarks. The genus name, *Karwinskia*, is in honor of Wilhelm Friedrich von Karwinski, a Bavarian botanist, who collected plants in Mexico in 1826. The species name, *humboldtiana*, honors Alexander von Humboldt (1769–1859), a Prussian naturalist who explored South America and Mexico, 1799–1804.

In Mexico this plant is known under many local names, such as Tullidora, Capulincillo, Capulincillo Cimarrón, Capulín, Palo Negrito, Margarita, Cacachila, China, Cacohila Silvestre, Frutillo Negrito, Cochila, and Margarita del Cero. The oily seeds are poisonous and when eaten cause paralysis in the limbs of human beings and domestic animals. It is reported that a decoction of the leaves and roots is less poisonous and is used locally in Mexico for fevers. The plant is easily propagated by root divisions.

Carolina Buckthorn

Rhamnus caroliniana Walt. [H]

Field Identification. Shrub or small tree attaining a height of 35 ft, with a diameter of 8 in.

Flowers. May–June, borne solitary or 2–10 in peduncled umbels, peduncles to 2/5 in. long or often absent, pedicels 1/8–1/4 in.; flowers perfect, small, greenish yellow; petals 5, each about 1/25 in. long or broad, apex broad and notched, base acute, concave; stamens 5, included, anthers and filaments less than 1/25 in. long; style equaling the calyx tube, stigma 3-lobed, ovary glabrous and 3-celled; calyx tube campanulate, about 1/12 in. long, 1/8 in. wide at apex, the 5 sepals glabrous and triangular, apices acuminate.

Fruit. Drupes August–October, persistent, sweet, spherical, 1/3–2/5 in. in diameter, red at first, at maturity black and lustrous, 3-seeded (occasionally 2–4-seeded); seeds 1/5–1/4 in. long, reddish brown, rounded almost equally at apex and base, rounded dorsally, inner side with a triangular ridge from the apex to notch at base.

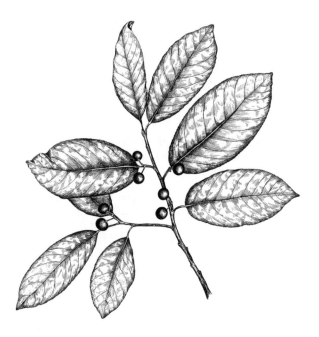

Leaves. Abundant, scattered along the branches, simple, alternate, deciduous, elliptic to broadly oblong, apex acute or acuminate, base cuneate to acute or rounded, sometimes inequilateral, margin indistinctly serrulate or subentire, rather thin, prominently parallel-veined; upper surface bright green, smooth and lustrous, pubescent to glabrous; lower surface velvety pubescent to only puberulent or glabrous, length of blade 2–6 in., width 1–2 in., turning yellow in the fall; petiole slender, ⅖–⅗ in., widened at base, glabrous or pubescent.

Twigs. Slender, young ones green to reddish, later gray; pubescent at first, glabrous later; sometimes terminating in a cluster of very small folded leaves.

Bark. Gray to brown, sometimes blotched, smoothish, furrows shallow.

Wood. Light brown, sapwood yellow, close-grained, fairly hard, rather weak, weighing 34 lb per cu ft.

Range. Most often in low grounds in eastern, central, and western Texas as far west as the Pecos River, Arkansas, Oklahoma, and

Louisiana; eastward to Florida, northward to North Carolina, and west to Missouri.

Remarks. The genus name, *Rhamnus*, is from an ancient Greek word. The species name, *caroliniana*, refers to the state of South Carolina where it grows. Other vernacular names are Yellow Buckthorn, Indian-cherry, Bog-birch, Alder-leaf Buckthorn, and Polecat-tree. The fruit is eaten by several species of birds, especially the catbird. The shrub appears susceptible to the crown rust of oats. The handsome leaves and fruit make the tree a good ornamental possibility. It is apparently adjustable to both moderately acid and alkaline soil types.

Smith Buckthorn

Rhamnus smithii Greene [H]

Field Identification. An upright, rounded, densely leafy shrub 3–15 ft.

Flowers. Dioecious, small, greenish, maturing April–May, solitary or in 2–3-flowered umbels in the axils of the leaves; petals 4 (sometimes absent), about ⅕₅ in. long, borne on the margin of a disk, deeply notched; stamens 4, inserted on the disk margin; ovary almost free, sometimes abortive, 2–4-celled, style small and short, stigma 2-parted; calyx campanulate, ⅕₅–⅟₁₂ in. long with 4 sepals; pedicels ⅟₁₂–⅕ in. long.

Fruit. Maturing June–August, drupe ¼–⅓ in. long, slightly longer than broad, black, subglobose, dry, dehiscent by a longitudinal slit; nutlets usually 2, apex rounded, base narrowed, surface finely reticulate, exterior with a groove about ⅕₅ in. wide.

Leaves. Appearing with the flowers from mixed buds, deciduous, opposite, alternate or fascicled, usually less than 1¼ in. long (rarely to 2¾ in.), elliptic to oblong or ovate to lanceolate, apex obtuse to acute, base rounded to cuneate or obtuse, margin serrulate to crenulate with glandular teeth, firm and thickish, surfaces pubescent with straight hairs or later glabrous, lower surface paler and green to yellowish green; petioles pubescent, ⅛–⅖ in.

Twigs. Slender, yellowish to gray or brown, younger ones pubescent, older ones smooth and glabrous, often lustrous; bud scales membranaceous, light brown, about ¼ in. long or less, margins fimbriate, apex obtuse, base truncate.

Range. Open hillsides, high mountain canyons, stream banks, at altitudes of 5,000–7,500 ft. In Trans-Pecos Texas in the Chisos and Davis mountains. In New Mexico in the Guadalupe, Sierra Blanca, and Sacramento mountains. Also in southern and western Colorado.

Remarks. The genus name, *Rhamnus*, is the ancient Greek name. The species name, *smithii*, is for B. H. Smith, who collected it at Pagosa Springs, Colorado. Smith Buckthorn was first introduced into cultivation in 1905. It is susceptible to crown rust of oats.

The plant is listed by some authors under the synonymous name of *R. fasciculata* Greene. However, others accept this name only in a varietal category as the Clustered Smith Buckthorn, *R. smithii* var. *fasciculata* (Greene) C. B. Wolf. The following key separates the species and variety in some instances: blades 1¼–2¾ in. long, apex acute, surface glabrous, green beneath, margin crenate indicate *R. smithii*; blades 1–1⅞ in. long, apex obtuse; surfaces pubescent, yellowish brown beneath, margin serrate are characteristic of *R. smithii* var. *fasciculata*.

Since the above variety occurs in the same ranges as the species and since intermediate forms connect the two, the segregation is sometimes dubious. *R. smithii* is also closely related to *R. lanceolata* Pursh, and further study may prove it to be a xerophytic variation of it.

Birch-leaf Buckthorn

Rhamnus betulaefolia Greene [H]

Field Identification. Upright rounded shrub, or sometimes a small tree to 20 ft, often branched near the base.

Flowers. In June, borne after the leaves appear, in peduncled, pubescent, axillary umbels; peduncles ⅙–1⅕ in. long, pedicels to ⅖ in. long, both elongate in fruit; petals 4–5 (or sometimes absent), small, greenish, about 1/25 in. long, notched, base narrowed, inserted on the disk; stamens 4–5, inserted on the edge of the disk, filaments about 1/25 in. long; ovary essentially superior, 2–3-celled, style equaling the calyx tube, stigma 2–3-lobed; calyx tube funnelform, about ⅛ in. long, lobes 5, triangular.

Fruit. Maturing July–October, drupe subglobose or somewhat depressed, about ⅓ in. in diameter, apex rounded, base narrowed, inner side with a triangular ridge, black to dark purple, glabrous and lustrous, flesh dry, 3-seeded; seeds dorsally rounded, plane on the 2 inner surfaces, peduncles ⅛–⅓ in. long, pubescent.

Leaves. Simple, alternate, deciduous, elliptic to oblong, apex rounded to obtuse or acute, base rounded or broadly cuneate, margins serrulate to subcrenate or, rarely, entire, blades 2–6 in. long, 1–1½ in. wide, rather thin, upper surface bright green, glabrous, and lustrous, lower surface paler and pubescent or glabrate, veins pinnately 10–11 pairs; petioles slender, pubescent, ⅕–⅖ in. long.

Twigs. Rather leafy, sometimes with embryonic leaves at the apex, young twigs pubescent and green to reddish, older ones and trunk gray to dark and glabrous.

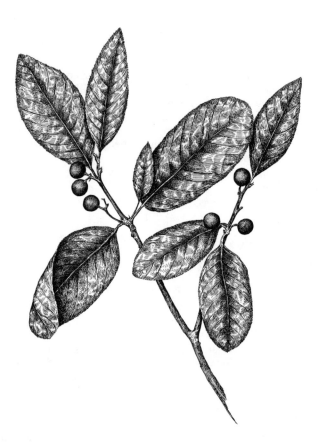

Range. Usually in moist canyons at altitudes of 4,000–7,500 ft. In Trans-Pecos Texas, New Mexico, and Arizona; north to Utah and Nevada; southward to Mexico in Sonora, Chihuahua, Durango, Tamaulipas, and Nuevo León.

Remarks. The genus name, *Rhamnus*, is the ancient Greek name, and the species name, *betulaefolia*, refers to the birchlike leaves. The young foliage is browsed by mule deer, and the seeds are eaten by a number of species of birds. The seed averages about 4,000 seeds per lb. They may be sown in fall or stratified for spring planting, or the plant reproduced by cuttings or grafts. Birch-leaf Buckthorn is closely related to the more northerly species, Cascara Buckthorn, *R. purshiana* DC., from which the drug cascara sagrada is obtained.

Obovate-leaf Buckthorn, *R. betulaefolia* var. *obovata* Kearney & Peebles, is a variety with obovate leaves and occurs in northern Arizona, Utah, and Nevada.

LINDEN FAMILY (Tiliaceae)

Carolina Linden

Tilia caroliniana Mill. [H]

Field Identification. Large tree with an irregular, rounded top.

Flowers. Borne on slender peduncles, pubescent, in 8–15-flowered cymes and subtended by conspicuous papery bracts; bracts linear, elliptic to obovate, cuneate at the base, rounded or acute at apex, somewhat pubescent at first, becoming glabrous later, 4–5 in. long, about ⅘ in. wide, decurrent or almost so to the peduncle

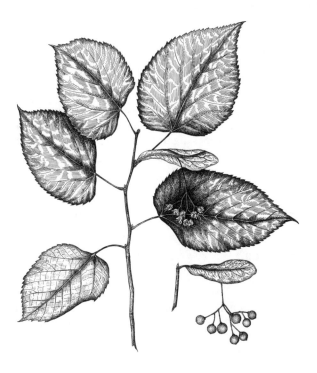

base; sepals 5, shorter than petals, ovate, acuminate, ciliate, brown-pubescent on the exterior, white-hairy within; petals 5, lanceolate, acuminate, somewhat longer than sepals; stamens many, with filaments forked at apex; staminodia about as long as sepals; ovary superior, 5-celled, with a slender style and 5-lobed stigma.

Fruit. Nutlet subglobose to ellipsoid, apiculate, tomentose, or pubescent, rather small, about ⅛ in. in diameter, 1–3-seeded.

Leaves. Alternate, simple, deciduous, blades 2⅓–4½ in. long, 1¾–3½ in. wide, broadly ovate, abruptly acuminate, base truncate or cordate and asymmetrical; margin coarsely dentate with glandular apiculate teeth; upper surface dark green, lustrous and glabrous at maturity, lower surface thinly tomentose with brownish fascicled hairs; leaves tomentose on both sides when young; petioles stout, glabrous or slightly pubescent, 1–1½ in.

Twigs. Slender, reddish brown, pubescent at first, glabrous later.

Bark. Gray, with shallow fissures and flat ridges.

Wood. Light-colored, soft, light, easily worked.

Range. Central and eastern Texas, southwestern Arkansas, and western Louisiana; eastward to Georgia and Florida, and north to North Carolina.

Remarks. The genus name, *Tilia*, is the classical name, and the species name, *caroliniana*, refers to the states of Carolina. Vernacular names are Basswood, Lime-tree, Whitewood, and Bee Basswood. The tree is a rapid grower and is often planted for ornament. The flowers make good honey, and the wood is used with other species for making interior finishing and woodenware.

MALLOW FAMILY (Malvaceae)

Shrub-althea

Hibiscus syriacus L. [H]

Field Identification. Much-branched shrub or small tree 3–18 ft. Often grown for ornament and developed into a large number of horticultural forms with single and double, variously colored flowers.

Flowers. Showy, perfect, solitary, axillary, on peduncles of variable length; bractlets subtending the calyx usually 5–7, ⅜–¾ in. long, linear to linear-spatulate; calyx longer or shorter than the bractlets; sepals 5, triangular ovate or lanceolate, about as long as the tube; petals 5, very variable in color in the many horticultural forms, white, pink, lavender, rose, with a crimson or purplish blotch at the base, 1¾–3 in. long, rounded to obovate, margins sometimes undulate; staminal column prominent with numerous anthers below, and apex 5-parted with capitate stigmas; ovary sessile, 5-celled, and loculicidally 5-valved.

Fruit. Capsule oblong-ovoid, apex drawn tightly, ¾-1 in. long, pubescent, more or less dry, larger than the calyx.

Leaves. Alternate, triangular to rhombic-ovate or elliptic to oval, blades 1½–4¾ in. long, margin variously crenate-toothed or notched with rounded or acutish teeth, usually more or less 3-lobed also; young leaves pubescent, when older becoming glabrous or nearly so; palmately veined with 3 veins more conspicuous; petioles generally shorter than the blades; winter buds minute. Some forms with variegated leaves are known.

Bark. Gray to brown, somewhat roughened.

Range. Cultivated in gardens and occasionally escaping to roadsides, thickets, and woods. Texas, Oklahoma, Arkansas, and Louisiana; eastward to Florida and northward to Missouri, Ohio, and Massachusetts. Also in coastal regions of Canada.

Remarks. The genus name, *Hibiscus*, is the ancient name of the European Marsh-mallow, and the species name, *syriacus*, is for Syria, where it was once supposed to be native. However, more recent investigations prove it to be originally from China and India. It is also known under the vernacular names of Rose-of-Sharon and Rose-mallow. It was introduced into cultivation about 1600.

CHOCOLATE FAMILY (Sterculiaceae)

Chinese Parasol-tree

Firmiana simplex W. F. Wight [H]

Field Identification. Cultivated shrub or tree to 35 ft, with a smooth green bark and a rounded crown.

Flowers. In a pubescent, terminal panicle 4–12 in. long; flowers monoecious, small, greenish yellow; petals absent; calyx petal-like, sepals 5, valvate, colored, linear to narrowly oblong, reflexed, ⅓–⅖ in. long; stamens united in a column, bearing a head of 10–15 sessile anthers; carpels 5, nearly distinct above, each terminating into a peltate stigma, carpels 2¼–4 in. long at maturity.

Fruit. A follicle, stipitate, leathery, carpels veiny, finely pubescent, distinct before maturity and spreading open into 5 leaflike bodies bearing 2–several seeds on their margins; seeds globular, pealike, about ¼ in. or less in diameter, albuminous; carpels rudimentary and free in the staminate flowers. A peculiar feature is the black or brown fluid that covers the fruit and is liberated when the follicle bursts.

Leaves. Alternate, simple, blades 4–12 in. broad and long, cordate to orbicular, palmately 3–5-lobed, lobes entire and acuminate, dull green and glabrous or lightly pubescent above, lower surface glabrous to tomentulose; petiole glabrous or pubescent, usually 5–18 in. long.

Twigs. Stout, smooth, grayish green, bark of trunk also smooth and green.

Range. A native of Japan and China. Cultivated in the United States and escaping to roadsides, woods, and thickets. From South Carolina to Florida and westward to Texas and California. Hardy as far north as Washington.

Remarks. The genus name, *Firmiana*, honors Karl Joseph von Firmian (1718–1782), at one time governor of Lombardy. The species name, *simplex*, refers to the lobed but simple leaves. It is also known as Varnish-tree, Phoenix-tree, and Bottle-tree. It is an excellent tree for lawn and shade and has been cultivated since 1757, being easily grown from seed.

A variety with creamy white, variegated leaves is known as *F. simplex* var. *variegata*. Two other species are cultivated in California.

TAMARISK FAMILY (Tamaricaceae)

French Tamarisk

Tamarix gallica L. [H]

Field Identification. Shrub with contorted branches, or a tree to 30 ft, with a twisted trunk.

Flowers. Borne in summer on the current wood, in white or pink racemes, which are grouped to form terminal panicles of variable length; pedicels about $\frac{1}{50}$ in. long; sepals 5, $\frac{1}{25}-\frac{1}{12}$ in. long, ovate; corolla petals 5, $\frac{1}{25}-\frac{1}{12}$ in. long, oblong, mostly deciduous from the mature fruit; stamens 5, filaments $\frac{1}{12}-\frac{1}{10}$ in., enlarged toward the base and attached to the corners of the 5-angled disk, anthers mucronate, 2-celled; ovary $\frac{1}{25}-\frac{1}{15}$ in. long, set on the disk; styles 3, about $\frac{1}{50}$ in. long, clavate.

Fruit. Capsule very small, $\frac{1}{12}-\frac{1}{8}$ in. long, dehiscing into 3 parts; seeds numerous, minute, tufted with hairs at apex.

Leaves. Foliage sparse, delicate, grayish green, scalelike, alternate, imbricate, $\frac{1}{50}-\frac{1}{8}$ in. long, deltoid to lanceolate, acute to acuminate, entire, and scarious, glabrous; bracts $\frac{1}{25}-\frac{1}{15}$ in. long.

Branches. Drooping and graceful, often sweeping the ground, young ones glabrous or glaucous, reddish to gray later.

Wood. Light-colored, close-grained, takes a high polish, often twisted or knotty.

Range. French Tamarisk was introduced to the United States from Europe. It now grows as an escape from cultivation from Texas eastward to Florida, westward to California, and north to Arkansas and South Carolina.

Remarks. The genus name, *Tamarix*, is the ancient name, probably with reference to the Tamaracine people of southern Europe, where the plant grew. The species name, *gallica*, refers to a Gallic tribe that lived where the plant grew. Other names are Salt-

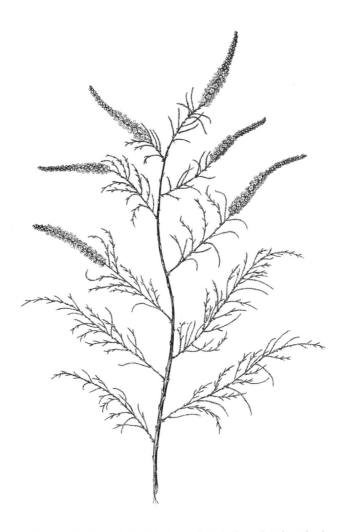

cedar, Manna-bush, Athel, Eshel, Asul, Athul, and Atle. The low-sweeping branches make excellent wildlife cover.

It is widely cultivated for ornament, erosion control, and wind-breaks in Texas and the Southwest generally. Preferring moist soil and an open sunny situation, it has adjusted to the Gulf Coast prairie areas because it has a high tolerance for saline or alkaline sites. It apparently does well in the coastal brackish, sandy marshes. It can be propagated readily from cuttings taken in early winter from hardwood of the previous summer.

African Tamarisk

Five-stamen Tamarisk

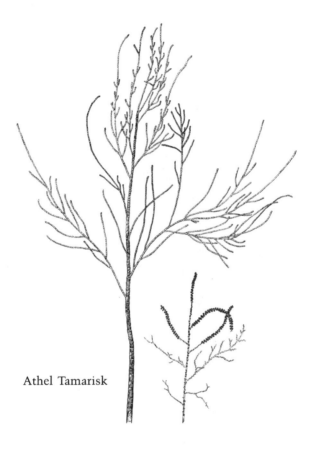

Athel Tamarisk

African Tamarisk, *T. africana* Poir., has black to dark purple bark, sessile leaves, and flowers borne in racemes 1¼–2¾ in. long; ¼–⅓ in. broad, smaller on green branches of the current year; bracts longer than pedicels. Flowers pentamerous; sepals subentire; the outer 2 slightly keeled and longer than the inner more obtuse ones; petals 5, ovate to broadly trulliform-ovate, about 1/12–⅛ in. long in vernal flowers, ⅛ in. long or more in aestival; staminal filaments inserted on gradually tapering lobes of disk. A native of the European and Mediterranean region. Grown in California, Arizona, Texas, and South Carolina.

Five-stamen Tamarisk, *T. pentandra* Pallas, is a shrub or small tree 10–15 ft high. The branches are long, slender, and plumose, the shoots purplish when young. The largest leaves 1/12–⅛ in. long, lanceolate, others very small, scalelike, crowded, rather

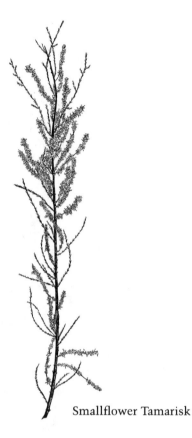

Smallflower Tamarisk

glaucous. Flowers rosy pink, usually borne August–September, about ⅛ in. wide, in cylindrical racemes 1–2 in. long; the current season's shoots transformed into slender panicles; bearing 5 stamens. A native of southeastern Europe. First cultivated in 1880 and is late flowering. It may be pruned back hard in the winter. Also listed as *T. pallasii*.

Athel Tamarisk, *T. aphylla* Karst., may be either a bush or tree to 25 ft high. The branches are fastigiate, long, slender, cylindrical-jointed. Leaves reduced to a very short sheath, minutely glandular-pitted and salt-secreting with a minute point. Flowers borne in July on more or less interrupted spikes, bisexual, nearly sessile, pink in color, about ⅛ in. broad. Also listed under the names of *T. articulata* or *T. orientalis*. A native of India and

Africa. Extensively cultivated in coastal Texas, Arizona, and California.

Smallflower Tamarisk, *T. parviflora* DC., has brown to deep purple bark and may be a shrub or small tree 12–18 ft high. Branches slender and dark purple. Leaves sessile, ovate, scalelike with hard points. Flowers April–May, pale pink in slender racemes about 1 in. long and ⅛–⅕ in. broad, often on the preceding year's branches; bracts diaphanous, longer than pedicels; sepals eroded-denticulate, the outer 2 trulliform or ovate, acute and keeled, the inner 2 ovate and obtuse; petals usually 4, parabolic or ovate, about 1/12 in. long; stamens 4 or sometimes more, emerging gradually from the disk lobes. A native of southeastern Europe. First cultivated in 1853. Introduced and widely cultivated in the United States.

CACTUS FAMILY (Cactaceae)

Lindheimer Prickly Pear

Opuntia lindheimeri Engelm. [H]

Field Identification. A heavy-bodied, thicket-forming cactus, with a definite cylindrical trunk, erect, or much lower and prostrate. Attaining a height of 3–12 ft.

Flowers. April–June, numerous, shallowly bowl shaped, usually 1 to an areole; sepals and petals numerous, intergrading, hardly distinct, yellow to orange or red, a plant usually producing only 1 shade of flowers, oval to obovate or spatulate, apices rounded or abruptly short-pointed, length ½–2½ in.; stamens numerous, much shorter than the petals; ovary inferior, 1-celled, ovules numerous on thick, fleshy stalks, placentas parietal, withered perianth crowning the ovary and later crowning the fruit; style longer than the stamens, single, thick, stigma lobes short.

Fruit. Ripening July–September, berry very variable in size and shape, clavate to oblong or globose, length ½–2½ in., red to purple, with scattered tufts of glochids; skin thin, rind thick, pulp juicy; seeds very numerous, about ⅛ in. long, flattened, curved, with a thick bony aril on the edge.

Leaves. Very small, ⅛–⅙ in. long, pointed, flattened, early deciduous.

Joints. Green to bluish green, orbicular or obovate, or sometimes asymmetrical, length to 11 in., flat, waxy, succulent; set with areoles 1–2⅓ in. apart, which produce dense tufts of yellow to brown barbed, minute glochids less than ³⁄₁₆ in. long; larger spines 1–6, usually 1–2, one erect or semierect, the others generally smaller and somewhat spreading, color of spines pale yellow to almost white, sometimes brown or black at base; some joints spineless or nearly so. Some forms are known that lack spines.

Range. From coastal southwestern Louisiana westward in drier regions of central Texas (not in east Texas woodlands). The type specimen was collected at New Braunfels. It is common around San Antonio, Corpus Christi, and Brownsville. It is not to be confused with *O. engelmannii* of Trans-Pecos Texas.

Remarks. The genus name, *Opuntia*, is the Latinized name for the town Opus in ancient Greece. The species name, *lindheimeri*, is in honor of Ferdinand Lindheimer, a German-born botanist, who collected extensively in Texas in 1836 and 1842.

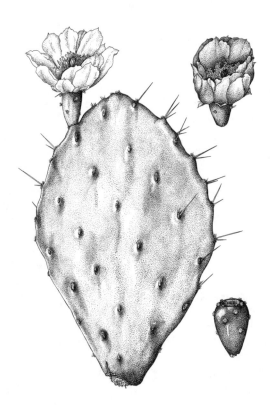

Spineless form

Opuntias are propagated easily by the joints. The joint is ex-posed to the sun a few days to callous the raw end, then laid flat on the surface of the ground. Roots develop from the lower side.

The plant and its relatives are known under many names in Latin-American countries, such as Nochtli, Culhua, Cancanopa, Pacal, Potzotz, Toat, Pare, Caha, Xantha, and more commonly Nopal. The fruit is known as *tuna*.

The Indians and Mexican people formerly used the plant exten-sively for food. The fruits may be eaten raw or made into a pre-serve. The joints, when young and tender, are cooked and served with dressing and pepper and are also made into candy. Syrup is made by boiling the ripe fruit and straining off the seed. The boiled and fermented juice is known as *colonche*. A thick paste made by boiling down the juice is known as *melcocha. Queso de tuna* (tuna cheese) is prepared from a pulp of the fruit seed. After evaporation, it is made into small cheeselike pieces. The Indians also believe that a tea made from the fruit will cure ailments caused by gallstones. Commercial alcohol has been made from the sap. The tender young joints are sometimes used as poultices to reduce inflammation. Juice of the joints is boiled with tallow in candlemaking to make the candles hard. The joints are made edible to cattle by burning off the spines. A number of animals and birds feed on the fruit. According to folklore, the coyote brushes the spines off the fruit with his tail before eating it.

The Nopal occupies a prominent place in the history and legend of Mexico. The Nopal and Caracara (Mexican Eagle) are the national emblems of Mexico. About 33 species of *Opuntia* are known in Texas, and about 250 species are found mostly in the southwestern United States, Mexico, and Central and South America.

LOOSESTRIFE FAMILY (Lythraceae)

Common Crapemyrtle

Lagerstroemia indica L. [H]

Field Identification. Commonly cultivated shrub or small tree to 35 ft, with a very smooth, fluted trunk.

Flowers. In showy, terminal panicles 2½–8 in. long, pedicels and peduncles bracted; corolla 1–1½ in. across; petals 5–7, but usually 6, purple, pink, white, red, lavender, or blue; stamens numerous, elongate, some upcurved; calyx of 5–8 sepals, shorter than the hypanthium; ovary 3–6-celled, style long and curved, stigma capitate.

Fruit. Capsule oval-globose, about ⅓ in. long; seeds with a winged apex.

Leaves. Opposite or alternate, deciduous, obovate-oval, entire, acute or obtuse, broad-cuneate or rounded at base, blades ½–2 in. long, subsessile, glabrous and lustrous above, paler and glabrous or pilose along veins beneath.

Twigs. Pale, glabrous, 4-angled.

Bark. Thin, exfoliating to expose a smooth, often convoluted, pale surface.

Range. A native of India. Cultivated extensively in Texas, Louisiana, Oklahoma, and Arkansas; eastward to Florida, and northward to Virginia. Also cultivated in California.

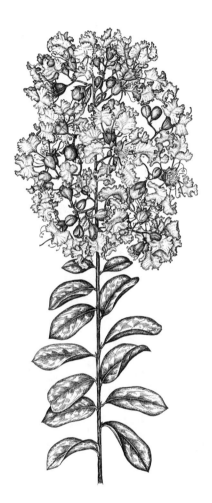

Remarks. The genus name, *Lagerstroemia*, is in honor of Magnus Lagerstroem (1696–1759), a Swedish friend of Linnaeus, and the species name, *indica*, is for India. Another vernacular name is Ladies' Streamer.

Some of the common color forms of crapemyrtle are Dwarf (*nana*), Dwarf Blue (*lavandula*), Pink, Purple (*purpurea*), Red (*magenta rubra*), and White (*alba*).

POMEGRANATE FAMILY (Punicaceae)

Pomegranate

Punica granatum L. [H]

Field Identification. Cultivated, clumped shrub or tree to 25 ft. The branches erect or ascending to form an irregularly shaped crown.

Flowers. In simple, axillary or terminal racemes with 1–5 solitary short-peduncled flowers; flowers to 2 in. across, perfect, perigy-

nous, showy, usually red (occasionally white or pink); calyx tubular to campanulate, later subglobose, persistent; 5–7-lobed; lobes valvate, ascending, fleshy, triangular to lanceolate, apex acute, stiffly persistent in fruit; petals 5–7, inserted on the upper part of the calyx between the lobes, imbricate, wrinkled, ⅝–1 in. long, suborbicular or obovate; stamens numerous, in several series, filaments filiform; style 1, stigma capitate; ovary inferior, embedded in the calyx tube, comprising several compartments in 2 series, ovules numerous.

Fruit. Berry maturing in September, pendulous, 2–4 in. in diameter, subglobose or depressed, crowned with the persistent calyx; rind thick, leathery, reddish yellow; pulp juicy, pink or red, acidulous; septa membranous, many-celled; seeds numerous, cotyledons convolute and auricled at base.

Leaves. Simple, deciduous, alternate, opposite or clustered, blades ¾–3½ in. long, oval or oblong or elliptic to lanceolate, apex obtuse or acute, base attenuate into a short wing, margin entire, surface bright green; main vein prominent below, impressed above, other veins inconspicuous, glabrous on both surfaces; petiole ⅛–⅓ in., grooved above, green to red; winter buds with 2 pairs of outer scales.

Twigs. Slender; younger ones green to reddish brown, somewhat striate or angular; older ones gray and more terete. Bark on older limbs and trunks gray to brown, smooth at first but eventually breaking into small, thin scales, shallowly reticulate.

Wood. White to yellowish, hard, close-grained, specific gravity about 0.93.

Range. Old fields, waste places, and abandoned homesites. A native of Arabia, Iran, Bengal, China, and Japan. Hardy in the United States as far north as Washington, D.C., but does best in subtropical southern regions. Escaping cultivation in the Gulf Coast states.

Remarks. The genus name, *Punica*, is from the Latin words for "Punic apple," and the species name, *granatum*, means "many-seeded apple." Known in the countries of Central and South America under the Spanish and Indian names of Granada de China, Granada Agria, Granado, Granada, Tzapyan, Yaga-zehi, and Yutnudidzi. The wood is sometimes used by engravers as a substitute for Boxwood (*Buxus*). The following varieties and forms are cultivated: Double Pomegranate, *P. granatum* forma *pleniflora* Hayne, has double scarlet flowers; Pale Pomegranate, *P. granatum* forma *albescens* DC., is a white-flowered form; Legrelle Pomegranate, *P. granatum* forma *legrellei* Vanh., is a form with double-striped red and yellowish white flowers; Yellow Pomegranate, *P. granatum* var. *flavescens* Sweet, is a yellow-flowered variety; and Dwarf Pomegranate, *P. granatum* var. *nana* (L.) Pers., is a low variety with smaller linear-lanceolate leaves and smaller flowers and fruit.

From the days of Solomon pomegranate has been used for making cooling drinks and sherbets; it is also eaten in its natural state. The astringent rind yields a black or red dye and has been used for tanning morocco leather and for ink. The fruit is sweet in the better varieties, and a spiced wine is made from the juice. The soft seeds are also eaten, sprinkled with sugar, or when dried, as a confection.

DOGWOOD FAMILY (Cornaceae)

Rough-leaf Dogwood

Cornus drummondii C. A. Meyer [H]

Field Identification. Irregularly branched shrub or small spreading tree.

Flowers. May–August, perfect, yellowish white, borne in terminal, spreading, long-peduncled cymes 1–3 in. across; peduncles 1-2 in. long, pubescent; individual pedicels ⅛–¾ in. long, branched, glabrous or pubescent; corolla ⅛–³⁄₁₆ in. across, short-tubular; petals 4, spreading, oblong-lanceolate, acute; calyx teeth 4, minute, much shorter than the hypanthium; stamens 4, exserted, filaments slender, white, longer than the pistil; style simple, slender, with a terminal somewhat capitate stigma; ovary inferior, 2-celled; annular ring viscid and reddish.

Fruit. Ripening August–October, drupe globular, about ¼ in. in diameter, white, style persistent, flesh thin; 1–2-seeded, seeds subglobose, slightly furrowed.

Leaves. Simple, opposite, deciduous, blades 1–5 in. long, ½–2½ in. broad, conspicuously veined, ovate to lanceolate or oblong to elliptic, apex acute or acuminate, base rounded or cuneate, margin entire, plane surface somewhat undulate; upper surface olive green and rather rough-pubescent; lower surface paler, pubescent, and veins prominent; petiole ⅕–¾ in. long, slender, rough-pubescent, green to reddish.

Twigs. Young ones green and pubescent, older ones reddish brown and glabrous.

Bark. On young branches and trunks rather smooth, pale gray to brown. On old trunks gray with narrow ridges and fissures, scales small.

Wood. Pale brown, with sapwood paler, heavy, hard, strong, durable, close-grained.

Range. Edges of thickets, streams, and fence rows. Central, southern, and eastern Texas, Oklahoma, Arkansas, and Louisiana; east to Alabama and northward to Ontario.

Remarks. The genus name, *Cornus*, is from *cornu* (a horn), in reference to the hard wood, and the species name, *drummondii*, is in honor of Thomas Drummond (1780–1835), a Scottish botanical explorer. Vernacular names are Cornel Dogwood, Small-flower Dogwood, and White Cornel. The word *dogwood* comes from the fact that a decoction of the bark of *C. sanguinea* was used in England to wash mangy dogs. Rough-leaf Dogwood was formerly listed by some authorities under the name of *C. asperifolia* Michx., but that name is no longer valid.

Rough-leaf Dogwood is sometimes used in shelter-belt planting in the prairie-plains region. It has been known in cultivation since 1836. The wood is used for small woodenware articles, especially shuttle blocks and charcoal. The fruit is known to be eaten by at least 40 species of birds, including bobwhite quail, wild turkey, and prairie chicken.

HEATH FAMILY (Ericaceae)

Texas Madrone

Arbutus texana Buckl. [H]

Field Identification. Tree hardly over 30 ft, and 1 ft in diameter, often only shrublike. Easily identified by the very smooth pink or white bark. The old bark scaling off in papery layers. Branches are usually crooked, stout, and spreading.

Flowers. February–March, borne in tomentose panicles about 2½ in. long; bracts scaly, ovate, acute, tomentose; calyx lobes 5, ovate, acute, scarious; corolla ovoid-urceolate, white or pink, 5-lobed; lobes obtuse, reflexed; stamens 10, filaments subulate, swollen and hairy at base; anthers short, compressed, 2-awned on the back, cell opening by a terminal pore; ovary 5-celled, granular, smooth or hairy, sessile or nearly so, disk 10-lobed; style simple with obscurely 5-lobed stigmas.

Fruit. Borne in clusters 2–3 in. long; body of fruit ¼–⅓ in. in diameter, subglobose, dark red to yellow, pubescent when young, waxy-granular, 5-celled; seeds numerous, white, small.

Leaves. Simple, alternate, persistent, mostly borne distally on twigs, blades 1–3 in. long, ⅔–1 in. wide, oblong to elliptic, ovate or oval, apex obtuse to rounded, base rounded or broadly cuneate; thick and leathery; upper surface dark green and glabrous; lower surface paler or glaucous, or somewhat pubescent, especially along the veins; venation inconspicuous, except the yellow mid-

vein; petioles stout, one-third to one-half as long as the leaf, green to reddish, pubescent to glabrous.

Bark. Very conspicuous, younger bark very smooth, pink or white. Older bark on lower parts of old trees generally dark brown to gray or black, breaking into rather small, short scales, but exfoliating in thin papery layers to expose the new bark.

Wood. Reddish brown, sapwood lighter, close-grained, hard, heavy, specific gravity about 0.75.

Range. On limestone or igneous hills and mountains. Central Texas, west Texas, and southeastern New Mexico. In Mexico in the states of Nuevo León, Chihuahua, Veracruz, Oaxaca, and Sinaloa; south into Guatemala.

Remarks. The genus name, *Arbutus*, is the classical name of a European species, and the species name, *texana*, refers to the state of Texas. Also known under the vernacular names of Texas Arbutus, Madroño, Naked Indian, Lady Legs, Manzanita, and Nuzu-ndu. The wood is used for tools, handles, rollers, fuel, and charcoal for gunpowder. The bark and leaves are astringent and are occasionally used medicinally in Mexico. The fruit is sweetish and is eaten by a number of species of birds. It is also browsed lightly by cattle and heavily by goats.

SAPODILLA FAMILY (Sapotaceae)

Woollybucket Bumelia

Bumelia lanuginosa (Michx.) Pers. [H]

Field Identification. Shrub or an irregularly shaped tree to 60 ft, with stiff, spinose branchlets.

Flowers. June–July, in small fascicles ¼–1½ in. across, pedicels hairy or subglabrous, ¹⁄₁₂–⅗ in. long; corolla white, petals 5, each 3-lobed, middle lobe longest, fragrant, ⅛–⅕ in. long, tube about ¹⁄₁₂ in. long; stamens 5, normal and fertile, also 5 sterile stamens (staminodia) that are deltoid-ovate, petaloid, and nearly equaling the corolla tube; ovary 5-celled, hairy, style 1; calyx 5-lobed, hairy or nearly glabrous, ¹⁄₁₂–⅛ in. long, lobes suborbicular or ovate.

Fruit. Berry September–October, borne on slender, drooping peduncles, subglobose or obovoid, ⅓–1 in. long, lustrous, black, fleshy; seed solitary, large, brown, rounded, scar small and nearly basal, ¼–½ in. long, no endosperm, cotyledons fleshy.

Leaves. Alternate or clustered, often on short lateral spurs, oblong-obovate, elliptic or wedge shaped, apex rounded or obtuse, base cuneate, margin entire, blade length 1–3 in., width ½–1 in., leathery, shiny green and smooth above, varying from rusty to white or gray-woolly beneath; petioles short, averaging about ½ in. long, tomentose.

Twigs. Gray to reddish brown, zigzag, slender, stiff, spinose, hairy at first with gray, white, or rusty tomentum.

Bark. Dark brown or grayish, fissured and reticulate into narrow ridges with thickened scales.

Wood. Yellow or brown, fairly hard, close-grained, weighing about 40 lb per cu ft.

Range. The species occurs in east Texas, Oklahoma, Arkansas, Louisiana, eastward to Florida, north to Kansas, Missouri, Illinois, and Virginia. In central and west Texas represented by its varieties.

Remarks. The genus name, *Bumelia*, is the ancient Greek name for the European Ash, and the species name, *lanuginosa*, refers to the woolly hairs of the leaf. Vernacular names are Woolly-buckthorn, Woolly Bumelia, Gum Elastic, Gum Bumelia, Chittamwood, False-buckthorn, and Blackhaw. The black fruit is edible, but not tasty, and produces stomach disturbances and

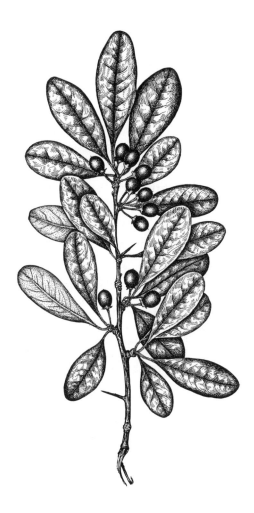

dizziness if eaten in quantity (at least this is the experience of the author). Birds are very fond of the fruit; in fact, they get it as soon as it is barely ripe. The wood is used in small quantities for tool handles and cabinetmaking. A gum is freely exuded from wounds on the trunk and branches. The tree has been in cultivation since 1806.

Some botanical authors have split *B. lanuginosa* into a number of varieties and forms according to color, density of hairs on the foliage, and flower parts.

One botanist believes that the most typical representatives of the species *lanuginosa* occur mostly east of the Mississippi River and have tawny or rufous hairs. Also, that the same species occurring west of the Mississippi River, and having gray or nearly white hairs, should be classified as the Oblong-leaf Woollybucket Bumelia, *B. lanuginosa* var. *oblongifolia* (Nutt.) Clark.

A variety with very long, silvery white hairs, which occurs from Oklahoma and east Texas to Nuevo León, Mexico, usually near the coast, is classified as Gum Woollybucket Bumelia, *B. lanuginosa* var. *albicans* Sarg.

A variety from central and west Texas, New Mexico, Arizona, and Mexico is classified as the Rigid Woollybucket Bumelia, *B. lanuginosa* var. *rigida* Gray. It has narrower leaves, ⅜–2 in. long, hairs gray or nearly white, occasionally tawny at first, the older leaves becoming less hairy, but the pedicels and sepals remaining hairy. The branches are quite rigid and spinescent, and the plant is usually less than 15 ft tall. When this variety becomes more glabrous on the leaves and flower parts it is classified by some authorities as Brazos Woollybucket Bumelia, *B. lanuginosa* var. *texana* Buckl., or by other authorities as a species under the name of *B. monticola* Buckl. Since the latter is more common in central and west Texas, southwestern Oklahoma, and adjacent Mexico than the Rigid Woollybucket Bumelia and seems to be more constant in its characters, it is described as a species by the author with the knowledge that it does have intergrades in certain localities.

Brazos Bumelia

Bumelia monticola Buckl. [H]

Field Identification. Spiniferous shrub, or small tree to 25 ft, with an irregular crown.

Flowers. May–June, pedicels ¼–½ in. long, hairy at first, glabrous later, flowers in fascicles; calyx green, hairy, lobes ovate, margin ciliate, shorter than corolla lobes; corolla short-campanulate, white; lobes 5, broad-ovate, rounded at apex, with a lanceolate appendage on each side at the base; stamens 5, filaments filiform, anthers sagittate; staminodia 5, petaloid, apex obtuse or rounded, margin erose or entire, longer than corolla lobes, style elongate, simple, stigmatic at apex.

Fruit. August–September, borne in fascicles on spurs ¼–⅓ in. long, black, oblong, obovoid or subglobose, apex rounded or apicu-

late; seed hardly over ⅜ in. long, oblong, smooth, obtuse or rounded at apices, straight or somewhat asymmetrical, light brown to white.

Leaves. Deciduous, fascicled on short spurs, blades 1–3 in. long, ⅓–1¼ in. wide, pubescent when young, glabrous at maturity, dark green, lustrous, slightly paler beneath, elliptic to oblong or spatulate, margin entire and barely revolute, apex obtuse, rounded or acute, base gradually narrowed, reticulate-veined; petiole ¼–½ in. long, slightly pubescent but glabrous later.

Twigs. Young twigs zigzag, reddish brown, smooth, the laterals often ending in stout, gray to reddish brown thorns; older twigs gray and smooth.

Bark. Gray, reddish brown beneath, broken into flat, narrow scales and shallow fissures.

Wood. Brown to yellowish, sapwood lighter, hard, moderately strong.

Range. In Texas mostly west of the Brazos River on the Edwards Plateau limestone hills. In Kerr, Kendall, Comal, Real, Uvalde, Palo Verde, Val Verde, Pecos, Brewster, Crockett, Callahan, Coleman, Shackleford, Terrell, and Brown counties. Also in Oklahoma. In Mexico in Coahuila.

Remarks. The genus name, *Bumelia*, is the ancient classical name for the ash tree. The species name, *monticola*, refers to its habitat of hilly or mountainous regions. Vernacular names used are Gum-elastic, Chittamwood, Mountain-gum, and Gum-buckthorn.

Some botanists have listed Brazos Bumelia under the names of *B. texana* Buckl., *B. lanuginosa* var. *texana* Buckl., or *B. riograndis* Lundell.

PERSIMMON FAMILY (Ebenaceae)

Common Persimmon

Diospyros virginiana L. [H]

Field Identification. Tree generally less than 40 ft, rarely reaching 70–100 ft. Habit of growth variable, usually disposed to an upright or drooping type with rounded or conical crown. Branches spreading or at right angles. Twigs self-pruning or some breaking with heavy fruit to form an irregularly shaped tree.

Flowers. April–June, staminate and pistillate on separate trees; pollen light and powdery, spread by wind and insects; staminate in 2–3-flowered cymes, tubular, ⅓–½ in. long, greenish yellow; stamens usually 16; pistillate solitary, sessile or short-peduncled, about ¾ in. long or less, stamens 8, some stamens abortive and some fertile; ovary 8-celled, styles 4, 2-lobed at apex; corolla fragrant, 4–5-lobed, greenish yellow, thick, lobes recurved.

Fruit. Berry persistent, variable as to season, locality, or individual tree, some early or some late (August–February). The very early or very late fruit generally smaller than fruit that ripens about when the leaves fall, seedless fruit also generally smaller; diameter generally ¾–1½ in., shape variable from subglobose or oblate to short-oblong; calyx thick, lobes ovate and recurved; color when

mature yellow to orange or dark red, often with a glaucous bloom, flesh pale and translucent, astringent and puckery to taste when green; when ripe somewhat softer and sweet with a high sugar content; 4–8-seeded, seeds large, oblong, flat, leathery, wrinkled, dark brown, about ½ in. long; some trees seedless.

Leaves. Deciduous, simple, alternate, entire, ovate-oblong to elliptic, apex acute or acuminate, base rounded, cuneate or subcordate, blade length 2–6 in., width 1–3 in., upper surface dark green and lustrous, lower surface paler and pubescent; petiole about 1 in. long or less, glabrous or pubescent.

Bark. Brown to black, fissures deep, ridges broken into rectangular checkered sections.

Wood. Dark brown to black, sapwood lighter, fine-grained, strong, hard.

Range. Thrives on almost any type of soil from sands to shales and mud bottomlands. Generally in the southeastern United States. Gulf states to Iowa and Connecticut. Seemingly the best zone is from Maryland, Virginia, and Carolinas westward through

Missouri and Arkansas. In Texas west to the valley of the Colorado River.

Remarks. The genus name, *Diospyros*, is translated "fruit of the gods," and the species name, *virginiana*, refers to the state of Virginia. Vernacular names are Jove's-fruit, Winter-plum, and Possum-wood. The fruit was known and appreciated by early settlers and explorers, being mentioned in writings of De Soto in 1539, Jan de Laet in 1558, and John Smith in the seventeenth century. The wood of Persimmon is used for handles and shoe lasts, but three-fourths of the supply is made into golf clubs and shuttles. Its hardness, smoothness, and even texture make it particularly desirable for these purposes. The tree is suitable for erosion control on deeper soils because of its deep root system, but this same characteristic makes it difficult to transplant. Also, the rapid spread of a new leaf-wilt disease introduces a factor of caution before extensive plantings are made.

The fruit is eaten by at least 16 species of birds, also by the skunk, raccoon, opossum, gray and fox squirrel, and white-tailed deer. Having a high carbohydrate content, fallen fruit is also useful in providing some forage for hogs. The bark is known to have astringent medicinal properties.

Texas Persimmon

Diospyros texana Scheele [H]

Field Identification. An intricately branched, smooth-barked shrub or tree up to 40 ft.

Flowers. Dioecious, small, solitary or in few-flowered clusters; corolla urn shaped, greenish white, pubescent, about ⅓ in. long; lobes 5, spreading, suborbicular, often notched at apex; stamens 16, included, anthers glabrous; ovary sessile, pubescent, 4–8-celled, style united with narrow stigmas; calyx lobes 5, ovate, obtuse, spreading or reflexed, thickened, pubescent.

Fruit. Depressed-globose, black, apiculate, pulp sweet when mature, astringent when green, about ¾–1 in. long; seeds 3–8, triangular, flattened, hard, shiny, about ⅓ in. long.

Leaves. Persistent, alternate, leathery, entire, oblong or obovate; apex obtuse, retuse, rounded or emarginate, abruptly narrowed at base, 1–2 in. long, dark green, glabrous above or somewhat pubescent, tomentose below.

Bark. Very smooth, gray, thin layers flaking off.

Wood. Heavy, black, compact, sapwood yellow, takes a high polish.

Range. In Texas and northern Mexico. In central and west Texas usually on rocky hills or the sides of ravines and canyons. Especially abundant in the Texas Edwards Plateau area. When near the coast usually on soils with lime composition because of marine shells. Probably reaching its easternmost limit in Harris County, near the coast. In Mexico in the states of Nuevo León, Coahuila, and Tamaulipas.

Remarks. The genus name, *Diospyros*, is translated "fruit of the gods," and the species name, *texana*, refers to the state of Texas. Vernacular names are Mexican Persimmon, Black Persimmon, Chapote, and Chapote Prieto. The fruit is somewhat smaller than that of the Common Persimmon but is likewise sweet and juicy at maturity and is eaten by many birds and mammals. The black juice is used to dye skins in Mexico, and the wood is used for tools and engraving blocks. It was also used in a craft now little practiced—that of ornamenting wooden objects by burning designs into them with an iron.

STORAX FAMILY (Styracaceae)

Sycamore-leaf Snow-bell

Styrax platanifolia Engelm. [H]

Field Identification. Shrub to 12 ft, open, irregular crown and slender branchlets.

Flowers. In axillary, semidrooping racemes 1½–2½ in. long, pedicels ¼–½ in. long, semiglabrous to pubescent, subtended by minute bracts; calyx, semiglabrous (or densely hairy in *S. platanifolia* var. *stellata*), shallowly 5-toothed; flowers perfect and regular; petals 5, oblong to elliptic or obovate, apex acute or obtuse, distinct, white; stamens 10, adnate to corolla base, filaments flattened; anthers elongate, linear, erect, introrse, sacs united; ovary superior, 3-celled or later 1-celled by abortion, ovules several in a cavity, style slender and united.

Fruit. Drupe maturing in June, borne singly or several in a cluster, peduncles ¼–½ in. long, slightly pubescent (or densely tomentose in *S. platanifolia* var. *stellata*); calyx tightly coherent to the fruiting base one-fourth to one-third the length, flaring widely from the clavate peduncles, margin set with remote, abruptly pointed, subulate teeth; surface semiglabrous to densely tomentose; body of fruit subglobose or obovate, ¼–⅜ in. long, the style persistent and apiculate; pericarp tough, leathery, dehiscent, flesh thin; seeds 1–2, about ¼ in. long, testa thin, oval to obovate, rounded or obtuse at apex and base, a ridge running from the hilum down the side.

Leaves. Simple, alternate, deciduous, blades 1½–3 in. long, about as broad, ovate or broadly heart shaped, margin entire or with short acute or obtuse lobes, apex acute to obtuse, base cordate or semitruncate; upper surface light to dark green, semilustrous to dull, semiglabrate or set with minute, scattered stellate hairs, veins numerous and finely reticulate; lower surface paler, reticulate veins more conspicuous than above, smooth or softly and densely stellate-hairy; petiole ¼–½ in. long, glabrate to stellate-hairy.

Twigs. Slender, when young brown and pubescent; with age brown to gray and glabrous.

Bark. Gray to black, when young smooth, on old trunks near the base broken into small scales.

Range. Wooded, rocky banks and ledges in central and western Texas—Spanish Pass in Kendall County, Enchanted Rock in Llano County, Little Blanco River in Blanco County, and Travis Peak in Travis County. The hairy variety, *S. platanifolia* var. *stellata* (Engelm.) Cory, has been collected 9 miles west of Boerne and in Sabinal Canyon 6½ miles north of Vanderpool.

Remarks. The genus name, *Styrax*, is the ancient Greek name, and the species name, *platanifolia*, refers to the sycamorelike foliage.

Specimens vary from quite glabrous to very densely stellate-hairy. However, these are connected by intermediate forms with varying degrees of hairiness. Those with copious stellate tomen-

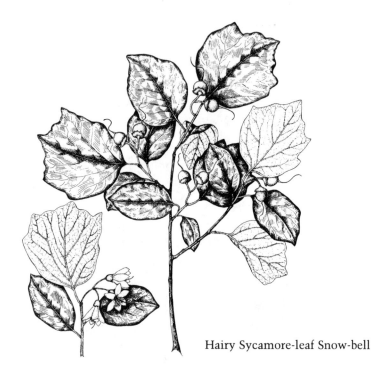

Hairy Sycamore-leaf Snow-bell

tum have been relegated to the status of a variety known as Hairy Sycamore-leaf Snow-bell, *S. platanifolia* var. *stellata* (Engelm.) Cory.

The snow-bells may be propagated by seeds or layers. Some species are grafted on the closely related *Halesia carolina*.

Texas Snow-bell

Styrax texana Cory [H]

Field Identification. Shrub to 15 ft, with slender and irregular branches; often appearing one-sided and unshapely because of its frequent occurrence on the faces of bluffs or cliffs.

Flowers. In spring, axillary, solitary or in clusters of 2–5; peduncles ½–¾ in. long, finely tomentulose; individual flower pedicels ¼–½ in. long; calyx ³⁄₁₆–¼ in. long, spreading at the apex, shallowly set with remote, minute teeth; corolla ½–¾ in. long, petals

5−6, distinct, white, elliptic to oblong, apex obtuse or acute; stamens equaling the petals, or shorter, included when the petals are not reflexed; style filiform, sometimes exceeding the corolla.

Fruit. Maturing August−September, peduncles finely tomentose, ¼−½ in. long, gradually expanded into the shallow, cup-shaped, minutely toothed calyx; fruit subglobose, about ⅜ in. long, green at first, brown-tomentose later, dehiscent into 2−3 valves; seed solitary, globose or slightly longer than wide, smooth, often with 1 or 2 shallow grooves on the side, dark lustrous-brown, about ⁵⁄₁₆ in. long.

Leaves. Simple, alternate, deciduous, blades 2−3 in. long, almost as broad, mostly oval or a few broadly elliptic, margin entire, base abruptly contracted into petiole, apex rounded or bluntly pointed, upper surface pale green and glabrous, veins delicate and impressed, lower surface conspicuously white with veins raised and more prominent; petiole ⅜−¾ in. long, green to reddish, grooved above, essentially glabrous.

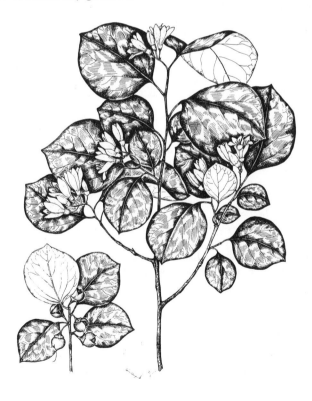

Twigs. Slender, when young reddish brown, older gray and glabrous, minutely white-scaly under the glass; bark of trunk smooth,
light gray to dark gray.

Range. Rare and local, confined to limestone areas of the central
Texas Edwards Plateau—in Edwards County on Polecat Creek
14½ miles southeast of Rocksprings, and also on Cedar Creek; and
in Real County, 3 miles north of Vance on Hackberry Creek near
old post office site.

Remarks. The genus name, *Styrax*, is the ancient Greek name,
and the species name, *texana*, refers to the state of Texas.

ASH FAMILY (Oleaceae)

Downy Forestiera

Forestiera pubescens Nutt. [H]

Field Identification. Sometimes a small tree to 15 ft, and 5 in. in
diameter, but usually only a straggling, irregularly shaped shrub.

Flowers. Polygamo-dioecious, appearing before the leaves in spring
from branches of the preceding year; clusters lateral, from bracts
that are obovate, ¹⁄₁₂–⅛ in. long, ciliate, densely pubescent; staminate fascicles greenish; sepals 4–6, small, early-deciduous; petals
absent; stamens 2–5; pistillate clusters on slender pedicels of
short spurs; ovary 2-celled, 2 ovules in each cell, style slender,
stigma capitate or somewhat 2-lobed.

Fruit. June–October, drupes pediceled, clustered, bluish black,
glaucous, ellipsoid, ¼–⅓ in. long, fleshy, 1-seeded; stone oblong to
ellipsoid, ribbed.

Leaves. Simple, opposite, deciduous, ½–1¾ in. long, varying from
elliptic to oblong or oval, margin obscurely serrulate, apex obtuse
or rounded, base cuneate or rounded; dull green and glabrous or
slightly pubescent above; lower surface densely soft-pubescent;
petioles short, yellowish green, pubescent.

Twigs. Green to yellowish and pubescent when young, older ones
light to dark gray and glabrous.

Range. Mostly in rich, moist soil along streams. New Mexico,
Texas, and Oklahoma; eastward to Florida.

Remarks. The genus name, *Forestiera*, honors the French physician and naturalist Charles Le Forestier, and the species name,

pubescens, refers to the soft-hairy leaves. Also known under the vernacular names of Devil's-elbow, Chaparral, Spring-herald, Spring-goldenglow, and Tanglewood. The shrub has no particular economic value but has been recommended for erosion control and wildlife cover. It has been cultivated since 1900. About 20 species of *Forestiera* are known, these being distributed in North America, the West Indies, and Central to South America. The various species are propagated by cuttings and seeds, and some are rooted by layering.

A variety, which is discussed immediately following, is *F. pubescens* Nutt. var. *glabrifolia* Shinners. It has sometimes been listed as *F. neomexicana* Gray.

New Mexico Forestiera

Forestiera pubescens Nutt. var. *glabrifolia* Shinners [H]

Field Identification. Erect, spreading shrubs or small trees to 12 ft, often clumped at the base and with semispinescent branches.

Flowers. March—May before the leaves in the axils of the last year's leaves; flowers small, polygamo-dioecious, crowded, the dense, sessile clusters subtended by 4 small bracts; petals absent; stamens 2—4, anthers oblong and yellow; ovary superior, ovate, 2-

celled, with 2 pendulous ovules in each cell; style slender, stigma somewhat 2-lobed; pistillate flowers with 2–4 sterile stamens.

Fruit. Ripening June–September, drupe ⅕–⅓ in. long, bluish black, ovoid to ellipsoid, obtuse, 1-celled and 1-seeded; seeds bony, germinating 40–70 percent.

Leaves. Simple, opposite, deciduous, spatulate-oblong to ovate-oblong, apex obtuse or short acuminate, base cuneate, margin minutely serrulate or sometimes entire toward the base, length ½–1¾ in., width ¼–¾ in., surfaces glabrous above and below, grayish green, membranous; petioles ⅛–¼ in. long, glabrous; smaller leaves sometimes fascicled at the base of the older ones.

Twigs. Stiff, lateral ones often shortened, gray to whitened, smooth, glabrous.

Range. New Mexico Forestiera is found on hillsides or mesas, or in moist valleys, at altitudes of 3,000–7,000 ft, from the northern parts of Trans-Pecos Texas to New Mexico, Arizona, Colorado, Utah, and westward into California.

Remarks. The genus name, *Forestiera*, honors Charles Le Forestier (d. *circa* 1820), a French naturalist and physician, and the variety name, *glabrifolia*, refers to the smooth foliage. It is also known as Desert Olive and Palo Blanco. The Hopi Indians are said to have made digging sticks of the branches. It has some ornamental value when mass planted with other plants along streams.

New Mexico Forestiera is also listed in the literature as *F. neomexicana* Gray. *F. neomexicana* var. *arizonica* Gray is not accepted. Instead, the listed characters of *arizonica* appear to make it a synonym for *F. pubescens*.

Net-leaf Forestiera

Forestiera reticulata Torr. [H]

Field Identification. A small to medium-sized shrub, with an irregular crown, and many small stems arising from the base; or more rarely a small spreading tree to 12 ft, with a single trunk.

Flowers. In short, crowded racemose clusters from the axils of last year's leaves; buds scaly, scales imbricate and straw-colored; flowers dioecious, petals absent, calyx of 4 minute greenish sepals; stamens 2–4, exserted, anthers oblong; ovary 2-celled, ovules 2 in

each cell, becoming a 1-celled and 1-seeded drupe; style slender, stigma somewhat 2-lobed or capitate.

Fruit. Borne in axillary, short clusters, from scales that are oval to ovate, acute to obtuse, ciliate, and ¹⁄₂₅−¹⁄₁₆ in. long; drupes on glabrous pedicels ¹⁄₈−³⁄₁₆ in. long, ovoid to ellipsoid or obovoid, asymmetrical, usually less than ¹⁄₄ in. long, tipped by the per-sistent style remnants, dark reddish brown; 1-celled and 1-seeded.

Leaves. Opposite, pairs ⅓–1 in. apart on the branchlets, length ½–1½ in., width ¼–⅘ in., coriaceous, ovate to short-oblong, a few oval; apex acute to obtuse, base rounded, margin entire or with obscure, appressed teeth mostly toward the apex; upper surface dull green, essentially glabrous, and finely reticulate; lower surface paler, glabrous, semiglaucous, reticulate-veiny and porulose-punctate under a glass; petioles mostly less than ¼ in. long, glabrous or puberulent.

Twigs. Slender, terete, rather straight; younger ones brown, glabrous or puberulent; older ones light to dark gray and glabrous; lenticels small, pale, and scattered.

Range. Dry hillsides and canyons. Texas and Mexico. In Texas on the Edwards Plateau, west to the Pecos River and perhaps beyond. Apparently nowhere abundant. Collected by Valery Havard at the mouth of the Pecos. Specimens examined by the author deposited in the Missouri Botanical Garden Herbarium by E. J. Palmer, No. 12974, from south and west slopes of high limestone hills at Montell, Uvalde County.

Remarks. The genus name, *Forestiera*, honors Charles Le Forestier (d. *circa* 1820), a French physician and naturalist at Saint-Quentin and first botany teacher of Poiret. The species name, *reticulata*, refers to the net-veined leaves. This shrub is not very well known.

Narrow-leaf Forestiera

Forestiera angustifolia Torr. [H]

Field Identification. Evergreen, dense, stiff, intricately branched shrub. Sometimes a small tree to 25 ft, with a short, crooked trunk.

Flowers. Polygamo-dioecious, inconspicuous, greenish, in clusters from scaly bracts; sepals 4, minute, early-deciduous; petals absent; staminate flowers sessile or nearly so; bracts imbricate, oval to ovate, margin fimbricate, yellowish green, about ¹⁄₁₆ in. long; stamens 2–4 in a cluster, conspicuously exserted, erect or spreading, ⅛–³⁄₁₆ in. long; anthers reddish brown, oblong, hardly over ⅛ in. long; pistil about ⅛ in. long, style slender and gradually swollen below into a 2-celled ovary, developing a stipelike base later, ovules 2 in each cavity.

Fruit. Drupe short-peduncled, oblong-ovoid, somewhat falcate, acute, ¼–½ in. long, black, 1-seeded, edible but astringent.

Leaves. On older twigs often clustered on short knotty spurs, on young shoots mostly opposite and more distant, persistent, linear to oblanceolate, apex obtuse, margin entire and somewhat revolute, leathery, light green and glabrous, veins obscure, somewhat porous, blade length ½–1¼ in., width ⅙–¼ in., sessile or nearly so.

Twigs. Gray, slender, stiff, smooth, sometimes spinescent; bark of older branches and trunk smooth and gray.

Range. On dry, well-drained hillsides, or along stony arroyos in Texas and Mexico. In Texas in the central, western, and southern portions. Also following the coastal shellbanks (limy soil) along the Gulf as far east as Chambers County. Rare in Harris County

but found on Hog Island at Tabbs Bay Ferry and at La Porte and
Seabrook close to the bayside. The coastal plant may be referable
to *F. texana* upon more investigation. In Mexico in the states of
Tamaulipas, Nuevo León, and Coahuila.

Remarks. The genus name, *Forestiera*, is in honor of Charles Le
Forestier, a French naturalist and physician, and the species name,
angustifolia, refers to the narrow, linear leaves. In Mexico it is
known as Panalero and Chaparral Blanco. The fruit is eaten by a
number of birds and mammals, including the scaled quail and
gray fox. The plant may be propagated by seeds and layers. It has
some possibility as an ornamental in close proximity to the Gulf,
in saline or limy soil, where plants are subject to heavy buffeting
by winds.

Japanese Privet

Ligustrum japonicum Thunb. [H]

Field Identification. A much cultivated evergreen, or deciduous in
cold climates, becoming a bushy shrub or small tree to 18 ft.

Sometimes escaping cultivation. Bark rather smooth and gray. Sometimes confused with *Ligustrum lucidum* Ait., but the latter has larger leaves, ovate-lanceolate in shape, with an acute or acuminate apex and a less glossy surface.

Flowers. Borne July–September, bisexual. Panicles terminal, to 4½ in. long. Corolla funnelform, the tube usually somewhat longer than the calyx; the 4 corolla lobes spreading; calyx campanulate, obscurely 4-toothed; stamens 2, slightly longer than the lobes, attached to the corolla tube; ovary 2-celled, with 2 ovules in each cell, or sometimes 1-seeded by abortion.

Fruit. A drupe-like berry, black, oblong or sometimes falcate.

Leaves. Opposite; 2–4 in. long; shape roundish-ovate to ovate-oblong; base rounded or broadly cuneate; margin entire; apices acute to obtuse; texture coriaceous; color dark green and glossy; with 4–5 pairs of lateral veins, the veins rather obscure beneath; midrib and margin sometimes reddish. Petiole ¼–½ in. long.

Twigs. Slender, gray to brown, minutely puberulent at first, but glabrous later and lenticellate.

Range. A native of Japan and Korea. Introduced into cultivation in 1845. A handsome, much cultivated, evergreen shrub or tree. Sometimes pruned for hedges or for rounded poodle forms.

Remarks. The genus name, *Ligustrum*, is from ancient Latin, and the species name, *japonicum*, is for its place of origin. Vernacular names are Privet-berry and Prim. The fruit is greedily eaten by the cedar waxwing and other birds.

Glossy Privet

Ligustrum lucidum Ait. [H]

Field Identification. A cultivated, evergreen, erect, large shrub or tree to 30 ft tall. The branches spreading and lenticellate. Trunk rather smooth and pale to dark gray or blotched gray or whitish.

Flowers. Borne July–August in terminal panicles 4–9 in. long, almost as wide. Flowers white, perfect, sessile or subsessile. Corolla salverform, with a rather short tube about as long as the calyx; lobes 4, spreading, about as long as the tube; calyx campanulate and obscurely 4-toothed; stamens 2, about as long as the corolla lobes; style cylindric, not exceeding the stamens; ovary 2-celled, cells 2-ovuled.

Fruit. A berrylike drupe, oblong, blue-black, about ⅜ in. long.

Leaves. Opposite, 3¼–5 in. long; shape ovate-lanceolate; apices acuminate to acute; margin entire; base usually broad-cuneate; venation with lateral veins usually 6–8 pairs that are distinct on both sides; veinlets often impressed; surface glabrous; winter buds ovoid, with about 2 outer scales. Petioles ⅓–¾ in. long.

Twigs. Slender, light to dark gray.

Range. Native to China, Korea, and Japan. Commonly planted in warm regions. Often planted for ornament in the Gulf Coast cities. Common in Houston. Introduced into cultivation in 1794.

Remarks. The genus name, *Ligustrum*, is the ancient Latin name. The species name, *lucidum*, refers to a shiny leaf surface. However, this has caused some confusion of names in the nursery trade, because the Japanese Privet, *Ligustrum japonicum* Thunb., has a much glossier leaf surface than *Ligustrum lucidum* Ait. Both *Ligustrum lucidum* and *Ligustrum japonicum* yield a white

wax, an exudation of the branches caused by the insect pe-lah;
therefore, they are cultivated in China.

Chinese Privet

Ligustrum sinense Lour. [H]

Field Identification. Shrub or small tree to 20 ft, and 5 in. in trunk
diameter. Trunks often clumped and inclined, branches slender
and spreading.

Flowers. Inflorescence March–May, fragrant, perfect; borne in
panicles that are terminal, narrow, elongate, 2–6 in. long and ½–

3 in. wide; corolla white, tubular, limb about ⅜ in. across, 4-lobed, lobes spreading, oblong or ovate, acute; stamens 2, filaments adnate to the corolla tube, exserted, longer than the prominent corolla lobes; pistil shorter than the stamens, stigma spatulate, flattened; calyx campanulate, about 1/12 in. long, glabrous, shallowly 4-lobed, lobes acute; pedicels 1/16–⅛ in. long, pubescent.

Fruit. Drupe bluish black, subglobose to oval or obovoid, seeds 1–2.

Leaves. Opposite, oval to elliptic, apex rounded to obtuse or slightly notched, base cuneate or rounded, margin entire, length 1–2 in., width ½–1 in., main vein apparent but others obscure; upper surface dark green and semilustrous, glabrous or slightly pubescent along the main vein; lower surface paler, glabrous or slightly pubescent on the main vein; petiole ⅛–½ in., pubescent.

Twigs. Slender, spreading, gray to brown, pubescent; older branches and trunk smooth, glabrous, and various shades of gray to brown, lenticels pale and scattered.

Range. A native of southeast Asia. Grown for ornament in Texas, Oklahoma, Arkansas, Louisiana, and elsewhere throughout the North Temperate Zone, sometimes escaping cultivation.

Remarks. The genus name, *Ligustrum*, is the ancient classical name, and the species name, *sinense*, refers to its Chinese origin. It is a handsome plant, much cultivated for hedges and screens in the South. A number of varieties have been listed.

Quihoui Privet

Ligustrum quihoui Carr. [H]

Field Identification. Shrub cultivated, slender, erect or spreading, to 10 ft.

Flowers. April–June, heavily scented, borne in narrow racemes 2–8 in. long and ½–1 in. wide, lateral branches of inflorescence ¼–½ in. long, rather densely flowered from the axils of smaller leaves below, usually leafless above; calyx sessile or nearly so, puberulent, shallowly 4-toothed; corolla white, tubular, about ⅛ in. long, the tube as long as the 4 lobes of the limb or longer, lobes ovate, acute to obtuse; stamens 2, much exserted, anthers short-oblong, about 1/16 in. long; pistil much shorter than the stamens, included or slightly exserted, simple, erect, stigma slightly capitate.

Fruit. Ripening September–November, bluish black, slightly glaucous, 3/16–1/4 in. long, subglobose or slightly flattened; seeds 1–2, about 3/16 in. long, short-oblong to oval; when 2-seeded the outer surfaces are rounded and sculptured and the inner faces plane.

Leaves. Opposite, simple, partly folded, 2/3–1½ in. long, 3/16–1/4 in. wide, linear to narrowly oblong or elliptic, margin entire; apex obtuse, sometimes slightly notched, base gradually narrowed; upper surface dark green and glabrous, lower surface paler and duller green, glabrous or barely puberulent on the midrib; leaves sessile or short-petiolate, glabrous or puberulent.

Twigs. Younger ones green and finely pubescent, older ones gray or pale brown and glabrous; bark gray, smooth, and with numerous pale lenticels.

Range. A native of China, cultivated in the Gulf Coast states, sometimes escaping.

Remarks. The genus name, *Ligustrum*, is the ancient classical name. The species name, *quihoui*, honors Antoine Quihou, a French botanist who worked in the late nineteenth century. The plant has been cultivated since 1862. It is an attractive shrub with erect or spreading stems and late-flowering habit. It grows well in the Houston area.

Fragrant Ash

Fraxinus cuspidata Torr. [H]

Field Identification. Shrub or small slender tree to 20 ft, sometimes forming thickets. Branches slender, smooth, gray.

Flowers. April–May, fragrant, borne in loose, terminal, glabrous panicles 3–4 in. long; corolla about ⅔ in. long, white, 4-petaled; petals linear-oblong, exceeding the anthers; anthers oblong, almost sessile; stigma 2-lobed, almost sessile, ovary 2-celled; calyx cup-shaped, about 1/16 in. long, teeth acute and apiculate.

Fruit. In drooping panicles 2–5 in. long; samaras on slender, glabrous peduncles ½–1 in. long, wing and seed together ¾–1¼ in. long, flattened, oblong-linear or spatulate, rounded or obtuse or notched at the apex, pale green.

Leaves. Compound, 3–5½ in. long, composed of 5–7 leaflets; leaflets delicate, lanceolate or narrowly ovate, long acuminate or cuspidate at the apex, cuneate at the base, margin sharply and remotely serrate, less so toward the apex and base, blades 1½–2½ in. long, ½–¾ in. wide; dark green, thin, glabrous above, paler beneath; long-petiolate, petiolules grooved above, slightly wing-margined, those of lateral leaflets ¼–½ in. long, those of the terminal leaflets ½–1 in. long.

Twigs. Slender, younger ones green to brown and glabrous, older ones gray, lenticels small.

Bark. Gray, smooth, rather tight, on old trunks broken into small, short scales and irregular fissures.

Range. In dry, well-drained soil at altitudes of 3,500–5,500 ft, on mountainsides of the grass, pinyon, and yellow pine belt. In Trans-Pecos Texas in rocky canyons of the Pecos and Devils rivers and the Rio Grande. Also in the Chisos Mountains of Brewster County. In New Mexico and Arizona. In Mexico in Nuevo León, Chihuahua, and Coahuila.

Remarks. The genus name, *Fraxinus*, is the ancient Latin name, and the species name, *cuspidata*, refers to the leaf apex. In Mexico it is known under the Spanish name of Fresno. This small western ash is unique in having floral fragrance and petals. Deer and livestock occasionally browse the foliage.

Arizona Fragrant Ash, *F. cuspidata* Torr. var. *macropetala* Rehd., is a variety occurring in the Grand Canyon area in Arizona and differing by having 3–7 broader, often ovate, entire leaflets, and larger flowers.

Gregg Ash

Fraxinus greggii Gray [H]

Field Identification. Western clump-forming shrub or small tree to 25 ft.

Flowers. Panicles ½–¾ in. long, individual flowers perfect or 1-sexed, on slender pedicels ⅛–¼ in. long, springing from brown-

pubescent, ovate, acuminate bracts; petals absent; calyx campanulate, scarious; stamens solitary or paired, filaments longer than
the calyx, anthers about ⅛ in. long; style short, stigmas with
reflexed stigmatic lobes, ovary rounded, longer than the calyx.

Fruit. Samaras ½–¾ in. long, on peduncles ⅛–³⁄₁₆ in. long; wing
narrowly elliptic or oblong, apex rounded, retuse or notched, often
tipped by the style remnant, extending at least part way down the
terete seed.

Leaves. Opposite, persistent, ¾–1½ in. long, odd-pinnate compound of 3 leaflets (rarely 5–7); leaflets sessile or nearly so, winged,
⅓–1 in. long, ⅛–¼ in. wide, terminal leaflet usually largest, spatulate, elliptic, oval, or narrowly ovate, apex obtuse, rounded or
notched, base gradually narrowed, margin entire or sparingly
crenate-serrate, sometimes revolute, thick and coriaceous, veins
inconspicuous, glabrous or puberulent, olive-green above, paler
beneath; petioles distinctly winged.

Twigs. Slender, young twigs dark green and puberulent; older twigs gray, glabrous or puberulent; lenticels small, rounded, raised, gray or brown.

Bark. Dark gray to black, mostly smooth, broken into thin scales on old trees.

Wood. Hard, heavy, close-grained, brown, sapwood lighter, specific gravity 0.79.

Range. On dry rocky hillsides and arroyo banks. Trans-Pecos Texas, rather abundant near Del Rio and Langtry in Val Verde County. In Brewster County in the Chisos Mountains at altitudes of 4,000–7,800 ft. Also near Mount Locke in Jeff Davis County. In New Mexico and southern Arizona. In Mexico in Nuevo León, Tamaulipas, Coahuila, and Zacatecas.

Remarks. *Fraxinus* is the ancient Latin name, and the species name, *greggii*, honors the botanist Josiah Gregg. Other vernacular names are Fresno, Escobillo, Barreta, and China. The wood is occasionally used for fuel, and the leafy twigs are used for crude brooms in Mexico.

Berlandier Ash

Fraxinus berlandieriana A. DC. [H]

Field Identification. Small round-topped tree of western distribution, seldom seen east of the Colorado River except in cultivation. Rarely over 30 ft.

Flowers. Dioecious, greenish, staminate and pistillate flowers on different trees; calyx of staminate flower obscurely 4-lobed; stamens 2, filaments short, anthers linear-oblong and opening laterally; calyx of pistillate flower campanulate, deeply cleft; ovary with a slender style and stigmas 2-lobed.

Fruit. Ripening in May. Samara spatulate to oblong-obovate, 1–1½ in. long, about ¼ in. wide; wing acute or acuminate at apex, decurrent down the seed body almost to the base, set in a deeply lobed calyx; samaras sometimes 3-winged.

Leaves. Deciduous, opposite, odd-pinnate, slender, petioled, 3–10 in. long; leaflets 3–5, petiolulate, elliptic, lanceolate or obovate, acuminate to acute at apex, cuneate or rounded at base, entire or remotely serrate, thickish, dark green, and glabrous above, glabrous or a few axillary hairs beneath, 3–4 in. long, ½–1½ in.

wide, petiolule of terminal leaflet longer than those of lateral leaflets. Leaflets fewer, smaller, more coarsely toothed, and more widely separated than those of White Ash or Green Ash.

Twigs. Green, reddish, or gray, with scattered lenticels, leaf scars small, raised, oval.

Bark. Gray or reddish, fissures shallow, and ridges narrow.

Wood. Light brown, sapwood lighter, close-grained, light, soft.

Range. Moist canyons and stream banks. Central Texas to Trans-Pecos Texas; southward in Mexico in Coahuila, Durango, and Veracruz.

Remarks. The genus name, *Fraxinus*, is the ancient Latin name, and the species name, *berlandieriana*, is in honor of the Swiss botanist Jean Louis Berlandier (1805–1851), who collected extensively in Mexico and Texas. Local names for the tree are Plumero, Fresno, and Mexican Ash. The wood has no particular commercial importance, but the tree is widely planted as an ornamental in western and southwestern Texas and Mexico.

Velvet Ash

Fraxinus velutina Torr. [H]

Field Identification. Slender tree with a diameter to 18 in. and a height of 50 ft, but generally only half that size, the branches spreading and forming a rounded crown. Velvet Ash is extremely variable in its form, size of leaflets, fruit, and the amount of hairiness. A number of varieties are recognized, some occurring with the species and connected by intergrades.

Flowers. Usually March–May with the unfolding leaves; dioecious, borne in long, pubescent panicles on slender pedicels; calyx densely pubescent, cup shaped, stamens short, anthers oblong and apiculate; ovary enveloped in the calyx, stigma lobes subsessile.

Fruit. Ripening in September, clusters often abundantly fruited, oblong to obovate or elliptic, about ¾ in. long and ⅙ in. wide, wing with apex rounded to acute or emarginate, seed terete, many-rayed, about ½ in. long.

Leaves. Rachis slender, grooved, pinnately compound, 4–5 in. long, composed of 3–5 leaflets, ovate to elliptic or obovate, apex acute, base cuneate to rounded, margin semientire to finely crenate-serrate above, thickened, when young densely tomentose, when older pale green and glabrous on the upper surface, tomentose beneath, midrib conspicuous, veins reticulate, length 1–1½ in., width ¾–1 in.; lateral petiolules to ⅙ in. long, terminal petiolule to ½ in. long.

Twigs. Densely tomentose at first, later glabrous and gray; leaf scars large, obcordate; buds about ⅛ in. long, acute, scales 6 or more, ovate to linear, tomentose, ¼–½ in. long.

Bark. Gray to brown or reddish, ⅓–½ in. thick, fissures deep, ridges broad and flat, scales small and thin.

Wood. Light brown, sapwood lighter, close-grained, rather soft, not strong, fairly heavy.

Range. Usually in mountain canyons at altitudes of 2,000–6,000 ft. Trans-Pecos Texas, New Mexico, Arizona, Utah, Nevada, and California. In Mexico in Baja California, Sonora, and Chihuahua.

Remarks. The genus name, *Fraxinus*, is the classical name of Ash, and the species name, *velutina*, refers to the velutinous (velvety) hairs of the leaves. Other names are Arizona Ash, Desert Ash, Smooth Oregon Ash, and Fresno. The wood is used for ax handles and in the manufacture of wagons. The tree is used in shelter-belt planting and in ornamental planting in arid regions of the Southwest. Velvet Ash has been in cultivation since 1900. It has some use as a food for wildlife.

Green Ash

Fraxinus pennsylvanica var. *subintegerrima* (Vahl) Fern. [H]

Field Identification. Spreading, round-topped tree attaining a height of 70 ft or more.

Flowers. Dioecious, borne in spring in slender-pediceled, terminal, glabrous panicles; no petals; staminate with a campanulate, obscurely toothed calyx; stamens 2, composed of short, terete filaments and linear-oblong, greenish purple anthers; calyx of pistil-

late flowers deeply cleft; ovary 2–3-celled, style elongate, with 2 green stigmatic lobes.

Fruit. Samaras in panicles; samaras flat, 1–2 in. long, ¼–⅓ in. wide, winged; wing decurrent down the side of seed body often past the middle, spatulate or oblanceolate; end of wing square, notched, rounded or acute; seed usually 1-celled, or rarely 2–3-celled.

Leaves. Deciduous, opposite, odd-pinnate compound, 8–12 in. long, rachis glabrous; leaflets 5–9 (usually 7) ovate to oblong-lanceolate, acute or acuminate at apex, cuneate at base, entire or irregularly serrate on margin, lustrous green on both sides or somewhat paler beneath; glabrous above, usually glabrous below or with scant pubescence on veins, 2–6 in. long, 1–2 in. wide.

Twigs. Gray, glabrous, terete; lenticels pale.

Bark. Brown, tight, ridges flattened, furrows shallow, scales thin and appressed.

Wood. Light brown, sapwood lighter, coarse-grained, heavy, hard, strong, weighing 44 lb per cu ft.

Range. Texas, New Mexico, Oklahoma, Arkansas, and Louisiana; eastward to Florida, northward to Nova Scotia, and west to Manitoba, Montana, Wyoming, Colorado, and Kansas.

Remarks. The genus name, *Fraxinus*, is the ancient name meaning ash tree. The variety name, *subintegerrima*, means "spaced between," with reference to the somewhat remote teeth of the leaf margin. Vernacular names are Water Ash, River Ash, Red Ash, Swamp Ash.

Green Ash is closely related to Red Ash, *F. pennsylvanica* Marsh., from which it is distinguished by the lustrous, green, lanceolate, sharply serrate leaves and glabrous twigs. Berlandier Ash, *F. berlandieriana* A. DC. is a closely related species of southwest Texas and Mexico often grown for ornament on the streets of Gulf Coast cities.

The wood is not as desirable as that of White Ash but is used for the same purposes, such as tool handles, furniture, interior finishing, cooperage, and wagons. A number of birds eat the seeds, and the foliage is browsed by white-tailed deer and cottontail.

Texas Ash

Fraxinus texensis (Gray) Sarg. [H]

Field Identification. Tree to 50 ft, 2–3 ft in diameter, with a short trunk and contorted branches.

Flowers. With the leaves in March, in large glabrous panicles, buds with ovate, rounded, brown to orange-colored scales, from the axils of last year's leaves; staminate and pistillate panicles separate; staminate with petals absent and a minute 4-lobed calyx; stamens 2, filaments short, anthers linear-oblong and apiculate, purplish; pistillate calyx with 4 deep, acute lobes; ovary attenuate into a slender style.

Fruit. Samara borne in compact panicles 2–3¾ in. long on slender pedicels ⅛–¼ in. long, fruit ½–1 in. long, 3/16–¼ in. wide, body rounded; wing terminal on the seed body or extending only slightly on the sides, apex rounded or notched (rarely with more than 1 wing).

Leaves. Odd-pinnate compound, 5–8 in. long; leaflets 5 (more rarely 7); petiolules ¼–1½ in. long, slender, yellowish green; blades elliptic to oblong or ovate to obovate, apex acute, base broadly cuneate or rounded, margins obscurely serrate or entire toward the base, length 1–3 in., width ¾–2 in.; upper surface olive green to dark green and glabrous; lower surface paler and often somewhat glaucous and glabrous, or with a few white hairs on the main vein.

Twigs. Numerous, stout, terete, green to reddish brown or gray, younger slightly puberulent, older glabrous, smooth; lenticels scattered, oblong, pale; leaf scars large, raised, with conspicuous fibrovascular bundles; buds acute, ovate, apex rounded or truncate, brown to orange, densely hairy.

Bark. Gray to brown or black, ½–¾ in. thick, furrows deep, the wide ridges confluent to give a netlike appearance.

Wood. Light brown, sapwood paler, strong, hard, heavy.

Range. From the Arbuckle Mountains of Oklahoma southward over the limestone Edwards Plateau of Texas. In Texas in Dallas, Tarrant, Travis, Bandera, Kerr, Edwards, and Palo Pinto counties. Collected by the author between Utopia and Tarpley.

Remarks. The genus name, *Fraxinus*, is the ancient Latin name, and the species name, *texensis*, refers to the state of Texas where it occurs. It is also known as Mountain Ash because of its growth on limestone hills. The wood is used for fuel or flooring, but is hardly abundant enough to be of commercial importance. It is a handsome tree and should be more extensively grown for ornament. It was first cultivated in 1901. Texas Ash is closely related to White Ash, *F. americana*, and some botanists consider it as only a variety of the latter.

White Ash

Fraxinus americana L. [H]

Field Identification. Tree attaining a height of 100 ft and a diameter of 3 ft. Records show that some trees have reached a height of 175 ft and a diameter of 5 to 6 ft, but such trees are no longer to be found. The general shape is rather narrow and rounded.

Flowers. Borne April–May, dioecious, with or before the leaves in staminate and pistillate panicles; staminate clusters short and dense; individual flowers minute, green to red, glabrous; no petals; calyx campanulate, 4-lobed; stamens 2–3, filaments short, anthers oblong-ovate and reddish; pistillate clusters about 2 in. long, slender, calyx deeply lobed; style split into 2 spreading, reddish purple stigmas.

Fruit. Ripening August–September. Samaras in dense clusters often 6–8 in. long; seed body terete; wing slightly extending down the body of the seed, but usually not at all, oblong or spatulate; often notched at the end, thin, smooth, flat, yellow to brown, 1–2½ in. long, about ¼ in. wide.

Leaves. Simple, opposite, deciduous, odd-pinnate compound, 8–13 in. long, leaflets 5–9, usually 7, ovate-lanceolate, acuminate or acute, rounded or cuneate at base, entire or crenulate-serrate on margin, dark lustrous green above, paler and whitish and glabrous or pubescent beneath, 3–5 in. long, 1½–3 in. wide; petiole glabrous.

Twigs. Green to brown or gray, stout, smooth with pale lenticels.

Bark. Light gray to dark brown, ridges narrow and separated by deep fissures into interlacing patterns.

Wood. Brown, sapwood lighter, close-grained, strong, hard, stiff, heavy, tough, weighing 41 lb per cu ft, seasons well, takes a good polish, moderately durable, shock resistant.

Range. Typical White Ash is distributed in Oklahoma, Arkansas, Texas, and Louisiana; eastward to Florida, northward to Nova Scotia, and west to Ontario, Minnesota, Michigan, and Nebraska.

Remarks. The genus name, *Fraxinus*, is the ancient Latin name, and the meaning of the species name, *americana*, is obvious. Also known as Small-seed White Ash, Cane Ash, Biltmore Ash, and Biltmore White Ash. It has been known in cultivation since 1724. It is an important timber tree and is widely planted as an ornamental. It is estimated that 45 percent of all ash lumber used is from the White Ash. The center of production is now the lower

Mississippi Valley. No differentiation is made in the lumber trade of the species of ash; however, the term "white ash" generally designates top quality ash. Ash wood is used for tanks, silos, toys, musical instruments, cabinets, refrigerators, millwork, sash, doors, frames, vehicle parts, farm utensils, woodenware, butter tubs, veneer, fuel, railroad crossties, sporting goods, furniture, cooperage, handles, ships, boats, railroad cars, and frame parts of airplanes. It usually grows in association with other hardwoods in well-drained soils on slopes. It is valuable in small tracts for woodland management. Although sometimes used, it is not as valuable for shelter-belt planting as Green Ash. The fruit is known to be eaten by a number of birds, including the purple finch and pine grosbeak, and the foliage is browsed by rabbit, porcupine, and white-tailed deer.

DOGBANE FAMILY (Apocynaceae)

Common Oleander

Nerium oleander L. [H]

Field Identification. Cultivated, clumped shrub to 18 ft, 3–8 in. in diameter at the base.

Flowers. Odorless, blooming during summer in compound, terminal cymes; flowers variously colored, and often double; corolla tube funnelform, dilated into a narrow campanulate throat with crownlike appendages 3–5-toothed; limb salverform, 1½–3 in. across, 5-lobed; lobes convolute in the bud, obliquely apiculate, twisted to the right; stamens 5, alternating with corolla lobes, filaments partly adnate to corolla tube; anthers with 2 basal tails, apex long-attenuate, hairy, 2-celled; styles united, slender, stigma simple, ovary superior and 2-carpellate; calyx of 5 persistent sepals, imbricate in the bud, lanceolate, acuminate, ⅙–¼ in. long.

Fruit. The 2 ovaries forming follicles, erect or nearly so, 4–8 in. long, seeds twisted.

Leaves. Numerous, opposite, or in whorls of 3–4, linear to elliptic, margin entire and often whitened, revolute, apex and base acute or acuminate, firm and leathery, many-nerved; dark green and glabrous with a conspicuous yellowish green main vein above; paler beneath with numerous, delicate, almost parallel lateral veins.

Twigs. Erect or arching, young ones green, older ones light brown to gray; lenticels numerous, oval.

Range. Cultivated in gardens in Texas and Louisiana, sometimes escaping cultivation. A native of Asia and widely distributed from the Mediterranean region to Japan. Cultivated throughout the tropics and subtropics.

Remarks. The genus name, *Nerium*, is from the Greek *neros* ("moist"), referring to places the wild plants grow. The species name, *oleander*, is from the Latin, meaning "olivelike," referring to the leaves. The flowers are poisonous if eaten by human beings, and the leaves have been known to kill cattle. They also contain a small amount of rubber. Oleander has been used for rat poison in Europe for many centuries. The symptoms of poisoning in human beings are abdominal pain, dilation of the pupil, vomiting, vertigo, insensibility, convulsive movements, small and slow pulse, and in fatal cases epileptiform convulsions with coma ending in death. The erratic pulsation of the heart in cases in which death has not followed has been pronounced, the pulse for 5 days remaining as low as 40 beats per minute. An infusion made from 4 ounces of the root is affirmed to have taken life. The active principle of the plant is a glycoside, oleandrin, which hydrolyzes into a gitoxigenin.

BORAGE FAMILY (Boraginaceae)

Anaqua

Ehretia anacua (Mier & Berland.) I. M. Johnst. [H]

Field Identification. Half-evergreen shrub or tree with a rounded head and attaining a height of 50 ft.

Flowers. March–April, but occasionally in fall after rains. Panicles 2–3 in. long, fragrant; bracts linear, acute, deciduous, about ¼ in. long; corolla small, white, about ¼ in. long, ⅓–½ in. across when open, tube short and campanulate, 5-lobed; lobes oval to ovate; calyx lobes 5, ovate to linear or lanceolate, acute at apex, almost as long as the corolla tube; stamens 5, adnate to the tube within, filaments filiform; ovary oblong, style split into 2 capitate stigmas.

Fruit. Drupe ¼–⅓ in. in diameter, globular, yellowish orange, juicy, sweet, edible, 2-celled and 2-seeded, stone separating into 2 bony nutlets rounded on the back and plane on the inner face, seeds terete and erect. A handsome tree when laden with the yellowish orange drupes.

Leaves. Simple, alternate, half-evergreen, oval to oblong or elliptic, margin entire or coarsely serrate above the middle, apex acute and sometimes apiculate, base cuneate or rounded, leathery, stiff, upper surface very roughened by small, crowded tubercles, upper surface dull olive green, glabrous or slightly pubescent, lower surface paler and pubescent, veins coarse, blade length 1–3½ in., width ¾–1½ in.; petiole stout, grooved, pubescent, ⅛–¼ in. long.

Twigs. Slender, crooked, brown to gray, when young with pale or brownish hairs, older glabrous; leaf scars small, obcordate and depressed; lenticels pale and numerous.

Bark. Thick, reddish brown to gray or black, broken into narrow, flat-topped ridges and deep fissures, the platelike scales exfoliating into gray or reddish flakes.

Wood. Light brown, sapwood lighter, close-grained, tough, heavy, hard, difficult to split, specific gravity about 0.64.

Range. Usually attaining its largest size in rich river valleys of central and south Texas. Only a shrub on poor, dry soil of hillsides. Southward into the Mexican states of Nuevo León, Tamaulipas, Coahuila, Guanajuato, and Veracruz. Occasionally as far east as Houston. Abundantly planted as shade trees in Victoria.

Remarks. The genus name, *Ehretia*, is in honor of George Dionysius Ehret (1708–1770), a German botanical artist. The species name, *anacua*, is a latinization of the vernacular name Anaqua. A scientific synonym no longer valid is *E. elliptica* DC. Other vernacular names are Anacahuite, Knackaway, Nockaway, Sugarberry, Manzanita, and Manzanillo. The wood is used for posts, wheels, spokes, axles, yokes, and tool handles. A number of birds and mammals feed upon the fruit. Anaqua is a desirable tree for ornamental planting in its native region. It forms persistent clumps by root suckers, which can be used for transplanting. It is drought resistant and comparatively free of disease. Of the 40 species of *Ehretia* known in the warm regions of the world, only a few are used in horticulture.

VERBENA FAMILY (Verbenaceae)

Lilac Chaste-tree

Vitex agnus-castus L. [H]

Field Identification. Cultivated, aromatic tree to 30 ft, often with many trunks from base. Branches slender and spreading outward to form a wide, broad-topped crown.

Flowers. May–September, panicled spikes conspicuous, terminal, dense, puberulent to pulverulent, 4–12 in. long, ½–1¼ in. wide; flowers sessile or very short-pediceled; corolla blue to purplish, ¼–⅓ in. long, funnelform; tube slightly curved, densely white-pubescent above the calyx; limb ⅕–¼ in. broad, slightly oblique, ciliate, white hairs at the limb sinuses, somewhat 2-lipped, 5-lobed, upper 2 lobes and lateral 2 lobes ovate and obtuse, lower lobe largest, obtuse to rounded; stamens 4, exserted, 2 sometimes longer than the others but not always, anthers with nearly parallel, arched or spreading sacs; stigma exserted, slender, 2-cleft; ovary 4-celled and 4-ovuled; calyx campanulate, ¹⁄₁₂–⅛ in. long, densely white-puberulent, irregularly and shallowly 5-toothed, teeth triangular and acute; bractlets and bracteoles linear-setaceous, ¹⁄₂₅–⅙ in. long.

Fruit. Small, globular, brown to black, ⅛–⅙ in. long, the persistent calyx membranous; stone 4-celled, no endosperm.

Leaves. Internodes 1¼–4 in. long, leaves decussate-opposite, deciduous, digitately compound of 3–9 (mostly 5–7) leaflets, blades 1¼–5 in., central one usually largest, linear to linear-elliptic or lanceolate, apex attenuate-acuminate; base gradually narrowed into a semiwing and channeled, sessile in the smaller leaves; mar-

gin entire or plane surface undulate-repand, texture thin; upper surface dull green and glabrous or minutely pulverulent; lower surface paler or almost whitened, puberulent, veins reticulate under magnification; petioles ½–3 in. long, densely grayish or reddish brown, puberulent to pulverulent or cinereous, resinous-granular.

Twigs. Slender, elongate, quadrangular, green to reddish brown or gray, grayish puberulent and pulverulent, pith stout.

Bark. Smooth, light to dark gray on young branches, on old trunks gray with broad ridges and shallow fissures.

Range. Dry, sunny situations, in various types of soils. From China and India, widely cultivated in Europe and Asia. In the United States cultivated from Texas eastward to Florida and northward to North Carolina. Sometimes escaping cultivation.

Remarks. The genus name, *Vitex*, is the ancient Latin name. The species name, *agnus-castus*, is from *agnus (lamb)* and *castus* (pure, holy, or chaste). Vernacular names are Monk's Pepper-tree, Wild Pepper, Indian Spice, Abraham's Balm, Hemp-tree, Sage-tree, Wild Lavender, Common Chaste-tree, True Chaste-tree, Tree of Chastity, Chaste Lamb-tree.

The seeds of the Chaste-tree are reported to be sedative. In Brazil a perfume is made from the flowers, and the aromatic leaves are used to spice food.

TRUMPET-CREEPER FAMILY
(Bignoniaceae)

Hardy Yellow Trumpet

Tecoma stans (L.) H. B. K. var. *angustata* Rehd. [H]

Field Identification. Irregular shrub or small tree to 24 ft high.

Flowers. Panicles or racemes 3–17-flowered, 3–5 in. long; pedicels ½₂–½ in. long; corolla bright yellow, funnelform-campanulate, 1–2 in. long; flared into a spreading limb about ¾ in. across, 5-lobed and slightly 2-lipped; lower lip 3-lobed, middle lobe the longest; upper lip 2-lobed, all lobes rounded; throat with faint dark streaks of orange; 4 stamens, 2 long and 2 short (sometimes with a fifth stamen bearing an abortive anther), attached to the corolla throat within, pubescent; anthers about ¼ in. across when spread in anthesis, hairy; pistil thinly spatulate but 2-cleft; ovary with numerous ovules borne in 2 rows in each cavity; calyx about ⅛–¼ in. long, tubular, 5-lobed; lobes triangular, acute or acuminate, glabrous.

Fruit. Capsule 4–6 in. long and ¼ in. wide, linear, flattened, acute, valves leathery, loculicidally dehiscent, pedicel about ½ in. long; seeds about ³⁄₁₆ in. long, flat and winged.

Leaves. Opposite, odd-pinnate, 4–8 in. long; leaflets 5–13 (usually 7–9) sessile or nearly so, lanceolate to elliptic or linear, acumi-

nate at apex, cuneate but rather asymmetrical at base, margin
sharply and coarsely serrate, surface usually glabrous and olive
green above, paler and glabrous or pubescent beneath (pubescent
to tomentose in the Velvety Yellow Trumpet, *T. stans* var.
velutina); petiole about ¼–½ in. long, winged and grooved by the
continuing leaf base.

Twigs. Young ones green, slender, older ones brown to gray,
striate, lenticels elongate.

Range. Well-drained, dry soil in full sun. The species, *stans*, grows
in western and southern Texas, New Mexico, Arizona, and Florida. Southward it is widely distributed through the countries of
Central and South America, and the West Indies.

Remarks. The genus name, *Tecoma*, is from an Indian name
meaning "pot tree." The species name, *stans*, signifies the upright
habit of this plant. English vernacular names are Yellow-bells,
Trumpet Flower, and Yellow-elder. In Mexico, Central and South

America, and the West Indies, there are many local names as
follows: Retamo, Retama, Tronodor, Tronodora, Trompetilla,
Trumpeta, Gloria, Kanlo, Xkanlol, Guie-bicki, Tulosuchil, Palo de
Arco, Flor de San Pedro, Corneta Amarilla, Nixtamaxochitl, Nex-
tamalxochill, Borla de San Pedro, Hierba de San Nicolás, Flor
Amarilla, Roble Amarillo, Miñona, Mazarca, Huachacata, Ichulili,
Saúco Amarillo, Ruibarba, Copete, Sardinillo, Fresno, Chirlobirlos,
Paulo Huesa, Tache, Tosto, Candillo, Garrocha, Garanguay Ama-
rillo, Guaram-guaran, San Andrés, Morchucha, and Tagualaishte.
The nectar is reported to be good bee food. The Indians made
bows from the wood. The plant is often cultivated for ornament.

Desert-willow

Chilopsis linearis (Cav.) Sweet [H]

Field Identification. Shrub or slender tree to 30 ft, with trunks
usually leaning.

Flowers. Mostly May–June, but blooming sporadically after rains
in other months, showy, perfect, in short panicles 2–4 in. long;
corolla funnelform-campanulate, slightly oblique, 1–1½ in. long,
5-lobate, lobes suborbicular and undulate on the margins, disposed in 2 lips; lower lip 3-lobed, dark pink or purple with the
central lobe longest; upper lip 2-lobed and pink, throat white,
yellow, or streaked purple (corolla variable in color shades from
white or purple); 4 stamens, 2 long and 2 short, included, adnate
to the wall of the corolla within; filaments filiform, glabrous;
anthers oblong, cells divergent at maturity; a solitary staminodium, shorter than the stamens, is also included; pistil simple,
usually longer than the stamens; ovary 2-celled, glabrous, lobes
flattened, ovate, rounded; ovules numerous; calyx splitting into 2
lips, lips about ¼ in. long, ovate, concave, acute, thin, papery,
pubescent or glabrous.

Fruit. Capsule borne on stout peduncles ½–1 in. long, linear, 4–12
in. long, about ¼ in. thick, subterete, striate, 2-valved, apiculate at
the apex, persistent; seeds numerous, compressed, oblong, about
⅓ in. long, in 2 ranks, extended into wings with long fimbriate
white hairs.

Leaves. Deciduous, opposite or alternate, linear to lanceolate, entire, thin, 3-nerved, 4–12 in. long, average length 3–5 in., ¼–⅓
in. wide, attenuate long-pointed at the ends, pubescent or glabrous, rather pale green on both sides, sometimes viscid-sticky;
petiole short or none, almost winged by the leaf base.

Twigs. Slender, green the first year, somewhat pubescent, later gray to reddish brown and glabrous.

Bark. Smooth and brown on young trunks, dark brown to black later and breaking into broad ridges with small scales, fissures irregular and rather deep.

Wood. Dark brown with lighter streaks, coarse-grained, soft, weak, rather durable in contact with the soil, specific gravity 0.59.

Range. The species, *linearis*, and its varieties grow along arid desert washes or dry arroyos from Texas north into New Mexico, west to Arizona and California, south into the Mexican states of Nuevo León, Tamaulipas, Zacatecas, Chihuahua, Sonora, Durango, and Baja California.

Remarks. The genus name, *Chilopsis*, is from the Greek words *cheilos* (lip) and *opsis* (likeness), with reference to the corolla lips. The species name, *linearis*, refers to the narrow leaves. Also known under the vernacular names of Flowering-willow, Willowleaf-catalpa, and Flor de Mimbre. These names arise from the fact that the flowers resemble those of the catalpa tree and the leaves are willowlike in appearance.

The wood is used for fence posts and fuel, and baskets are woven from the twigs. It is reported that in Mexico a decoction of the flowers is used for coughs and bronchial disturbances. The flowers also make good honey. The foliage is unpalatable to live-stock and is eaten only under stress. Various birds consume the winged seeds, which average about 75,000 per lb. Only about half the seeds are viable, and according to United States Forest Service data only about 4,000 usable plants can be obtained from a pound of seed. The tree grows readily from cuttings and is being planted extensively for ornament.

One botanist has separated two varieties of the Desert-willow. One of these is referred to as the Western Desert-willow, *C. linearis* var. *arcuata* Fosberg, with curved, glabrous leaves about $\frac{1}{12}$–$\frac{1}{6}$ in. wide. This variety is found from New Mexico north to Nevada, west to California, and south to Sonora, Mexico. The other variety is known as the Sticky Desert-willow, *C. linearis* var. *glutinosa* (Engelm.) Fosberg. It is reported as having straight, viscid leaves $\frac{1}{4}$–$\frac{1}{3}$ in. wide and is listed as occurring in Texas, New Mexico, and Mexico. A white-flowered horticultural form, *C. linearis* forma *alba*, is popular.

The trees of the Texas Big Bend area appear to fit the description of the Sticky Desert-willow, but those of the northern Trans-Pecos area show wide foliage variations, the extremes being viscid and nonviscid, straight and curved, and wider or narrower leaves. The intergrades between the two varieties are rather numerous.

MADDER FAMILY (Rubiaceae)

Common Button-bush

Cephalanthus occidentalis L. [H]

Field Identification. Shrub or small tree to 18 ft, growing in low areas, often swollen at the base.

Flowers. June–September. Borne on peduncles 1–3 in. long, white, sessile, clustered in globular heads 1–1½ in. in diameter; corolla

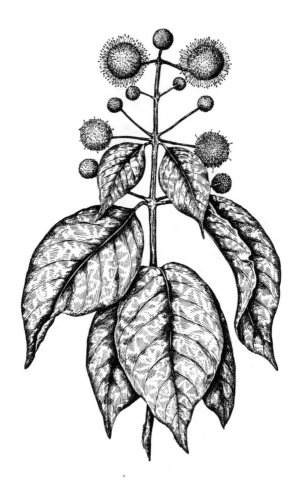

¼–½ in. long, tubular with 4 short, ovate, spreading lobes; stamens 4, inserted in corolla throat, anthers oblong; style slender, exserted; stigma capitate; ovary 2-celled; calyx tube obpyramidal with 4–5 rounded sepals.

Fruit. September–October. Round cluster of reddish brown nutlets; nutlets dry, obpyramidal, ¼–⅓ in. long.

Leaves. Opposite, or in whorls of 3, simple, deciduous, short-petioled, ovate or lanceolate-oblong, acuminate or acute at apex, rounded or narrow at base, entire; blades 2–8 in. long, 1–3 in.

wide, dark green and glabrous above or somewhat hairy beneath; petioles glabrous, stout, ½–¾ in. long; stipules small, triangular.

Twigs. Dark reddish brown, lustrous, glaucous when young; lenticels pale and elongate.

Bark. Thin, smooth, gray to brown, later with flattened ridges and deep fissures.

Range. New Mexico, Oklahoma, Texas, Arkansas, and Louisiana; eastward to Florida, and throughout North America from southern Canada to the West Indies. Also in eastern Asia.

Remarks. The Greek genus name, *Cephalanthus*, means "head flower," and the species name, *occidentalis*, means "western." Vernacular names for the shrub are Spanish Pincushion, Riverbrush, Swampwood, Button-willow, Crane-willow, Little-snowball, Pinball, Box, Button-wood, Pond-dogwood, Uvero, and Crouperbush. It is frequently cultivated as an ornamental shrub and provides good bee food. According to stomach records, the nutlet is eaten by at least 25 species of birds, mostly water birds. The wood is of no economic value.

HONEYSUCKLE FAMILY (Caprifoliaceae)

American Elder

Sambucus canadensis L. [H]

Field Identification. Stoloniferous shrub with many stems from the base, or under favorable conditions a tree to 30 ft. Stems thinly woody with a large white pith.

Flowers. Borne May–July in conspicuous, large, terminal, convex or flattened cymes, sometimes as much as 10 in. across. Peduncles and pedicels striate, green at first, reddish later. Corolla white, ⅕–¼ in. wide, tube short and expanding into 5 lobes; lobes ovate to oblong, rounded, about ⅛ in. long; calyx minute, 5-lobed; stamens 5, exserted, inserted at the base of the corolla; filaments slender, white, about ⅛ in. long, anthers oblong, yellow; style short, depressed, 3-parted; ovary inferior, 4-celled and 1-seeded.

Fruit. Drupe berrylike, deep purple or black, subglobose, ⅙–¼ in. in diameter, bittersweet, 4-celled, seed roughened.

Leaves. Deciduous, opposite, 4–12 in. long, odd-pinnate compound of 5–11 (usually 5–7) leaflets; rachis glabrous or pubescent;

leaflets elliptic to lanceolate or ovate to oval, apex acute or acuminate, base rounded or broadly cuneate, margin sharply serrate, blades 2–6 in. long, width 1–2 in.; petiolules ⅛–¼ in. long, pubescent; upper surface lustrous, bright green, and glabrous; lower surface paler, barely or copiously pubescent.

Stems. Smooth to angular or grooved, green to red when young, older stems reddish, yellowish, or gray, bark sometimes with warty protuberances, nodes sometimes enlarged; external woody layer thin, pith large and white.

Range. In rich moist soil, along streams, low places, fence rows. In Oklahoma, Arkansas, Texas, and Louisiana; eastward to Florida and Georgia, northward to Nova Scotia, and westward to Kansas and Manitoba.

Remarks. The genus name, *Sambucus*, is the classical Latin name, and the species name, *canadensis*, refers to Canada, where the plant grows at its most northern limit. It is also known under the local names of Elder-berry, Common Elder, Sweet Elder, Pie Elder, and Elder-blow. The various parts of the plant have been used for food or medicine in domestic practice. The fruit is made into pies, wines, and jellies. The flowers are used to flavor candies and jellies, and the Indians made a drink by soaking them in water. The dried leaves have been used as an insecticide, and the bark in preparing a black dye. The stems, with the pith removed, were formerly used as drains in tapping maple sugar, and children make whistles, flutes, and popguns from them. The plant has considerable value as a wildlife food, being eaten by about 45 species of birds, especially the gallinaceous birds, such as the quail, pheasant, and prairie chicken. It is also browsed by white-tailed deer and is considered highly palatable to livestock; however, its use by livestock should be investigated further. The writer has noted that in some localities it is browsed, but in other localities the cattle refuse to touch it even under stress conditions.

Rusty Blackhaw Viburnum

Viburnum rufidulum Raf. [H]

Field Identification. An irregularly branched shrub or tree to 40 ft, with opposite, finely serrate, shiny leaves.

Flowers. In flat cymes 2–6 in. across with 3–4 stout rays and minute subulate bracts and bractlets; corolla small, ¼–⅓ in. in diameter, regular; petals 5, rounded orbicular or oblong, white; stamens 5, attached to the corolla, exserted, anthers oblong and introrse; pistil with style absent and stigmas 1–3, sessile on the ovary, ovary 3-celled, only 1 cell maturing.

Fruit. Ripe July–October, in drooping clusters, drupes ⅓–½ in. long, oblong to obovoid, bluish black, glaucous; seed solitary, flattened, oval to ovate, ridged toward one end.

Leaves. Simple, opposite, deciduous, or half-evergreen southward, dark green, leathery, shiny above, paler below with red hairs on veins, margin finely serrate, elliptic to obovate or oval, apex rounded to acute or obtuse, base cuneate or rounded, 1½–4 in. long, 1–2½ in. broad, petiole grooved, wing-margined, clothed with red hairs, length ½–¾ in.

Bark. Rather rough, ridges narrow and rounded, fissures narrow, breaking into dark reddish brown or black squarish plates.

Twigs. Young ones gray with reddish hairs, older ones reddish brown, more glabrous.

Wood. Fine-grained, hard, heavy, strong, with a disagreeable odor.

Range. In river-bottom lands or dry uplands. Oklahoma, Arkansas, Texas, and Louisiana; eastward to Florida, northward to Virginia, and west to Kansas.

Remarks. The genus name, *Viburnum*, is the classical name of the Wayfaring-tree, *V. lantana* L., of Eurasia, which is often cultivated. The species name, *rufidulum*, refers to the rufous-red hairs on young parts. This character prompted the use of the name *V. rufotomentosum* Small at one time. Some vernacular names are Rusty Nanny-berry, Southern Nanny-berry, Blackhaw, Southern Blackhaw. The roots or stems of either *V. rufidulum* Raf. or *V. prunifolium* have been used to make a drug. The tree is worthy of cultivation because of the lustrous leaves, cymes of white flowers in April, and bluish black fruit in October. The wood is of no particular value.

DIAGRAMS

Inflorescence

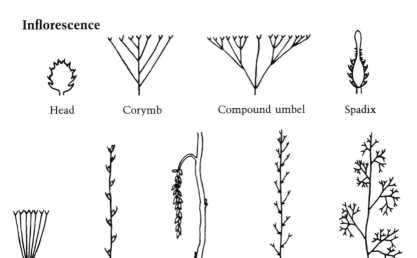

Head   Corymb   Compound umbel   Spadix

Umbel   Spike   Catkin   Raceme   Panicle

Leaf Apices

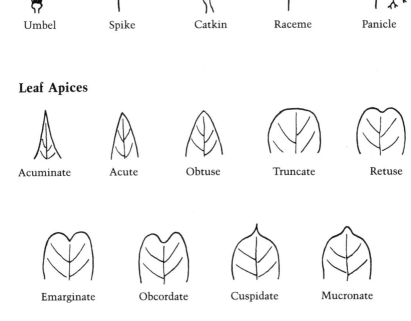

Acuminate   Acute   Obtuse   Truncate   Retuse

Emarginate   Obcordate   Cuspidate   Mucronate

Leaf Margins

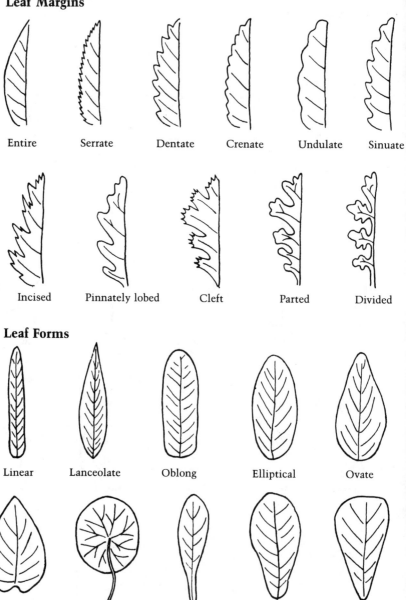

Entire Serrate Dentate Crenate Undulate Sinuate

Incised Pinnately lobed Cleft Parted Divided

Leaf Forms

Linear Lanceolate Oblong Elliptical Ovate

Cordate Orbicular Spatulate Obovate Cuneate

Flower Parts

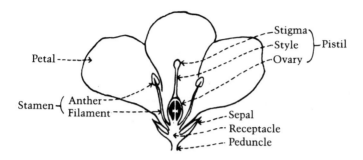

GLOSSARY

A- (prefix). Without, lacking.

Abaxial. On the dorsal side, away from the axis.

Aberrant. Not normal, atypical.

Abortive. Imperfectly developed.

Abruptly acuminate. Suddenly pointed from a rounded or truncate apex.

Abruptly pinnate. A pinnate leaf ending with a pair of leaflets; even-pinnate.

Acaulescent. Without a stem aboveground.

Accrescent. Increasing in size with age.

Accumbent. Lying against and face to face.

Acerose. Needlelike.

Achene. A small, dry, hard, one-seeded, indehiscent fruit.

Acicular. Bristlelike.

Acidulous. Slightly acid or bitter.

Acorn. The fruit of oaks.

Acotyledonous. Without cotyledons.

Acrid. Bitter or sharp tasting, usually referring to the fruit or sap.

Acropetal. Borne in succession toward the apex, as in certain inflorescences.

Acuminate. Referring to an acute apex whose sides are concave.

Acute. Terminating with a sharp angle.

Adherent. Referring to two dissimilar parts or organs which touch but are not fused.

Adnate. Grown together; organically united.

Adventive. A recent, perhaps temporary, introduction, not as yet naturalized, or barely so.

Aerenchyma. Spongy respiratory tissue in stems of many aquatic plants, characterized by large intercellular spaces.

Aerial. Parts above the ground or water.

Aggregate. Referring to a type of fruit with a cluster of ripened coherent ovaries.

Alkaloid. An organic base produced in some plants, sometimes with medicinal or poisonous properties.

Allergic. Subject to irritation by foreign substances.

Alpine. At high elevations; above the tree line.

Alternate. Placed singly at different levels on the axis.

Alternation of generations. Alternate sexual and asexual generations.

Alveola. Surface cavity of carpel or seed.

Ament. A catkin or scaly-bracted, often pendulous, spike of naked or reduced flowers.

Amplexicaul. Clasping the stem.

Ampliate. Expanded or enlarged.

Anastomosing. Netted; said of leaf blades with cross veins forming a network.

Anatropous. Referring to an ovule's position when the micropyle is close to the point of funiculus attachment.

Androecium. Stamens, in the collective sense.

Androgynous. Bearing staminate and pistillate flowers in the same inflorescence.

Androphore. Supporting stalk of a group of stamens.

Angulate. Angled.

Annulus. A ring-shaped part or organ.

Anterior. Away from the axis; the front; toward a subtending leaf or bract.

Anther. The polleniferous part of a stamen.

Anther cells. The actual chambers or locules of an anther.

Anther sac. Pollen sac of an anther.

Antheriferous. Having anthers.

Anthesis. Time of expansion of a flower; pollination time.

Anthocarp. A fruit condition in which at least a portion of the perianth is united with the ovary wall itself.

Antrorse. Directed upward.

Apetalous. Lacking petals.

Apex. The top or termination of a part or organ.

Apiculate. Ending in a short pointed tip.

Apomixis. Reproduction without sexual union.

Appendages. Various subsidiary or secondary outgrowths.

Appressed. Closely and flatly pressed against.

Approximate. Adjacent or close.

Aquatic. Growing in water.

Arachnoid. Bearing weak, tangled, cobwebby hairs.

Arboreal. Referring to trees, treelike.

Arborescent. Like tees in size and growth habit.

Arcuate. Somewhat curved.

Arenicolous. Sand loving.

Areole, areola (pl. *areolae*). An open space or island formed by anastomosing veins in a foliar organ; spine-bearing area of cactus.

Aril. An appendage or complete additional covering of the seed, arising as an outgrowth from hilum or funicle.

Aristate. With a stiff, bristlelike appendage.

Articulated. Jointed and cleanly separating to leave a scar.

Ascending. Growing upward, but not erect.

Asexual. Without sex, reproduction without sexual union, such as by cuttings, buds, bulbs, etc.

Assurgent. Ascending.

Asymmetric. Not symmetrical; with no plane of symmetry.

Atypical. Not typical.

Attenuate. Slenderly tapering.

Auricle. Earlike attachment, such as at the base of some leaves or petals.

Auriculate. Furnished with auricles.

Autophytic. Having chlorophyll, self-sustaining.

Axial. Referring to the axis.

Axil. The upper angle formed by a leaf with the stem, or veins with other veins.

Axile. Situated on the axis.

Axillary. Situated in an axil.

Axis. The center line of any organ; the main stem.

Baccate. Berrylike; bearing berries.

Banner. Upper or posterior petal of a papilionaceous flower.

Barb. A bristlelike hooked hair or projection.

Bark. External tissues of woody plants, especially the dead corky layer external to the cortex or bast in trees.

Basal. At or near the base.

Beak. A narrow pointed outgrowth of a fruit, a petal, etc.

Berry. A fruit in which the ovary becomes a fleshy or pulpy mass enclosing one or more seeds, as is seen in the tomato.

Bi- (prefix). Two or two-parted.

Bifid. Cleft into two lobes.

Biglandular. With two glands.

Bilabiate. Two-lipped, as in some irregular corollas.

Bipinnate. Twice pinnate.

Bisexual. Having both sex organs in the same flower.

Biternate. Twice ternate.

Blade. The expanded portion of a leaf.

Brackish. Partially saline.

Bract. A more or less modified leaf subtending a flower or belonging to a cluster of flowers.

Bracteole. A small bract or bractlet.

Bractlet. The bract of a pedicel.

Bud. The rudimentary state of a shoot; an unexpanded flower.

Bud scales. Modified leaves protecting a bud, often dry, resinous or viscid.

Caducous. Falling early.

Caliche. A hard calcareous soil.

Callose. Bearing a callus.

Callus. A thickened or hardened protuberance or region.

Calyculus. Usually in the Compositae, referring to the short outer sepallike phyllaries of an involucre.

Calyx. The outer perianth whorl of the flower.

Campanulate. Bell-shaped.

Canaliculate. Having one or a few prominent longitudinal grooves.

Cancellate. With cross hatching or latticed ridges.

Canescent. Hoary with a gray pubescence.

Capillary. Hairlike.

Capitate. In a head, or headlike.

Capsule. A dry dehiscent fruit composed of more than one carpel.

Carina. A dorsal ridge or keel.

Carpel. A simple pistil, or one member of a compound pistil; the ovule-bearing portion of a flower, believed to be of foliar origin.

Cartilaginous. Firm or tough tissue, suggestive of animal cartilage.

Caruncle. A seed protuberance; a small hard aril.

Catkin. A delicate, scaly bracted, usually pendulous, spike of flowers; an ament.

Caudate. Long-attenuate; taillike.

Caudex. Enlarged basal part of stems, or combined root and stem.

Caulescent. Having an evident stem, as contrasted to acaulescent.

Cauline. Borne on the stem.

Centrifugal inflorescence. Flowers developing from the center outward; a determinate type, such as a cyme.

Centripetal inflorescence. Flowers developing from the outer edge toward the center; an indeterminate type, such as a corymb.

Cespitose, caespitose. In tufts.

Chaff. A small scale, as is found on the receptacle of many Compositae.

Chaparral. A type of low scrub, commonly with dense twiggy, thorny habit and evergreen leaves.

Chartaceous. Like old parchment; papery.

Ciliate. Bearing marginal hairs.

Ciliolate. Bearing short marginal hairs.

Cinereous. Ashy gray.

Circinate. Referring to a leaf that is coiled from the tip toward the base, the lower surface outermost.

Cirrhus. A tendril.

Clambering. Leaning on other plants or objects, not self-supporting.

Clasping. Enveloping the stem partially or wholly at the base, as leaf bases, bracts, stipules, etc.

Clavate. Club-shaped.

Claw. Narrowed petiolelike base of a petal or sepal.

Cleft. Incised or cut nearly or quite to the middle.

Cleistogamous. Said of flowers that are self-fertilized without expanding; modified or reduced flowers.

Climber. Plant seeking support by twining or by tendrils.

Coalescent. Grown together, as in similar parts.

Coat. Covering of a seed.

Coherent. Having similar parts in close contact but not fused.

Column. A body formed by the union of parts, such as a union of stamens to form the staminal column in Malvaceae.

Coma. A hair tuft, usually at the apex of seeds.

Commisure. A line of coherence, such as where two carpels are joined.

Compound leaf. A leaf with the blade divided into two or more leaflets.

Compressed. Flattened.

Concavo-convex. Convex on one side and concave on the other.

Concolorous. The same in color.

Conduplicate. Folded lengthwise.

Cone. An inflorescence of flowers or fruit with overlapping scales.

Confluent. Gradually passing into each other.

Congested. Crowded, as flowers in a dense inflorescence.

Conic. Cone-shaped.

Coniferous. Cone-bearing.

Connate. Said of similar parts which are united, at least at the base.

Connective. Extension of the filament of a stamen connecting the anther lobes.

Connivent. Arched inward so that the tips meet.

Consimilar. Alike.

Constricted. Narrowed between wider portions.

Contiguous. Adjacent or adjoining similar or dissimilar parts, not fused.

Contorted. Twisted.

Contracted. Narrowed or shortened.

Convergent. Tending toward a single point, as with leaf veins approaching each other.

Convolute. Rolled together, as with petals in buds of certain plants.

Copious. Abundant, plentiful.

Cordate. Heart-shaped, as in some leaves.

Coriaceous. Leathery in texture.

Corneous. Horny, as in margins of some leaves.

Corniculate. Hornlike in appearance.

Cornute. Spurred or horned.

Corolla. The inner perianth whorl of a flower.

Corona. A crownlike structure on the corolla and the stamens.

Coroniform. Crown-shaped, applied to the pappus of certain Compositae.

Corrugate. Strongly wrinkled.

Corymb. A flat-topped or convex open flower cluster, with its marginal flowers opening first.

Costa. A thickened vein or midrib.

Cotyledon. Plant embryo leaf, usually rich in stored food.

Creeping. Referred to a trailing shoot which strikes root along most of its length.

Crenate. Dentate with the teeth much rounded.

Crenulate. The diminutive of crenate.

Crest. A crown or elevated ridge, often entirely or partly of hair.

Crispate. Crisped or crumpled.

Cross-pollination. Transfer of pollen from flower to flower.

Crown. Usually referring to the branches and foliage of a tree; or thickened bases of stems.

Cruciform. Shaped like a cross.

Crustaceous. Dry and brittle.

Cucullate. Hood-shaped.

Cuneate. Wedge-shaped.

Cupulate. Cup-shaped, as the involucre of an acorn.

Cuspidate. Having a sharp rigid point.

Cyathium. A specialized form of inflorescence of some of the Euphorbias.

Cylindric. Elongate and circular in cross section.

Cylindroid. Like a cylinder but elliptic in cross section.

Cymbiform. Boat-shaped.

Cyme. A usually broad and flattish inflorescence with its central or terminal flowers blooming earliest.

Cymose. Cymelike.

Cymule. A small cyme.

Deciduous. Not persistent, not evergreen.

Declined. Turned downward or outward, as in some stamens.

Decompound. Several times divided, as in repeatedly compound leaves and inflorescences.

Decumbent. Reclining, but ascending at the apices.

Decurrent. Extensions downward, as of some petioles or leaves along the stem.

Decurved. Curved downward.

Decussate. Leaves opposite, with each pair at a right angle to the pair above or below.

Deflexed. Bent downward.

Dehiscent. Opening regularly by valves.

Deltoid. Triangular.

Dentate. Toothed, specifically when teeth have sharp points and spreading bases.

Denticulate. Minutely toothed.

Denudate. Becoming bare.

Depressed. Flattened from above.

Dermatitis. Irritation or inflammation of the skin.

Determinate. Having fixed limits, as in an inflorescential axis ending with a bud; also referring to a cymose, or centrifugal, inflorescence.

Diadelphous. With stamens in two groups.

Dichotomous. Forked in pairs.

Didymous. Twice, two-lobed, in pairs.

Didynamous. With four stamens in two pairs of differing length.

Diffuse. Spreading.

Digitate. Said of a compound leaf in which all the leaflets arise from one point.

Dilated. Expanded or enlarged.

Dimidiate. Reduced to one-half, often by abortion.

Dimorphic. Having two forms.

Dioecious. Unisexual, with the two kinds of flowers on separate plants.

Diploid. Having the somatic number of chromosomes; twice as many as in the germ cells after reduction.

Disarticulate. Breaking at a joint.

Disc, disk. Outgrowth of the receptacle or hypanthium within the perianth, often composed of fused nectaries; central portion of the head in Compositae.

Disciform. Disk-shaped.

Discoid. Referring to a rayless head of flowers, as in some Compositae.

Discolored. Usually of two colors, as in leaf surfaces.

Dissected. Deeply cut or divided into many narrow segments, as in some leaves.

Distal. The apex of an organ, the part most distant from the axis.

Distended. Swollen.

Distichous. In two vertical ranks.

Distinct. Separate, not united.

Diurnal. Opening during the day.

Divaricate. Widely spreading.

Divergent. Spreading apart.

Divided. Lobed to near the base.

Division. Segment of a parted or divided leaf.

Dorsal. Upon or relating to the back or outer surface of an organ.

Dorsifixed. Attached to the dorsal side.

Drupe. A fleshy or pulpy fruit in which the inner portion is hard and stony, enclosing the seed.

Drupelet. A small drupe.

E- (prefix). Without or lacking a structure or organ.

Echinate. Prickly.

Ecology. Science dealing with plants in relation to their environment.

Eglandular. Without glands.

Ellipsoid. Referring to the geometric figure obtained by rotating an ellipse on its longer axis.

Elliptic. Of the form of an ellipse.

Elongate. Lengthened, drawn out.

Emarginate. Referring to a notch, usually of a leaf apex.

Embryo. A young plant, still enclosed in the seed.

Endemic. Known only in a limited geographical area.

Endocarp. Inner layer of the pericarp of the ovary or fruit.

Endosperm. Part of the seed outside the embryo; the albumen or stored food.

Ensiform. Sword-shaped.

Entire. Without toothing or divisions.

Ephemeral. Lasting for only a short period.

Epidermis. The superficial layer of cells.

Epigaeous, epigeous. Growing on the ground, or close to the ground.

Epigynous. Attached to or borne on the pistil, as in some stamens or petals.

Erose. Irregularly toothed.

Estipulate. Exstipulate.

Exalbuminous. Without albumen or endosperm, the embryo filling the seed instead.

Excavated. Referring to some pitted or channeled seeds.

Excurrent. Prolongation of nerves into awns or mucros of a leaf or fruit body; also the prolongation of the main stem or axis of a plant in certain conifers.

Excurved. Curved outward.

Exfoliating. Referring to bark separating into strips or flakes.

Exocarp. The outer layer of pericarp.

Exogenous. Growth by increase of tissue beneath the expanding bark; the cambium region in dicotyledonous woody plants; as opposed to endogenous growth by internal multiplication of tissues in monocotyledonous plants.

Expanded. Spreading, opened to the greatest extent.

Explanate. Flattened out.

Exserted. Projecting beyond an envelope, as stamens from a corolla.

Exstipulate. Lacking stipules.

Extra-axillary. Being near the axil but not truly axillary, as in some flowers.

Extrafloral. Outside the flower, as extrafloral nectaries.

Extrorse. Directed outward.

Exudate. An excretion of wax, gum, sap, etc.

Faceted. Usually applied to seeds with several plane surfaces.

Facial. On the plane surface or face rather than the margin.

Falcate. Sickle- or scythe-shaped.

Farinose. Covered with mealy or floury particles.

Fascicle. A close bundle or cluster.

Fastigiate. Having closely set erect branches.

Faveolate. Honeycombed.

Feather-veined. With secondary veins branching from the main vein.

Fertile. Applied to flowers with pistils capable of producing seeds, or to stamens with functional pollen.

Fetid. Malodorous.

Fibrilla. A very small fringe.

Fibrillose. Having fine fibers, as the leaf margins of some Yuccas.

Fibrous. Bearing a resemblance to fibers, or possessing fibers, as in fibrous roots.

Filament. The part of a stamen which supports the anther.

Filamentose. Having threadlike structures; threadlike.

Filiferous. Bearing threads.

Filiform. Thread-shaped.

Fimbriate. Fringed, frayed at the ends or on the margin.

Flabellate. Fan-shaped.

Flaccid. Lax, limp, flabby.

Flexuose, flexuous. Zigzag, or bent in an alternating manner.

Floccose. Clothed with tufts of soft woolly hairs.

Flora. Referring to flowers.

Floret. A small flower, as in the disk flowers of Compositae.

Floriferous. Having flowers, usually abundantly.

Floristic. Referring to the aggregate aspects of the vegetation, as to species, abundance, and distribution in a geographical sense.

Fluted. Regularly marked by alternating ridges and groovelike depressions.

Foliaceous. Leaflike in texture and appearance.

Foliate. Referring to leaves as opposed to leaflets.

Foliolate. Referring to the leaflets in a compound leaf, such as bifoliolate or trifoliolate.

Follicle. A dry fruit opening along the single suture, the product of a simple pistil.

Fruit. Seed-bearing part of a plant.

Frutescent. Shrubby.

Fugacious. Referring to early-deciduous parts, such as petals or sepals of certain plants.

Fulvous. Tawny, dull yellow.

Functional. Able to produce normally.

Funiculus. The stalk attaching ovule to ovary wall or placenta.

Funnelform. Shaped like a funnel.

Fuscous. Dark brownish gray.

Fusiform. Spindle-shaped.

Gamopetalous. Referring to the petals being more or less united.

Gamosepalous. Referring to the sepals being more or less united.

Geminate. In pairs, twins.

Gene. A unit of inheritance which occupies a fixed place on a chromosome.

Geniculate. Bent like a knee joint.

Gibbous. Swollen or inflated on one side.

Glabrate. Somewhat glabrous or becoming glabrous.

Glabrous. Smooth; pubescence or hairs absent.

Gland. A secreting protuberance or appendage.

Glandular. Bearing glands, or of the nature of a gland.

Glaucous. Covered with a white, waxy bloom.

Globose. Globular, spherical.

Glochid. A hair or minute prickle, often with retrorse or hooklike projections, as in some cacti.

Glomerate. In a headlike or crowded inflorescence.

Glomerule. A small headlike inflorescence.

Glutinous. Gluelike, sticky.

Graduated. Rows or series of bracts, or phyllaries, of different size, as on the involucre of some Compositae.

Granules. Small particles on the surface of a plant, such as resinous granules, wax granules, etc.

Gynoecium, gynecium. The total female element of a flower.

Gynophore. The stalk of a pistil.

Habitat. The environment of a plant.

Halophyte. A plant tolerant of saline conditions.

Haploid. Possessing half of the diploid number of chromosomes, as in the germ cells after the reduction division.

Hastate. Halberd-shaped; sagittate, but with the basal lobes more or less at right angles.

Head. A spherical or flat-topped inflorescence of sessile or nearly sessile flowers borne on a common receptacle.

Heartwood. The oldest wood, inclosing the pith; the hard central, often deeply colored, portion of a tree trunk.

Hermaphrodite. Bisexual.

Heterogamous. Having two or more kinds of flowers with respect to the distribution of sex organs.

Heteromorphic. Unlike in form or size, as sometimes the length of stamens or pistils on different plants of the same species.

Heterostylous. Having styles of different length or character.

Hexamerous. With the parts in sixes.

Hilum. The scar of a seed, marking the point of attachment.

Hip. Fruit in *Rosa*, composed of swollen hypanthium bearing achenes within.

Hirsute. Covered with rather coarse or stiff hairs.

Hirsutulous. Finely or minutely hirsute.

Hispid. Beset with rigid or bristly hairs or with bristles.

Hispidulous. Minutely hispid.

Hoary. Densely grayish white pubescent.

Homochromous. Of uniform color.

Homogeneous. Of the same kind, uniform.

Homomorphic. Of uniform size and shape.

Hood. A concave organ, usually referring to certain petals.

Hyaline. Very thin and translucent.

Hybrid. Product of genetically dissimilar parents.

Hybridization. The production of a hybrid.

Hydrophilous. Referring to a tendency to grow in water.

Hydrophyte. An aquatic plant.

Hypanthium. Upward or outward extension of receptacle derived from fused basal portions of perianth and androecium.

Hypogynous. Inserted beneath the gynoecium, but free from it.

Imbricate. Overlapping.

Immersed. Submerged.

Imparipinnate. Pinnate with a single terminal leaflet; odd-pinnate.

Imperfect. Diclinous; lacking functional stamens or pistils.

Implicate. Twisted together or interwoven.

Impressed. Lying below the general surface; as, impressed veins.

Incanous. Hoary with whitish pubescence.

Incised. Cut sharply, irregularly, and more or less deeply.

Included. Not protruding, not exserted.

Incomplete. Descriptive of flowers in which one or more perianth whorls are wanting.

Incurved. Curved inward.

Indehiscent. Not opening.

Indeterminate. Applied to inflorescences in which the flowers open progressively from the base upward.

Indigenous. Native to an area.

Indument. A covering of hairs or wool.

Induplicate. Having the edges folded together.

Indurate. Hardened.

Inequilateral. Asymmetrical.

Inferior. Usually referring to an ovary being adnate to and appearing as if below the calyx.

Infertile. Not fertile or viable.

Inflated. Bladderlike.

Inflexed. Bent inward.

Inflorescence. A flower cluster; the disposition of flowers.

Inframedial. Below the middle, but not at the base.

Infrastaminal. Below the stamens.

Inodorous. Lacking odor.

Inserted. Attached to or growing out of.

Inter- (prefix). Between.

Intercostal. Between the ribs, veins, or nerves.

Internode. That portion of stem lying between two successive nodes.

Interrupted. Referring to an inflorescence with sterile intervals, mostly of varying length, between the flowers.

Intricate. Densely tangled, as in some branches.

Introflexion. State of being inflexed.

Introrse. Turned inward; facing the axis.

Intrusion. Protruding or projecting inward.

Inverted. Reversed, opposite to the normal direction.

Investing. Enclosing or surrounding.

Involucel. A secondary involucre, subtending a secondary division of an inflorescence as in Umbelliferae.

Involucral. Belonging to an involucre.

Involucre. One or more series of bracts, surrounding a flower cluster or a single flower.

Involute. With edges rolled inward.

Irregular. Said of flowers that are not bilaterally symmetrical.

Joint. A node; a unit of a segmented stem as in *Opuntia.*

Keel. The united pair of petals in a papilionaceous flower; a central or dorsal ridge.

Laciniate. Cut into lobes separated by deep, narrow, irregular incisions.

Lanate, lanuginose. Covered with matted hairs or wool.

Lanceolate. Shaped like a lance head.

Lanulose. Short-woolly.

Leaf. The usually thin and expanded organ borne laterally on the stem; in a strict sense inclusive of the blade, petiole, and stipules; but in common practice referred to the blade only.

Leaflet. A single division of a compound leaf.

Legume. A dry fruit, the product of a simple unicarpellate pistil, usually dehiscing along 2 lines of suture.

Lenticels. Corky growths on young bark.

Lenticular. Having the shape of a double convex lens.

Lepidote. Covered with minute scales or scurf.

Liana. A climbing woody plant.

Ligneous. Woody.

Ligulate. Tongue-shaped.

Ligule. Usually referring to an expanded ray flower in the Compositae.

Limb. The ultimate or uppermost extension of a gamopetalous corolla or calyx; distinct from the tube or throat.

Linear. Long and narrow.

Lingulate. Tongue-shaped.

Lip. One of the (usually two) divisions of an unequally divided corolla or calyx.

Littoral. Growing near the sea.

Lobe. Any segment or division of an organ.

Lobed. Divided into lobes, or having lobes.

Lobulate. With small lobes.

Locule. A compartment of an anther, ovary, or fruit.

Loculicidal. Longitudinally dehiscent dorsally, midway between the septa.

Loment. A fruit of the Leguminosae usually constricted between the seeds, the one-seeded indehiscent portions breaking loose.

Longitudinal. Lengthwise.

Lunate. Crescent-shaped.

Lyrate. Lyre-shaped, or a pinnatifid form with the terminal lobe usually longest.

Marcescent. Persistent after withering.

Marginal. On or pertaining to the margin of a plane organ.

Mealy. Farinose or floury.

Medial, median. Referring to or at the middle.

Membranaceous, membranous. Thin, rather soft, and more or less translucent.

Meniscoid. Concavo-convex, like a watch crystal.

Mericarp. A one-seeded indehiscent carpel of a fruit whose carpels separate at maturity.

-Merous (suffix). Referring to the number of parts; as 4-merous.

Mesophyte. Plant requiring a moderate amount of water.

Microphyllous. Small-leaved.

Midnerve. The central vein or rib.

Midrib. The main rib of a leaf.

Monadelphous. Union of all stamens by their filaments.

Moniliform. Necklacelike.

Monochasial. Applied to a cymose inflorescence with one main axis.

Monochromatic. Of one color.

Monoecious. With stamens and pistils in separate flowers, but on the same plant.

Monopodial. Applied to a stem having a single continuous axis.

Montane. Growing in the mountains.

Mottled. Spotted or blotched.

Mucilaginous. Sticky and moist.

Mucro. A short and small abrupt tip.

Mucronate. Tipped with a mucro.

Mucronulate. Diminutive of mucronate.

Multicipital. With several or numerous stems from a single caudex or taproot.

Multifoliolate. Referring to a compound leaf with numerous leaflets.

Multiple fruit. One that results from the aggregation of ripened ovaries into one mass.

Muricate. With surfaces bearing hard sharp tubercles.

Muriculate. Diminutive of muricate.

Naked. Lacking a customary part or organ; flowers without a perianth, a receptacle without chaff, a stem without leaves, etc.

Nectariferous. Producing nectar.

Nectary. A gland, or an organ containing the gland, which secretes nectar.

Nerve. An unbranched vein.

Neuter. Referring to flowers lacking stamens or pistils; or in some flowers of the Compositae having an ovary but lacking style or stigmas.

Nigrescent. Turning black.

Nocturnal. Night blooming.

Nodding. Arching downward.

Node. The joint of a twig; usually a point bearing a leaf or leaflike structure.

Nut. A hard, indehiscent, one-celled and one-seeded fruit.

Ob- (prefix). Inversely, upside down, as an obovate leaf (inversely ovate), etc.

Obcordate. Inverted heart-shaped.

Oblanceolate. Lanceolate with the broadest part toward the apex.

Oblique. Slanting; with unequal sides.

Oblong. Longer than broad and with nearly parallel sides.

Obovate. Inverted ovate.

Obovoid. Appearing as an inverted egg.

Obsolete. Not evident; very rudimentary; vestigial.

Obtuse. Blunt.

Ochroleucous. Yellowish white.

Ocrea. A tubular sheath formed by the union of a pair of stipules.

Odd-pinnate. A pinnate leaf with a single terminal leaflet.

Opposite. Opposed to each other, such as two opposite leaves at a node.

Orbicular. Circular.

Organ. A part of a plant with a definite function, as a leaf, stamen, etc.

Oval. Broadly elliptical.

Ovary. The part of the pistil that contains the ovules, or seeds after fertilization.

Ovate. Egg-shaped, with the broader end closer to the stem.

Ovoid. Referring to a solid object of ovate or oval outline.

Ovulate. Bearing ovules; referring to the number of ovules.

Ovule. The body which after fertilization becomes the seed.

Palea. A chaffy bract on the receptacle of Compositae.

Pallid. Pale or light colored.

Palmate. Said of a leaf radiately lobed or divided.

Palmatifid. Palmately cleft or lobed.

Palmatisect. Palmately divided.

Palustrine. Growing in wet ground.

Panicle. A branched raceme.

Pannose. Feltlike, covered with closely interwoven hairs.

Papilionaceous. Descriptive of the flowers of certain legumes having a standard, wings, and keel petals; resembling a sweet pea.

Papilla. A small soft protuberance on leaf surfaces, etc.

Papillate. Bearing papillae.

Pappus. Modified calyx of certain Compositae, often elaborate in the fruit, consisting of hairs, bristles, awns, or scales.

Parcifrond. A long leafy usually sterile shoot of a floricane, arising from below the ordinary floral branches.

Parietal. Attached to the wall within the ovary.

Parted. Cleft nearly to the base.

Parthenogenetic. Asexual development of an egg, without fertilization by a male sex cell.

Parti-colored. Variegated.

Pectinate. With narrow, toothlike divisions.

Pedate. Palmate, with the lateral lobes or divisions again divided.

Pedicel. The stalk of a single flower in a cluster.

Pedicellate. Borne on a pedicel.

Peduncle. Primary flower stalk supporting either a cluster or a solitary flower.

Pedunculate. Borne on a peduncle.

Pellucid. Transparent or nearly so.

Peltate. Referring to a leaf blade in which the petiole is attached to the lower surface, instead of on the margin as in the garden nasturtium.

Pendent. Hanging or drooping.

Pendulous. More or less hanging.

Pentagonal. Five-angled.

Pentamerous. Of five parts, as a flower with five petals.

Perennial. Usually living more than two years.

Perfect. Referring to a flower having both pistil and stamens.

Perfoliate. A sessile leaf whose base passes around the stem.

Perforate. Pierced with holes; dotted with translucent openings which resemble holes.

Perianth. The floral envelope, usually consisting of distinct calyx and corolla.

Pericarp. The outer wall of an ovary after fertilization, hence of the fruit.

Perigynous. Referring to petals and stamens whose bases surround the pistil, or pistils, and are borne on the margin of the hypanthium, as in some Rosaceae.

Persistent. Said of leaves that are evergreen, and of flower parts and fruits that remain attached to the plant for protracted lengths of time.

Petal. The unit of the corolla.

Petaloid. Resembling a petal.

Petiole. The stalk of a leaf.

Petiolar. Relating to or borne on the petiole, as a petiolar gland.

Petiolate. Having a petiole.

Petiolulate. Having a petiolule.

Petiolule. The footstalk of a leaflet.

Phyllary. One of the bracts of the involucre in Compositae.

Pilose. Hairy, especially with long soft hairs.

Pinnae. The primary divisions of a pinnate leaf.

Pinnate. Descriptive of compound leaves with the leaflets arranged on opposite sides along a common rachis.

Pinnatifid. Pinnately cleft, the clefts not extending to the midrib.

Pinnatilobate. Pinnately lobed.

Pinnatisect. Pinnately divided, the clefts extending to the midrib.

Pinnule. A leaflet or ultimate segment of a pinnately decompound leaf.

Pistil. The seed-bearing organ of the flower, consisting of ovary, stigma, and style.

Pistillate. Provided with pistils, but lacking functional stamens.

Pith. The central tissue of a (usually exogenous) stem, composed of thin-walled cells.

Placenta. The structure in an ovary to which the ovules are attached.

Plano-convex. Flat on one side, convex on the other.

Pleiochasium. A compound cyme with more than two branches at each division.

Plicate. Folded into plaits.

Plumose. Having fine hairs on each side like the plume of a feather.

Pluriseriate. In many series.

Pod. Any dry and dehiscent fruit.

Pollen. The male germ cells, contained in the anther.

Pollen sac. Pollen-bearing chamber of the anther.

Pollination. Deposition of pollen upon the stigma.

Polygamo-dioecious. Essentially dioecious, but with some flowers of other sex or perfect flowers on same individual.

Polygamous. With both perfect and unisexual flowers on the same individual plant or on different individuals of the same species.

Polygonal. With several sides or angles.

Polymorphic. With a number of forms, as, a very variable species.

Polyploid. With chromosome number in the somatic nuclei greater than the diploid number, sometimes accompanied by increased size and vigor of the plant.

Pome. A kind of a fleshy fruit of which the apple is the typical form.

Pore. A small opening, as found in certain anthers or fruits.

Porrect. Reaching or extending perpendicular to the surface, as with spines of some cacti.

Posterior. Toward the rear, behind, toward the axis.

Prickle. A rigid, straight or hooked, outgrowth of the bark or epidermal tissue.

Procumbent. Lying on the ground.

Prominent. Higher than the adjacent surface, as in prominent veins.

Prophyllum. A bracteole.

Prostrate. Flat on the ground.

Proximal. Near the base or axis, the opposite of distal.

Pruinose. Covered with a white bloom or powdery wax.

Puberulent. Very slightly pubescent.

Pubescence. A covering of short hairs.

Pubescent. Covered with hairs, especially if short, soft, and downlike.

Pulverulent. Powdered, appearing as if covered by minute grains of dust.

Punctate. Dotted with depressions or translucent internal glands or colored spots.

Pungent. Sharply and stiffly pointed; bitter or hot to the taste.

Pyriform. Pear-shaped.

Quadrangular. Four-angled.

Quadrate. Square.

Raceme. A single indeterminate inflorescence of pediceled flowers upon a common more or less elongated axis.

Racemose. Resembling a raceme; in racemes.

Rachis. The axis of a compound leaf or of an inflorescence.

Radial. Developing around a central axis.

Raphe. In anatropous ovules, the ridge formed by the fusion of a portion of the funicle to the ovule coat; ridge often persistent and prominent in seeds.

Ray. Usually referring to the more or less strap-shaped flowers in the head of Compositae.

Receptacle. The expanded portion of the axis that bears the floral organs.

Reclining. Bending or curving toward the ground.

Recurved. Curved downward or backward.

Reduced. Not normally or fully developed in size.

Reflexed. Abruptly bent or turned downward.

Regular. Uniform in shape or distribution of parts; radically symmetrical.

Remote. Referring to leaves or flowers which are distant or scattered on the stem.

Reniform. Kidney-shaped.

Repand. Having a somewhat undulating margin.

Repent. Prostrate, with the creeping stems rooting at the nodes.

Reticulate. Forming a network.

Retrorse. Turned downward or backward.

Retuse. Rounded and shallowly notched at the apex.

Revolute. Rolled or turned downward or toward the under surface.

Rhizome. A prostrate stem under the ground, rooting at the nodes and bearing buds on nodes.

Rhombic. With equal sides forming oblique angles.

Rib. A primary vein.

Rigid. Stiff.

Rosette. A cluster of basal leaves appearing radially arranged.

Rostrate. With a beaklike point.

Rotate. Wheel-shaped, usually referring to a flattened, short-tubed, sympetalous corolla.

Rotund. Rounded in shape.

Rudiment. A vestige, a much reduced organ, often nonfunctional.

Rufous. Reddish brown.

Rugose. Wrinkled.

Runcinate. Sharply incised pinnately, the incisions retrorse.

Runner. A stolon.

Sagittate. Shaped like an arrowhead.

Salient. Conspicuously projecting, as salient teeth or prominent ribs.

Salverform. Referring to a sympetalous corolla, with the limb at right angles to the tube.

Samara. An indehiscent winged fruit as in the maples and elms.

Scaberulous. Minutely scabrous.

Scabrous. Rough to the touch.

Scale. A leaf much reduced in size, or an epidermal outgrowth.

Scandent. Climbing.

Scape. A flower-bearing stem rising from the ground, the leaves either basal or scattered on the scape and reduced to bracts.

Scarious. Thin and dry.

Schizocarp. Referring to a septicidally dehiscent fruit with one-seeded carpels.

Sclerotic. Hardened, stony.

Scurf. Small scales, usually borne on a leaf surface or on stems.

Secondary. The second division, as in branches or leaf veins.

Secund. One-sided.

Seed. A ripened ovule.

Segment. Part of a compound leaf or other organ, especially if the parts are alike.

Self-pollination. Pollination within the flower.

Semi- (prefix). Approximately half; partly or nearly.

Sepal. A unit of the calyx.

Septicidal. Splitting or dehiscing through the partitions.

Septum (pl. *septa*). A partition or crosswall.

Seriate. Arranged in rows or whorls.

Sericeous. Bearing straight silky hairs.

Serrate. Having sharp teeth pointing forward.

Serrulate. Serrate with small fine teeth.

Sessile. Without stalk of any kind.

Seta (pl. *setae*). A bristle.

Sheath. A tubular structure, such as a leaf base enclosing the stem.

Shoot. A young branch.

Shrub. A woody plant with a number of stems from the base, usually smaller than a tree.

Silicle. A silique broader than long.

Silique. A long capsular fruit typical of the Cruciferae, the two valves separating at maturity.

Silky. Covered with close-pressed soft and straight hairs.

Simple. In one piece or unit, not compound.

Sinuate. Deeply or strongly wavy.

Sinus. The cleft or recess between two lobes.

Solitary. Alone, single.

Somatic. Referring to the body, or to all cells except the germ cells.

Spatulate. Gradually narrowed downward from a rounded summit.

Spherical. Round.

Spike. A racemose inflorescence with the flowers sessile or nearly so.

Spine. Modification of a stipule, petiole, or branch to form a hard, woody, sharp-pointed structure.

Spinescent. Ending in a spine.

Spiniferous. Bearing spines.

Spinulose. With small spines.

Spur. A tubular or saclike projection of the corolla or calyx, sometimes nectar bearing; a short, compact twig with little or no internodal development.

Squamella. A small scale, usually as in the pappus of some Compositae.

Squamose. Bearing scales.

Squamulose. Diminutive of squamose.

Stamen. The pollen-bearing organ, usually two or more in each flower.

Staminal column. A column or tube formed by the coalescence of the filaments of the stamens.

Staminate. Bearing stamens but lacking pistils.

Staminodium (pl. *staminodia*). A sterile stamen, often reduced or otherwise modified.

Standard. Usually referring to the upper or posterior petal of a papilionaceous corolla; a banner.

Stellate. Having the shape of a star; starlike.

Stem. Main axis of the plant.

Sterile. Unproductive.

Stigma. That part of the pistil which receives the pollen.

Stigmatic. Relating to the stigma.

Stipe. A stalklike support of a pistil or of a carpel.

Stipel. The stipule of a leaflet in compound leaves.

Stipitate. Having a stipe.

Stipulate. Having stipules.

Stipule. An appendage at the base of a petiole or on each side of its insertion.

Stolon. A branch or shoot given off at the summit of a root.

Stoma. A minute orifice in the epidermis of a leaf.

Stone. The hard endocarp of a drupe.

Striate. With fine grooves, ridges, or lines.

Strict. Erect and straight.

Strigillose. Diminutive of strigose.

Strigose. Bearing hairs which are usually stiff, straight, and appressed.

Strobile. An inflorescence or cone with imbricate bracts or scales.

Style. Upward extension of the ovary terminating with the stigma.

Sub- (prefix). Under, below, less than.

Subshrub. Perennial plant with lower portions of stems woody and persistent.

Subtend. Adjacent to an organ, under or supporting; referring to a bract or scale below a flower.

Subulate. Awl-shaped.

Succulent. Juicy.

Sucker. A stem originating from the roots or lower stem.

Suffrutescent. Slightly shrubby or woody at the base.

Suffruticose. Referring to a slightly shrubby plant; especially applied to low subshrubs.

Sulcate. Grooved or furrowed.

Superior. Above or over; applied to an ovary when free from and positioned above the perianth.

Supra- (prefix). Above.

Suture. Line of dehiscence; a groove denoting a natural union.

Symmetric. Divisible into equal and like parts; referring to a regular flower having the same number of parts in whorl or series.

Sympetalous. Petals more or less united.

Sympodial. Development by simultaneous branching rather than by only a main continuous axis.

Taproot. The main or primary root.

Taxonomy. The science of classification.

Tendril. Usually a slender organ for climbing, formed by modification of leaf, branch, inflorescence, etc.

Terete. Circular in transverse section.

Terminal. At the end, summit, or apex.

Ternate. Divided into three parts.

Testa. The outer seed coat.

Tetragonal. Four-angled.

Tetrahedral. Four-sided.

Theca. Anther sac.

Thorn. A sharp-pointed modified branch.

Throat. The orifice of a sympetalous or gamopetalous corolla.

Thyrse. A shortened panicle with the main axis indeterminate and the lateral flower clusters cymose; loosely, a compact panicle.

Tomentellous. Diminutive of tomentose.

Tomentose. Densely hairy with matted wool.

Tomentulose. Slightly pubescent with matted wool.

Toothed. Having teeth; serrate.

Tortuous. Zigzag or bent in various directions.

Torulose. Cylindrical and constricted at intervals.

Torus. The receptacle, or thickened terminal axis, of a flower head, especially in the Compositae.

Toxic. Poisonous.

Trailing. Growing prostrate but not rooting at the nodes.

Translucent. Transmitting light but not transparent.

Transpiration. Passage of water vapor outward, mostly through the stomata.

Transverse. A section taken at right angles to the longitudinal axis.

Tri- (prefix). In three parts, as trilobate (3-lobed); trifid (3-cleft).

Trichome. A hair arising from an epidermal cell.

Trichotomous. Three-branched or forked.

Truncate. Ending abruptly, as if cut off transversely.

Trunk. The main stem or axis of a tree below the branches.

Tube. A hollow cylindric organ, such as the lower part of a sympetalous calyx or corolla, the upper part usually expanding into a limb.

Tuber. A thickened underground stem usually for food storage and bearing buds.

Tubercle. A small tuberlike body.

Tumid. Inflated or swollen.

Turbinate. Top-shaped.

Turgid. Swollen.

Twining. Climbing by means of the main stem or branches winding around an object.

Ultimate. The last or final part in a train of progression, as the ultimate division of an organ.

Umbel. An inflorescence with numerous pedicels springing from the end of the peduncle, as with the ribs of an umbrella.

Umbilicate. Depressed in the center.

Umbo. A central raised area or hump.

Uncinate. Scythe-shaped, sometimes referring to hooked hairs or prickles.

Undershrub. A low plant generally woody only near the base.

Undulate. With a wavy surface or margin.

Unequally pinnate. Pinnate with an odd terminal leaflet.

Uni- (prefix). Solitary or one only; such as unifoliate (with one leaflet) or unilocular (with one cell).

Unilateral. One-sided.

Uniseriate. In one series, or in one row or circle.

Unisexual. Of one sex, either staminate or pistillate only.

Urceolate. Pitcher-shaped, usually with a flaring mouth and constricted neck.

Utricle. An achenelike fruit, but with a thin, loose outer seed covering.

Vallecula (pl. *valleculae*). A channel or groove between the ridges on various organs, such as on stems or fruits.

Valve. One of the pieces into which a capsule splits.

Vascular. Referring to the conductive tissue in the stems or leaves.

Vascular bundle. A bundle or group of vascular tubes or ducts.

Vegetative. Nonreproductive, as contrasted to floral.

Veins. Ramifications or threads of fibrovascular tissue in a leaf, or other flat organ.

Velutinous. Covered with dense velvety hairs.

Venation. A system of veins.

Venose. Veiny.

Ventral. Belonging to the anterior or inner face of an organ; the opposite of dorsal.

Ventricose. Asymmetrically swollen.

Vernation. Arrangement of leaves in a bud.

Verrucose. Covered with wartlike excrescences.

Versatile. Swinging free, usually referring to an anther attached above its base to a filament.

Verticil (adj. *verticillate*). A whorl of more than two similar parts at a node; leaves, stems, etc.

Verticillate. Disposed in a whorl.

Vesicle (adj. *vesicular*). A small inflated or bladderlike structure.

Vespertine. Opening in the evening.

Vestigial. A rudimentary, usually nonfunctioning, or underdeveloped organ.

Villosulous. Diminutive of villous.

Villous, villose. Bearing long soft hairs.

Virgate. Straight and wandlike.

Viscid. Glutinous or sticky.

Viviparous. Precocious development, such as the germination of seeds or buds while still attached to the parent plant.

Whorl. Cyclic arrangement of like parts.

Wing. Any membranous or thin expansion bordering or surrounding an organ.

Woolly. Clothed with long and tortuous or matted hairs.

Xeric. Characterized by aridity.

Xerophilous. Drought resistant.

Xerophyte. A desert plant or plant growing under xeric conditions.

INDEX

Abele, 26
Abraham's Balm, 353
Abrojo, 279
Acacia, 174–190
  amentacea, 176
  berlandieri, 182–184
  constricta, 176–178
  constricta var. *paucispina*, 178
  farnesiana, 180–182
  greggii, 184–186, 188
  rigidula, 174–176
  roemeriana, 189–190
  schaffneri, 180
  tortuosa, 178–180
  vernicosa, 178
  wrightii, 187–188
Acacia
  All-thorn, 178
  Berlandier, 182–184
  Black-brush, 174–176
  Catclaw, 182, 184–186, 188
  de Aguijote, 205
  Gregg, 186
  Long-flowered, 186
  Mescat, 176–178
  Roemer, 189–190
  Round-flowered, 190
  Schaffner, 180
  Spineless Mescat, 178
  Sweet, 180–182
  Three-thorned, 200
  Viscid, 178
  White-thorn, 178
  Wright, 187–188
Acacia-catclaw, 182
Acer negundo, 261–263
Aesculus, 263–267
  arguta, 263–265
  glabra, 265
  glabra var. *arguta*, 265
  pavia, 265–267
  pavia var. *flavescens*, 267
Agarita, 119
Agrillo, 119, 246, 255
Agrito, 119, 255

Ague-bark, 229
Ailanthus altissima, 232–234
Alamo, 31
Albizia julibrissin, 190–192
Albizia, Silk-tree, 190–192
Algerita, 119
Alligator-tree, 127
Allspice, Wild, 123
Allthorn, Spiny, 124–125
Althea, Shrub, 290–292
Amole de Bolita, 269
Amygdalus persica, 165
Anacacho Bauhinia, 211–212
Anacahuite, 351
Anaqua, 349–351
Appalachian-tea, 257
Apple
  Hedge, 117
  Horse, 117
Arbor-vitae, Oriental, 10–11
Arbutus texana, 308–309
Arbutus, Texas, 309
Aroma, 182
Aroma Amarilla, 182
Ash
  Arizona, 341
  Arizona Fragrant, 336
  Berlandier, 338–339, 343
  Biltmore, 346
  Biltmore White, 346
  Cane, 346
  Desert, 341
  Fragrant, 335–336
  Green, 341–343, 347
  Gregg, 336–338
  Hoop, 95
  Maple, 263
  Mexican, 339
  Mountain, 345
  Prickly, 230
  Red, 343
  River, 343
  Sea, 230
  Small-seed White, 346
  Smooth Oregon, 341

Swamp, 343
Texas, 343–345
Velvet, 340–341
Wafer, 229
Water, 343
White, 343, 345–347
Asul, 295
Athel, 295
Athul, 295
Atle, 295
Ayume, 247

Barreta, 338
Basswood, 290
  Bee, 290
Bastard-elm, 95
Bauhinia congesta, 211–212
Bead-tree, 236
Bean
  Big-drunk, 220
  Coral, 220
Bearberry, 261
Beaverwood, 95
Benjamin-bush, 123
Benzoin aestivale, 123
Bihi, 182
Bilsted, 127
Binorama, 182
Bird-of-paradise, 207
Blackhaw, 310, 362
  Southern, 362
Bog-birch, 285
Bois d'Arc, 117
Borla de San Pedro, 355
Bottle-tree, 293
Box, 359
Boxwood, 305
Brazil, 276
Broussonetia papyrifera, 108–109
Buckeye
  Canyon, 271
  False, 271
  New Mexican, 271
  Ohio, 265
  Red, 265–267
  Scarlet, 267
  Spanish, 271
  Texas, 263–265, 271
  Woolly, 267
  Yellow Woolly, 267
Buckthorn
  Alder-leaf, 285

Birch-leaf, 287–289
Carolina, 283–285
Cascara, 288
Clustered Smith, 287
False, 310
Gum, 314
Obovate-leaf, 289
Smith, 285–287
Texas, 279
Woolly, 310
Yellow, 285
Bumelia, 310–314
  lanuginosa, 310–312
  lanuginosa var. albicans, 312
  lanuginosa var. oblongifolia, 312
  lanuginosa var. rigida, 312
  lanuginosa var. texana, 312, 314
  monticola, 312–314
  riograndis, 314
  texana, 314
Bumelia
  Brazos, 312–314
  Brazos Woollybucket, 312
  Gum, 310
  Gum Woollybucket, 312
  Oblong-leaf Woollybucket, 312
  Rigid Woollybucket, 312
  Woolly, 310
  Woollybucket, 310–312
Buttonball-tree, 129
Button-bush, Common, 357–359
Button-willow, 359
Button-wood, 129, 359
Buxus, 305

Cacachila, 283
Cacheto de aroma, 182
Cacohila Silvestre, 283
Caesalpinia gilliesii, 206–207
Caha, 301
Calentano, 205
Cambrón, 205
Camphor-tree, 119–121
Cancanopa, 301
Candillo, 355
Canyon-buckeye, 271
Capul, 96
  Negro, 276
Capulín, 247, 276, 283
Capulincillo, 283
  Cimarrón, 283
Carolina-tea, 257

Carya, 49–54
  illinoensis, 49
  texana, 53–54
  tomentosa, 51–53
Cassena, 257
  Evergreen, 257
Cassie, 182
Cassine, 257
Cassio-berry-bush, 257
Castor-bean, 236–238
Castor-oil-plant, 238
Catclaw, 176
  Mimosa, 184
  Round-flowered, 184, 190
  Texas, 188
  Thornless, 184
  Tree, 188
Caupulin, 158
Cedar
  Atlas, 5
  Carolina, 13
  Deodar, 4–6
  Lebanon, 5
  Mountain, 17
  Red, 12–13, 15
  Salt, 294–295
  Texas, 17
Cedar Brake, 17
Cedro, 17
  Rojo, 15
Cedrus, 4–6
  atlantica, 5
  deodara, 4–6
  libani, 5
Celtis, 88–96
  laevigata, 89–93
  laevigata var. *anomala*, 91
  laevigata var. *brachyphylla*, 91
  laevigata var. *brevipes*, 93
  laevigata var. *reticulata*, 93
  laevigata var. *smallii*, 91–92
  laevigata var. *texana*, 91
  lindheimeri, 88–89
  occidentalis, 93–95
  occidentalis var. *crassifolia*, 93
  pallida, 95–96
Cephalanthus occidentalis,
  357–359
Cercidium, 200–204
  macrum, 202–204
  texanum, 200–202, 203–204
Cercis canadensis, 207–211

forma *alba*, 209
forma *glabrifolia*, 209
forma *plena*, 209
var. *mexicana*, 209, 210, 211
var. *pubescens*, 209
var. *texensis*, 209, 210, 211
Cercocarpus, 172–174
  argenteus, 174
  breviflorus, 174
  eximius, 174
  montanus, 172–174
  montanus var. *argenteus*, 174
  montanus var. *paucidentatus*,
    174
  parvifolius var. *breviflorus*, 174
  parvifolius var. *paucidentatus*,
    174
  paucidentatus, 174
Chaparral, 96, 186, 276, 279,
  323
  Berry, 119
  Blanco, 329
  Prieto, 176, 178, 279
Chapote, 317
  Prieto, 317
Chaste-tree
  Common, 353
  Lamb-tree, 353
  Lilac, 351–353
  True, 353
Cherry
  Black, 154–157
  Cabinet, 158
  Common Choke, 157–158
  Eastern Choke, 158
  Escarpment Black, 156–157
  Indian, 285
  Mountain, 162
  Mountain Black, 156
  Rum, 156, 158
  Western Choke, 158
  Whiskey, 158
  Wild Black, 158
Chilopsis, 355–357
  linearis, 355–357
  linearis forma *alba*, 357
  linearis var. *arcuata*, 357
  linearis var. *glutinosa*, 357
China, 283, 338
China-berry, 235–236, 273
  Texas Umbrella, 236
China-plum, 172

China-tree, 236, 273
  Wild, 269
Chirlobirlos, 355
Chittamwood, 310, 314
Chocolate del Indio, 257
Chokeberry
  Black, 158
  California, 158
  Eastern, 158
Christmas-berry, 257
Cinnamomum camphora, 119–121
Citrus trifoliata, 224–226
Cloth-of-Gold, 205
Cochila, 283
Cola de Zorillo, 229
Colorín, 220
Colubrina texensis, 273–274
Colubrina, Texas, 273–274
Condalia, 275–278
  hookeri, 275–276
  lycioides, 279
  viridis, 276–278
  viridis var. *reedii*, 278
Condalia
  Bluewood, 275–276
  Green, 276–278
  Lote-bush, 278–279
  Reed's Green, 278
Copal, 234
Copete, 355
Cornel, White, 308
Corneta Amarilla, 355
Cornus, 306–308
  asperifolia, 308
  drummondii, 306–308
  sanguinea, 308
Corona de Cristo, 125
Correosa, 255
Cotinus, 240–242
  coggygria, 242
  obovatus, 240–242
Cottonwood
  Eastern, 27, 29–31
  Great Plains, 26–27
  Southern, 31
  Texas Great Plains, 28–29
  Yellow, 31
Coyotillo, Humboldt, 281–283
Crab
  Iowa, 168
  Prairie, 168
Crab-apple

Prairie, 166–168
  Western, 168
Crane-willow, 359
Crapemyrtle
  Common, 302–303
  Dwarf, 303
  Dwarf Blue, 303
  Pink, 303
  Purple, 303
  Red, 303
  White, 303
Crataegus, 130–154
  crus-galli, 136, 145–147
  glabriuscula forma *desertorum*,
    135, 144–145
  greggiana, 140, 151–152
  montigava, 150
  reverchonii, 137, 147–149
  rivularis, 141, 152–154
  sutherlandensis, 135, 141–143
  sutherlandensis var. *spinescens*,
    143
  tracyi, 138, 149–150
  uvaldensis, 152
Crouper-bush, 359
Crown-of-thorns, 205
Cuji Cimarrón, 182
Culhua, 301
Cupressus, 8–10
  horizontalis, 10
  sempervirens, 8–10
  sempervirens var. *fastigiata*, 10
  sempervirens var. *horizontalis*,
    10
  sempervirens var. *stricta*, 10
Currant, Wild, 119
Cypress
  Black, 8
  Columnar Italian, 10
  Common Bald, 6–8
  Gulf, 8
  Italian, 8–10
  Red, 8
  Southern, 8
  Spreading Italian, 10
  Swamp, 8
  Tidewater Red, 8
  White, 8
  Yellow, 8

Date, Chinese, 281
Desert Olive, 325

Desert-willow, 355–357
  Sticky, 357
  Western, 357
Devil Claws, 186
Devil's-elbow, 323
Devil's Walkingstick, 234
Diospyros, 314–318
  texana, 316–318
  virginiana, 314–316
Dogwood
  Cornel, 308
  Pond, 359
  Rough-leaf, 306–308
  Small-flower, 308
  Swamp, 228–229
Don Quixote Lance, 19

Ehretia, 349–351
  anacua, 349–351
  elliptica, 351
Elder
  American, 359–361
  Common, 100, 360
  Pie, 360
  Sweet, 360
  Yellow, 354
Elder-berry, 360
Elder-blow, 360
Elm
  American, 98–100
  Androssow Siberian, 106
  Basket, 102
  Bastard, 95
  Cedar, 101–102
  Chinese, 105, 106–107
  Common, 100
  Cork, 104
  False, 95
  Gray, 98
  Indian, 98
  Lime, 102
  Moose, 98
  Narrow Siberian, 105
  Red, 98, 102, 104
  Rock, 98, 100
  Scotch, 106
  Scrub, 102
  Siberian, 104–106
  Slippery, 97–98
  Soft, 98, 100
  Southern Rock, 102
  Swamp, 100

Sweet, 98
Texas, 102
Wahoo, 104
Water, 100, 104
Weeping Siberian, 105
White, 100
Winged, 102–104
Witch, 104
Enebro, 17
Eriobotrya japonica, 170–172
  var. *variegata*, 172
Erythrina herbacea, 220
Escobillo, 338
Eshel, 295
Espilla, 205
Espinillo, 182, 205
Espinillo de España, 205
Espiño, 182
  Blanco, 182
  Real de España, 205
Eve's Necklace, 222
Eysenhardtia, 216–218
  angustifolia, 218
  texana, 216–218

False-buckeye, 271
False-buckthorn, 310
False-elm, 95
Fence Flowers, Barbados, 205
Fever-bush, 123
Finisache, 182
Firecracker Plant, 267
Firethorn
  Narrow-leaf, 168–170
  Scarlet, 170
Firmiana simplex, 292–294
  var. *variegata*, 294
Fish-poison-bush, 267
Flor
  Amarilla, 355
  de Mimbre, 357
  de Rayo, 205
  de San Pedro, 355
Flowering-willow, 357
Forestiera, 322–329
  angustifolia, 327–329
  neomexicana, 323, 325
  neomexicana var. *arizonica*, 325
  pubescens, 322–323, 325
  pubescens var. *glabrifolia*, 323, 324–325
  reticulata, 325–327

Forestiera
  Downy, 322–323
  Narrow-leaf, 327–329
  Net-leaf, 325–327
  New Mexico, 324–325
Fraxinus, 335–347
  americana 343, 345–347
  berlandieriana, 338–339, 343
  cuspidata, 335–336
  cuspidata var. *macropetala*, 336
  greggii, 336–338
  pennsylvanica, 343
  pennsylvanica var. *subinteger-
      rima*, 341–343, 347
  texensis, 343–345
  velutina, 340–341
Fresno, 336, 338, 339, 341, 355
Frigolito, 220
Frijolillo, 220
Frijollito, 220
Frutillo Negrito, 283

Gabia, 182
Garabata, 96
Garanguay Amarillo, 355
Garrocha, 355
Garrya, 43–45
  ovata, 43–45
  ovata var. *lindheimeri*, 45
  wrightii, 45
Gatuña, 186
Gavia, 176
Gigantillo, 178
Gleditsia triacanthos, 198–200
Gloria, 355
Goldenrain-tree, 271–273
Granada, 305
  Agria, 305
  de China, 305
Granado, 305
Granjeno, 96
  Huasteco, 96
Guacopano, 205
Guajacum, 224
Guajillo, 184
Guaram-guaran, 355
Guayacán, 224
Guichi-belle, 205
Guie-bicki, 355
Guisache, 182
Guisache Yondino, 182

Gum
  Buckthorn, 314
  Bumelia, 310
  California Red, 127
  Elastic, 310, 314
  Mountain, 314
  Rabbit, 230
  Red, 127
  Star-leaf, 127
  White, 127
Gum-wood, 127

Hackberry
  Arizona Sugar, 93
  Common, 93–95
  Desert, 96
  Lindheimer, 88–89
  Net-leaf Sugar, 92, 93
  Scrub Sugar, 91
  Small Sugar, 91–92
  Spiny, 95–96
  Sugar, 89–93
  Texas Sugar, 91
  Uvalde Sugar, 91
Halesia carolina, 320
Hamdek-kiup, 116
Haw, Purple, 276
Hawthorn
  Cock's-spur, 145–147
  Gregg, 151–152
  Reverchon, 147–149
  River, 152–154
  Smooth Western, 144–145
  Spiny Sutherland, 143
  Sutherland, 141–143
  Tracy, 149–150
Heavenward-tree, 234
Hedge-apple, 117
Hemp-tree, 353
Hercules-club, 229–230
  Texas, 231–232
Hibiscus syriacus, 290–292
Hickory
  Bigbud, 53
  Black, 53–54
  Buckley, 54
  Bullnut, 53
  Fragrant, 53
  Hardbark, 53
  Mockernut, 51–53
  Pignut, 54

Red, 53
White, 53
Whitebark, 53
Whiteheart, 53
Hierba de San Nicolás, 355
Hinsach, 182
Hog-plum, 274
Holly
    American, 258–259
    Christmas, 259
    Deciduous, 261
    Emetic, 257
    Evergreen, 257
    Meadow, 261
    Possum-haw, 259–261
    Prairie, 261
    Welk, 261
    White, 259
    Yaupon, 256–258
    Yule, 259
Honey-ball, 182
Honey-locust, Common, 198–200
Honey-shucks, 200
Hoop-ash, 95
Hop-tree
    Baldwin, 228, 229
    Common, 226–229
    Three-leaf, 228
Horse-apple, 117
Horsebean, 205
Huachacata, 355
Huajilla, 184, 186
Huisache, 178, 182
    Chino, 180
    de la Semilla, 182
Huisachillo, 178–180
Huixachin, 182

Ichulili, 355
Ilex, 256–261
    decidua, 259–261
    opaca, 258–259
    vomitoria, 256–258
Illinois Nut, 51
Indian
    Blackdrink, 257
    Naked, 309
    Nuts, 4
    Spice, 353
Indian-cherry, 285
Indian-lilac, 236

Jaboncillo, 269
Japanese-plum, 172
Jaray, 41
Jerusalem-thorn, 204–206
Jove's-fruit, 316
Judas-tree, 209
Juglans, 45–49
    microcarpa, 47–49
    nigra, 45–47
Jujube, Common, 279–281
Junco, 125, 205
Junco Marion, 205
Juniper
    Ashe, 15–17
    Red, 13
    River, 15
    Rocky Mountain, 13–15
    Western, 15
Juniper-bush, 13
Juniper-tree, 95
Juniperus, 12–17
    ashei, 15–17
    virginiana, 12–13
    virginiana var. *scopulorum*,
        13–15

Kalmia latifolia, 220
Kanlo, 355
Karwinskia humboldtiana,
    281–283
Kidneywood, Texas, 216–218
Kinnikinnick, 247
Knackaway, 351
Koeberlinia spinosa, 124–125
Koelreuteria paniculata, 271–273

Ladies' Streamer, 303
Lady Legs, 309
Lagerstroemia, 302–303
    alba, 303
    indica, 302–303
    lavendula, 303
    magenta rubra, 303
    nana, 303
    purpurea, 303
Lambrisco, 247
Lamb-tree, Chaste, 353
Lantrioco, 247
Largancillo, 178
Laurel, Mountain, 220
Laurus nobilis, 220

Lavender, Wild, 353
Lead-tree
  Golden-ball, 194–195
  Gregg, 192–194
Lemita, 246
Leucaena, 192–195
  greggii, 192–194
  retusa, 194–195
Ligustrum, 329–335
  japonicum, 329–330, 331
  lucidum, 330–332
  quihoui, 333–335
  sinense, 332–333
Lilac
  Chaste-tree, 251–253
  Indian, 236
Lime-tree, 290
Limoncito, 226
Linden, Carolina, 289–290
Lindera benzoin, 121–123
  var. pubescens, 123
  var. xanthocarpa, 123
Liquidambar styraciflua, 125–127
Little-snowball, 359
Lluvia de Oro, 205
Locust
  Black, 213–214
  False-acacia, 214
  Green, 214
  Honey, 198–200, 214
  New Mexico, 215–216
  Pea-flower, 214
  Post, 214
  Red, 214
  Red-flowering, 214
  Silver, 214
  Sweet, 200
  Thorny, 200
  White, 214
  Yellow, 214
Logwood, 276
Loquat, 170–172

Maclura pomifera, 116–117
Madrone, Texas, 308–309
Madroño, 309
Mahogany
  Shaggy Mountain, 174
  Silver Mountain, 174
  True Mountain, 172–174
Mahonia trifoliolata, 118–119

Mahonia, Laredo, 118–119
Manna-bush, 295
Manzanillo, 351
Manzanita, 309, 351
Maple
  Ashleaf, 263
  Black, 263
  Box-elder, 261–263
  Manitoba, 263
  Red River, 263
  Sugar, 263
Maple-ash, 263
Margarita, 283
  del Cero, 283
Matitas, 182
Matoral, 184
Mazarca, 355
Melia azedarach, 235–236
  forma umbraculiformis, 236
Mesquite
  Extranjero, 205
  Honey, 196–198
  Torrey, 198
Mexican-buckeye, 269–271
Mimosa, 192, 195
  Texas, 186
Miñona, 355
Mock-orange, 117
Monillo, 271
Mora, 116
Morchucha, 355
Morea, 114
Morera, 114
Morus, 109–116
  alba, 112–114
  alba var. tatarica, 112
  microphylla, 114–116
  nigra, 111–112
  rubra, 109–111
Mountain-gum, 314
Mountain-laurel, 220
  Texas, 220
Mulberry
  Black, 111–112
  Common Paper, 108–109
  Dwarf, 116
  Mexican, 116
  Mountain, 116
  Red, 109–111, 114, 116
  Russian, 114
  Silkworm, 114

Texas, 114–116
White, 112–114
Wild, 116

Naked Indian, 309
Nanny-berry
  Rusty, 362
  Southern, 362
Negra, 188
Negundo aceroides, 263
Nerium oleander, 347–349
Nettle-tree, 95
New Mexican-buckeye, 271
Nextamalxochill, 355
Nixtamaxochitl, 355
Nochtli, 301
Nockaway, 351
Nogal, 49
Nogalillo, 49
Nopal, 301
Nuzu-ndu, 309

Oak
  Barren, 84
  Bastard, 67, 71
  Black, 84
  Blackjack, 81–82
  Bluejack, 82–84
  Box, 60
  Boynton, 64–65
  Branch, 60
  Bray Chinquapin, 58
  Bur, 54–56
  Bur Scrub, 56
  Canyon, 71
  Chestnut, 58
  Chinkapin, 58
  Chinquapin, 56–58
  Cinnamon, 82
  Cross, 60
  Drummond Post, 62–64
  Durand, 66–67
  Gray, 72, 74
  Harvard, 74
  Havard Shin, 74–76
  High-ground Willow, 82
  Hill, 87
  Holly, 257, 259, 261
  Iron, 60, 84
  Jack, 84
  Lacey, 69–71

Leopard, 85
Limestone, 74
Limestone Durand, 67–69, 71
Live, 78–79, 81
Mohr, 72–74, 76
Mossycup, 56
Mountain, 71
Overcup, 56
Pin, 58
Post, 59–60, 74, 76
Red, 85, 87
Rock, 58, 71, 87
Rough, 60
Sand, 76
Sandjack, 82
Sand Post, 60–62
Scrub, 58, 72, 74, 77, 84
Scrub Live, 79–81
Shin, 74, 77
Shinnery, 76
Shrub, 58
Shrub Live, 71–72
Shumard, 84–86
Smoky, 71
Spanish, 85, 87
Spotted, 85, 87
Texas, 86–87
Texas Red, 87
Turkey, 82
Upland Willow, 82
Vasey, 76–77
White, 56
Yellow, 58
Ocote, 4
Oleander, Common, 347–349
Olive, Desert, 325
One-berry, 95
Opopanax, 182
Opossum-tree, 127
Opuntia lindheimeri, 299–302
Orange
  Bitter, 226
  Trifoliate, 224–226
  Wild, 230
Osage-orange, 116–117

Pacal, 301
Palma
  Christi, 238
  de Dátiles, 19
  Loca, 19

Pita, 19
Palo
  Amarillo, 119
  Blanco, 89, 269, 325
  de Arco, 355
  de Rayo, 205
  Negrito, 283
Paloverde, 205
  Border, 202–204
  Texas, 200–202, 203–204
Panalero, 329
Paradise Flower, 186
Parasol-tree, Chinese, 292–294
Pare, 301
Parkinsonia aculeata, 204–206
Paulo Huesa, 355
Peach, 163–165
Pear
  Common, 165–166
  Prickly, 299–302
Pecan, 49–51
Pelá, 182
Pencil-wood, 13
Pepper, Wild, 353
Pepper-tree, Monk's, 353
Pepperwood, 230
Persea borbonia, 220
Persimmon
  Black, 317
  Common, 314–316, 317
  Mexican, 317
  Texas, 316–318
Phoenix-tree, 293
Pickaway-anise, 229
Pillenterry, 230
Pinball, 359
Pine
  Nut, 4
  Pinyon, 2–4
Pino, 4
Piñon, 4
Piñones, 4
Pinus, 2–4
  cembroides, 3
  cembroides var. *edulis*, 4
  edulis, 2–4
Pistache, Texas, 242–244
Pistacia, 242–244
  mexicana, 244
  texana, 242–244
Pita, 19

Plane-tree
  American, 127–130
  Smooth American, 129–130
Platanus occidentalis, 127–130
  var. *glabrata*, 130
Plum
  Big-tree, 163
  Chicksaw, 160–162
  Japanese, 172
  Mexican, 162–163
  Oklahoma, 158–160
  Sour, 160
  Winter, 316
Plumero, 339
Podocarpus, 1–2
  longifolia, 2
  macrophylla, 1–2
Poinciana, Paradise, 206–207
Polecat-tree, 285
Pomegranate, 304–306
  Double, 305
  Dwarf, 306
  Legrelle, 305
  Pale, 305
  Yellow, 306
Poncirus trifoliata, 225–226
Pond-dogwood, 359
Popinach, 182
Poplar
  Black, 23–24
  Carolina, 31
  Euphrates, 38
  Necklace, 31
  Water, 31
  White, 24–26
Populus, 23–31
  acuminata, 27
  alba, 24–26
  deltoides, 27, 29–31
  euphratica, 38
  nigra var. *italica*, 23–24
  sargentii, 26–27, 28
  sargentii var. *texana*, 28–29
Porlieria angustifolia, 222–224
Porlieria, Texas, 222–224
Possum-wood, 316
Potatochip-tree, 229
Potzotz, 301
Prairie-grub, 229
Prickly-ash, Yellow, 230
Prickly Pear, Lindheimer, 299–302

Pride-of-India, 236, 273
Prim, 330
Privet
  Chinese, 332–333
  Glossy, 330–332
  Japanese, 329–330, 331
  Quihoui, 333–335
Privet-berry, 330
Prosopis, 196–198
  glandulosa, 196–198
  glandulosa var. *torreyana*, 198
Prunus, 154–165
  angustifolia, 160–162
  gracilis, 158–160
  mexicana, 162–163
  persica, 163–165
  serotina, 154–157
  serotina var. *eximia*, 156–157
  virginiana, 157–158
Ptelea, 226–229
  baldwinii, 228, 229
  trifoliata, 226–229
  trifoliata var. *mollis*, 226
Punica granatum, 304–306
  forma *albescens*, 305
  forma *legrellei*, 305
  forma *plentiflora*, 305
  var. *flavescens*, 306
  var. *nana*, 306
Pyracantha, 168–170
  angustifolia, 168–170
  coccinea, 170
Pyrus, 165–168
  communis, 165–166
  ioensis, 166–168

Quail-bush, 246
Quercus, 54–87
  austrina, 67
  boyntonii, 64–65
  drummondii, 60, 62–64
  durandii, 66
  durandii var. *austrina*, 67
  durandii var. *breviloba*, 67
  fusiformis, 79–81
  glaucoides, 69–71
  grisea, 72
  havardii, 74–76
  incana, 81–82
  macrocarpa, 54–56
  macrocarpa var. *depressa*, 56

macrocarpa var. *olivaeformis*, 56
margaretta, 60–62, 63, 64
marilandica, 82–84
mohriana, 72–74
muhlenbergii, 56–58
muhlenbergii var. *brayi*, 58
pungens var. *vaseyana*, 76–77
shumardii, 84–86
sinuata, 66–67, 69
sinuata var. *breviloba*, 67–69, 71
stellata, 59–60
stellata var. *boyntonii*, 65
stellata var. *margaretta*, 60, 63
texana, 86–87
turbinella, 71–72
undulata var. *vaseyana*, 77
vaseyana, 77
virginiana, 78–79, 80
virginiana var. *fusiformis*, 81
Quinine-tree, 229

Redbud
  Double Eastern, 209
  Eastern, 207–211
  Hairy Eastern, 209
  Mexican, 209, 210, 211
  Smooth Eastern, 209
  Texas, 209, 210, 211
  White Eastern, 209
Red-cedar, 15
  Colorado, 15
  Eastern, 12–13, 15
  Mountain, 15
  Western, 15
Retama, 205, 355
  de Cerda, 205
Retamo, 355
Rhamnus, 283–289
  betulaefolia, 287–289
  betulaefolia var. *obovata*, 289
  caroliniana, 283–285
  fasciculata, 286
  lanceolata, 287
  purshiana, 288
  smithii, 285–287
  smithii var. *fasciculata*, 287
Rhus, 244–255
  aromatica var. *flabelliformis*, 244–246
  choriophylla, 248

copallina, 248–249, 251
copallina var. *lanceolata,*
    249–252
copallina var. *latifolia,* 249
copallina var. *leucantha,* 24
glabra, 252–254
microphylla, 254–255
sempervirens, 246–248
trilobata, 245–246
virens, 247
Ricinus communis, 236–238
Rim-ash, 95
River-brush, 359
Robinia, 213–216
    neomexicana, 215-216
    pseudo-acacia, 213–214
Roble Amarilla, 355
Rock Brush, 218
Rose-mallow, 292
Rose-of-Sharon, 292
Ruibarba, 355
Rulac negundo, 263

Sabino, 17
Sabino-tree, 8
Sage-tree, 353
Salix, 31–43
    amphibia, 43
    babylonica, 36–38
    caroliniana, 41–43
    chapmanii, 43
    exigua, 38–40
    exigua var. *nevadensis,* 40
    exigua var. *stenophylla,* 39–40
    floridana, 43
    fluviatilis, 36
    goodingii, 34
    harbisonii, 43
    interior, 35–36
    longifolia, 36
    longipes, 43
    longipes var. *venulosa,* 43
    longipes var. *wardii,* 43
    marginata, 43
    nigra, 31–33, 41–42
    nigra var. *vallicola,* 33–35
    nigra var. *wardii,* 43
    occidentalis, 43
    occidentalis var. *longipes,* 43
    taxifolia, 40–41
    wardii, 43
Salt-cedar, 294–295

Sambucus canadensis, 359–361
San Andrés, 355
Sapindus saponaria var. *drummon-*
    dii, 268–269
Sapium sebiferum, 238–240
Sardinillo, 355
Sassafras albidum, 220
Sauce, 41
Saúco Amarillo, 355
Sauz, 41
Savin, Red, 13
Scrub, Sand, 76
Senhalanac, 252
Shinnery, Panhandle, 76
Shoe-make, 252
Shrub-althea, 290–292
Shrubby-trefoil, 228
Silktassel
    Lindheimer, 45
    Mexican, 43–45
    Wright, 45
Silk-tree, 192
    Albizia, 190–192
Silver-chain, 214
Skunk-bush, 229
    Sumac, 244–246
Smoke-tree
    American, 240–242
    European, 242
Snap-bush, 123
Snow-bell
    Hairy Sycamore-leaf, 320
    Sycamore-leaf, 318–320
    Texas, 320–322
Soapberry, Western, 268–269
Soap-bush, 224
Soap-plant, Indian, 269
Sophora, 218–222
    affinis, 220–222
    secundiflora, 218–220
Sophora
    Mescal-bean, 218–220
    Texas, 220–222
South-sea-tea, 257
Spanish
    Bayonet, 19
    Dagger, 19
    Pincushion, 359
Spanish-buckeye, 271
Spice-bush
    Common, 121–123
    Hairy Common, 123

Yellow-berry Common, 123
Spice-wood, 123
Spring-goldenglow, 323
Spring-herald, 323
Squaw-bush, 246
Stain-walnut, 127
Sting Tongue, 230
Styrax, 123, 318–322
   benzoin, 123
   plantanifolia, 318–320
   plantanifolia var. *stellata*, 320
   texana, 320–322
Subin, 182
Sugarberry, 351
Sumac
   Black, 249, 251
   Chinese, 234
   Dwarf, 249
   Evergreen, 246–248
   Flame-leaf, 248–249, 251
   Ill-scented, 246
   Lance-leaf, 251
   Lemonade, 246
   Limestone, 251
   Little-leaf, 254–255
   Mountain, 249, 251
   Pennsylvania, 252
   Prairie Flame-leaf, 249–252
   Prairie Shining, 251
   Red, 252
   Scarlet, 252
   Shining, 249
   Skunk-bush, 244–246
   Sleek, 253
   Small-leaf, 255
   Smooth, 249, 252–254
   Three-leaf, 246
   Tobacco, 247
   Tree, 251
   Upland, 249, 252–253
   White, 252
   White Flame-leaf, 249
   Winged, 249, 255
Swampwood, 359
Sweet-bean, 200
Sweetgum, American, 125–127
Sycamore, 127–130

Tache, 355
Tagualaishte, 355
Tallow-tree
   Chinese, 238–240

Vegetable, 240
Tamaichia, 247
Tamarisk
   African, 296, 297
   Athel, 297, 298–299
   Five-stamen, 296, 297–298
   French, 294–299
   Smallflower, 298, 299
Tamarix, 294–299
   africana, 296, 297
   aphylla, 297, 298–299
   articulata, 298
   gallica, 294–299
   orientalis, 298
   pallasii, 298
   parviflora, 298, 299
   pentandra, 296, 297–298
Tanglewood, 323
Tarais, 41
Taray, 41
   de Río, 41
Tascate, 17
Taxate, 17
Taxodium distichum, 6–8
Taxus macrophylla, 2
Tear Blanket, 230
Tecoma, 353–355
   stans, 353–355
   stans var. *velutina*, 354
Tehuistle, 269
Texas-buckeye, 271
Thorn, Crucifixion, 125
Thorn-tree, 200
Three-thorned-acacia, 200
Thuja orientalis, 10–11
Tilia caroliniana, 289–290
Toat, 301
Tongue-bush, 230
Toothache, 230
Tosto, 355
Tree of Chastity, 353
Tree-of-heaven, 232–234
Tree-of-the-Gods, 234
Trompetilla, 355
Tronodor, 355
Tronodora, 355
Trumpet
   Flower, 354
   Hardy Yellow, 353–355
   Velvety Yellow, 354
Trumpeta, 355
Tullidora, 283

Tulosuchil, 355
Tzapyan, 305
Tzitzi, 116

Uisatsin, 182
Ulmus, 97–107
  alata, 102–104
  americana, 98–100
  coreana, 107
  crassifolia, 101–102
  fulva, 98
  glabra, 106
  parvifolia, 105, 106–107
  pumila, 100, 104–106
  pumila forma *androssowi*, 106
  pumila var. *arborea*, 105
  pumila var. *pendula*, 105
  rubra, 97–98
  shirasawana, 107
  sieboldii, 107
Uña de Cabra, 182
Uña de Gato, 186, 188, 216
Ungnadia speciosa, 269–271
Uvero, 359

Vara Prieta, 178
Varnish-tree, 273, 293
  False, 234
Viburnum, 361–362
  prunifolium, 362
  rufidulum, 361–362
  rufotomentosum, 362
Viburnum, Rusty Blackhaw,
  361–362
Vinegar-tree, 252
Vinorama, 182
Vitex agnus-castus, 351–353

Wafer-ash, 229
Wahoo-tree, 195
Wait-a-bit, 230
Walnut
  Dwarf, 49
  Eastern Black, 45–47
  English, 47
  Little, 49
  Stain, 127
  Texas Black, 47–49
Water-ash, 263
Water-beech, 129
Whitewood, 290

Willow
  Acequia, 39
  Babylon Weeping, 36–38
  Basket, 39
  Black, 34
  Button, 359
  Carolina, 43
  Coastal Plain, 41–43
  Coyote, 38–40
  Crane, 359
  Desert, 355–357
  Dudley, 34
  Flowering, 357
  Garb, 38
  Gooding, 34
  Gray, 39
  Gulf Black, 31–33, 41–42
  Long-leaf, 36
  Napoleon, 38
  Narrow-leaf, 36, 39
  Narrow-leaf Coyote, 39–40
  Nevada Coyote, 40
  Osier, 36
  Pussy, 33
  Red, 36
  Riverbank, 36
  Sand-bar, 35–36, 39
  Scythe-leaved, 33
  Shrub, 36
  Slender, 39
  Swamp, 33
  Ward, 43
  Weeping, 38
  Western Black, 33–35
  White, 36
  Yew-leaf, 40–41
Willowleaf-catalpa, 357
Wingseed, 229
Winterberry, 261
Winter-plum, 316
Woolly-buckthorn, 310

Xantha, 301
Xkanlol, 355
Xkantiriz, 182

Yabo, 205
Yaga-zehi, 305
Yapon, 257
Yellow-bells, 354
Yellow-elder, 354

Yellow-opopanax, 182
Yellowwood, 117
    Prickly, 230
Yew, Japanese, 1–2
Yopan, 257
Yopon del Indio, 257
Youpon, 257
Yucca, 17–22
    thompsoniana, 21–22
    torreyi, 19–21
    treculeana, 17–19
Yucca
    Thompson, 21–22
    Torrey, 19–21
    Trecul, 17–19, 21
Yutnudidzi, 305

Zanthoxylum, 229–232
    carolinianum var. *fruticosum*,
        232
    clava-herculis, 229–230, 232
    clava-herculis var. *fruticosum*,
        232
    hirsutum, 231–232
Ziziphus, 279–281
    jujuba, 279–281
    jujuba var. *inermis*, 281
    lycioides, 279
    obtusifolia, 278–279
Zubin, 182
Zubin-ché, 182